Bibliography of Resources in Bilingual Education: Curricular Materials

BIBLIOGRAPHY OF RESOURCES IN BILINGUAL EDUCATION

Curricular Materials

NATIONAL CLEARINGHOUSE FOR BILINGUAL EDUCATION

This document is published by InterAmerica Research Associates, Inc., pursuant
to contract NIE 400-77-0101 to operate the National Clearinghouse for Bilingual
Education. The National Clearinghouse for Bilingual Education is jointly
funded by the National Institute of Education and the Office of Bilingual
Education and Minority Languages Affairs, U.S. Department of Education.
Contractors undertaking such projects under government sponsorship are
encouraged to express their judgment freely in professional and technical
matters; the views expressed in this publication do not necessarily reflect
the views of the sponsoring agencies.

InterAmerica Research Associates, Inc. d/b/a
National Clearinghouse for Bilingual Education
1300 Wilson Boulevard, Suite B2-11
Rosslyn, Virginia 22209
(703) 522-0710 / (800) 336-4560

Cover design by J. Nick Davis, Sans Serif Graphics, Arlington, Virginia

ISBN: 0-89763-016-5
First printing 1980
Printed in USA

10 9 8 7 6 5 4 3 2 1

CONTENTS

Introduction..ix

Bibliography of Resources in Bilingual Education: Curricular Materials........1

Indexes...287
    Author Index, 289
    Index to Languages, 295
    Index to Subjects, 299
    Index to Series Titles, 309
    Index to Titles, 311

INTRODUCTION

Bibliography of Resources in Bilingual Education: Curricular Materials is
a collection of over 400 entries describing instructional products for use
in bilingual education programs. These entries were derived from the bibliographic file of the computerized database that is being developed by the
National Clearinghouse for Bilingual Education. This file is indexed with
descriptors from the ERIC Thesaurus and is searchable through the Clearinghouse
following procedures used for accessing the ERIC system. Each entry contains
complete author, title, language, and availability information, as well as
a thorough abstract describing the contents of the material. In each case,
the availability source (AV), not the Clearinghouse, should be contacted for
further information. This document is fully indexed according to the entry
number (AN) by author, language, subject, series title, and title.

Reproduced below is a typical entry, with explanations of the two-character
field labels used:

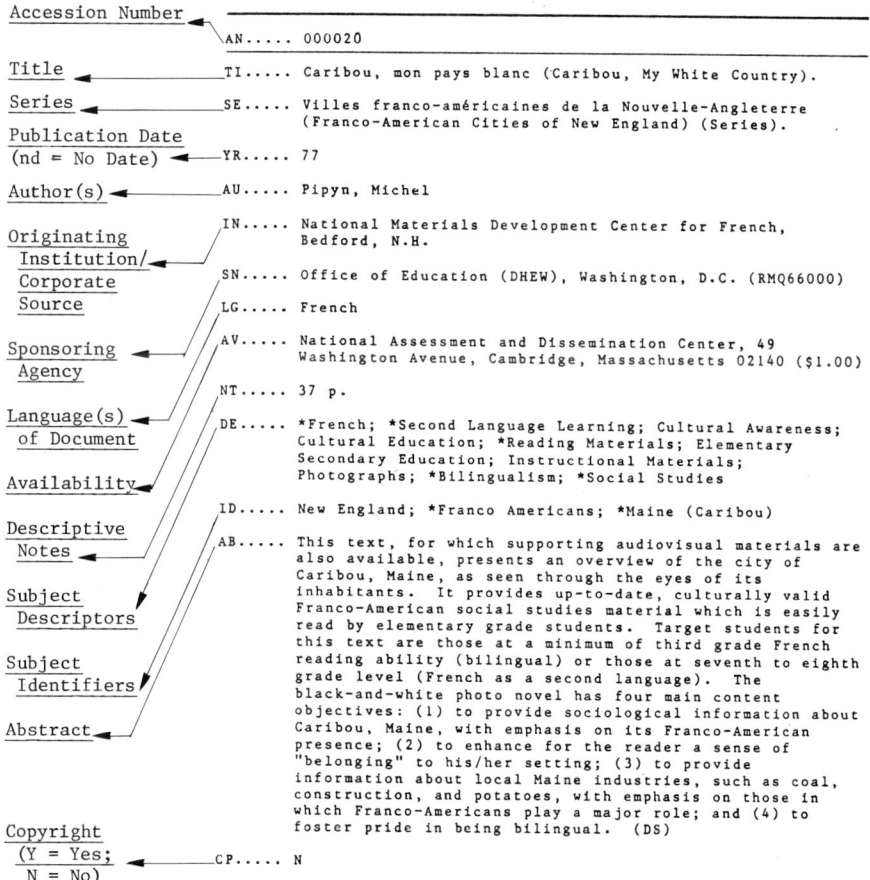

ix

Additional field labels not shown in the sample record include the following:

ER = ERIC Accession Number
NO = Grant, Contract, Project, or Report Number
SO = Source Journal Citation
GS = Geographic Source
IS = Issue (C = Curricular; N = Noncurricular; J = Journal)
PT = Publication Type
GV = Government Level (Official Documents)

The bibliographic file is continually being expanded with new entries, and the Clearinghouse will produce publications which derive from that file, such as this one, from time to time.

One of the activities of the National Clearinghouse for Bilingual Education is to publish documents addressing the specific information needs of the bilingual education community. Subsequent Clearinghouse products will similarly seek to contribute information and knowledge that can assist in the education of minority culture and language groups in the United States.

                                    National Clearinghouse for Bilingual Education

Bibliography of Resources in Bilingual Education: Curricular Materials

AN..... 000006

TI..... Un Jacques Cartier errant: Pièce en un acte (An Errant Jacques Cartier: One-Act Play).

YR..... 77

AU..... Chabot, Grégoire

IN..... National Assessment and Dissemination Center, Cambridge, Mass.; National Materials Development Center for French, Bedford, N.H.

SN..... Office of Education (DHEW), Washington, D.C. (RMQ66000)

LG..... French

AV..... National Assessment and Dissemination Center, 49 Washington Avenue, Cambridge, Massachusetts 02140 ($1.00)

NT..... ii, 31 p.

DE..... *French; *Drama; *Reading Materials; Glossaries; History; *Instructional Materials; Ethnic Groups; Intermediate Grades; Elementary Secondary Education; Regional Dialects; Language Instruction; Group Activities

ID..... *Franco Americans; Cartier (Jacques)

AB..... In a humorous vein, this one-act play treats the history and present plight of the Franco-American people. It is designed to be read or presented in 45 minutes. The text of the play is followed by a Franco-American/Standard French glossary, a brief biography of Jacques Cartier, and a design of a set for this play. The language of the text is Franco-American French. (AM)

CP..... N

AN..... 000007

TI..... My New Friend, David.

YR..... 78

AU..... Takemoto, Alan, ill.

IN..... California State Univ., Los Angeles, National Dissemination and Assessment Center. (BBB15398); Asian American Bilingual Center, Berkeley, Calif. (BBB13628)

SN..... Office of Education (DHEW), Washington, D.C. (RMQ66000)

LG..... Chinese; English

AV..... National Dissemination and Assessment Center, California State University, 5151 State University Drive, Los Angeles, California 90032

NT..... 19 p.

DE.....	*Chinese; *Reading Materials; Elementary Education; *Instructional Materials; Childrens Literature; *Chinese Americans; Asian Americans; Primary Education
AB.....	This reader is intended for use in a bilingual education setting at the elementary level. Each page consists of a black-and-white illustration accompanied by an English and a Chinese text. The story recounts the friendship between a Hispanic boy and a Chinese-American boy who meet in San Francisco's Chinatown. (AM)
CP.....	N

AN.....	000008
TI.....	Laika paignidia kai tragoudia (Folk Poems and Rhymes).
YR.....	77
AU.....	Spiridakis, Eugenia; Marinos, Giorgios, ill.
IN.....	Northeast Center for Curriculum Development, Bronx, N.Y.; National Assessment and Dissemination Center, Cambridge, Mass.
SN.....	Office of Education (DHEW), Washington, D.C. (RMQ66000)
LG.....	Greek
AV.....	National Assessment and Dissemination Center, 49 Washington Avenue, Cambridge, Massachusetts 02140 ($2.00)
NT.....	90 p.
DE.....	*Greek; *Folk Culture; Childrens Literature; *Reading Materials; Language Instruction; *Folklore Books; *Poetry; Anthologies; Games; Instructional Materials; Childrens Games; Puns; Dance; Elementary Education; Primary Education; Music Activities; Singing
AB.....	Songs, dances, games, riddles, jokes, puns, and satire taken from Greek folklore are collected in this illustrated anthology. It is designed to be read aloud to children in the primary grades or to be read independently by older children. (AM)
CP.....	N

AN.....	000013
TI.....	Antoine ou la leçon des choses (Antoine or the Lesson of Things).
YR.....	[77]

AU..... Pipyn, Michel; Heikens, Joanna, ill.

IN..... National Assessment and Dissemination Center, Cambridge, Mass.; National Materials Development Center for French, Bedford, N.H.

SN..... Office of Education (DHEW), Washington, D.C. (RMQ66000)

LG..... French

AV..... National Assessment and Dissemination Center, 49 Washington Avenue, Cambridge, Massachusetts 02140 ($4.00)

NT..... [33] p.

DE..... *French; Childrens Literature; Elementary Education; *Reading Materials; *Instructional Materials; *Physical Environment; *Language Instruction; Self Concept; Grade 5; Grade 6

AB..... This reader, illustrated in color, is designed for use in a French bilingual education setting at the grade 5-6 level. The story incorporates environmental awareness and positive self-concept. (AM)

CP..... N

AN..... 000014

TI..... Bai Hoc Trac Nghiem Thanh Ngu Anh Van (Tests on English Idioms).

YR..... 74

AU..... Tran Van Dien

LG..... English; Vietnamese

AV..... Grand Rapids Public Schools, Bilingual Department, 143 Bostwick N.E., Grand Rapids, Michigan 49503 ($3.75)

NT..... 134 p.
For related documents, see 000015-17.

DE..... *Vietnamese; *Idioms; *Instructional Materials; *Language Tests; Sentences; Language Instruction; *Secondary Language Learning; *English (Second Language); Autoinstructional Aids

AB..... This bilingual book of tests on English idioms is part of a publication project to provide language materials for Vietnamese-speaking people. The book is divided into elementary, intermediate, and advanced sections, with each consisting of lists of idioms used in sentence context and corresponding multiple-choice tests. An answer key is provided. (DS)

CP..... Y

AN..... 000015

TI..... Hoc Anh-Van Bang Thanh-Ngu (Learning English by Idioms).

YR..... [57]

AU..... Tran Van Dien

LG..... English; Vietnamese

AV..... Grand Rapids Public Schools, Bilingual Department, 143 Bostwick N.E., Grand Rapids, Michigan 49503 ($4.95)

NT..... 226 p.
For related documents, see 000014 and 16-17.

DE..... *Vietnamese; *Idioms; *Instructional Materials; *Sentences; Verbs; *English (Second Language); *Second Language Learning; Language Instruction; Autoinstructional Aids

AB..... This bilingual book on English idioms is part of a publication project to provide language materials for Vietnamese-speaking people. Features of the book include: (1) a list of English contractions, (2) common English verbs and examples illustrating their use in sentences, (3) common English words and examples of their use in sentences, and (4) a list of idioms with examples. (DS)

CP..... N

AN..... 000016

TI..... Van Pham Anh Ngu Thuc Hanh: Bai Hoc (Practical English Grammar).

YR..... Sep77

AU..... Tran Van Dien

LG..... Vietnamese

AV..... Grand Rapids Public Schools, Bilingual Department, 143 Bostwick N.E., Grand Rapids, Michigan 49503 ($6.95)

NT..... 457 p.
For related documents, see 000014-15 and 17.

DE..... Vietnamese; *Instructional Materials; *English (Second Language); *Second Language Learning; *Grammar; Adjectives; Pronouns; Adverbs; Verbs; Sentences; Form Classes (Languages)

AB..... This bilingual book on English grammar is part of a publication project to provide language materials to Vietnamese-speaking people. Grammar concepts covered include: (1) nouns; (2) articles; (3) adjectives; (4) pronouns; (5) prepositions; (6) adverbs; (7)

conjunctions; (8) verbs; (9) verb tenses; (10) direct and indirect speech; and (11) sentences, clauses, and phrases. A list of irregular verbs is appended. (DS)

CP..... N

AN..... 000017

TI..... Van Pham Anh Ngu Thuc Hanh: Bai Tap (English Grammar Exercises).

YR..... Sep77

AU..... Tran Van Dien

LG..... English; Vietnamese

AV..... Grand Rapids Public Schools, Bilingual Department, 143 Bostwick N.E., Grand Rapids, Michigan 49503 ($3.50)

NT..... 160 p.
For related documents, see 000014-16.

DE..... Vietnamese; *Instructional Materials; *English (Second Language); *Second Language Learning; *Pattern Drills (Language); *Grammar; *Language Instruction; Autoinstructional Aids; Nominals; Adjectives; Pronouns; Adverbs; Verbs; Sentences; Form Classes (Languages)

AB..... This bilingual book of English grammar exercises is part of a publication project to provide language materials for Vietnamese-speaking people. The exercises follow the format of the companion text and cover the following: (1) nouns; (2) articles; (3) adjectives; (4) pronouns; (5) prepositions; (6) adverbs; (7) conjunctions; (8) verbs; (9) verb tenses; (10) direct and indirect speech; and (11) sentences, clauses, and phrases. (DS)

CP..... N

AN..... 000018

TI..... Introduction to Choctaw.

YR..... 77

AU..... Jacob, Betty; Nicklas, Dale; Spencer, Betty Lou

IN..... Southeastern Oklahoma State Univ., Durant. Choctaw Bilingual Education Program.

SN..... Office of Education (DHEW), Washington, D.C. (RMQ66000)

LG..... Choctaw; English

AV..... National Dissemination and Assessment Center, 7703 North Lamar Boulevard, Austin, Texas 78752 (ISBN 0-089417-300-6; $4.25)

NT..... xx, 224 p.

DE..... Secondary Education; Higher Education; *Choctaw; *Textbooks; *Grammar; Vocabulary; American Indian Languages; *Instructional Materials; Sentence Structure; Glossaries; *Language Instruction; *Second Language Learning; Pronunciation; Phonology; Cultural Background; Cultural Education; Spelling; Uncommonly Taught Languages

AB..... The essentials of Choctaw grammar and basic Choctaw vocabulary are presented in this textbook designed for the university and secondary level. The first teaching unit is a guide to spelling and pronunciation. Each subsequent teaching unit consists of (1) pattern sentences, (2) words to master, (3) dialect notes, (4) grammar rules and exercises, (5) sentence patterns, and (6) hints for building word power. In addition, sections on Choctaw history or language history are scattered throughout the text. A glossary is appended. (DS)

CP..... Y

AN..... 000019

TI..... El Cuento de la gran piñata (The Story of the Big Piñata).

YR..... 77

AU..... Álvarez, Gerarda; Gutiérrez, Ralph, ill.

IN..... Mesa Community Coll., Ariz. (BBB13901)

LG..... Spanish

AV..... Mesa Community College, Mesa, Arizona

NT..... [16] p.

DE..... Elementary Education; Intermediate Grades; *Instructional Materials; *Spanish; *Language Instruction; *Reading Materials; Vocabulary; Cultural Education; Childrens Literature

ID..... Mexico

AB..... This reader, intended for use in a bilingual education setting at the elementary level, describes the celebration of Christmas in Mexico. The book is illustrated by black-and-white drawings, and a vocabulary guide is provided. (JB)

CP..... Y

AN..... 000020

TI..... Caribou, mon pays blanc (Caribou, My White Country).

SE..... Villes franco-américaines de la Nouvelle-Angleterre (Franco-American Cities of New England) (Series).

YR..... 77

AU..... Pipyn, Michel

IN..... National Materials Development Center for French, Bedford, N.H.

SN..... Office of Education (DHEW), Washington, D.C. (RMQ66000)

LG..... French

AV..... National Assessment and Dissemination Center, 49 Washington Avenue, Cambridge, Massachusetts 02140 ($1.00)

NT..... 37 p.

DE..... *French; *Second Language Learning; Cultural Awareness; Cultural Education; *Reading Materials; Elementary Secondary Education; Instructional Materials; Photographs; *Bilingualism; *Social Studies

ID..... New England; *Franco Americans; *Maine (Caribou)

AB..... This text, for which supporting audiovisual materials are also available, presents an overview of the city of Caribou, Maine, as seen through the eyes of its inhabitants. It provides up-to-date, culturally valid Franco-American social studies material which is easily read by elementary grade students. Target students for this text are those at a minimum of third grade French reading ability (bilingual) or those at seventh to eighth grade level (French as a second language). The black-and-white photo novel has four main content objectives: (1) to provide sociological information about Caribou, Maine, with emphasis on its Franco-American presence; (2) to enhance for the reader a sense of "belonging" to his/her setting; (3) to provide information about local Maine industries, such as coal, construction, and potatoes, with emphasis on those in which Franco-Americans play a major role; and (4) to foster pride in being bilingual. (DS)

CP..... N

AN..... 000021

TI..... Sur les traces de l'héritage français en Nouvelle-Angleterre: Boston (In Search of the French Heritage in New England: Boston).

YR..... 77

AU..... Quintal, Claire; Moisan, Richard, photo.; Blais,
        Danielle, trans.

IN..... National Materials Development Center for French,
        Bedford, N.H.

SN..... Office of Education (DHEW), Washington, D.C. (RMQ66000)

LG..... English; French

AV..... National Assessment and Dissemination Center, 49
        Washington Avenue, Cambridge, Massachusetts 02140 ($1.00)

NT..... 39 p.
        For companion teacher's guide, see 000022.

DE..... *Cultural Education; *French; Photographs; *Instructional
        Materials; *History Instruction; Cultural Awareness;
        Secondary Education; *Reading Materials; Second Language
        Learning

ID..... New England; *Franco Americans; *Massachusetts (Boston)

AB..... Historical information about the French influence in the
        Boston, Mass., area, especially during the Revolutionary
        and post-Revolutionary periods of American history, is
        presented in this text illustrated with black-and-white
        photographs. The material is designed to foster student
        pride in the French cultural heritage in America and is
        intended for students at the secondary level and above
        who have at least an intermediate reading ability in
        French. It may also be used as a cultural reader for
        French language reinforcement/enrichment. The text, in
        French only, outlines significant persons, places, and
        events and is supplemented by maps and illustrations in
        addition to the photographs. A French-French glossary
        follows the reading material. (DS)

CP..... N

AN..... 000022

TI..... Sur les traces de l'héritage français en
        Nouvelle-Angleterre: Boston. Livret du maître (In Search
        of the French Heritage in New England: Boston. Teacher's
        Guide).

YR..... 77

AU..... Quintal, Claire; Moisan, Richard, photo.; Blais,
        Danielle, trans.

IN..... National Materials Development Center for French,
        Bedford, N.H.

SN..... Office of Education (DHEW), Washington, D.C. (RMQ66000)

LG..... English; French

AV..... National Assessment and Dissemination Center, 49
        Washington Ave., Cambridge, Massachusetts 02140 ($1.50)

NT..... 40 p.
        For companion text, see 000021.

DE..... *Cultural Education; *Teaching Guides; *French;
Instructional Materials; *History Instruction; Cultural
Awareness; Secondary Education; Reading Materials; Second
Language Learning

ID..... New England, *Franco Americans; *Massachusetts (Boston)

AB..... The English version of a text for secondary students with
at least an intermediate reading ability in French is
provided in this teacher's manual. The reading material
is intended to foster student pride in the French
cultural heritage in America and presents historical
information about the French influence in the Boston,
Mass., area, especially during the Revolutionary and
post-Revolutionary periods. It may also be used as
cultural reading material for French language
reinforcement/enrichment. A model pre- and posttest is
presented at the end of the teacher's guide. (DS)

CP..... N

AN..... 000023

TI..... The Well of Time: Eighteen Short Stories from Philippine
Contemporary Literature.

YR..... 78

AU..... Laygo, Teresito M., comp.

IN..... Berkeley Unified School District, Calif. Asian American
Bilingual Center. (BBB13628); California State Univ., Los
Angeles. National Dissemination and Assessment Center.
(BBB15398)

SN..... Office of Education (DHEW), Washington, D.C. (RMQ66000)

AV..... National Dissemination and Assessment Center, California
State University, 5151 State University Drive, Los
Angeles, California 90032 ($4.95)

NT..... 229 p.
For accompanying teacher's handbook, see 000024.

DE..... *Short Stories; *Adolescent Literature; Senior High
Schools; Twentieth Century Literature; *Folk Culture;
*Cultural Awareness; Cultural Education; *Literature
Appreciation; *Reading Materials; Learning Experience

ID..... Philippines; *Filipino Literature

AB..... Filipino cultural heritage is conveyed in this collection
of 18 short stories written by several generations of
Filipino writers. They offer a variety of images of
Filipino culture, both urban and rural, and of lifestyles
in the Northern and Southern Philippines, allowing the
reader to sample the experience of the Filipino people.
The stories are intended for use by students in the 9th
through the 12th grades. Students will learn to
empathize with experiences rendered in language,
appreciate the writer's art and craft, and understand the
short-story form. Four cultural or experimental
categories tie the stories together with the theme of the

Filipino's search for unity in diversity: (1) Home and the Native Country, (2) Of Identity and Family, (3) A Sense of History, and (4) Of Change and Values. Brief biographies of the writers are included. (JB)

CP..... Y

AN..... 000024

TI..... The Well of Time: Teacher's Handbook.

YR..... 78

AU..... Laygo, Teresito M., comp.

IN..... Berkeley Unified School District, Calif. Asian American Bilingual Center. (BBB13628); California State Univ., Los Angeles. National Dissemination and Assessment Center. (BBB15398)

SN..... Office of Education (DHEW), Washington, D.C. (RMQ66000)

AV..... National Dissemination and Assessment Center, California State University, 5151 State University Drive, Los Angeles, California 90032 ($4.85)

NT..... 65 p.
For accompanying short stories, see 000023.

DE..... *Short Stories; *Teaching Guides; *Folk Culture; Cultural Education; *Cultural Awareness; *Instructional Materials; Senior High Schools; Twentieth Century Literature; *Adolescent Literature; Reading Materials

ID..... Philippines; *Filipino Literature

AB..... Information for the teacher is provided in this handbook which accompanies a collection of short stories for the 9th- to 12th-grade student. The 18 stories in the reader provide background material in the Philippine cultural environment and encourage analysis and classroom discussion. The introduction to the teacher's manual contains a questionnaire which covers specific aspects of the students' reading experience (i.e., awareness of ethnic relevance, formal artistic values, empathy, and thematic or conceptual response) and a self-evaluation checklist of the short story for the teacher. The handbook includes a brief introduction to the Filipino storyteller's art and the Philippine short story, supplemental readings on three short stories, and study guides for each of the stories. (JB)

CP..... Y

AN..... 000026

TI..... The Muppet Gallery.

YR..... 78

AU..... Bailey, Joe; Geiss, Tony; Kingsley, Emily; Korr, David; Moss, Jeff; Stiles, Norman; Cushman, Dean, ed.

IN..... Children's Television Workshop, New York, N.Y. Community Education Services.

SN..... Office of Education (DHEW), Washington, D.C. (RMQ66000)

NO..... C 300-76-0100

AV..... Children's Television Workshop, Community Education Services, Dept. A, One Lincoln Plaza, New York, New York 10023

NT..... 25 p.

DE..... *Emotional Development; *Play; Social Behavior; Pretend Play; *Childrens Television; *Educational Television; Children; Parents; *Parent Participation; Social Development; Social Relations; Role Playing; Enrichment Activities; Instructional Aids; Television Viewing; Television Curriculum; *Affective Behavior

ID..... *Sesame Street; Muppets

AB..... This booklet is intended to give parents or those involved with child care a better understanding of how the Muppets illustrate the Sesame Street instructional goals. Each Muppet has been designed to personify characteristics with which children can identify. The show teaches viewers about emotions, feelings, and how individuals work together within society. This book includes color pictures of all the major Muppets and a few of the minor characters. A brief character sketch and a story from the show illustrate how the Muppets make their instructional point. The final section includes directions for Muppet masks and suggestions for role-playing activities that concern social and affective skills, such as recognizing and labeling emotions, coping with failure, entering social groups, understanding different points of view, cooperation, sharing, and conflict resolution. (JB)

CP..... Y

AN..... 000027

TI..... La Choza de cotense (The Burlap Hut).

SE..... Miami Linguistic Readers: Plateau Level 1-3 (Series).

YR..... Apr71

AU..... Robinett, Ralph F.; Nash, Rose L., ill.; Granado, Eusebia, trans.

IN..... Dade County Public Schools, Miami, Fla. (HWP20100); Southeastern New Mexico Bilingual Program, Artesia, N. Mex.

LG..... Spanish

AV..... Southeastern New Mexico Bilingual Program, Artesia, New Mexico

NT..... 32 p.

DE..... *Instructional Materials; *Reading Materials; *Spanish; Vocabulary; *Reading Instruction; Language Instruction; Primary Education; *Childrens Books

AB..... This illustrated reader for the primary grades uses animal characters to tell a story in Spanish; a variety of basic vocabulary words is used. (JB)

CP..... Y

AN..... 000028

TI..... Beto y Tito (Beto and Tito).

SE..... Miami Linguistic Readers: Level 1-A (Series).

YR..... Mar71

AU..... Robinett, Ralph F.; Nash, Rose L., ill.; Granado, Eusebia, trans.

IN..... Southeastern New Mexico Bilingual Program, Artesia, N. Mex.; Dade County Public Schools, Miami, Fla. (HWP20100)

LG..... Spanish

AV..... Southeastern New Mexico Bilingual Program, Artesia, New Mexico

NT..... 23 p.

DE..... *Childrens Books; *Spanish; *Reading Instruction; Language Instruction; *Reading Materials; *Instructional Materials; Primary Education

AB..... This illustrated Spanish reader for the primary grades uses eight vocabulary words in a story of two canine friends. (JB)

CP..... Y

AN..... 000032

TI..... Bonjour papillon (Hello Butterfly).

YR..... 77

AU..... Dugas, Donald G.; Ogrydziak, Dan, ill.

IN..... National Assessment and Dissemination Center, Cambridge, Mass.; National Materials Development Center for French, Bedford, N.H.

SN..... Office of Education (DHEW), Washington, D.C. (RMQ66000)

LG..... French

AV..... National Assessment and Dissemination Center, 49 Washington Avenue, Cambridge, Massachusetts 02140

NT..... 21 p.

DE..... *Reading Materials; Elementary Education; *Instructional Materials; Childrens Literature; *French; *Language Instruction

AB..... This coloring book is designed for use in a French bilingual setting at the elementary level. Three related stories are told with French captions. (DS)

CP..... N

AN..... 000033

TI..... Le Vieil homme et l'enfant (The Old Man and the Child).

YR..... [77]

AU..... Pipyn, Michel; Ganin, Barbara, ill.; Mora, Diane, ill.; Aqua, Karen, ill.

IN..... National Assessment and Dissemination Center, Cambridge, Mass.; National Materials Development Center for French, Bedford, N.H.

SN..... Office of Education (DHEW), Washington, D.C. (RMQ66000)

LG..... French

AV..... National Assessment and Dissemination Center, 49 Washington Avenue, Cambridge, Massachusetts 02140 ($8.75)

NT..... 70 p.

DE..... *Reading Materials; Elementary Education; *Instructional Materials; *French; Childrens Literature; *Language Instruction

AB..... This storybook with color illustrations is for use in a French bilingual education setting at the elementary level. Three parts comprise the reader: (1) the title story; (2) a skit about a trip to a museum; and (3) a dictionary in pictures. (DS)

CP..... N

AN..... 000034

TI..... Un Mot de chez-nous (A Word from Our Home).

YR..... 76

AU..... Dubé, Normand; Jalbert, Paul, ill.

IN..... National Assessment and Dissemination Center, Cambridge, Mass.; National Materials Development Center for French, Bedford, N.H.

SN..... Office of Education (DHEW), Washington, D.C. (RMQ66000)

LG..... French

AV..... National Assessment and Dissemination Center, 49 Washington Avenue, Cambridge, Massachusetts 02140

NT..... 80 p.

DE..... *French; *Supplementary Reading Materials; *Poetry; Secondary Education; Higher Education; Language Instruction

ID..... Acadians

AB..... Poems which may be used as supplementary reading materials in a French bilingual education setting are presented in this compilation of works by an Acadian poet. Illustrations are scattered throughout the book. (DS)

CP..... N

AN..... 000035

TI..... Langue française: Enseignement élémentaire, 5e (French Language: Elementary Education, 5th).

YR..... 66

AU..... Giroux, Emile

LG..... French

AV..... Les Editions FM, Québec, Canada

NT..... 318 p.

DE..... *French; *Textbooks, *Grammar, *Vocabulary; Elementary Education; *Instructional Materials; *Language Instruction; Grade 5

AB..... This textbook for a French language class is intended for use at the fifth grade level of the Canadian educational system. It is geared to students whose first language is French and provides grammar and vocabulary instruction. Individual units are composed of: (1) a reading selection; (2) vocabulary; (3) phonetics; (4) a recitation; (5) grammar; (6) verb conjugation; (7) sentence diagrams; (8) sentence patterns; and (9) a composition exercise. A grammatical index, verb conjugation list, and subject index are provided. Color illustrations are interspersed throughout the text. (DS)

CP..... Y

AN..... 000036

TI..... Aprendemos con gusto. Actividades en español para niños bilingües (Let's Have Fun Learning. Activities in Spanish for Bilingual Children).

YR..... 76

AU..... Herbert, Charles H.; Otis, David L.; Powell, Lilia M.; Sancho, Anthony R.; Smith, Tana

IN..... San Bernadino County Schools, Calif. Regional Project Office. (BBB07971)

SN..... Office of Education (DHEW), Washington, D.C. (RMQ66000)

LG..... English; Spanish

AV..... National Assessment and Dissemination Center, 7703 North Lamar Boulevard, Austin, Texas 78752 ($3.00)

NT..... 123 p.

DE..... *Spanish Speaking; *Lesson Plans; Instructional Materials; Elementary Education; *Teaching Guides; *Group Activities; Creative Activities; *Spanish; Art Activities; Mathematics; Reading; Science Activities; Writing; Social Studies; Language Usage; Bilingual Students

AB..... Lesson plans in the form of task cards designed to implement Spanish language usage in the classroom in many areas of instruction are presented in this manual for teachers. The 70 lessons are intended to provide groups of bilingual children with activities that will promote self-motivated learning and may be used in first through sixth grades. The activities are designed to utilize the children's dominant language regardless of its origin or local dialect and can be performed by the children regardless of level of language competency. The materials call for small groups of four to six children to work together on a given task card activity in the areas of art, math, reading, science, writing, and social studies. Suggestions are provided for adaptation, preparation, and evaluation of task cards based on the models in the manual. Each task card contains information on the activity's purpose, preparation of materials, materials, and instructions. (DS)

CP..... Y

AN..... 000045

TI..... Loca, Eco Tentokorkvtes. Terrapin Race.

YR..... 78

AU..... Factor, Susannah, trans.; Chuleewah, Quannah, ill.

IN..... East Central Univ., Ada, Okla. Seminole Bilingual
       Education Project; National Dissemination and Assessment
       Center, Austin, Tex.

SN..... Office of Education (DHEW), Washington, D.C. (RMQ66000)

LG..... English; Seminole

AV..... National Dissemination and Assessment Center, 7703 North
       Lamar Boulevard, Austin, Texas 78752 (ISBN 0-89417-302-2;
       $1.00)

NT..... 25 p.

DE..... *Reading Materials; *Instructional Materials; *Language
       Instruction; *Reading Instruction; Primary Education;
       American Indian Languages

ID..... *Seminole; Coloring Books

AB..... This reader and coloring book for the primary grades is
       written in Seminole and English. It tells the story of a
       turtle who wins a race with a deer. Facing pages contain
       text in both English and Seminole and an illustration.
       (JB)

CP..... N

AN..... 000046

TI..... Jim: L'histoire de Jim Caron jeune homme racontée par
       lui-même (à 101 ans) (Jim: The Story of Jim Caron the
       Young Man As Told by Jim Caron at 101).

YR..... 77

AU..... Olivier, Julien; Lefebvre, Suzanne, ill.

IN..... National Assessment and Dissemination Center, Cambridge,
       Mass.; National Materials Development Center for French,
       Bedford, N.H.

SN..... Office of Education (DHEW), Washington, D.C. (RMQ66000)

LG..... French

AV..... National Assessment and Dissemination Center, 49
       Washington Avenue, Cambridge, Massachusetts 02140 ($1.25;
       cassette $1.50)

NT..... 54 p.

DE..... *French; Instructional Materials; *Interviews;
       Vocabulary; Autobiography; Tape Recordings; *Oral
       History; Reading Materials; Speech Communication;
       *Standard Spoken Usage; Elementary Secondary Education;
       Regional Dialects; Language Instruction; Intermediate
       Grades; Junior High Schools

ID..... *Franco Americans

AB..... This text is designed for grades six through eight in a
       French bilingual setting. It consists of an edited

version of the oral memoirs of an old Franco-American, born in Canada, who resides in New England. The text is illustrated by black-and-white photographs and drawings. A tape recording taken from the original interview complements the text. (AM)

CP..... N

AN..... 000048

TI..... Antoine ou le silence des choses (Antoine or the Silence of Things).

YR..... [7?]

AU..... Pipyn, Michel; Heikens, Joanna, ill.

IN..... National Assessment and Dissemination Center, Cambridge, Mass.; National Materials Development Center for French, Bedford, N.H.

SN..... Office of Education (DHEW), Washington, D.C. (RMQ66000)

LG..... French

AV..... National Assessment and Dissemination Center, 49 Washington Avenue, Cambridge, Massachusetts 02140 ($4.00)

NT..... [35] p.

DE..... *French; Instructional Materials; *Reading Materials; Childrens Literature; Elementary Education; Cultural Education; *History; Cultural Background; *Language Instruction

ID..... *Acadians

AB..... This reader, illustrated in color, is designed for use in a French bilingual education setting on the elementary level. It conveys background information on Acadian history. (AM)

CP..... N

AN..... 000049

TI..... Le Journal d'un skidoo (The Diary of a Skidoo).

YR..... 77

AU..... Dugas, Don; Ogrydziak, Dan, ill.

IN..... National Assessment and Dissemination Center, Cambridge, Mass.; National Materials Development Center for French, Bedford, N.H.

SN..... Office of Education (DHEW), Washington, D.C. (RMQ66000)

LG..... French

AV..... National Assessment and Dissemination Center, 49
Washington Avenue, Cambridge, Massachusetts 02140 ($1.25)

NT..... 33 p.

DE..... *French; *Reading Materials; *Instructional Materials;
Childrens Literature; Language Instruction; Intermediate
Grades; Junior High Schools; Elementary Secondary
Education

ID..... *Franco Americans

AB..... This illustrated reader is intended for use in a
bilingual education setting, for grades six to eight. It
tells the story of the adventures of a snowmobile
belonging to a Franco-American man. (AM)

CP..... N

AN..... 000051

TI..... Chinese Cultural Resource Book (For Elementary Bilingual
Teachers).

YR..... Jan76

AU..... Kwok, Irene; Chin, Wayne, ill.

IN..... San Francisco Unified School District, Calif. Chinese
Bilingual Pilot Program. (BBB12945); Berkeley Unified
School District, Calif. Asian American Bilingual Center.
(BBB13628); National Assessment and Dissemination
Center, Cambridge, Mass.

SN..... Office of Education (DHEW), Washington, D.C. (RMQ66000)

LG..... Chinese; English

AV..... National Assessment and Dissemination Center, 49
Washington Avenue, Cambridge, Massachusetts 02140 ($3.50)

NT..... iv, 32 p.
Rev. ed.

DE..... Teacher Developed Materials; *Resource Materials;
*Instructional Materials; Elementary Education; Social
Sciences; Classroom Games; Supplementary Reading
Materials; Art Activities; Music Activities; *Class
Activities; *Cultural Activities; *Chinese; Poetry;
*Chinese Culture; Short Stories; Folk Culture; Folklore
Books; Childrens Literature; Cultural Education

ID..... Recipes

AB..... Intended to provide a resource for selected aspects of
the ethnic heritage of children in kindergarten through
sixth grade Chinese bilingual bicultural programs, this
book is to be used in conjunction with other materials in
a social science curriculum. The 206 stories, poems,
songs, games, art projects, and recipes are related to
the 5 major Chinese festivals: Moon Festival, Winter
Festival, Chinese New Year, Ching Ming, and Dragon Boat
Festival. Some materials are also related to seasonal,

transportation, and family topics. The story section includes Chinese legends, myths, and folktales. Each item is illustrated and presented in both English and modern Chinese. A 41-citation bibliography is included. (JS)

CP..... N

AN..... 000052

TI..... La Estrella perdida (The Missing Star).

YR..... [7?]

AU..... Cohen, Allen Stephen; Puigdollers, Carmen, trans.; Cancel, Luis R., ill.; Carmen García, María del, ed.

IN..... Northeast Center for Curriculum Development, Bronx, N.Y.

SN..... Office of Education (DHEW), Washington, D.C. (RMQ66000)

LG..... Spanish

AV..... National Assessment and Dissemination Center, 49 Washington Avenue, Cambridge, Massachusetts 02140 ($1.00)

NT..... [19] p.
For an English version of this book, see 000053.

DE..... *Spanish; *Childrens Literature; Illustrations; *Reading Materials; Elementary Education; *Instructional Materials; Puerto Rican Culture

ID..... Puerto Rico

AB..... This reader in Spanish, designed for grades one to five, recounts adventures of the star on the Puerto Rican flag. It is illustrated in black and white. (DS)

CP..... N

AN..... 000053

TI..... The Missing Star.

YR..... [7?]

AU..... Cohen, Allen Stephen; Cancel, Luis R., ill.; Rodríguez, Aurea E., ed.; Puigdollers, Carmen, trans.

IN..... Northeast Center for Curriculum Development, Bronx, N.Y. (BBB17015)

SN..... Office of Education (DHEW), Washington, D.C. (RMQ66000)

AV..... National Assessment and Dissemination Center, 49 Washington Avenue, Cambridge, Massachusetts 02140 ($1.00)

NT..... [19] p.
For a Spanish version of this book, see 000052.

DE..... *Childrens Literature; *Reading Materials; Illustrations; Elementary Education; *Instructional Materials; Puerto Rican Culture

ID..... Puerto Rico

AB..... This reader, designed for grades one to five, recounts adventures of the star on the Puerto Rican flag. It is illustrated in black and white. (DS)

AN..... 000054

TI..... Vamos a jugar con letras (Let's Play with Letters).

YR..... 77

AU..... Cadilla de Ruibal, Carmen Alicia; Maldonado, Juan, ill.

IN..... Northeast Center for Curriculum Development, Bronx, N.Y. (BBB17015)

SN..... Office of Education (DHEW), Washington, D.C. (RMQ66000)

LG..... Spanish

AV..... National Assessment and Dissemination Center, 49 Washington Avenue, Cambridge, Massachusetts 02140 ($1.00)

NT..... 30 p.

DE..... *Spanish; *Letters (Alphabet); Primary Education; *Spanish Speaking; Word Lists; Illustrations; *Reading Instruction; *Reading Materials; *Beginning Reading

AB..... In this visual aid for both reading and writing designed for Spanish-speaking children at the kindergarten to first grade level, each letter of the Spanish alphabet is illustrated with black-and-white drawings of objects and word lists which reinforce that particular letter. (DS)

CP..... N

AN..... 000055

TI..... Pintando también se aprende: Aspectos de la cultura puertorriqueña (You Learn by Coloring, Too: Aspects of Puerto Rican Culture).

YR..... 77

AU..... Cadilla de Ruibal, Carmen Alicia; Maldonado, Juan, ill.

IN..... Northeast Center for Curriculum Development, Bronx, N.Y. (BBB17015)

SN..... Office of Education (DHEW), Washington, D.C. (RMQ66000)

LG..... Spanish

AV..... National Assessment and Dissemination Center, 49 Washington Avenue, Cambridge, Massachusetts 02140 ($1.25)

NT..... v, 38 p.

DE..... *Puerto Rican Culture; *Puerto Ricans; *Reading Materials; *Cultural Education; *Spanish; *Instructional Materials; History; Geography; Folklore; Primary Education

ID..... *Coloring Books

AB..... A collection of vignettes dealing with Puerto Rican culture is presented as a reading and coloring book for Puerto Rican children and children of Hispanic origin in general at the kindergarten to first grade level. Each set of facing pages covers a different topic in the history, geography, customs, and traditions of Puerto Rico. Readings, either prose or poetry, are on the left, illustrations on the right. Questions to elicit student responses to the text and pictures follow each reading. (DS)

CP..... N

AN..... 000056

TI..... Practice Exercises in Everyday English for Advanced Foreign Students.

YR..... 57

AU..... Dixson, Robert J.

AV..... Simon and Schuster, Inc., 1230 Avenue of the Americas, New York, New York 10020

NT..... 208 p.

DE..... *English (Second Language); *Grammar; Idioms; Workbooks; Language Instruction; *Foreign Students; Textbooks, *Second Language Learning; *Instructional Materials; *Pattern Drills (Language)

AB..... Grammar and idiomatic principles of English are explained, and exercises based on those principles are provided in this drill book for students of English as a second language at the advanced level. The text's emphasis is on everyday practice rather than theory. Elementary and intermediate material is reviewed, and the lessons are graded, moving from easier to more difficult material. Sections in each lesson are: (1) grammar/idioms; (2) exercises; and (3) word study. An appendix containing sample verb conjugations and principal parts of common irregular verbs is provided, along with a subject index. (DS)

CP..... Y

AN..... 000057

TI..... Social Studies: English-Spanish.

SE..... Learning Achievement Packages (Series).

YR..... 75

AU..... Markatos, John

IN..... Calexico Intercultural Design, Calif.

SN..... Office of Education (DHEW), Washington, D.C. (RMQ66000)

LG..... English; Spanish

AV..... National Dissemination and Assessment Center, 7703 North Lamar Boulevard, Austin, Texas 78752 ($3.00)

NT..... vi, 133 p.

DE..... *Spanish; *Social Studies; *Curriculum Guides; *Instructional Materials; Grade 12; Senior High Schools; Adult Education; Political Science; Legal Education; Government (Administrative Body); Civics; Learning Difficulties; Language Handicaps

AB..... This publication contains 2 social studies curriculum units designed to deal with the learning problems of students with special language difficulties, in grade 12 or in adult education classes. Entitled "An Idea Becomes a Law" and "The State: Forms of Government and Political Systems," the units inform students of the legislative function of Congress and the various basic forms of governments and political systems. Each unit is presented first in English and then in Spanish and contains an information guide for the teacher, information for the student, pre- and posttests, model worksheets and exercises, suggested additional materials, and a bibliography. (DS)

CP..... N

AN..... 000058

TI..... Mexican American Studies: English-Spanish.

SE..... Learning Achievement Packages (Series).

YR..... 76

AU..... Astacio, Ramón; Iruegas, Efraín; Hernández, Gloria J., ed.

IN..... Calexico Intercultural Design, Calif.

SN..... Office of Education (DHEW), Washington, D.C. (RMQ66000)

LG..... English; Spanish

AV..... National Dissemination and Assessment Center, 7703 North Lamar Boulevard, Austin, Texas 78752 ($3.00)

NT..... viii, 126 p.

DE..... *Spanish; *Mexican American History; *Curriculum Guides; *Instructional Materials; Grade 7; Grade 8; Grade 9; Grade 10; Grade 11; Grade 12; Secondary Education; Adult

Education; Language Handicaps; Learning Difficulties; High Schools; *Mexican Americans; *Area Studies

AB..... This publication contains Mexican-American studies curriculum units designed to deal with the learning problems of students with special language difficulties, in grades 7 through 12 or in adult education classes. The units, presented first in English and then in Spanish, are intended to give students a broader background in Mexican civilization and cover three pre-Hispanic cultures: the Olmec, the Maya, and the Aztec. Each unit contains an information guide for the teacher, information for the student, pre- and posttests, model worksheets and exercises, suggested additional materials, and a bibliography. (DS)

CP..... N

AN..... 000059

TI..... Las Formas geométricas (Geometric Shapes).

YR..... 77

AU..... Fuller, Elizabeth Valenzuela

IN..... Mesa Community Coll., Ariz. (BBB13901)

LG..... Spanish

AV..... Mesa Community College, Bilingual Teachers Aide Program, 1833 West Southern Avenue, Mesa, Arizona 85202

NT..... [11] p.

DE..... *Primary Education; *Spanish; Instructional Materials; *Geometric Concepts; Mathematical Concepts; Reading Materials

AB..... This reader, intended for primary-level mathematics instruction in a Spanish bilingual setting, introduces seven geometric shapes. A brief vocabulary list completes the volume. (JS)

CP..... Y

AN..... 000060

TI..... Mathématiques I: Volume 1 (Mathematics I: Volume 1).

YR..... May73

AU..... Bradley, Ruth; Coussan, Odette; Begnaud, Noëmi; Price, Kathleen; Bachelier, Raymond; Pétreault, Marie-Claude; Granger, Jean-Michel; Bernard, David, ill.; Desjardins, Peggy, ill.

IN..... Lafayette Parish Bilingual Program, La.

SN..... Office of Education (DHEW), Washington, D.C. (RMQ66000)

AV..... Lafayette Parish Bilingual Program, 400 Willow Street,
        Lafayette, Louisiana 70501

NT..... [99] leaves
        For Volume 2, see 000061.

DE..... *French; *Mathematics Curriculum; *Curriculum Guides;
        *Teaching Guides; Visual Aids; Learning Activities;
        *Mathematics Instruction; Grade 1; Primary Education;
        Lesson Plans; Concept Teaching

AB..... This mathematics program for grade one was designed to
        permit French-speaking children to learn basic concepts
        in their native language. It is used in conjunction with
        the primary mathematics curriculum adopted by the
        Lafayette, La., school system. The lessons are written
        for 30-minute periods every other day, but may be adapted
        to meet the needs of particular children. Each of the 30
        lessons in this volume contains a statement of purpose,
        materials needed, vocabulary, development of review and
        lesson, and an exercise. The black-and-white patterns
        which accompany the lessons may be used as masters for
        transparencies, flannel board cutouts, ditto sheets, or
        other visuals. (Author/DS)

CP..... N

AN..... 000061

TI..... Mathématiques I: Volume 2 (Mathematics I: Volume 2).

YR..... May73

AU..... Bradley, Ruth; Coussan, Odette; Begnaud, Noëmi; Price,
        Kathleen; Bachelier, Raymond; Pétreault, Marie-Claude;
        Granger, Jean-Michel; Bernard, David, ill.; Desjardins,
        Peggy, ill.

IN..... Lafayette Parish Bilingual Program, La.

SN..... Office of Education (DHEW), Washington, D.C. (RMQ66000)

LG..... French

AV..... Lafayette Parish Bilingual Program, 400 Willow Street,
        Lafayette, Louisiana 70501

NT..... [77] leaves
        For Volume 1, see 000060.

DE..... *French; *Mathematics Curriculum; *Curriculum Guides;
        *Teaching Guides; Grade 1; Visual Aids; Learning
        Activities; *Mathematics Instruction; Primary Education;
        *Lesson Plans; Concept Teaching

AB..... This mathematics program for grade one was designed to
        permit French-speaking children to learn basic concepts
        in their native language. It is used in conjunction with
        the primary mathematics curriculum adopted by the
        Lafayette, La., school system. The lessons are written
        for 30-minute periods every other day, but may be adapted
        to meet the needs of particular children. Each of the 27
        lessons in this volume contains a statement of purpose,

materials needed, vocabulary, development of review and
lesson, and an exercise. The black-and-white patterns
which accompany the lessons may be used as masters for
transparencies, flannel board cutouts, ditto sheets, or
other visuals. (DS)

CP..... N

AN..... 000062

TI..... Kindergarten: Curriculum Guide. Kindergarten: Livre du maître.

YR..... May72

AU..... Bradley, Ruth; Coussan, Odette; Fanjeaux, Francis; Price, Kathleen; Begnaud, Noëmi; Bernard, David, ill.

IN..... Lafayette Parish Bilingual Program, La.

SN..... Office of Education (DHEW), Washington, D.C. (RMQ66000)

LG..... French

AV..... Lafayette Parish Bilingual Program, 400 Willow Street, Lafayette, Louisiana 70501

NT..... [132] leaves
For related documents covering the rest of the school year, see 000063-65.

DE..... *Kindergarten; *Curriculum Guides; *French; *Teaching Guides; *Learning Activities; Social Development; Art; Mathematics; Physical Education; Music; Visual Aids; Primary Education; Early Childhood Education; *Lesson Plans, Concept Teaching

ID..... Acadians

AB..... Guides in curriculum areas of social living, art, mathematics, physical education, and music are contained in this manual designed to permit French-speaking kindergarten children to learn basic concepts and develop vocabulary in their native language. The activities are grouped to relate monthly to the school calendar; this handbook covers September and October. Patterns for visuals to accompany the daily guides are printed in black and white and may be used as flannel board cutouts, ditto stencils, or transparencies. (DS)

AN..... 000063

TI..... Kindergarten: Livre du maître. Novembre-décembre-janvier (Kindergarten: Teacher's Manual. November-December-January).

YR..... May72

AU..... Bradley, Ruth; Coussan, Odette; Fanjeaux, Francis; Price, Kathleen; Begnaud, Noëmi; Bernard, David, ill.

IN..... Lafayette Parish Bilingual Program, La.

SN..... Office of Education (DHEW), Washington, D.C. (RMQ66000)

LG..... French

AV..... Lafayette Parish Bilingual Program, 400 Willow Street, Lafayette, Louisiana 70501

NT..... [91] leaves
For related documents covering the rest of the school year, see 000062 and 64-65.

DE..... *Kindergarten, *Curriculum Guides; *French; *Teaching Guides; *Learning Activities; Social Development; Art; Mathematics; Physical Education; Music; Visual Aids; Lesson Plans; Early Childhood Education; Primary Education; Concept Teaching

AB..... Guides in curriculum areas of social living, art, mathematics, physical education, and music are contained in this manual designed to permit French-speaking kindergarten children to learn basic concepts and develop vocabulary in their native language. The activities are grouped to relate monthly to the school calendar; this handbook covers November, December, and January. Patterns for visuals to accompany the daily guides are printed in black and white and may be used as flannel board cutouts, ditto stencils, or transparencies. (DS)

CP..... N

AN..... 000064

TI..... Kindergarten: Livre du maître. Avril-mai (Kindergarten: Teacher's Manual. April-May).

YR..... May72

AU..... Bradley, Ruth; Coussan, Odette; Fanjeaux, Francis; Price, Kathleen; Begnaud, Noëmi; Bernard, David, ill.

IN..... Lafayette Parish Bilingual Program, La.

SN..... Office of Education (DHEW), Washington, D.C. (RMQ66000)

LG..... French

AV..... Lafayette Parish Bilingual Program, 400 Willow Street, Lafayette, Louisiana 70501

NT..... [75] leaves
For related documents covering the rest of the school year, see 000062-63 and 65.

DE..... *Kindergarten; *Curriculum Guides; *French; Bilingual Education; *Teaching Guides; *Learning Activities; Social Development; Art; Mathematics; Physical Education; Music; Visual Aids; *Lesson Plans; Early Childhood Education; Primary Education

AB..... Guides in curriculum areas of social living, art, mathematics, physical education, and music are contained

in this manual designed to permit French-speaking
kindergarten children to learn basic concepts and develop
vocabulary in their native language. The activities are
grouped to relate monthly to the school calendar; this
handbook covers April and May. Patterns for visuals to
accompany the daily guides are printed in black and white
and may be used as flannel board cutouts, ditto stencils,
or transparencies. (DS)

CP..... N

AN..... 000065

TI..... Kindergarten: Livre du maître. Février-mars
(Kindergarten: Teacher's Manual. February-March).

YR..... May72

AU..... Bradley, Ruth; Coussan, Odette; Fanjeaux, Francis; Price,
Kathleen; Begnaud, Noëmi; Bernard, David, ill.

IN..... Lafayette Parish Bilingual Program, La.

SN..... Office of Education (DHEW), Washington, D.C. (RMQ66000)

LG..... French

AV..... Lafayette Parish Bilingual Program, 400 Willow Street,
Lafayette, Louisiana 70501

NT..... [101] leaves
For related documents covering the rest of the school
year, see 000062-64.

DE..... *Kindergarten; *Curriculum Guides; *French; *Teaching
Guides; *Learning Activities; Social Development; Art;
Mathematics; Physical Education; Music; Visual Aids;
*Lesson Plans; Early Childhood Education; Primary
Education

AB..... Guides in curriculum areas of social living, art,
mathematics, physical education, and music are contained
in this manual designed to permit French-speaking
kindergarten children to learn basic concepts and develop
vocabulary in their native language. The activities are
grouped to relate monthly to the school calendar; this
handbook covers February and March. Patterns for visuals
to accompany the daily guides are printed in black and
white and may be used as flannel board cutouts, ditto
stencils, or transparencies. (DS)

CP..... N

AN..... 000066

TI..... Coyote, the Millionaire.

YR..... Aug76

AU..... Weahkee, Laurie; Weahkee, Sonny

IN..... Native American Materials Development Center, Albuquerque, N. Mex.

SN..... Office of Education (DHEW), Washington, D.C. (RMQ66000)

AV..... National Dissemination and Assessment Center, 7703 North Lamar Blvd., Austin, Texas 78752 ($1.00)

NT..... 12 p.

DE..... *Childrens Literature; *Childrens Art; *Navajo; *Reading Materials; Elementary Education; American Indians; *Student Developed Materials

AB..... This reader is designed for use in a Native American education setting. The text is accompanied by children's stick-figure drawings. (AM)

CP..... N

AN..... 000067

TI..... Social Living I: Curriculum Guide. Livre du maître (Teacher's Manual).

YR..... [nd]

AU..... Bradley, Ruth; Coussan, Odette; Bachelier, Raymond; Bachelier, Guy; Schlickling, Janine; Price, Kathleen; Begnaud, Noëmi; Calais, Gayle; Bernard, David, ill.

IN..... Lafayette Parish Bilingual Program, La.

SN..... OED

LG..... French

AV..... Lafayette Parish Bilingual Program, 400 Willow Street, Lafayette, Louisiana 70501

NT..... [109] leaves; For volumes 2 and 3, see BE000068 and BE000069

DE..... *French; *Social Development; *Curriculum Guides; *Lesson Plans; *Teaching Guides; Visual Aids; Grade 1; Primary Education; Learning Activities; Concept Teaching; Illustrations

AB..... This curriculum guide contains social living materials intended for use and/or adaptation with first-grade French-speaking children. Each guide is planned for a lesson of approximately 30 minutes' duration. Major groups of lessons are entitled "self-identification," "autumn,""Halloween," "safety rules," and Thanksgiving." Individual lessons are composed of a statement or purpose, materials needed, vocabulary, and lesson development. Black-and-white patterns for visuals to accompany the guides are designed for optional use as flannel board cutouts, ditto stencils, transparencies, etc. (Author/DS)

CP..... N

AN..... 000068

TI..... Social Living I: Volume 2.

YR..... [nd]

AU..... Bradley, Ruth; Coussan, Odette; Bachelier, Raymond; Bachelier, Guy; Schlickling, Janine; Price, Kathleen; Begnaud, Noëmi; Calais, Gayle; Bernard, David, ill.

IN..... Lafayette Parish Bilingual Program, La.

SN..... Office of Education (DHEW), Washington, D.C. (RMQ66000)

LG..... French

AV..... Lafayette Parish Bilingual Program, 400 Willow Street, Lafayette, Lousisana 70501

NT..... [156] leaves; For Volumes 1 and 3, see 000067 and 69.

DE..... *French; *Social Development; *Curriculum Guides; *Teaching Guides; *Lesson Plans; Visual Aids; Grade 1; Primary Education; Learning Activities; Concept Teaching

AB..... This curriculum guide contains social living materials intended for use and/or adaptation with first grade French-speaking children. Each guide is planned for a lesson of approximately 30 minutes duration. Major groups of lessons are entitled "the school and its surroundings," "winter," "Christmas," "everyday clothes and Sunday clothes," "the parts of the body," "the family," "public services," and "Mardi Gras." Individual lessons are composed of a statement of purpose, materials needed, vocabulary, and lesson development. Black-and-white patterns for visuals to accompany the guides are designed for optional use as flannel board cutouts, ditto stencils, transparencies, etc. (Author/DS)

CP..... N

AN..... 000069

TI..... Social Living: Volume 3.

YR..... [nd]

AU..... Bradley, Ruth; Coussan, Odette; Bachelier, Raymond; Bachelier, Guy; Schlickling, Janine, Price, Kathleen; Begnaud, Noëmi; Calais, Gayle; Bernard, David, ill.

IN..... Lafayette Parish Bilingual Program, La.

SN..... Office of Education (DHEW), Washington, D.C. (RMQ66000)

LG..... French

AV..... Lafayette Parish Bilingual Program, 400 Willow Street, Lafayette, Louisiana 70501

NT..... [103] leaves; For volumes 1 and 2, see BE000067 and BE000068

DE..... *French; *Social Development; *Curriculum Guides; *Teaching Guides; *Lesson Plans; Visual Aids; *Grade 1; Primary Education; Learning Activities; Cultural Education

ID..... Acadians

AB..... This curriculum guide contains social living materials intended for use and/or adaptation with first-grade French-speaking children. Each guide is planned for a lesson of approximately 30 minutes duration. Major groups of lessons are entitled: "The Acadian heritage," "spring," "Easter," "animals," "transportation," "summer," and "the seasons." Individual lessons are composed of a statement of purpose, materials needed, vocabulary, and lesson development. Black-and-white patterns for visuals to accompany the guides are designed for optional use as flannel board cutouts, ditto stencils, transparencies, etc. (Author/DS)

CP..... N

AN..... 000070

TI..... Sesame Street Activities.

YR..... 76

AU..... O'Connor, Jane, ed.; Merril, Abby, ill.

IN..... Children's Television Workshop, New York, N.Y. (BBB03935)

SN..... Office of Education (DHEW), Washington, D.C. (RMQ66000)

NO..... C 300-76-0100

AV..... Children's Television Workshop, One Lincoln Plaza, New York, New York 10023

NT..... 65 p.

DE..... *Creative Activities; *Enrichment Activities; *Learning Activities; Activity Units; *Instructional Materials; Early Childhood Education; Children's Games; Educational Games; Television Viewing; *Children's Television; Group Activities

ID..... Muppets; *Sesame Street

AB..... This book is based on the instructional goals of the television series, Sesame Street. It provides a way of linking the educational content of the show with learning activities that can be conducted before or after the program. The manual is divided into four content areas: (1) The Child and His World, which contains activities relating to body parts, emotions, etc.; (2) Using Symbols, which contains activities on letters and numbers; (3) Learning Skills; and (4) Bilingual/Bicultural Activities. The last section discusses the instructional goals of the Sesame Street program. (JS)

CP..... Y

AN.....	000101

TI..... El Cuento de la nota musical (The Story of the Musical Note).

YR..... 77

AU..... Allen, Shauna; Keith, Lapita, ill.

IN..... Mesa Community Coll., Ariz. (BBB13901)

LG..... Spanish

AV..... Mesa Community College, Bilingual Teachers Aide Program, 1833 West Southern Avenue, Mesa, Arizona 85202

NT..... [16] p.

DE..... Primary Education; *Music Education; Childrens Literature; *Spanish; *Reading Materials; *Instructional Materials; Elementary Education; *Language Instruction; Vocabulary

AB..... This reader, intended for use in the bilingual classroom at the primary grade level, introduces the concept of the musical notes in Spanish. The book is illustrated with black-and-white drawings. (JB)

CP..... Y

AN.....	000102

TI..... Un Libro de pinturas de la revolución de México (A Picture Book of the Mexican Revolution).

YR..... [nd]

AU..... Pfeiffer, Theresa

IN..... Mesa Community Coll., Ariz. (BBB13901)

LG..... Spanish

AV..... Mesa Community College, Bilingual Teachers Aide Program, 1833 West Southern Ave., Mesa, Arizona 85202

NT..... [16] p.

DE..... Primary Education; Elementary Education; *Spanish; *Mexicans; *Reading Materials; *Instructional Materials; *History

ID..... Mexico; *Coloring Books; *Hidalgo (Miguel)

AB..... This reader, intended for use in a bilingual education setting at the primary grade level, is about Miguel Hidalgo and the Mexican revolution. It is illustrated in black and white and could be used as a coloring book. (JB)

CP..... N

AN..... 000103

TI..... Aprendemos de carreras (We Learn About Careers).

YR..... 77

AU..... Randall, Clint; VanBuskirk, Sue

IN..... Mesa Community Coll., Ariz. (BBB13901)

LG..... Spanish

AV..... Mesa Community College Bilingual Teachers Aide Program, 1833 West Southern Ave., Mesa, Arizona 85202

NT..... 26 leaves

DE..... Primary Education; Elementary Education; *Spanish; *Reading Materials; Vocabulary; *Career Awareness; *Instructional Materials

ID..... Coloring Books

AB..... This reader, intended for use in a bilingual education setting on the primary level, introduces children to different occupations. Each occupation is presented with a black-and-white illustration and a brief description. (JB)

CP..... Y

AN..... 000104

TI..... Graciela camina a la escuela (Graciela Walks to School).

YR..... 77

AU..... Stewart, Julieta; Echeveste, Irene, ill.

IN..... Mesa Community Coll., Ariz. (BBB13901).

LG..... Spanish

AV..... Mesa Community College, Bilingual Teachers Aide Program, 1833 West Southern Avenue, Mesa, Arizona 85202

NT..... 19 p.

DE..... Elementary Education; Primary Education; *Instructional Materials; *Reading Materials; Vocabulary; *Spanish; *Safety Education; *Traffic Safety

ID..... Coloring Books

AB..... This reader, intended for use in the bilingual education classroom at the primary grade level, teaches children about safety on the streets. It explains how to obey traffic lights and how to cross streets safely. It is illustrated in black and white and includes a vocabulary list. (JB)

CP..... Y

AN..... 000105

TI..... Learning English Uno: Conforme a los objetivos del programa oficial (Learning English One: Corresponding to the Objectives of the Official Program).

SE..... Educación media básica. Primer grado (Intermediate Basic Education. First Grade) (Series).

YR..... Aug75

AU..... Vallejo, Bernardo

LG..... English; Spanish

AV..... Editorial Trillas, S.A., Av. 5 de Mayo 43-105, Mexico 1, D.F.

NT..... 176 p.

DE..... *Grammar; *English (Second Language); Secondary Education; *Instructional Materials; Classroom Materials; *Language Instruction; *Textbooks; Spanish Speaking; *Second Language Learning

AB..... This grammar is intended for first year English instruction on the secondary level and is designed to be used with Spanish-speaking students. It is composed of eight units and two review units. The eight units consist of basic structures followed by conversation and reading comprehension drills. Eight songs, an English-Spanish vocabulary, and an index of objectives contained in each unit complete the volume. (AM)

CP..... Y

AN..... 000106

TI..... Kindergarten Bilingual Resource Handbook.

YR..... Feb74

IN..... Lubbock Public Schools, Tex.

SN..... Office of Education (DHEW), Washington, D.C. (RMQ66000)

LG..... English; Spanish

AV..... National Dissemination and Assessment Center, 7703 North Lamar Boulevard, Austin, Texas 78752 ($4.50)

NT..... xi, 187 p.
        Rev. ed.

DE..... *Bilingual Education; Primary Education; *Kindergarten; *Educational Resources; *Curriculum Design; Teacher Developed Materials; *Instructional Materials; Evaluation Criteria; Evaluation Methods; Bilingual Students; Learning Activities; Bilingual Teacher Aides; Teaching Methods

AB..... This handbook is intended to assist kindergarten teachers who work with bilingual children and contains activities which are appropriate to these children's age group and cultural background. Suggestions are provided for the following: (1) curriculum design and schedules; (2) teacher aides and room arrangements; (3) teaching oral language, social studies, numerical concepts, science, health, art, music, and physical education; (4) resource and activity units; (5) bilingual resource materials; (6) constructing various instructional aids; (7) evaluating children's development; and (8) purchasing instructional materials. A 10-item bibliography completes the volume. (AM)

CP..... N

AN..... 000108

TI..... A Casa do Manuel (Manuel's House).

YR..... 77

AU..... Miranda Correia, Luis de; Mattos, William J., ill.

IN..... National Assessment and Dissemination Center, Cambridge, Mass.

SN..... Office of Education (DHEW), Washington, D.C. (RMQ66000)

LG..... Portuguese

AV..... National Assessment and Dissemination Center, 49 Washington Avenue, Cambridge, Massachusetts 02140 ($1.75)

NT..... vi, 60 p.

DE..... *Instructional Materials; *Portuguese; Grammar; Elementary Education; *Second Language Learning; *Reading Materials; *Language Instruction; Childrens Literature; Health Education; Housing; Time; Eating Habits

AB..... This illustrated reader is intended for students of Portuguese as a second language on the elementary level. Concepts of the house, time, hygiene, and meals are conveyed. Questions relating to the readings and a brief grammar section complete the book. (AM)

CP..... N

AN..... 000109

TI..... Aquí se habla español (Spanish is Spoken Here).

YR..... [nd]

AU..... Cohen, Allen Stephen; Rodríguez, Aurea E., ed.; Rosario, Idalia, ill.

IN..... Curriculum Adaptation Network for Bilingual/Bicultural Education, Bronx, N.Y. Northeast Regional Adaptation Center. (BBB11922)

SN..... Office of Education (DHEW), Washington, D.C. (RMQ66000)

AV..... National Assessment and Dissemination Center, 49 Washington Avenue, Cambridge, Massachusetts 02140 ($1.00)

NT..... 19 p.

DE..... *Childrens Literature; Elementary Education; *Cultural Education; Cultural Environment; *Instructional Materials; Story Reading; Spanish Speaking; *Puerto Ricans; *Ethnic Groups; *Reading Materials

ID..... New York (New York)

AB..... This reader, illustrated in black and white, conveys the importance of multilingualism through the story of a Puerto Rican boy in New York City. A short vocabulary list is appended. (AM)

CP..... N

AN..... 000110

TI..... Taga the Great.

YR..... 73

AU..... Baker, Frances S.

IN..... Trust Territory of the Pacific Islands. Dept. of Education, Saipan. (LXA93761); California State Univ., Los Angeles. National Dissemination and Assessment Center. (BBB15398)

SN..... Office of Education (DHEW), Washington, D.C. (RMQ66000)

AV..... National Dissemination and Assessment Center, California State University, Los Angeles, 5151 State University Drive, Los Angeles, California 90032 ($2.65); Superintendent of Documents, U.S. Government Printing Office, Washington, D.C. 20402 (Stock no. 1978-785-301/1902-M,1078,9-I)

NT..... 81 p.

DE..... *Legends; Folk Culture; Intermediate Grades; Grade 5; *Childrens Literature; *Reading Materials; Reading Instruction; *Social Studies; Elementary Education; *Instructional Materials

ID..... *Mariana Islands; *Taga

AB..... This reader, intended to accompany the fifth grade social studies unit of the Mariana school system, recounts the story of Taga, a legendary hero of the Pacific Islands. Black-and-white drawings and photographs illustrate the book. (JB)

CP..... N

AN.....	000111
TI.....	English Language Arts Units: Teacher's Guide.
YR.....	Mar78
AU.....	Thompson, Jean; Pérez, Carlos, ed.
IN.....	National Dissemination and Assessment Center, Austin, Tex.; Fort Worth Public Schools, Tex. Bilingual Education Program.
SN.....	Office of Education (DHEW), Washington, D.C. (RMQ66000)
AV.....	National Dissemination and Assessment Center, 7703 North Lamar Blvd., Austin, Texas 78752 (ISBN 0-89417-342-1; $2.00)
NT.....	vii, 76 p. For accompanying student's book, see 000112.
DE.....	*Language Arts; Vocabulary; *Teaching Guides; Puns; Metaphors; Figurative Language; Mexican Americans; Literature; Puzzles; Intermediate Grades; Folk Culture; Cultural Factors; *Vocabulary Development; Grade 6; Elementary Education; Spanish; Childrens Literature; Spanish Speaking; *Lesson Plans; Learning Activities; *English (Second Language); *Instructional Materials
ID.....	Language Functions
AB.....	This teacher's guide is designed to accompany the student's language arts unit and was developed for the bilingual multicultural upper elementary classroom, especially for the sixth grade. Eleven units deal with English language development and ten with literature relevant to Spanish-speaking children. Each unit contains information about the following for the teacher: (1) general background on the lesson; (2) concept to be conveyed; (3) lesson objectives; (4) vocabulary; (5) materials; (6) learning activities; (7) evaluation; and (8) enrichment activities. An answer key is provided, as are suggested reading lists for the teacher and for the student. (JB)
CP.....	N

AN.....	000112
TI.....	English Language Arts Units: Student's Book.
YR.....	Mar78
IN.....	National Dissemination and Assessment Center, Austin, Tex. Fort Worth Public Schools, Tex. Bilingual Education Program.
SN.....	Office of Education (DHEW), Washington, D.C. (RMQ66000)
LG.....	English; Spanish

AV..... National Dissemination and Assessment Center, 7703 North Lamar Blvd., Austin, Texas 78752 (ISBN 0-89412-343-X; $2.00)

NT..... iii, 87 p.
For accompanying teacher's guide, see 000111.

DE..... *Language Arts; Workbooks; *Vocabulary Development; Vocabulary; Mexican Americans; Spelling; Figurative Language; Literature; Folk Culture; Cultural Factors; Puzzles; Puns; Metaphors; Intermediate Grades; *English (Second Language); Elementary Education; *Childrens Literature; *Reading Materials; Spanish; *Instructional Materials; Spanish Speaking; Learning Activities

ID..... Language Functions

AB..... This vocabulary and literature guide was designed for the bilingual multicultural upper elementary classroom, especially for the sixth grade. Section one, dealing with vocabulary development, consists of the following units: (1) "The Alphabet"; (2) "How to Fill Out A Form"; (3) "Our Changing Language"; (4) "The Language of Mathematics"; (5) "The Language of Religion"; (6) "The Language of Politics"; (7) "How Can I Find It in the Dictionary If I Don't Know How to Spell It?"; (8) "Different Ages, Different Words"; and (9) "Vocabulary for Cooking." Section two consists of the following units, which deal with literature relevant to Spanish-speaking children: (1) "Language of Poetry"; (2) "My First Day at School"; (3) "Too Early"; (4) "Just Wait"; (5) "The Sleeping Uncle"; (6) "El Nacimiento"; (7) "El Agua, el viento y la verdad"; (8) "The Record"; and (9) "El Tío Candido." (JB)

CP..... N

AN..... 000115

TI..... How to Write Criterion-Referenced Tests for Spanish-English Bilingual Programs.

YR..... Aug78

AU..... Tombari, Martin; Mangino, Evangelina

IN..... National Dissemination and Assessment Center, Austin, Tex.

SN..... Office of Education (DHEW), Washington, D.C. (RMQ66000)

LG..... English; Spanish

AV..... National Dissemination and Assessment Center, 7703 North Lamar Blvd., Austin, Texas 78752 (ISBN 0-89417-519-X; $3.00)

NT..... 125 p.

DE..... *Criterion Referenced Tests; Educational Objectives; Bilingual Education; *Testing; Programed Texts; *Teaching Guides; Programed Instruction; *Test Construction

AB..... This module is intended to serve as a step-by-step guide to writing criterion-referenced tests. It can be used by teachers, curriculum writers, and students as a text in a college course, as a module in an inservice training program, as a self-paced learning guide, or as a professional reference tool. The following skills necessary to constructing a criterion-referenced test form a hierarchy; i.e., one step is prerequisite to the next: (1) write instructional objectives, (2) rewrite poorly written objectives, (3) prepare a content outline, (4) write test items that match objectives, and (5) write various item types. Each step is presented in individual units with examples and exercises. The last chapter contains a list of relevant questions and answers related to criterion-referenced testing. The concepts are presented in English and summarized in Spanish. (JB)

CP..... N

AN..... 000119

TI..... Construindo o mundo: 1. Porquê trabalhar? (Building the World: 1. Why Work?).

YR..... [nd]

AU..... Almeida, Onésimo; Cramer, Sharon

IN..... Massachusetts Dept. of Education, Boston. Educational Television.

SN..... Fall River Public Schools, Mass. (BBB03090)

LG..... Portuguese

AV..... National Assessment and Dissemination Center, 49 Washington Ave., Cambridge, Massachusetts 02140 (set of 5 workbooks and filmstrips $19.00)

NT..... 22 p.
For units 2-5, see 000120-123.

DE..... *Portuguese; Portuguese Americans; *Workbooks; *Filmstrips; *Work Attitudes; Job Skills; Jobs; Job Market; Job Training; *Career Awareness; Career Education; Career Opportunities; Careers; Intermediate Grades; Junior High Schools; *Instructional Materials; Grade 5; Grade 6; Grade 7; Grade 8

AB..... This workbook in Portuguese and accompanying 35mm color filmstrip are part of a career awareness set designed for use in grades five through eight. Students are encouraged to be proud of the work they will do and to develop a sense of its contribution to society. The set covers the topics of why people work, attitudes toward work, job requirements, and job opportunities. Objectives, pre- and posttests, and suggested activities are included in the workbooks. (CO)

CP..... N

AN.....	000120

TI..... Construindo o mundo: 2. O Trabalho é uma forma de realizacao (Building the World: 2. Work is a Form of Realization).

YR..... [nd]

AU..... Almeida, Onésimo; Cramer, Sharon

IN..... Massachusetts Department of Education, Boston. Educational Television.

SN..... Fall River Public Schools, Mass. (BBB03090)

LG..... Portuguese

AV..... National Assessment and Dissemination Center, 49 Washington Ave., Cambridge, Massachusetts 02140 (set of 5 workbooks and filmstrips $19.00)

NT..... 18 p.
For units 1 and 3-5, see 000119 and 121-123.

DE..... *Portuguese; Portuguese Americans; *Workbooks; *Filmstrips; *Work Attitudes; Job Skills; Jobs; Job Market; Job Training; *Career Awareness; Career Education; Career Opportunities; Careers; Intermediate Grades; Junior High Schools; *Instructional Materials; Grade 5; Grade 6; Grade 7; Grade 8

AB..... This workbook in Portuguese and accompanying 35mm color filmstrip are part of a career awareness set designed for use in grades five through eight. Students are encouraged to be proud of the work they will do and to develop a sense of its contribution to society. The set covers the topics of why people work, attitudes toward work, job requirements, and job opportunities. Objectives, pre- and post·tests, and suggested activities are included in the workbooks. (CO)

CP..... N

AN.....	000121

TI..... Construindo o mundo: 3. O Trabalho transforma o mundo (Building the World: 3. Work Transforms the World).

YR..... [nd]

AU..... Almeida, Onésimo; Cramer, Sharon

IN..... Massachusetts Department of Education, Boston. Educational Television.

SN..... Fall River Public Schools, Mass. (BBB03090)

LG..... Portuguese

AV..... National Assessment and Dissemination Center, 49 Washington Ave., Cambridge, Massachusetts 02140 (set of 5 workbooks and filmstrips $19.00)

NT..... 19 p.
For units 1-2 and 4-5, see 000119-120 and 122-123.

DE..... *Portuguese; Portuguese Americans; *Workbooks;
*Filmstrips; *Work Attitudes; Job Skills; Jobs; Job
Market; Job Training; *Career Awareness; Career
Education; Career Opportunities; Careers; Intermediate
Grades; Junior High Schools; *Instructional Materials;
Grade 5; Grade 6; Grade 7; Grade 8

AB..... This workbook in Portuguese and accompanying 35mm color
filmstrip are part of a career awareness set designed for
use in grades five through eight. Students are
encouraged to be proud of the work they will do and to
develop a sense of its contribution to society. The set
covers the topics of why people work, attitudes toward
work, job requirements, and job opportunities.
Objectives, pre- and posttests, and suggested activities
are included in the workbooks. (CO)

CP..... N

AN..... 000122

TI..... Construindo o mundo: 4. O que há a fazer? (Building the
World: 4. What is There to Do?).

YR..... [nd]

AU..... Almeida, Onésimo; Cramer, Sharon

IN..... Massachusetts Department of Education, Boston.
Educational Television.

SN..... Fall River Public Schools, Mass. (BBB03090)

LG..... Portuguese

AV..... National Assessment and Dissemination Center, 49
Washington Ave., Cambridge, Massachusetts 02140 (set of 5
workbooks and filmstrips $19.00)

NT..... 13 p.
For units 1-3 and 5, see 000119-121 and 123.

DE..... *Portuguese; Portuguese Americans; Jobs; *Workbooks;
*Filmstrips; Work Attitudes; Job Skills; Job Market; Job
Training; *Career Awareness; Career Education; *Career
Opportunities; *Careers; Intermediate Grades; Junior High
Schools; *Instructional Materials; Grade 5; Grade 6;
Grade 7; Grade 8

AB..... This workbook in Portuguese and accompanying 35mm color
filmstrip are part of a career awareness set designed for
use in grades five through eight. Students are
encouraged to be proud of the work they will do and to
develop a sense of its contribution to society. The set
covers the topics of why people work, attitudes toward
work, job requirements, and job opportunities.
Objectives, pre- and posttests, and suggested activities
are included in the workbooks. (CO)

CP..... N

```
AN..... 000123
```

TI..... Construindo o mundo: 5. O que e que tu vais fazer?
        (Building the World: 5. What Are You Going to Do?).

YR..... [nd]

AU..... Almeida, Onésimo; Cramer, Sharon

IN..... Massachusetts Department of Education, Boston.
        Educational Television.

SN..... Fall River Public Schools, Mass. (BBB03090)

LG..... Portuguese

AV..... National Assessment and Dissemination Center, 49
        Washington Ave., Cambridge, Massachusetts 02140 (set of 5
        workbooks and filmstrips $19.00)

NT..... 14 p.
        For units 1-4, see 000119-22.

DE..... *Portuguese; Portuguese Americans; Jobs; *Workbooks;
        *Filmstrips; Work Attitudes; Job Skills; Job Market; Job
        Training; *Career Awareness; Career Education; *Career
        Opportunities; Careers; Intermediate Grades; Junior High
        Schools; *Instructional Materials; Grade 5; Grade 6;
        Grade 7; Grade 8

AB..... This workbook in Portuguese accompanying a 35mm color
        filmstrip is part of a career awareness set designed for
        use in grades five through eight. Students are
        encouraged to be proud of the work they will do and to
        develop a sense of its contribution to society. The set
        covers the topics of why people work, attitudes toward
        work, job requirements, and job opportunities.
        Objectives, pre- and posttests, and suggested activities
        are included in the workbook. (CO)

CP..... N

```
AN..... 000124
```

TI..... Entre dois mundos: Vida quotidiana de criancas
        portuguesas na América (Between Two Worlds: Daily Life
        of Portuguese Americans).

YR..... 77

AU..... Meneses, Fernando de; Machado, Magdalena, ill.

IN..... National Assessment and Dissemination Center, Cambridge,
        Mass.

SN..... Office of Education (DHEW), Washington, D.C. (RMQ66000)

LG..... Portuguese

AV..... National Assessment and Dissemination Center, 49
        Washington Ave., Cambridge, Massachusetts 02140 ($2.50)

NT..... x, 129 p.
For accompanying teacher's guide, see 000537.

DE..... *Portuguese; *Portuguese Americans; *Cultural Awareness;
Instructional Materials; *Reading Materials; High
Schools; Secondary Education; *Cultural Education;
Cultural Differences; Grade 7; Grade 8; Grade 9; Grade
10; Grade 11; Grade 12; Humanistic Education; Adolescent
Literature

AB..... This black-and-white illustrated reader is designed for
use in Portuguese bilingual classes at the secondary
level. The stories about Portuguese children in the
United States focus on their problems and experiences,
especially as they relate to "cultural shock." The
materials are useful for cultural awareness and affective
education. (CO)

CP..... N

AN..... 000125

TI..... Lenguaje. III Unidad generadora: La Convivencia. Libro
del maestro (Language. Unit III: Living Together.
Teacher's Guide).

YR..... 76

AU..... Iribarren, Norma C.; Iribarren, Leonel O., ed.;
Martínez, Jesús, ill.

IN..... Midwest Materials Development Center, Milwaukee, Wis.

SN..... Office of Education (DHEW), Washington, D.C. (RMQ66000)

LG..... Spanish

AV..... National Assessment and Dissemination Center, Cambridge,
Mass. ($1.00)

NT..... 41 p.
For companion workbook, see 000126.

DE..... *Spanish; *Instructional Materials; *Teaching Guides;
Spanish Speaking; Spanish Americans; Cultural Awareness;
Verbs; *Reading Comprehension; Social Studies; Folk
Culture; Language Instruction; Grade 4; Grade 5;
Intermediate Grades; *Pattern Drills (Language)

AB..... This teacher's manual is designed to be used with the
workbook of the same title in bilingual Spanish-English
classes at the grade four to five level. They are part
of a set of books dealing with Latin Americans living in
the United States. Languages, folklore, and social
studies concepts are covered, with emphasis on reading
comprehension, analysis of principal ideas, and use of
verbs through exercises. Objectives, methodologies, and
classroom activities are given in the teacher's guide.
(CO)

CP..... N

AN.....	000126

TI.....	Lenguaje. III Unidad generadora: La Convivencia. Libro del alumno (Language. Unit III: Living Together. Workbook).
YR.....	76
AU.....	Iribarren, Norma C.; Iribarren, Leonel O., ed.; Martínez, Jesús, ill.
IN.....	Midwest Materials Development Center, Milwaukee, Wis.
SN.....	Office of Bilingual Education (DHEW/OE), Washington, D.C. (BBB12883)
LG.....	Spanish
AV.....	National Assessment and Dissemination Center, 49 Washington Ave., Cambridge, Massachusetts 02140 ($1.00)
NT.....	44 p. For companion teacher's guide, see 000125.
DE.....	*Spanish; *Instructional Materials; *Workbooks; *Spanish Speaking; Spanish Americans; Cultural Awareness; Verbs; *Reading Comprehension; Social Studies; Folk Culture; Language Instruction; Grade 4; Grade 5; Intermediate Grades; *Pattern Drills (Language)
AB.....	This workbook is designed to be used with the teacher's manual of the same title in bilingual Spanish-English classes in grades four and five. They are part of a set of books dealing with Latin Americans living in the United States. Language, folklore, and social studies concepts are covered, with emphasis on reading comprehension, analysis of principal ideas, and use of verbs through exercises. (CO)
CP.....	N

AN.....	000129

TI.....	Doing Things with Language: Informing.
YR.....	77
AU.....	Urzúa, Carole
IN.....	National Dissemination and Assessment Center, Austin, Tex.
SN.....	Office of Education (DHEW), Washington, D.C. (RMQ66000)
AV.....	National Dissemination and Assessment Center, 7703 North Lamar Blvd., Austin, Texas 78752 (ISBN 0-89417-304-9; $4.50)
NT.....	12 p. 45 cards

DE..... *Language Arts; *Language Usage; Child Language; *Speech
Communication; *Speech Skills; Communication Skills;
Language Skills; Language Enrichment; Self Expression;
*Teaching Guides; *Learning Activities; Verbal Ability;
Elementary Education

ID..... *Language Functions

AB..... This kit is part of an innovative series of activities
designed to encourage children to use oral language in
natural, spontaneous ways. The activities which make up
this kit address the specific language aim of
"informing," and are printed on color-coded cards so that
the teacher may sequence them according to the needs of
individual students. The four colors correspond to the
four modes of informing: description, narration,
classification, and evaluation. Each card describes one
activity and materials needed for carrying it out, and
often includes suggestions for expanding the original
activity. (AM)

CP..... N

AN..... 000130

TI..... Puerto Rican History, Civilization, and Culture: A
Mini-Documentary.

YR..... 76

IN..... National Dissemination and Assessment Center, Austin,
Tex.

SN..... Office of Education (DHEW), Washington, D.C. (RMQ66000)

AV..... National Dissemination and Assessment Center, 7703 North
Lamar Blvd., Austin, Texas 78752 ($3.00)

NT..... vii, 97 p.

DE..... Secondary Education; Intermediate Grades; *Puerto Rican
Culture; *History; Music; Food; Architecture;
Bibliographies; Biographies; Folk Culture; *Cultural
Education; *Instructional Materials; *Social Studies;
Literature; Economic Development

ID..... *Puerto Rico

AB..... This publication was compiled from a number of smaller
manuscripts dealing with various aspects of Puerto Rican
culture, history, and civilization. Its purpose is to
provide middle school and high school students with a
basic knowledge of Puerto Rico from its discovery to the
present form of government. The chapters deal with Puerto
Rican history, economic development, culture, music,
pastimes, cultural centers, foods, important dates and
holidays, flora and fauna, famous people, and
architecture. Appended are a 40-item bibliography of
sources of information on Puerto Rico and a bibliography
of books available in Spanish by Puerto Rican authors
including 150 citations. (JB)

CP..... N

AN..... 000135

TI..... Buscando hallarás, Libro II: Guía para el maestro (Look and You Will Find, Book II: Teacher's Guide).

SE..... Qué bonito es leer II (How Nice It Is to Read II) (Series).

YR..... Feb78

IN..... Curriculum Adaptation Network for Bilingual/Bicultural Education, San Antonio, Tex. Southwest Regional Adaptation Center. (BBB11923); National Dissemination and Assessment Center, Austin, Tex.

SN..... Office of Education (DHEW), Washington, D.C. (RMQ66000)

LG..... Spanish

AV..... National Dissemination and Assessment Center, 7703 North Lamar Blvd., Austin, Texas 78752 ($4.50)

NT..... xv, 186 p.
For companion reader and workbook, see 000136-137.

DE..... *Curriculum Guides; Diagnostic Tests; Educational Objectives; *Instructional Materials; *Language Instruction; Language Tests; Primary Education; *Reading Instruction; Reading Materials; Reading Tests; *Spanish; *Teaching Guides; Teaching Methods; Grade 2

AB..... This teacher's manual is intended for bilingual Spanish-English reading instruction in the second grade. An introduction to the series is followed by a discussion of the course objectives and diagnostic testing. The teacher's guide follows the structure of the reader which contains eight stories: some have animals as main characters and the others deal with different cultures. (CO)

CP..... N

AN..... 000136

TI..... Buscando hallarás, Libro II: Libro de lectura (Look and You Will Find, Book II: Reader).

SE..... Qué bonito es leer II (How Nice It Is to Read II) (Series).

YR..... Feb78

IN..... Curriculum Adaptation Network for Bilingual/Bicultural Education, San Antonio, Tex. Southwest Regional Adaptation Center. (BBB11923); National Dissemination and Assessment Center, Austin, Tex.

SN..... Office of Education (DHEW), Washington, D.C. (RMQ66000)

LG..... Spanish

AV..... National Dissemination and Assessment Center, 7703 North Lamar Blvd., Austin, Texas 78752 ($1.50)

NT..... 100 p.
For companion teacher's guide and workbook, see 000135 and 137.

DE..... Children's Books; *Instructional Materials; *Language Instruction; Primary Education; *Reading Instruction; *Reading Materials; *Spanish; Grade 2; Childrens Literature

AB..... This Spanish reader is designed to be used as a supplement to second grade bilingual reading instruction. The book, illustrated in black and white, consists of eight stories: some of the stories have animals as main characters; the others deal with different cultures. (CO)

CP..... N

AN..... 000137

TI..... Buscando hallarás, Libro II: Cuaderno de ejercicios (Look and You Will Find, Book II: Workbook).

SE..... Qué bonito es leer II (How Nice It Is to Read II) (Series).

YR..... Feb78

IN..... Curriculum Adaptation Network for Bilingual/Bicultural Education, San Antonio, Tex. Southwest Regional Adaptation Center. (BBB11923); National Dissemination and Assessment Center, Austin, Tex.

SN..... Office of Education (DHEW), Washington, D.C. (RMQ66000)

LG..... Spanish

AV..... National Dissemination and Assessment Center, 7703 North Lamar Blvd., Austin, Texas 78752 ($1.00)

NT..... 44 p.
For companion teacher's guide and reader, see 000135-136.

DE..... *Spanish; *Workbooks; *Reading Instruction; Reading Materials; Primary Education; *Language Instruction; Language Skills; Grade 2; *Pattern Drills (Language); Punctuation; Grammar; Phonology; Spelling; Reading Comprehension

AB..... This black-and-white illustrated workbook is intended for bilingual Spanish-English reading instruction in the second grade. It contains exercises designed to help the student practice punctuation, grammar, phonology, spelling, and reading comprehension. A glossary is included. (CO)

CP..... N

AN.....	000138

TI.....	Noche del sol, Libro III: Guía para el maestro (Night of the Sun, Book III: Teacher's Guide).
SE.....	Qué bonito es leer II (How Nice It Is to Read II) (Series).
YR.....	Mar78
IN.....	Curriculum Adaptation Network for Bilingual/Bicultural Education, San Antonio, Tex. Southwest Regional Adaptation Center. (BBB11923); National Dissemination and Assessment Center, Austin, Tex.
SN.....	Office of Education (DHEW), Washington, D.C. (RMQ66000)
LG.....	Spanish
AV.....	National Dissemination and Assessment Center, 7703 North Lamar Blvd., Austin, Texas 78752 ($4.50)
NT.....	xii, 135 p. For companion reader and workbook, see 000139-140.
DE.....	*Curriculum Guides; Educational Objectives; Primary Education; *Instructional Materials; *Language Instruction; *Reading Intruction; Reading Materials; Reading Tests; *Spanish; *Teaching Guides; Teaching Methods; Grade 2
AB.....	This teacher's manual is intended for bilingual Spanish-English reading instruction in the second grade. An introduction to the series is followed by a discussion of the course objectives. The guide follows the structure of the reader which contains seven stories about sharing, cooperation, and daily living. A glossary is included. (CO)
CP.....	N

AN.....	000139

TI.....	Noche del sol, Libro III: Libro de lectura (Night of the Sun, Book III: Reader).
SE.....	Qué bonito es leer II (How Nice It Is to Read II) (Series).
YR.....	Mar78
IN.....	Curriculum Adaptation Network for Bilingual/Bicultural Education, San Antonio, Tex. Southwest Regional Adaptation Center. (BBB11923); National Dissemination and Assessment Center, Austin, Tex.
SN.....	Office of Education (DHEW), Washington, D.C. (RMQ66000)

LG..... Spanish

AV..... National Dissemination and Assessment Center, 7703 North Lamar Blvd., Austin, Texas 78752 ($1.50)

NT..... 55 p.
For companion teacher's guide and workbook, see 000138 and 140.

DE..... Childrens Books; *Instructional Materials; *Language Instruction; Primary Education; *Reading Instruction; *Reading Materials; *Spanish; Grade 2; Childrens Literature

AB..... This Spanish reader is designed to be used as a supplement to second grade bilingual reading instruction. The book, illustrated in black and white, consists of seven stories dealing with sharing, cooperating, and daily living. (CO)

CP..... N

AN..... 000140

TI..... Noche del sol, Libro III: Cuaderno de ejercicios (Night of the Sun, Book III: Workbook).

SE..... Qué bonito es leer II (How Nice It Is to Read II).

YR..... Mar78

IN..... Curriculum Adaptation Network for Bilingual/Bicultural Education, San Antonio, Tex. Southwest Regional Adaptation Center. (BBB11923); National Dissemination and Assessment Center, Austin, Tex.

SN..... Office of Education (DHEW), Washington, D.C. (RMQ66000)

LG..... Spanish

AV..... National Dissemination and Assessment Center, 7703 North Lamar Blvd., Austin, Texas 78752 ($1.00)

NT..... 54 p.
For companion teacher's guide and reader, see 000138-139.

DE..... *Spanish, *Workbooks; *Reading Instruction; *Reading Materials; Primary Education; *Language Instruction; Language Skills; *Pattern Drills (Language); Grade 2; Punctuation; Grammar; Phonology; Spelling; Reading Comprehension

AB..... This black-and-white illustrated workbook is intended for bilingual Spanish-English reading instruction in the second grade. The workbook contains exercises designed to help the student practice punctuation, grammar, phonology, spelling, and reading comprehension. A glossary is included. (CO)

CP..... N

AN.....	000141
TI.....	Hombres y lugares, Libro IV: Guía para el maestro (People and Places, Book IV: Teacher's Guide).
SE.....	Qué bonito es leer II (How Nice It Is to Read II) (Series).
YR.....	May78
IN.....	Curriculum Adaptation Network for Bilingual/Bicultural Education, San Antonio, Texas, Southwest Regional Adaptation Center. (BB11923); National Dissemination and Assessment Center, Austin, Tex.
SN.....	Office of Education (DHEW), Washington, D.C. (RMQ66000)
LG.....	Spanish
AV.....	National Dissemination and Assessment Center, 7703 North Lamar Blvd., Austin, Texas 78752 ($4.50)
NT.....	xi, 114 p. For companion reader and workbook, see 000142-143.
DE.....	*Curriculum Guides; Educational Objectives; *Instructional Materials; *Language Instruction; Primary Education; Reading Materials; *Spanish; *Teaching Guides; Teaching Methods; Grade 2; *Reading Instruction
AB.....	This teacher's manual is intended for bilingual Spanish-English reading instruction in the second grade. An introduction to the series is followed by a discussion of the course objectives. The guide follows the structure of the reader which contains seven stories about going on vacation and about famous persons of the past and present. (CO)
CP.....	N

AN.....	000142
TI.....	Hombres y lugares, Libro IV: Libro de lectura (People and Places, Book IV: Reader).
SE.....	Qué bonito es leer II (How Nice It Is to Read II) (Series).
YR.....	May78
IN.....	Curriculum Adaptation Network for Bilingual/Bicultural Education, San Antonio, Tex. Southwest Regional Adaptation Center. (BB11923); National Dissemination and Assessment Center, Austin, Tex.
SN.....	Office of Education (DHEW), Washington, D.C. (RMQ66000)
LG.....	Spanish

AV..... National Dissemination and Assessment Center, 7703 North
       Lamar Blvd., Austin, Texas 78752 ($1.50)

NT..... 65 p.
       For companion teacher's guide and workbook, see
       000141 and 143.

DE..... Childrens Books; Elementary Education; *Instructional
       Materials; *Language Instruction; Primary Education;
       *Reading Instruction; *Reading Materials; *Spanish; Grade
       2

AB..... This Spanish reader is designed to be used as a
       supplement to second grade bilingual reading instruction.
       The book, illustrated in black and white, consists of
       seven stories about going on vacation and about famous
       persons of the past and present. (CO)

CP..... N

AN..... 000143

TI..... Hombres y lugares, Libro IV: Cuaderno de ejercicios
       (People and Places, Book IV: Workbook).

SE..... Qué bonito es leer II (How Nice It Is to Read II)
       (Series).

YR..... May78

IN..... Curriculum Adaptation Network for Bilingual/Bicultural
       Education, San Antonio, Tex. Southwest Regional
       Adaptation Center. (BBB11923); National Dissemination and
       Assessment Center, Austin, Tex.

SN..... Office of Education (DHEW), Washington, D.C. (RMQ66000)

LG..... Spanish

AV..... National Dissemination and Assessment Center, 7703 North
       Lamar Blvd., Austin, Texas 78752 ($1.00)

NT..... 42 p.
       For companion teacher's guide and reader, see 000141-142.

DE..... *Spanish; *Workbooks; *Reading Instruction; Reading
       Materials; Primary Education; *Language Instruction;
       Language Skills; Punctuation; *Pattern Drills (Language);
       Grammar; Phonology; Spelling; Reading Comprehension;
       Grade 2

AB..... This black-and-white illustrated workbook is intended to
       be used for bilingual Spanish-English reading instruction
       in the second grade. The workbook contains exercises
       designed to help the student practice punctuation,
       grammar, phonology, spelling, and reading comprehension.
       A glossary is included. (CO)

CP..... N

```
AN..... 000149

TI..... Un Sueño musical (A Musical Dream).

YR..... [7?]

AU..... Guardarrama, Eduardo; Rodríguez, Aurea E., ed.;
        Puigdollers, Carmen, ed.; Rosario, Idalia, ill.

IN..... Northeast Center for Curriculum Development, Bronx, N.Y.;
        National Assessment and Dissemination Center, Cambridge,
        Mass.

SN..... Office of Education (DHEW), Washington, D.C. (RMQ66000)

LG..... Spanish

AV..... National Assessment and Dissemination Center, 49
        Washington Avenue, Cambridge, Massachusetts 02140 ($2.50)

NT..... 16 p.

DE..... *Spanish; *Reading Materials; *Instructional Materials;
        Primary Education; Childrens Books; Childrens Literature;
        *Puerto Rican Culture; *Cultural Education; Cultural
        Awareness; Music Education

ID..... Puerto Rico

AB..... Bright color illustrations characterize this Spanish
        reader designed for use in bilingual classes at the
        primary level. The story includes cultural information
        about Puerto Rico's musical heritage. (CO)

CP..... N
```

```
AN..... 000152

TI..... Gin gonee? Dots'il-aanee? (What Is It? What Can You Do
        With It?).

SE..... Dinaakk'a bidots'uhdil-eeghee (Units in Language
        Learning) (Series).

YR..... 77

AU..... Jones, Eliza; Boffa, J. Leslie; ill.

IN..... Alaska Univ., Anchorage. National Bilingual Materials
        Development Center. (BBB16750)

SN..... Office of Education (DHEW), Washington, D.C. (RMQ66000)

NO..... G G007605457

LG..... Koyukon Athapascan

AV..... National Bilingual Materials Development Center,
        University of Alaska, 2223 Spenard Road, Anchorage,
        Alaska 99503 ($1.30; supplies are limited)
```

NT..... 28 p.

DE..... *Athapascan Languages; Alaska Natives; Uncommonly Taught Languages; Elementary Education; *Reading Materials; *Instructional Materials; *Childrens Books; *Language Instruction; *American Indians

ID..... Alaska (Koyukon)

AB..... This illustrated reader in Central Koyukon Athapascan, like others in the series, uses a question-and-answer approach to teach language to Alaskan children at the elementary level. Content is relevant to daily activities in Alaskan villages. A vocabulary list is included. (SH)

CP..... N

AN..... 000155

TI..... Leyendas puertorriqueñas: Adaptaciones (Puerto Rican Legends: Adaptations).

YR..... [7?]

AU..... Rodríguez, Aurea; Puigdollers, Carmen; Ramos, Ernesto, ill.

IN..... Northeast Center for Curriculum Development, Bronx, N.Y.; National Assessment and Dissemination Center, Cambridge, Mass.

SN..... Office of Education (DHEW), Washington, D.C. (RMQ66000)

LG..... Spanish

AV..... National Assessment and Dissemination Center, 49 Washington Avenue, Cambridge, Massachusetts 02140 ($1.75)

NT..... 36 p.

DE..... *Spanish; *Instructional Materials; *Reading Materials; Childrens Literature; *Puerto Rican Culture; Cultural Education; Intermediate Grades; *Legends; *Folklore Books; Childrens Books; Grade 5; Grade 6; Word Lists

ID..... Puerto Rico

AB..... Four Puerto Rican folk tales are included in this black-and-white illustrated reader designed for use in bilingual Spanish-English classes at the fifth to sixth grade level. A word list, with Spanish definitions, is included for each story. (CO)

CP..... N

AN..... 000156

TI..... Tolón: El gatito glotón (Tolón: The Gluttonous Kitten).

YR..... 77

AU..... Cadilla de Ruibal, Carmen Alicia; Rosario, Idalia, ill.; Ramos, Ernesto, ill.

IN..... National Assessment and Dissemination Center, Cambridge, Mass.; Northeast Center for Curriculum Development, Bronx, N.Y.

SN..... Office of Education (DHEW), Washington, D.C. (RMQ66000)

LG..... Spanish

AV..... National Assessment and Dissemination Center, 49 Washington Avenue, Cambridge, Massachusetts 02140 ($1.00)

NT..... 20 p.

DE..... Grade 3; Primary Education; *Spanish; *Reading Materials; *Instructional Materials; Childrens Literature; *Childrens Books

AB..... This black-and-white illustrated Spanish reader is designed for use in bilingual classes at the third grade level. A short vocabulary with Spanish definitions is included. (CO)

CP..... N

AN..... 000169

TI..... Los Amigos del tío Santiago (The Friends of Uncle Santiago).

YR..... [7?]

AU..... Cadilla, Carmen Alicia; Ramos Nieves, Ernesto, ill.

IN..... Northeast Center for Curriculum Development, Bronx, N.Y.; National Assessment and Dissemination Center, Cambridge, Mass.

SN..... Office of Education (DHEW), Washington, D.C. (RMQ66000)

LG..... Spanish

AV..... National Assessment and Dissemination Center, 49 Washington Avenue, Cambridge, Massachusetts 02140 ($2.00)

NT..... 19 p.

DE..... *Spanish; *Reading Materials; *Instructional Materials;
Primary Education; *Childrens Books; Childrens
Literature; Grade 1; Grade 2; Grade 3; Puerto Rican
Culture; Cultural Education

ID..... *Puerto Rico

AB..... This color-illustrated reader, written in Spanish, is
designed for use in bilingual Spanish classes at the
grade one to three level. The objective of the story is
to teach children about frogs and their contribution to
Puerto Rican agriculture. A vocabulary list with Spanish
definitions is included. (CO)

CP..... N

AN..... 000173

TI..... Kiko coquí 1 (Kiko the Tree Frog 1).

YR..... [nd]

AU..... Cadilla de Ruibal, Carmen Alicia; Román, Neil, ill.

IN..... Northeast Center for Curriculum Development, Bronx, N.Y.;
National Assessment and Dissemination Center, Cambridge,
Mass.

SN..... Office of Education (DHEW), Washington, D.C. (RMQ66000)

LG..... Spanish

AV..... National Assessment and Dissemination Center, 49
Washington Avenue, Cambridge, Massachusetts 02140 (set of
5 books: $5.25)

NT..... [16] p.
For the other readers in this set, see 000174-177.

DE..... *Spanish; *Reading Materials; *Instructional Materials;
Primary Education; *Childrens Books; Childrens
Literature; Grade 1; Grade 2; Grade 3

ID..... Puerto Rico

AB..... This color-illustrated reader, written in Spanish, is one
of a set of five featuring a Puerto Rican tree frog. The
books are designed for bilingual Spanish classes in
grades one to three. A vocabulary list with Spanish
definitions is included. (CO)

CP..... N

AN..... 000174

TI..... Kiko coquí 2: Fiesta en Loiza Aldea (Kiko the Tree Frog
2: Festival in Loiza Aldea).

YR..... [nd]

AU..... Cadilla de Ruibal, Carmen Alicia; Román, Neil, ill.

IN..... Northeast Center for Curriculum Development, Bronx, N.Y.;
National Assessment and Dissemination Center, Cambridge,
Mass.

SN..... Office of Education (DHEW), Washington, D.C. (RMQ66000)

LG..... Spanish

AV..... National Assessment and Dissemination Center, 49
Washington Avenue, Cambridge, Massachusetts 02140 (set of
5 books: $5.25)

NT..... [12] p.
For the other readers in this set, see 000173 and
175-177.

DE..... *Spanish; *Reading Materials; *Instructional Materials;
Primary Education; *Childrens Books; Childrens
Literature; Grade 1; Grade 2; Grade 3

ID..... Puerto Rico

AB..... This color-illustrated reader, written in Spanish, is one
of a set of five featuring a Puerto Rican tree frog. The
books are designed for bilingual Spanish classes in
grades one to three. A vocabulary list with Spanish
definitions is included. (CO)

CP..... N

AN..... 000175

TI..... Kiko coquí 3: En San Juan (Kiko the Tree Frog 3: In San
Juan).

YR..... [nd]

AU..... Cadilla de Ruibal, Carmen Alicia; Román, Neil, ill.

IN..... Northeast Center for Curriculum Development, Bronx, N.Y.;
National Assessment and Dissemination Center, Cambridge,
Mass.

SN..... Office of Education (DHEW), Washington, D.C. (RMQ66000)

LG..... Spanish

AV..... National Assessment and Dissemination Center, 49
Washington Avenue, Cambridge, Massachusetts 02140 (set of
5 books: $5.25)

NT..... [12] p.
For the other readers in this set, see 000173-174 and
176-177.

DE..... *Spanish; *Reading Materials; Primary Education;
*Instructional Materials; *Childrens Books; Childrens
Literature; Grade 1; Grade 2; Grade 3

ID..... Puerto Rico

AB..... This color-illustrated reader, written in Spanish, is one
of a set of five featuring a Puerto Rican tree frog. The
books are designed for bilingual Spanish classes in
grades one to three. A vocabulary list with Spanish
definitions is included. (CO)

CP..... N

AN..... 000176

TI..... Kiko coquí 4: Como en los cuentos (Kiko the Tree Frog
4: Like in a Story).

YR..... [nd]

AU..... Cadilla de Ruibal, Carmen Alicia; Román, Neil, ill.

IN..... Northeast Center for Curriculum Development, Bronx, N.Y.;
National Assessment and Dissemination Center, Cambridge,
Mass.

SN..... Office of Education (DHEW), Washington, D.C. (RMQ66000)

LG..... Spanish

AV..... National Assessment and Dissemination Center, 49
Washington Avenue, Cambridge, Massachusetts 02140 (set
of 5 books: $5.25)

NT..... [12] p.
For the other readers in this set, see 000173-175 and 177.

DE..... *Spanish; *Reading Materials; *Instructional Materials;
Primary Education; *Childrens Books; Childrens
Literature; Grade 1; Grade 2; Grade 3

ID..... Puerto Rico

AB..... This color-illustrated reader, written in Spanish, is one
of a set of five featuring a Puerto Rican tree frog. The
books are designed for bilingual Spanish classes in
grades one to three. A vocabulary list with Spanish
definitions is included. (CO)

CP..... N

AN..... 000177

TI..... Kiko coquí 5: El recibimiento en Nueva York (Kiko the
Tree Frog 5: The Reception in New York).

YR..... [nd]

AU..... Cadilla de Ruibal, Carmen Alicia; Román, Neil, ill.

IN..... Northeast Center for Curriculum Development, Bronx, N.Y.;
National Assessment and Dissemination Center, Cambridge,
Mass.

SN..... Office of Education (DHEW), Washington, D.C. (RMQ66000)

LG..... Spanish

AV..... National Assessment and Dissemination Center, 49
Washington Avenue, Cambridge, Massachusetts 02140 (set of
5 books: $5.25)

NT..... [16] p.
For the other readers in this set, see 000173-176.

DE..... *Spanish; *Reading Materials; *Instructional Materials;
Primary Education; *Childrens Books; Childrens
Literature; Grade 1; Grade 2; Grade 3

ID..... Puerto Rico

AB..... This color-illustrated reader, written in Spanish, is one
of a set of five featuring a Puerto Rican tree frog. The
books are designed for bilingual Spanish classes in
grades one to three. A vocabulary list with Spanish
definitions is included. (CO)

CP..... N

AN..... 000180

TI..... Education physique I et II (Physical Education I and II).

YR..... Jul72

AU..... Bradley, Ruth; Coussan, Odette; Marchal, Alain; Marchal,
Danièle; Begnaud, Noëmi

IN..... Lafayette Parish Bilingual Program, La.

SN..... Office of Education (DHEW), Washington, D.C. (RMQ66000)

LG..... French

AV..... Lafayette Parish Bilingual Program, 400 Willow Street,
Lafayette, Louisiana 70501

NT..... [103] leaves in various pagings

DE..... Grade 1; Grade 2; *Curriculum Guides; *French; Games;
Playground Activities; *Physical Education; *Physical
Activities; Physical Recreation Programs; Primary
Education

ID..... Franco Americans

AB..... This guide contains directions for the development of
selected skills important to the physical growth of young
children. Some skills are introduced in the primary
grades with plans for their progression of difficulty to
spiral in the grades that follow. Some are so basic as
to be mastered in the first and second grades. Each
activity is planned for 30 minutes duration with 15
minutes for the exercises and 15 minutes for the game.
The plan provides for 12 weeks of exercises and games
suited to the development of the prescribed skills with
the degree of difficulty progressing from week 1 to week
12. Twelve weeks of indoor games and rhythmic activities
are also provided. (Author/SH)

CP..... N

AN..... 000181

TI..... Les Arts et la littérature chez les Franco-Américains de la Nouvelle-Angleterre: Module expérimental destiné aux élèves dans les écoles-secondaires américaines (Arts and Literature of the Franco-Americans of New England: Experimental Module for American Secondary School Students).

YR..... 77

AU..... Chassé, Paul; Olivier, Julien; Albert, Renaud S.; Quintal, Claire

IN..... National Materials Development Center for French, Bedford, N.H.; National Assessment and Dissemination Center, Cambridge, Mass.

SN..... Office of Education (DHEW), Washington, D.C. (RMQ66000)

LG..... French

AV..... National Assessment and Dissemination Center, 49 Washington Avenue, Cambridge, Massachusetts 02140 ($1.25)

NT..... 46 p.

DE..... *Literature; Fine Arts; *French; *Instructional Materials; Cultural Education; *Reading Materials; *Literature Appreciation; Secondary Education

ID..... *Franco Americans; New England

AB..... The contribution of Franco-Americans to the arts and literature is examined in this pamphlet, part of an audiovisual experimental module for American secondary school students. The volume is designed to accompany a set of slides and a cassette. Short biographies of famous Franco-Americans, including Lucien Gosselin, Lorenzo de Nevers, Juliette Albert, Rudy Vallée, Rosaire Dion-Lévesque, Camille Lessard-Bissonnette, Anna Duval-Thibault and Jean-Louis Kérouac, are featured, as well as selected portions of their novels and poetry. (SH)

CP..... N

AN..... 000182

Tl..... Chants et jeux K-I-II (Songs and Games K-I-II).

YR..... Aug72

AU..... Bradley Ruth; Coussan, Odette; Schlickling, Jean Claude; Price, Kathleen; Begnaud, Noëmi; Bernard, David, ill.

IN..... Lafayette Parish Bilingual Program, La.

SN..... Office of Education (DHEW), Washington, D.C. (RMQ66000)

LG..... French

AV.....	Lafayette Parish Bilingual Program, 400 Willow Street, Lafayette, Louisiana 70501
NT.....	[125] leaves in various pagings For related document, see BE000183.
DE.....	*French; Childrens Games; Illustrations; Classroom Games; *Games; *Singing; *Music Activities; Vocal Music; Kingergarten; Grade 1; Grade 2; Primary Education; *Instructional Materials
ID.....	*Franco Americans; *Acadians; French Canadians
AB.....	This publication contains songs and games representative of Acadian culture and is intended to accompany the social studies program for kindergarten, first grade, and second grade. Illustrations which accompany the songs and games are intended to increase comprehension and may be used for transparencies or ditto copies for coloring. (SH)
CP.....	N

AN.....	000183
TI.....	Chants et danses III (Songs and Dances III).
YR.....	May73
AU.....	Bradley, Ruth; Price, Kathleen; Calais, Gayle; Begnaud, Noëmi; Marchal, Alain; Marchal, Danièle; Fanjeaux, Francis; Pétreault, Marie-Claude; D'Entresangle, Serge; Desjardins, Peggy, ill.
IN.....	Lafayette Parish Bilingual Program, La.
SN.....	Office of Education (DHEW), Washington, D.C. (RMQ66000)
LG.....	French
AV.....	Lafayette Parish Bilingual Program, 400 Willow Street, Lafayette, Louisiana 70501
NT.....	[95] leaves in various pagings For related document, see BE000182.
DE.....	French Canadians; *French; *Singing; *Dance; *Music Activities; Illustrations; *Instructional Materials; Grade 3; Folk Culture; *Cultural Education; Primary Education
ID.....	Acadians; *Franco Americans
AB.....	This publication contains songs and dances representative of French, Acadian, and Canadian culture and is intended to be used in connection with a third grade social studies program. Illustrations accompany the music in order to aid in the comprehension of the songs and dances. (SH)
CP.....	N

AN.....	000184
TI.....	Berlin: Ville industrielle du nord (Berlin: Industrial City of the North).
SE.....	Villes franco-américaines de la Nouvelle-Angleterre (Franco-American cities of New England) (Series).
YR.....	77
AU.....	Hagel, Phyllis
IN.....	National Materials Development Center for French, Bedford, N.H.
SN.....	Office of Education (DHEW), Washington, D.C. (RMQ66000); National Assessment and Dissemination Center, Cambridge, Mass.
LG.....	French
AV.....	National Assessment and Dissemination Center, 49 Washington Avenue, Cambridge, Massachusetts 02140
NT.....	30 p.
DE.....	*Instructional Materials; *French Photographs; *Reading Materials; Second Language Learning; Elementary Secondary Education; *Social Studies; Cultural Awareness; Cultural Education
ID.....	New England; *Franco Americans; *New Hampshire (Berlin)
AB.....	The first in a series of materials dealing with cities in New England with a distinct Franco-American character, this text and supporting audiovisual materials present an overview of Berlin, New Hampshire. The Franco-American character, principal industries, and historical/tourist attractions of the city are presented in the form of photographs and narration geared to elementary grade bilingual students or high school students learning French as a second language. (SH)
CP.....	N

AN.....	000185
TI.....	L'Eau (Water).
YR.....	Feb73
IN.....	Lafayette Parish Bilingual Program, La.
SN.....	Office of Education (DHEW), Washington, D.C. (RMQ66000)
LG.....	French
AV.....	Lafayette Parish Bilingual Program, 400 Willow Street, Lafayette, Louisiana 70501
NT.....	[10] leaves

DE..... *French; *Language Instruction; *Reading Materials; Grade 3; *Student Developed Materials; Primary Education; Illustrations; Social Studies; Water Resources; *Instructional Materials

AB..... Third graders in a social studies class conducted in French wrote and illustrated this booklet. The children's black-and-white illustrations, captioned in French, depict the uses of water. (SH)

CP..... N

AN..... 000186

TI..... Les Ressources naturelles (Natural Resources).

YR..... Feb73

IN..... Lafayette Parish Bilingual Program, La.

SN..... Office of Education (DHEW), Washington, D.C. (RMQ66000)

LG..... French

AV..... Lafayette Parish Bilingual Program, 400 Willow Street, Lafayette, Louisiana 70501

NT..... 5 leaves

DE..... *French; *Language Instruction; *Reading Materials; Grade 3; *Instructional Materials; Social Studies; Illustrations; *Student Developed Materials; Natural Resources; Primary Education

AB..... Third graders in a social studies class conducted in French wrote and illustrated this booklet. The children's black-and-white illustrations are accompanied by captions, in French, depicting cotton cultivation and fishing. (SH)

CP..... N

AN..... 000187

TI..... Nos plantations (Our Plantings).

YR..... Feb73

IN..... Lafayette Parish Bilingual Program, La.

SN..... Office of Education (DHEW), Washington, D.C. (RMQ66000)

LG..... French

AV..... Lafayette Parish Bilingual Program, 400 Willow Street, Lafayette, Louisiana 70501

NT..... 10 leaves

DE.....	*French; *Language Instruction; *Reading Materials; Grade 3; *Instructional Materials; Illustrations; Plant Growth; Social Studies; *Student Developed Materials; Primary Education
AB.....	Third graders in a social studies class conducted in French wrote and illustrated this booklet. The children's black-and-white illustrations are accompanied by captions, in French, depicting the process of growing plants. (SH)
CP.....	N

AN.....	000188
TI.....	Le Temps: La campagne (The Weather: The Country).
YR.....	Feb73
IN.....	Lafayette Parish Bilingual Program, La.
SN.....	Office of Education (DHEW), Washington, D.C. (RMQ66000)
LG.....	French
AV.....	Lafayette Parish Bilingual Program, 400 Willow Street, Lafayette, Louisiana 70501
NT.....	[16] leaves in various pagings
DE.....	*French; *Language Instruction; *Reading Materials; Grade 3; *Instructional Materials; *Student Developed Materials; Social Studies; Illustrations; Primary Education; *Workbooks; Pattern Drills (Language); Rural Environment
ID.....	Weather
AB.....	Third graders in a social studies class conducted in French wrote and illustrated this booklet. The children's black-and-white illustrations, captioned in French, depict weather and country life. The reading material is followed by several exercises aimed at strengthening French language skills. (SH)
CP.....	N

AN.....	000189
TI.....	Lafayette.
YR.....	Feb73
IN.....	Lafayette Parish Bilingual Program, La.
SN.....	Office of Education (DHEW), Washington, D.C. (RMQ66000)
LG.....	French

AV..... Lafayette Parish Bilingual Program, 400 Willow Street, Lafayette, Louisiana 70501

NT..... [20] leaves in various pagings

DE..... *French; *Language Instruction; *Reading Materials; Social Studies; Grade 3; *Student Developed Materials; *Workbooks; Primary Education; Pattern Drills (Language); Illustrations; *Instructional Materials

ID..... *Louisiana (Lafayette)

AB..... This booklet was written and illustrated by third grade pupils in a social studies class taught in French. The children's black-and-white illustrations are accompanied by captions, in French, depicting life in Lafayette, Louisiana. The reading material is followed by several exercises aimed at strengthening French language skills. (SH)

CP..... N

AN..... 000313

ER..... ED108490

TI..... Language Development Resources for Bilingual Bicultural Education: An Aid to Primary Teachers of Mexican American Children.

YR..... May75

IN..... National Dissemination and Assessment Center, Austin, Tex.; Arizona Univ., Tucson. Experienced Teacher Fellowship Program. (BBB11970)

SN..... Office of Education (DHEW), Washington, D.C. (RMQ66000)

LG..... English; Spanish

AV..... National Dissemination and Assessment Center, 7703 North Lamar Boulevard, Austin, Texas 78752 ($4.50); ERIC Document Reproduction Service, P.O. Box 190, Arlington, Virginia 22210 ($13.32; microfiche $0.76)

NT..... viii, 243 p.
Rev. ed.

DE..... Audiovisual Aids; Bibliographies; Biculturalism; Classroom Games; Classroom Materials; Community Resources; *Learning Activities; *Mexican Americans; Primary Education; *Resource Materials; Spanish Speaking; *Instructional Materials; *Spanish; *Language Arts

AB..... This resource guide is designed as an aid to primary teachers of Mexican American children. Teachers may use these materials to implement programs designed for the particular needs of their students. Besides including basic introductory material, the volume provides suggestions for parent involvement, classroom learning activity centers, and extensive resource materials. Suggested types of activity centers include the following: art, book, communication, discussion, game, listening, puppet, role playing, sensitivity, viewing, cooking, and field trips. Each learning center activity outlines the teacher's and the children's parts and refers to other centers for possible extended learning. Bilingual resources include: (1) stories, poems, and lists of books and audiovisual materials in English and Spanish; (2) community resource suggestions; and (3) cultural awareness materials for the teacher. Appendixes cite suggested community resources, books, records, films, filmstrips, references for English as a second language, and books mentioned in the text. (Author/DS)

CP..... N

AN..... 000436

TI..... Las Actividades de Sesame Street (Activities of Sesame Street).

YR..... 76

AU..... Rodríguez, Roberto; Umpierre, Helga; O'Connor, Jane, ed.; Barden, Anne, ill.

IN..... Children's Television Workshop, New York, N.Y. Community Education Services Div.

SN..... Office of Education (DHEW), Washington, D.C. (RMQ66000)

NO..... C 300-76-0100

LG..... Spanish

AV..... Children's Television Workshop, Community Education Services, Dept. A, One Lincoln Plaza, New York, New York 10023

NT..... 68 p.
Cover title: Actividades.

DE..... *Instructional Materials; *Teaching Guides; *Childrens Television; *Enrichment Activities; Instructional Aids; Television Curriculum; Preschool Education; Learning Activities; Educational Games; *Educational Television; *Spanish; Parent Participation

ID..... *Sesame Street

AB..... This manual is designed for parents and educators working with preschool children in formal and informal learning environments. It contains many activities based on the Sesame Street curriculum and can be used independently or together with the television broadcast. Activities are grouped under the headings: (1) "The Child and His World," (2) "Using Symbols," and (3) "Learning Skills." A goal statement, bilingual and bicultural objectives, and objectives for use with mentally retarded children are included. The text is in Spanish and contains black-and-white illustrations. (CO)

CP..... Y

AN.....	000479
TI.....	Oh! Canada.
YR.....	Aug77
AU.....	Kirschbaum, Gabrielle; Kronby, Madeline; Boka, Geo, ill.
IN.....	Foster Advertising Company, Ltd.; Canadian Office of the Commissioner of Official Languages, Ottawa, (Ontario). (BBB14777)
LG.....	English; French
AV.....	Commissioner of Official Languages, Ottawa, Ontario, Canada K1A 0T8
NT.....	Game board with 5 cards; sound disc, ca. 10 min., 33-1/3 rpm, mono., 7 in.; comic book, 32 p.; activity book, 30 p. For companion cassette sound track, see 000480.
DE.....	*Childrens Games; *Educational Games; *Learning Activities; *Bilingual Students; French; English; Comics (Publications); Phonotape Recordings; Creative Activities; Geography; History; Cross Cultural Training; Vocabulary; Music; Singing; Fantasy; Childrens Literature; Vocabulary Development; Second Language Learning; Word Lists; Fiction; *Learning Modules; Elementary Education
ID.....	*Canada
AB.....	This kit, designed for use by Canadian children, teaches the geography and history of the Canadian provinces and territories using basic French and English vocabularies. Kit materials, housed in a folding game board, include: (1) explanation and rules of the bilingual word game; (2) four cards of English and French phrases of varying difficulties to be translated during the game; (3) a comic book describing the adventures of four Canadian youngsters on a tour of Canada; (4) a record containing four French-English songs; and (5) a book composed of activities, crossword puzzles, games, tongue twisters, riddles, song music and lyrics to accompany the records, and a list of vocabulary items used throughout the kit. (SH)
CP.....	Y

AN.....	000480
TI.....	Oh! Canada: Piste sonore. Sound track.
YR.....	76
IN.....	Canadian Office of the Commissioner of Official Languages, Ottawa (Ontario). (BBB14777)
LG.....	English; French
AV.....	Commissioner of Official Languages, Ottawa, Ontario, Canada K1A 0T8 (Free)

NT..... 2 sound cassettes, 120 min.
        For companion kit, see 000479.

DE..... *Magnetic Tape Cassettes; Bilingualism; *Sound Tracks;
        Geographic Regions; Geography; Fiction; Comics
        (Publications); *Fantasy; *Childrens Literature;
        Vocabulary; Vocabulary Development; French; English;
        *Bilingual Students; Learning Modules

ID..... *Canada

AB..... This sound track of the Oh! Canada Adventure Kit comic
        book begins with a short introduction, followed by 13
        episodes relating the adventures of 4 Canadian youngsters
        in each province and territory of Canada. Teachers may
        use each episode as the basis for a single,
        self-contained lesson. The live voices accompanied by
        music and sound effects enable pupils to hear native
        speakers and can help even preschool children enjoy the
        comic book by following only the pictures. (SH)

CP..... Y

AN..... 000481

TI..... Gabino Gatito y el siluro (Gabino Gatito and the
        Catfish).

SE..... Miami Linguistic Readers: Level 1-B (Series).

YR..... Mar71

AU..... Granado, Eusebia, trans.; Nash, Rose L., ill.

IN..... Dade County Public Schools, Miami, Fla. (HWP20100);
        Southeastern New Mexico Bilingual Program, Artesia.

LG..... Spanish

AV..... Southeastern New Mexico Bilingual Program, Artesia, New
        Mexico

NT..... 23 p.

DE..... *Spanish; *Reading Materials; Reading Instruction;
        *Childrens Books; Primary Education; Childrens
        Literature; *Instructional Materials

AB..... This Spanish reader, illustrated in black and white, is
        designed for use in a bilingual program at the primary
        level. (CO)

CP..... Y

AN..... 000486

TI..... Beginning Cherokee.

YR..... 77

AU..... Holmes, Ruth Bradley; Smith, Betty Sharp

AV..... University of Oklahoma Press, 1005 Asp Avenue, Norman, Oklahoma 73019 (ISBN 0-8061-1463-0; $6.95)

NT..... xiii, 332 p.
Second ed.
Cherokee title follows English title.

DE..... Autoinstructional Aids; *American Indian Languages; *Cherokee; *Language Instruction; Language Guides; Basic Vocabulary; Vocabulary Development; Verbs; *Textbooks; Nominals; Pronouns; Sentence Structure; Syntax; Grammar; Vocabulary; Cultural Education; Second Language Learning; Uncommonly Taught Languages; *Instructional Materials

AB..... In 27 lessons, this textbook combines an everyday vocabulary of words and phrases, gradual familiarity with the Cherokee syllabary, and an introduction to Cherokee verb- and noun-building methods. Each lesson constitutes a semi-independent unit which can be mastered by a student working alone or by an entire class. A study guide serves as a table of contents, providing lesson and page numbers, syllabary rows, phrase numbers, verbs, and a brief description of the subject matters for each lesson. Appendixes enlarge upon subjects of unusual difficulty or interest such as verb structure, pronouns, Indian names for plants and animals, numbers, and the alphabet. Cherokee-English and English-Cherokee glossaries define vocabulary used in the text and list page and lesson references. The text uses the Oklahoma dialect of Cherokee. (SH)

CP..... Y

AN..... 000513

TI..... Games Without Losers: Learning Games and Independent Activities for Elementary Classrooms.

YR..... 75

AU..... Liu, Sarah; Vittitow, Mary Lou

IN..... Incentive Publications, Nashville, Tenn.

AV..... Incentive Publications, Box 12522, Nashville, Tennessee 37212 (ISBN 0-913916-17-X; $5.00)

NT..... 107 p.

DE..... *Language Arts; Writing Skills; Syntax; Primary Education; Classroom Games; *Educational Games; Reading Readiness; *Mathematics; *Sciences; Social Studies; Spelling; Language Development; *Learning Activities; *Individual Study

AB..... These games, for use in the elementary classroom, are designed to satisfy the needs of children with different levels of experiences and proficiency. The activities can be carried out independently by the student and are designed to be self-correcting. Areas covered include word attack and analysis, reading readiness, language comprehension, spelling and writing, science and social studies, and math. Each game covers the subject area,

```
            skill reinforced, adaptability, materials, directions for
            construction, and directions for playing. A
            black-and-white illustration for each game, a title
            index, and a list of helpful hints are also included.
            (JB)

CP..... Y
```

```
AN..... 000522

TI..... Reading Norwegian.

YR..... 76

AU..... Haugen, Einar, ed.

IN..... Spoken Language Services, Inc., Ithaca, N.Y. (QPX01650)

LG..... English; Norwegian

AV..... Spoken Language Services, Inc., P.O. Box 783, Ithaca, New
        York 14850 (ISBN 0-87950-172-3)

NT..... vii, 200 p.
        Reprint of the 1940 ed. published by F.S. Crofts, New York.

DE..... *Norwegian; *Reading Materials; *Language Instruction;
        *Instructional Materials; Foreign Language Books;
        Vocabulary; Textbooks; *Second Language Learning;
        Uncommonly Taught Languages; *Short Stories

AB..... Five stories are included in this beginning reader
        designed to be used by someone who has completed an
        introductory course in Norwegian. The stories were
        chosen for interest and have been rewritten somewhat to
        make them easy to read. The stories inform students of
        city and country life in Norway and the experiences of
        Norwegians who have emigrated to the United States. A
        comprehensive Norwegian-English list of vocabulary found
        in the text is included, as are English introductions to
        each story. (CO)

CP..... Y
```

```
AN..... 000523

TI..... Spoken Dutch: Basic Course, Units 1-12.

YR..... 44

AU..... Bloomfield, Leonard

IN..... Linguistic Society of America, Washington, D.C.
        (BBB10235); American Council of Learned Societies, New
        York, N.Y. (BBB02837)

LG..... English; Dutch

AV..... Spoken Language Services, Inc., P.O. Box 783, Ithaca, New
        York 14850
```

NT..... ix, 236 p.
         Cover title: Spoken Dutch: Book One.

DE..... *Conversational Language Courses; *Dutch; Independent
         Study; Language Instruction; Textbooks; *Instructional
         Materials; Cultural Education; Language Skills; Modern
         Languages; Uncommonly Taught Languages; Speech
         Communication; Vocabulary; Listening Comprehension;
         Grammar; Pronunciation; Speech Skills; *Second Language
         Learning; *Autoinstructional Aids; *Standard Spoken Usage

AB..... This course in spoken Dutch is intended for use in
         introductory conversational classes. The course is
         divided into five parts, and this book contains the first
         two. Each part contains five learning units and one
         devoted to review. Each unit contains sections
         including: (1) basic sentences, (2) word study, (3)
         listening comprehension, and (4) conversation exercises.
         The lessons, based on cultural experiences commonly
         shared by the Dutch, are structured for indepenent study.
         Dutch-English and English-Dutch word lists are included.
         The text is designed for use either with a native speaker
         or with accompanying recordings. (CO)

CP..... Y

AN..... 000524

TI..... Spoken Arabic (Saudi).

YR..... 77

AU..... Van Wagoner, Merrill Y.; Satterthwait, Arnold; Rice,
         Frank

IN..... Spoken Language Services, Inc., Ithaca, N.Y. (QPX01650)

LG..... Arabic; English

AV..... Spoken Language Services, Inc., P.O. Box 783, Ithaca, New
         York 14850 (ISBN 0-87950-410-2)

NT..... 159 p.

DE..... *Arabic; *Conversational Language Courses; Independent
         Study; Language Instruction; Textbooks; *Instructional
         Materials; Cultural Education; Language Skills; Speech
         Communication; Vocabulary; Listening Comprehension;
         Grammar; Pronunciation; Speech Skills; *Second Language
         Learning; *Uncommonly Taught Languages;
         *Autoinstructional Aids

AB..... This course in spoken Saudi Arabic is intended for use in
         introductory conversational classes or for independent
         study. It consists of a key to pronounciation, 12 units,
         a list of numbers, a list of verbs, and an English-Arabic
         vocabulary. Each of the 12 units is divided into the
         following sections: (1) basic sentences, (2) review, (3)
         grammar, (4) conversation, and (5) Arabic-English
         vocabulary. Recordings are available to supplement the
         text. (CO)

CP..... Y

AN.....	000525

TI.....	Spoken Romanian: Standard Colloquial Romanian, Book One.
YR.....	74
AU.....	Agard, Frederick B.; Petrescu-Dimitriu, Magdalena
IN.....	Spoken Language Services, Inc., Ithaca, N.Y. (QPX01650)
LG.....	English; Romanian
AV.....	Spoken Language Services, Inc., P.O. Box 783, Ithaca, New York 14850 (ISBN 0-87950-315-7)
NT.....	iv, 129 p.
DE.....	*Conversational Language Courses; *Romanian; Independent Study; Language Instruction; Textbooks; *Instructional Materials; Cultural Education; Language Skills; Speech Communication; Vocabulary; Grammar; Pronunciation; Modern Languages; Listening Comprehension; Speech Skills; *Autoinstructional Aids; Uncommonly Taught Languages; *Standard Spoken Usage; *Second Language Learning
AB.....	This course in spoken Romanian is intended for use in introductory conversational classes. The course is divided into 12 units, including 2 review units. The units cover grammar, reading, vocabulary, and conversational practice. A section on pronunciation and spelling is appended, as well as a Romanian-English list containing words and idioms not found repeatedly in the text. Tape recordings are available to supplement the text. (CO)
CP.....	Y

AN.....	000526

TI.....	Spoken Portuguese: Basic Course, Units 1-2. A Self-Teaching Guide.
YR.....	May44
AU.....	Reno, Margarida F.; Cioffari, Vincenzo, ed.
IN.....	Spoken Language Services, Inc., Ithaca, N.Y. (QPX01650)
LG.....	English; Portuguese
AV.....	Spoken Language Services, Inc., P.O. Box 783, Ithaca, New York 14850
NT.....	viii, 204 p. Cover title: Spoken Portuguese: Book One. Transcription by Robert A. Hall, Jr.
DE.....	Independent Study; *Portuguese; Language Instruction; Textbooks; Conversational Language Courses; Language Skills; Modern Languages; Cultural Education;

             *Instructional Materials; Grammar; Speech Communication;
             Pronunciation; Speech Skills; Vocabulary;
             *Autoinstructional Aids; *Second Language Learning;
             *Standard Spoken Usage

AB..... This course in spoken Portuguese is intended for use in
        introductory conversational classes. The course is
        divided into five parts, and this book contains the first
        two. Each part consists of five learning units and one
        devoted to review. Each unit contains sections
        including: (1) basic sentences, (2) word study, (3)
        listening comprehension, (4) conversation exercises, and
        (5) vocabulary lists. The lessons are structured for
        independent study, and the text can be used either with
        the accompanying recordings or with the help of a native
        speaker. (CO)

CP..... Y

AN..... 000527

TI..... Spoken Chinese: Book One.

YR..... 76

AU..... Hockett, Charles F.; Fang, Chaoying

IN..... American Council of Learned Societies, New York, N.Y.
        (BBB02837); Linguistic Society of America, Washington,
        D.C. (BBB10235); Spoken Language Services, Inc., Ithaca,
        N.Y. (QPX01650)

LG..... English; Mandarin

AV..... Spoken Language Services, Inc., P.O. Box 783, Ithaca, New
        York 14850 (ISBN 0-87950-031-X)

NT..... vi, 231 p.

DE..... *Mandarin Chinese; Chinese; Language Instruction;
        *Instructional Materials; Textbooks; *Second Language
        Learning; *Autoinstructional Aids; *Conversational
        Language Courses; Grammar; Speech Communication;
        Pronunciation; Speech Skills; Uncommonly Taught
        Languages; Vocabulary; Independent Study; *Standard
        Spoken Usage

AB..... This is one of a series of self-teaching textbooks
        initially prepared for the armed forces and now available
        to the general public. The text is divided into two main
        sections, each consisting of five lessons and a review.
        Each lesson is divided into several sections: basic
        sentences, word study, pronunciation practice, grammar,
        and conversational situations. Each of the two main
        sections is followed by a checklist containing all of the
        vocabulary introduced in the lessons. An answer section
        is appended. These 12 units, which make up Book One, are
        designed to be used with the help of a native speaker of
        Chinese or with accompanying recordings. (CO)

CP..... Y

AN..... 000528

TI..... Spoken Persian.

YR..... 73

AU..... Obolensky, Serge; Panah, Kambiz Yazdan; Nouri, Fereidoun Khaje

IN..... Spoken Language Services, Inc., Ithaca, N.Y. (QPX01650)

LG..... English; Persian

AV..... Spoken Language Services, Inc., P.O. Box 783, Ithaca, New York 14850 (ISBN 0-87950-295-9)

NT..... 387 p.

DE..... *Persian; *Conversational Language Courses; Independent Study; Language Instruction; Textbooks; *Instructional Materials; Cultural Education; Language Skills; Speech Communication; Vocabulary; Listening Comprehension; Grammar; Pronunciation; Speech Skills; *Autoinstructional Aids; Uncommonly Taught Languages; *Second Language Learning; *Standard Spoken Usage

AB..... This course in spoken Persian is intended for use in introductory conversational classes. The text is divided into 12 units, each containing sections on: (1) basic sentences, (2) grammar, (3) drills, and (4) orthography. Tape recordings are available to supplement the text. (CO)

CP..... Y

AN..... 000529

TI..... Spoken Hausa.

YR..... 76

AU..... Cowan, J. Ronayne; Schuh, Russel G.

IN..... Spoken Language Services, Inc., Ithaca, N.Y. (QPX01650)

LG..... English; Hausa

AV..... Spoken Language Services, Inc., P.O. Box 783, Ithaca, New York 14850 (ISBN 0-87950-401-3)

NT..... 378 p.

DE..... *Hausa, *Conversational Language Courses; Independent Study; Language Instruction; Textbooks; *Instructional Materials; Language Skills; Speech Communication; Vocabulary; Listening Comprehension; Grammar; Pronunciation; Speech Skills; *Autoinstructional Aids; *Second Language Learning; *Standard Spoken Usage

AB..... This course in spoken Hausa is intended for use in introductory conversational classes. It is basically patterned after the aural-oral method with increased

emphasis on oral comprehension and pronunciation for
loosely controlled conversation at the first-year level.
The text is divided into 25 units, 3 of which are review
units, and can be used over a 2-year period. The units
cover conversation, grammar, pronunciation, and
comprehension exercises. Recordings are available to
supplement the text. A list of selected references on
the Hausa language includes five dictionaries, three
grammars, four readers, and journal and newspaper
citations. (CO)

CP..... Y

AN..... 000531

ER..... ED127825

TI..... Social Studies, Book I: A Bilingual Multicultural Guide, English-Spanish.

YR..... Jun75

AU..... Mata, José G.

IN..... Fort Worth Independent School District, Tex. Bilingual Education Program. (BBB13287)

SN..... Office of Bilingual Education (DHEW/OE), Washington, D.C. (BBB12883)

LG..... English; Spanish

AV..... National Dissemination and Assessment Center, 7703 North Lamar Boulevard, Austin, Texas 78752 ($3.50); ERIC Document Reproduction Service, P.O. Box 190, Arlington, Virginia 22210 ($10.03; microfiche $0.83; ED127825)

NT..... 199 p.
For Book II, see 000532.

DE..... *Curriculum Guides; Elementary Education; Social Studies; *Lesson Plans; *Mexican Americans; *Units of Study (Subject Fields); Behavioral Objectives; Citizenship; Consumer Education; Government Role; Government (Administrative Body); Instructional Materials; *Social History

AB..... This is the first of two social science guides designed for the bilingual multicultural classroom. Although originally intended for the fifth grade, it is also appropriate for use in other elementary grades and possibly in some junior high school classes. The guide may be used independently or as a supplement to other social studies programs. Activities may be done in writing or orally; in English or in Spanish; and with the entire class, in small groups, or individually. Fifteen curriculum lessons are presented: (1) "Studying Man: Adaptation"; (2) "The Legend of the Eagle and the Serpent"; (3) "The Building of a City -- Tenochtitlan"; (4) "All Occupations Are Important"; (5) "Ways of Buying"; (6) "The Explorations and Development of the Southwest"; (7) "Mexican Americans: Contributions, Successes, Challenges"; (8) "Lincoln, Juarez, King"; (9)

"Who Is a Citizen?"; (10) "The Power of the Vote"; (11) "The Legislature -- Making Laws to Run a Nation"; (12) "The Presidency -- Executing the Laws"; (13) "The Judiciary -- Interpreting the Laws"; (14) "Why People Use Drugs"; and (15) "Places of Worship in My Barrio." The lessons present concept, behavioral objectives, vocabulary, recommended materials and ways to use them, activities, evaluation, and optional activities. A bibliography and an answer key for worksheets are also included. (Author/DS)

CP..... N

AN..... 000532

ER..... ED123895

TI..... Social Studies, Book II: A Bilingual Multicultural Guide, English-Spanish.

YR..... Nov75

AU..... Cedillo, Gustavo F.

IN..... Fort Worth Independent School District, Tex. Bilingual Education Program. (BBB13287)

SN..... Office of Bilingual Education (DHEW/OE), Washington, D.C. (BBB12883)

LG..... English; Spanish

AV..... National Dissemination and Assessment Center, 7703 North Lamar Boulevard, Austin, Texas 78752 ($3.50); ERIC Document Reproduction Service, P.O. Box 190, Arlington, Virginia 22210 ($10.03; microfiche $0.83; ED123895)

NT..... 195 p.
For Book I, see 000531.

DE..... *Curriculum Guides; Elementary Education; *Lesson Plans; *Social Studies; Units of Study (Subject Fields); Behavioral Objectives; Consumer Education; *Cultural Education; Cultural Traits; Economics; Government (Administrative Body); Learning Activities; Racial Differences; Social Relations

AB..... This is the second of two social science guides designed for the bilingual multicultural classroom. Although originally intended for the sixth grade, it is also appropriate for use in other elementary grades and possibly in some junior high school classes. The guide may be used independently or as a supplement to other social studies programs. Activities may be done in writing or orally; in English or in Spanish; and with the entire class, in small groups, or individually. Eight curriculum lessons are presented: (1) "The Three Human Racial Stocks: Some Facial Physical Traits"; (2) "Cultural Traits: Differences and Similarities"; (3) "Has Our Culture Changed?"; (4) "One Individual: Numerous Groups"; (5) "We Have Wants and Needs"; (6) "The Law of Supply and Demand"; (7) "Your Government and Mine"; and (8) "Settlements Without Violence." The lessons present concept, behavioral objectives, vocabulary, recommended

```
         materials and ways to use them, activities, evaluation,
         and optional activities.  A bibliography and an answer
         key for worksheets are also provided.  (Author/DS)

CP.....  N
```

```
AN.....  000533

TI.....  Leamos sobre veinte ocupaciones!   Twenty Trades to Read
         About.

YR.....  Oct78

AU.....  Lamatino, Robyn; Mintz, Adin, ed.; Mintz, Adin, trans.

IN.....  Rutgers, The State Univ. New Brunswick, N.J. Curriculum
         Lab. (QAT77005)

SN.....  New Jersey State Dept. of Education, Trenton. Div. of
         Vocational Education. (QAT59178)

LG.....  English; Spanish

AV.....  New Jersey Vocational-Technical Curriculum Laboratory,
         Building 4103, Kilmer Campus, Rutgers University, New
         Brunswick, New Jersey 08903

NT.....  ii, 154 p.

DE.....  *Career Awareness; *Spanish; *English (Second Language);
         *Workbooks; Instructional Materials; Language
         Instruction; *Occupations; Secondary Education; Adult
         Basic Education; Reading Materials; Trade and Industrial
         Education; Reading Instruction; Second Language Learning;
         Vocational Education; *Spanish Speaking

AB.....  This Spanish-English bilingual supplementary workbook is
         designed specifically for Spanish-speaking students of
         English as a second language (ESL).  The 20 chapters in
         the book contain successively more English.  Each chapter
         begins with a story in both Spanish and English.  The
         units deal with auto body work, auto mechanics, baking,
         carpentry and cabinetmaking, electrical trades, fashion
         design, commercial foods, health occupations, ornamental
         horticulture, plumbing, painting and decorating, machine
         shop, upholstery, welding, cosmetology, and diesel
         mechanics.  The workbook can be used for vocational
         career exploration, simulation practice, and ESL
         instruction.  The stories and exercises are written in
         two different type colors.  Black-and-white illustrations
         accompany each unit.  (CO)

CP.....  N
```

```
AN.....  000537

TI.....  Entre dois mundos: Vida quotidiana de criancas
         portuguesas na América (Between Two Worlds:  Daily Life
         of Portuguese Americans). Teacher's Guide.

YR.....  78
```

AU..... Meneses, Fernando de; Machado, Magdalena, ill.

IN..... National Assessment and Dissemination Center, Cambridge, Mass.

SN..... Office of Education (DHEW), Washington, D.C. (RMQ66000)

AV..... National Assessment and Dissemination Center, 49 Washington Avenue, Cambridge, Massachusetts 02140

NT..... v, 84 p.
For companion text, see 000124.

DE..... *Teaching Guides; *Portuguese Americans; Portuguese; *Cultural Awareness; *Instructional Materials; High Schools; Secondary Education; *Cultural Education; Cultural Differences; Humanistic Education

AB..... This teacher's guide is designed for use in Portuguese bilingual classes at the secondary level. The accompanying text contains stories about Portuguese children in the United States and focuses on their problems and experiences, especially as they relate to "cultural shock." The materials are useful for cultural awareness and affective education classes. (CO)

CP..... N

AN..... 000539

TI..... Pu-nvt-tv e-ten-hes-se (Animal Friends).

YR..... Sep78

AU..... Harjo, Edmond A.

IN..... East Central University, Ada, Okla. Seminole Bilingual Education Project.

SN..... Office of Education (DHEW), Washington, D.C. (RMQ66000)

LG..... English; Seminole

AV..... National Dissemination and Assessment Center, 7703 North Lamar Boulevard, Austin, Texas 78752 (ISBN 0-89417-376-6)

NT..... 14 p.

DE..... *Childrens Literature; *Reading Materials; American Indian Languages; Primary Education; *Language Instruction; Uncommonly Taught Languages; Instructional Materials

ID..... *Coloring Books; *Seminole

AB..... This reader and coloring book is intended for Seminole language instruction on the elementary level. Black-and-white illustrations are accompanied by Seminole captions. English translations of each of the captions precede the illustrations. (SH)

CP..... N

AN..... 000549

TI..... SCDC Spanish Curricula Units: Grade 1-4.

YR..... 73-78

IN..... National Dissemination and Assessment Center, Austin, Tex.; Spanish Curricula Development Center, Miami Beach, Fla. (BBB06110)

SN..... Office of Education (DHEW), Washington, D.C. (RMQ66000)

LG..... English; Spanish

AV..... National Dissemination and Assessment Center, 7703 North Lamar Boulevard, Austin, Texas 78752

NT..... In various editions
237 volumes

DE..... Grade 1; Grade 2; Grade 3; Grade 4; Primary Education; *Spanish; *Instructional Materials; *Language Arts; *Second Language Learning; *Fine Arts; Social Sciences; *Sciences; Mathematics

AB..... This curriculum package supports Spanish-English bilingual bicultural programs in the first through fourth grades. Instructional materials come in five strands or areas of instruction: (1) language arts, which includes a basal reading program to extend the language that Spanish-dominant children bring from home and incorporates language analysis, creative writing, and oral-language development; (2) Spanish as a second language (SL), which utilizes an aural-oral approach; (3) fine arts, which includes a music-oriented curriculum for grades one through three and a cultural arts program for grade four; (4) social science, reflecting basic social science concepts within different cultures; and (5) science/math, in which a process approach is utilized and basic concepts and skills are identified and developed. Units are composed of 4 "kits," each designed for use over a period of instruction of 2-3 weeks. Unit components may include: (1) a teacher's guide, (2) a supplement of visual aids, (3) a ditto packet, (4) readers or songbooks, (5) criterion-referenced test manuals for student and teacher, (6) an audio cassette of songs, and (7) a set of two hand puppets. (DS)

CP..... N

AN..... 000550

TI..... Las Matemáticas: Lenguaje universal (Mathematics: The Universal Language). Teacher's Guide 1.

SE..... Aguila Volante Series: Levels 1-3.

YR..... 78

AU..... Osborn, Faye; Alvarez, Verónica; O'Dell, Evelyn Villa; Holiday, Roberta, ed.; Díaz, Luis C., ed.; Chambers, Steve, ill.

IN..... National Dissemination and Assessment Center, Austin, Tex.

SN..... Office of Education (DHEW), Washington, D.C. (RMQ66000)

LG..... English; Spanish

AV..... National Dissemination and Assessment Center, 7703 North Lamar Boulevard, Austin, Texas 78752 (ISBN 89417-585-8)

NT..... xi, 280 p.
For companion workbooks, see 000551-555.

DE..... Grade 6; Intermediate Grades; *Mathematics Instruction; *Mathematics Materials; *Arithmetic; Addition; Subtraction; Multiplication; Division; *Teaching Guides; *Spanish; Instructional Materials; Numbers; Number Systems

AB..... This teacher's guide, designed for use in sixth grade bilingual Spanish mathematics instruction, is divided into sections corresponding to five student booklets which cover: (1) numbers and numeration, (2) addition and subtraction of whole numbers, (3) multiplication and division of whole numbers, (4) factors and multiples, and (5) measurement. Each section contains an overview, the behavioral objectives of the section, contrastive features of the American and Hispanic systems, the lessons, patterns and activities, and tests. The instructions are presented in both Spanish and English. This guide is part of a sequential course of study which can be used as a basic course or as a supplement to other texts. (CO)

CP..... Y

AN..... 000551

TI..... Las Matemáticas: Lenguaje universal. Números y numeración (Mathematics: The Universal Language. Numbers and Numeration).

SE..... Aguila Volante Series: Level 1.

YR..... Oct78

IN..... National Dissemination and Assessment Center, Austin, Tex.

SN..... Office of Education (DHEW), Washington, D.C. (RMQ66000)

LG..... English; Spanish

AV..... National Dissemination and Assessment Center, 7703 North Lamar Boulevard, Austin, Texas 78752 (ISBN 89417-585-8)

NT..... 87 p.
For teacher's guide and other workbooks, see 000550 and 552-.

DE..... Grade 6; Intermediate Grades; *Spanish; *Mathematics Instruction; *Mathematics Materials; Arithmetic; *Instructional Materials; *Workbooks; Numbers; *Number Concepts

AB..... This workbook, designed for use in sixth grade bilingual Spanish mathematics instruction, contains eight lessons covering: (1) the set, number, and numeral; (2) graphing on a number line; (3) place value; (4) using exponents; (5) expanded notation; (6) flow charts; (7) rounding numbers; and (8) Roman numerals. A review, a glossary, and a reference chart relating other selected texts to this booklet are appended. Instructions are presented in both Spanish and English. (CO)

CP..... Y

AN..... 000552

TI..... Las Matemáticas: Lenguaje universal. Factores y múltiplos (Mathematics: The Universal Language. Factors and Multiples).

SE..... Aguila Volante Series: Level 2c.

YR..... Oct78

IN..... National Dissemination and Assessment Center, Austin, Tex.

SN..... Office of Education (DHEW), Washington, D.C. (RMQ66000)

LG..... English; Spanish

AV..... National Dissemination and Assessment Center, 7703 North Lamar Boulevard, Austin, Texas 78752 (ISBN 89417-585-8)

NT..... 63 p.
For teacher's guide and other workbooks, see 000550-551 and 553-555.

DE..... Grade 6; Intermediate Grades; *Spanish; *Mathematics Instruction; *Mathematics Materials; Arithmetic; *Instructional Materials; *Workbooks; *Number Systems

AB..... This workbook, designed for use in sixth grade bilingual Spanish mathematics instruction, contains 13 lessons on factors and multiples. A review, a glossary, and a reference chart relating other selected texts to this booklet are appended. Instructions are in both Spanish and English. (CO)

CP..... Y

AN..... 000553

TI..... Las Matemáticas: Lenguaje universal. Suma y resta de números enteros (Mathematics: The Universal Language. Addition and Subtraction of Whole Numbers).

SE..... Aguila Volante Series: Level 2a.

YR..... Oct78

IN..... National Dissemination and Assessment Center, Austin, Tex.

SN..... Office of Education (DHEW), Washington, D.C. (RMQ66000)

LG..... English; Spanish

AV..... National Dissemination and Assessment Center, 7703 North Lamar Boulevard, Austin, Texas 78752 (ISBN 89417-585-8)

NT..... 70 p.
For teacher's guide and other workbooks, see 000550-552 and 554-555.

DE..... Grade 6; Intermediate Grades; *Spanish; Mathematics Instruction; *Mathematics Materials; Arithmetic; Instructional Materials; *Workbooks; *Addition; *Subtraction; *Whole Numbers

AB..... This workbook, designed for use in sixth grade bilingual Spanish mathematics instruction, contains 13 lessons on the addition and subtraction of whole numbers. A review, a glossary, and a reference chart relating other selected texts to this booklet are appended. Instructions are presented in both Spanish and English. (CO)

CP..... Y

AN..... 000554

TI..... Las Matemáticas: Lenguaje universal. Multiplicación y división de números enteros (Mathematics: The Universal Language. Multiplication and Division of Whole Numbers).

SE..... Aguila Volante Series: Level 2b.

YR..... Oct78

IN..... National Dissemination and Assessment Center, Austin, Tex.

SN..... Office of Education (DHEW), Washington, D.C. (RMQ66000)

LG..... English; Spanish

AV..... National Dissemination and Assessment Center, 7703 North Lamar Boulevard, Austin, Texas 78752 (ISBN 89417-585-8)

NT..... 82 p.
For teacher's guide and other workbooks, see 000550-553 and 555.

DE..... Grade 6; Intermediate Grades; *Spanish; *Mathematics Instruction; *Mathematics Materials; Arithmetic; *Instructional Materials; *Workbooks; Multiplication; Division; *Whole Numbers

AB..... This workbook, designed for use in sixth grade bilingual Spanish mathematics instruction, contains 15 lessons on multiplication and division of whole numbers. A review, a glossary, and a reference chart relating other selected

          texts to this booklet are appended.   Instructions are in
          both Spanish and English. (CO)

CP..... Y

AN..... 000555

TI..... Las Matemáticas: Lenguaje universal. La Medida.
          (Mathematics: The Universal Language. Measurement).

SE..... Aguila Volante Series: Level 3.

YR..... Oct78

IN..... National Dissemination and Assessment Center, Austin,
          Tex.

SN..... Office of Education (DHEW), Washington, D.C. (RMQ66000)

LG..... English; Spanish

AV..... National Dissemination and Assessment Center, 7703 North
          Lamar Boulevard, Austin, Texas 78752 (ISBN 89417-585-8)

NT..... 76 p.
          For teacher's guide and other workbooks, see 000550-554.

DE..... Grade 6; Intermediate Grades; *Spanish; *Mathematics
          Instruction; *Mathematics Materials; Arithmetic;
          Instructional Materials; *Workbooks; *Measurement;
          *Metric System

AB..... This workbook, designed for use in sixth grade bilingual
          Spanish mathematics instruction, contains 14 lessons on
          measurement: (1) hours of the day, (2) minutes, (3)
          shortcuts to minutes, (4) measurement by pictures, (5)
          small to large measurement by pictures, (6) changing
          larger units of measure to smaller units, (7) changing
          smaller units of measure to larger units, (8) using
          measures of time, (9) using dry measure, (10) using
          liquid measure, (11) using measures of weight, (12) using
          measures of length, (13) adding measurements, and (14)
          subtracting measurements. A review, a glossary, and a
          reference chart relating other selected texts to this
          booklet are appended. Instructions are presented in both
          Spanish and English. (CO)

CP..... Y

AN..... 000557

ER..... ED149640

TI..... Así aprendemos: Libro I. Libro de lectura (This Is How
          We Learn: Book I. Reader).

SE..... Qué bonito es leer, II (How Nice It Is To Read, II)
          (Series).

YR..... Jan78

IN..... National Dissemination and Assessment Center, Austin, Tex.; Curriculum Adaptation Network for Bilingual/Bicultural Education, San Antonio, Tex. Southwest Regional Adaptation Center. (BBB11923)

SN..... Office of Education (DHEW), Washington, D.C. (RMQ66000)

LG..... Spanish

AV..... National Dissemination and Assessment Center, 7703 North Lamar Boulevard, Austin, Texas 78752 (ISBN 0-89417-306-5; $1.50); ERIC Document Reproduction Service, P.O. Box 190, Arlington, Virginia 22210 ($4.67; microfiche $0.83; ED149640)

NT..... 81 p.
For teacher's guide and workbook, see 000558-559.

DE..... Childrens Books; *Instructional Materials; *Language Instruction; Primary Education; *Reading Instruction; *Reading Materials; *Spanish; Vowels

AB..... This Spanish reader is designed to be used as a supplement to second grade bilingual reading instruction. The book consists of seven stories, the first having to do with vowels, the following three with school, and the last three with the family. (CO)

CP..... N

AN..... 000558

ER..... ED149642

TI..... Así aprendemos: Libro I. Guía para el maestro (This Is How We Learn: Book I. Teacher's Guide).

SE..... Qué bonito es leer, II (How Nice It Is to Read, II) (Series).

YR..... Jan78

IN..... National Dissemination and Assessment Center, Austin, Tex.; Curriculum Adaptation Network for Bilingual/Bicultural Education, San Antonio, Tex. Southwest Regional Adaptation Center. (BBB11923)

SN..... Office of Education (DHEW), Washington, D.C. (RMQ66000)

LG..... Spanish

AV..... National Dissemination and Assessment Center, 7703 North Lamar Boulevard, Austin, Texas 78752 (ISBN 0-89417-308-1; $4.50); ERIC Document Reproduction Service, P.O. Box 190, Arlington, Virginia 22210 ($10.03; microfiche $0.83; ED149642)

NT..... lxiii, 186 p.
For reader and workbook, see 000557 and 559.

DE..... Curriculum Guides; Diagnostic Tests; Educational Objectives; Elementary Education; Instructional

Materials; *Language Instruction; Language Tests; Primary Education; *Reading Instruction; Reading Materials; Reading Tests; *Spanish; *Teaching Guides; *Teaching Methods; Vocabulary

AB..... In this teacher's manual, an introduction to the series is followed by a discussion of course objectives and diagnostic testing of reading. The guide follows the structure of the companion reader, which consists of seven stories dealing with vowels, school, and family. A glossary completes the volume. (CO)

CP..... N

AN..... 000559

ER..... ED149641

TI..... Así aprendemos: Libro I. Cuaderno de ejercicios (This Is How We Learn: Book I. Workbook).

SE..... Qué bonito es leer, II (How Nice It Is to Read, II) (Series).

YR..... Jan78

IN..... National Dissemination and Assessment Center, Austin, Tex.; Curriculum Adaptation Network for Bilingual/Bicultural Education, San Antonio, Tex. Southwest Regional Adaptation Center. (BBB11923)

SN..... Office of Education (DHEW), Washington, D.C. (RMQ66000)

LG..... Spanish

AV..... National Dissemination and Assessment Center, 7703 North Lamar Boulevard, Austin, Texas 78752 (ISBN 0-89417-307-3; $1.00); ERIC Document Reproduction Service, P.O. Box 190, Arlington, Virginia 22210 ($2.06; microfiche $0.83; ED149641)

NT..... 37 p.
For reader and teacher's guide, see 000557-558.

DE..... Childrens Books; Educational Games; Elementary Education; *Instructional Materials; *Language Instruction; Language Skills; Phonology; Primary Education; *Reading Comprehension; *Reading Instruction; Reading Materials; *Spanish; Spelling; *Workbooks; Pattern Drills (Language)

ID..... Language Exercises

AB..... This workbook is intended to be used for bilingual Spanish-English reading instruction in the second grade. As a followup to the stories contained in the reader, the workbook provides drawing games, word games, punctuation exercises, and other exercises designed to practice grammar, phonology, spelling, and reading comprehension skills. A glossary completes the workbook. (CO)

CP..... N

AN..... 000560

TI..... Activity Supplement for Puedo Leer: Teacher's Guide. Program for Initial Reading in Spanish for Bilingual Children.

YR..... Feb75

AU..... López, Sara

IN..... National Dissemination and Assessment Center, Austin, Tex.

SN..... Office of Education (DHEW), Washington, D.C. (RMQ66000)

AV..... National Dissemination and Assessment Center, 7703 North Lamar Boulevard, Austin, Texas 78752 ($3.50); ERIC Document Reproduction Service, P.O. Box 190, Arlington, Virginia 22210 ($10.78; microfiche $0.76; price includes set of cards; ED108502)

NT..... v, 162 p.
For related documents, see 000561-562.

DE..... Basic Reading; *Consonants; Educational Games; Primary Education; Instructional Aids; *Instructional Materials; Language Instruction; Learning Activities; Phonics; Reading Games; Reading Instruction; *Spanish; Supplementary Reading Materials; *Teaching Guides; *Vowels; *Prereading Experience

AB..... This teacher's guide is part of an activity supplement intended to accompany the "Puedo Leer -- I Can Read" training manual for initial reading in Spanish for bilingual students. The guide provides suggestions for a wide variety of prereading activities and approaches, expanding on the activities in the training manual. The two main sections of the teacher's guide consist of introductions to vowels and consonants, followed by reinforcement and followup activities such as word games and composition exercises. The second part of the activity supplement, a set of cards, accompanies the section on consonants. (CO)

CP..... N

AN..... 000561

TI..... Activity Supplement for Puedo Leer: Use of Charts: Program for Initial Reading in Spanish for Bilingual Children.

YR..... Feb75

AU..... López, Sara

IN..... National Dissemination and Assessment Center, Austin, Tex.

SN..... Office of Education (DHEW), Washington, D.C. (RMQ66000)

- AV..... National Dissemination and Assessment Center, 7703 North Lamar Boulevard, Austin, Texas 78752 ($3.00); ERIC Document Reproduction Service, P.O. Box 190, Arlington, Virginia 22210 ($10.78; microfiche $0.76; price includes teacher's guide; ED108502)

- NT..... 54 cards, 8-1/2"x11".
  For related documents, see 000560 and 562.

- DE..... *Alphabet Cards; Instructional Media; Instructional Materials; *Spanish; Supplementary Reading Materials; *Consonants; *Basic Reading; Educational Games; Primary Education; Language Instruction; Learning Activities; Reading Games; Phonics

- AB..... These cards, together with a companion teacher's guide, form an activity supplement to the "Puedo Leer -- I Can Read" training manual. The set is designed for initial reading instruction in Spanish in a bilingual program. The exercises on the cards are to be used after the introduction of each consonant. Syllables, words, and sentences using each consonant appear in the exercises. Strategies for the use of the cards are included. (CO)

- CP..... N

- AN..... 000562

- TI..... Puedo Leer. I Can Read. Initial Reading in Spanish for Bilingual Children.

- YR..... Aug75

- AU..... Herbert, Charles H.; Sancho, Anthony R.

- IN..... San Bernardino County Schools, Calif. Regional Project Office. (BBB07971)

- SN..... Office of Education (DHEW), Washington, D.C. (RMQ66000)

- AV..... National Dissemination and Assessment Center, 7703 North Lamar Boulevard, Austin, Texas 78752 ($3.50)

- NT..... x, 121 p.
  Rev. ed.
  For activity supplement, see 000560-561.

- DE..... Consonants; Vowels; Educational Games; Learning Activities; *Spanish; *Basic Reading; *Reading Instruction; Instructional Materials; *Teaching Guides; Primary Education; Phonics; Reading Games; Language Instruction; *Prereading Experience; Grade 1

- AB..... This manual contains information about the "Puedo Leer -- I Can Read" series, the basic rationale of the program, and lesson outlines for teaching initial reading in Spanish to first grade Spanish children. The manual is based on research reports from four project sites in Texas and Mexico. This volume is one of the components of the program designed to train classroom teachers to teach reading to monolingual Spanish-speaking children or to Spanish-speaking children with limited-English-speaking facility. It includes sections on prereading, concept development, and lesson plans with suggestions for activities, games, and other devices for teaching initial reading skills in Spanish. (CO)

CP..... N

AN..... 000563

ER..... ED156817

TI..... Teacher Training Pack for a Course on Cultural Awareness.

YR..... 76

AU..... Curt, Carmen Judith Nine

IN..... National Assessment and Dissemination Center, Cambridge, Mass.; Northeast Center for Curriculum Development, Bronx, N.Y. (BBB17015)

SN..... Office of Education (DHEW), Washington, D.C. (RMQ66000)

AV..... National Assessment and Dissemination Center, 49 Washington Avenue, Cambridge, Massachusetts 02140 ($2.00); ERIC Document Reproduction Service, P.O. Box 190, Arlington, Virginia 22210 ($3.50; microfiche $0.83)

NT..... 52 p.
For related document, see 000564.

DE..... *Course Content; *Course Organization; *Cultural Awareness; *Nonverbal Communication; *Teaching Guides; Communication Skills; Course Evaluation; Elementary Secondary Education; Ethnicity; Teacher Education; Cross Cultural Studies; Cultural Education

AB..... This book is a teacher's guide for a course on cultural awareness. The general objectives of the course are given, along with a listing of the required texts. The first section deals with cultural identity. Objectives of this part of the course and a series of activities the teacher can undertake to promote cultural identity are described. The second section deals with various modes of nonverbal communication and their cultural significance. A course evaluation questionnaire is included, as well as three tests on cultural identity and nonverbal communication to be given to the course participants a semester after the course is taken. The followup activities focus on attitudes and facts relating to Puerto Rican and other Latin American cultures. (CO)

CP..... Y

AN..... 000564

TI..... Non-verbal Communication in Puerto Rico.

YR..... 76

AU..... Curt, Carmen Judith Nine

IN..... National Dissemination and Assessment Center, Austin, Tex.; Northeast Center for Curriculum Development, Bronx, N.Y. (BBB17015)

SN..... Office of Education (DHEW), Washington, D.C. (RMQ66000)

AV..... National Assessment and Dissemination Center, 49 Washington Avenue, Cambridge, Massachusetts 02140 ($2.00)

NT..... ii, 71 p.
For related document, see 000563.

DE..... *Nonverbal Communication; *Puerto Ricans; *Puerto Rican Culture; *Cultural Awareness; Cross Cultural Studies; *Teacher Education; *Cultural Differences

ID..... Puerto Rico

AB..... This text includes observations made by the author over a period of several years regarding the contrasts that exist between Anglo-American and Latin American cultures in the area of nonverbal communication. The emphasis is placed on the author's native Puerto Rican culture. Included in the text are: (1) a paper on nonverbal communication in Puerto Rico; (2) a speech on nonverbal communication in the English as a second language classroom; (3) sections on smiling, staring, eye contact, silence versus noise, clothes, money matters, laughter and play, frankness versus reticence, greetings, farewells, and interruptions; and (4) a case study done on Puerto Rican children in New York. A bibliography of 15 citations is appended. (CO)

CP..... Y

AN..... 000565

ER..... ED109900

TI..... Poesías infantiles: Primer grado (Children's Poems: First Grade).

YR..... Mar74

IN..... National Dissemination and Assessment Center, Austin, Tex.; Curriculum Adaptation Network for Bilingual/Bicultural Education, Bronx, N.Y. Northeast Regional Adaptation Center (BBB11921)

SN..... Office of Education (DHEW), Washington, D.C. (RMQ66000)

LG..... Spanish

AV..... National Dissemination and Assessment Center, 7703 North Lamar Boulevard, Austin, Texas 78752 ($1.50); ERIC Document Reproduction Service, P.O. Box 190, Arlington, Virginia 22210 ($1.95; microfiche $0.76; ED109900)

NT..... 24 p.

DE..... Childrens Books; *Childrens Literature; *Instructional Materials; *Poetry; Primary Education; Reading Comprehension; *Reading Materials; Reading Skills; *Spanish; Kindergarten; Grade 1; Grade 2; Grade 3

AB..... This collection of original poems and riddles in Spanish is designed for use in Spanish-English bilingual education in the primary grades. The material is intended to reinforce learning skills of decoding, comprehension, and interpretation. (Author/DS)

CP..... N

AN..... 000566

TI..... Mi ambiente y yo (My Environment and Me): An Aural-Oral Activity Guide.

YR..... 73

AU..... Canales, Estella; García, Inés; Garza, Olivia; Godoy, Viola; Garza, Beatriz de la, ed.; Pérez, Carlos, ed.; Perkins, Carolita, ill.

IN..... Corpus Christi Independent School District, Tex. (XPT83183); National Dissemination and Assessment Center, Austin, Tex.

SN..... Office of Education (DHEW), Washington, D.C. (RMQ66000)

LG..... English; Spanish

AV..... National Dissemination and Assessment Center, 7703 North Lamar Boulevard, Austin, Texas 78752 ($5.00)

NT..... vii, 247 p.

DE..... Classroom Games; Cultural Awareness; Intonation; Kindergarten; *Teaching Guides; Latin American Culture; *Learning Activities; Lesson Plans; Music Techniques; Oral Communication; Pattern Drills (Language); Preschool Education; Pronunciation; *Spanish; Spanish Speaking; Vocabulary; Curriculum Guides; *Cultural Education; *Audiolingual Skills

AB..... This aural-oral guide is designed especially for use at the preschool and kindergarten levels. The teacher of Spanish-speaking children may use it as a series of lesson plans or scripts around such topics as school, the family, and pets. Vocabulary enrichment, syntactical drill patterns, and pronunciation and intonation exercises are provided. The book uses songs, games, and folklore of the Spanish American culture to promote the children's knowledge of and pride in their heritage. (Author/DS)

CP..... N

AN.....	000567
ER.....	ED127820
TI.....	Libro de lectura: Nivel A (Reader: Level A).
YR.....	Jul75
AU.....	Yeats, Alid; López, Erleen; Baca, Nina; Hernández, Lucille, ill.; Hill, Patti, ill.
IN.....	Albuquerque Public Schools, N. Mex. (QII9293); National Dissemination and Assessment Center, Austin, Tex.
SN.....	Office of Education (DHEW), Washington, D.C. (RMQ66000)
LG.....	Spanish
AV.....	National Dissemination and Assessment Center, 7703 North Lamar Boulevard, Austin, Texas 78752 ($1.50); ERIC Document Reproduction Service, P.O. Box 190, Arlington, Virginia 22210 ($4.67; microfiche $0.83; ED127820)
NT.....	77 p. For Level B and C readers and supplement, see 000568-570.
DE.....	Childrens Literature; Cultural Context; Cultural Traits; Elementary Education; *Reading Materials; *Instructional Materials; *Social Studies; *Spanish; Vocabulary; *Natural Sciences; Weather; Grade 1; Grade 2
AB.....	This is the first in a series of four reading books written in Spanish and designed for use in elementary bilingual education programs. Level A is geared to first and second grade students. The stories are divided into two sections: "Estudios Sociales" (Social Studies) and "La Naturaleza" (Nature). The five stories in the first section deal with such topics as the home, school, and cleaning. The five stories in the second section deal mainly with the seasons and aspects of the weather. Each story is followed by a list of new words and is illustrated with black-and-white and color drawings. (DS)
CP.....	N

AN.....	000568
ER.....	ED127821
TI.....	Libro de lectura: Nivel B (Reader: Level B).
YR.....	Jul75
AU.....	Yeats, Alid; López, Erleen; Baca, Nina; Hernández, Lucille, ill.; Fuentevilla, Mercy, ill.; Hill, Patti, ill.

IN.....	Albuquerque Public Schools, N. Mex. (QII01293); National Dissemination and Assessment Center, Austin, Tex.
SN.....	Office of Education (DHEW), Washington, D.C. (RMQ66000)
LG.....	Spanish
AV.....	National Dissemination and Assessment Center, 7703 North Lamar Boulevard, Austin, Texas 78752 ($1.50); ERIC Document Reproduction Service, P.O. Box 190, Arlington, Virginia 22210 ($4.67; microfiche $0.83; ED127821)
NT.....	93 p. For Level A and C readers and supplement, see 000567 and 569-570.
DE.....	Childrens Literature; *Community Relations; Community Services; Cultural Context; Cultural Education; Cultural Traits; Elementary Education; *Instructional Materials; *Reading Materials; *Social Studies; *Spanish; Vocabulary; Professional Occupations; Grade 2; Grade 3
AB.....	This is the second in a series of four reading books written in Spanish and designed for use in elementary bilingual education programs. Level B is geared to second and third grade students. The stories are divided into two sections: "Estudios Sociales" (Social Studies) and "La Comunidad" (The Community). The stories in the first section have to do with activities in the home, particularly chores and helping; most of the stories in the second section deal with important community figures, such as the nurse, the fireman, the doctor, the mailman, the dentist, and the policeman. Each story is followed by a list of new words and is illustrated with black-and-white and color drawings. (DS)
CP.....	N

AN.....	000569
ER.....	ED127822
TI.....	Libro de lectura: Nivel C (Reader: Level C).
YR.....	Jul75
AU.....	Yeats, Alid; Baca, Niña; Saavedra, Frances; Hayakawa, Linda; Vigil, Tonie, ill.; Saavedra, Frances, ill.; Hernández, Lucille, ill.; Fuentevilla, Mercy, ill.; Hill, Patti, ill.
IN.....	Albuquerque Public Schools, N. Mex. (QII01293); National Dissemination and Assessment Center, Austin, Tex.
SN.....	Office of Education (DHEW), Washington, D.C. (RMQ66000)
LG.....	Spanish
AV.....	National Dissemination and Assessment Center, 7703 North Lamar Boulevard, Austin, Texas 78752 ($2.00); ERIC Document Reproduction Service, P.O. Box 190, Arlington, Virginia 22210 ($7.35; microfiche $0.83; ED127822)

NT..... 129 p.
For Level A and B readers and supplement, see 000567-568 and 570.

DE..... Childrens Literature; Educational Games; Elementary Education; Enrichment Activities; *Instructional Materials; *Language Enrichment; Language Skills; Puzzles; *Reading Materials; *Spanish; Vocabulary; *Natural Sciences; Grade 4; Grade 5

AB..... This is the third in a series of four reading books written in Spanish and designed for use in elementary bilingual education programs. Level C is geared to fourth and fifth grade students. The reader contains nine stories, most of which deal with some aspect of nature study, such as plants or insects. Each story is followed by a list of new vocabulary and enrichment exercises and activities in the form of fill-ins, definitions, puzzles, and experiments. The text is illustrated with black-and-white drawings. (DS)

CP..... N

AN..... 000570

ER..... ED127823

TI..... Libro de lectura: Suplemento (Reader: Supplement).

YR..... Jul75

AU..... Saavedra, Frances; Saavedra, Frances, ill.; Hill, Patti, ill.

IN..... Albuquerque Public Schools, N. Mex. (QII01293); National Dissemination and Assessment Center, Austin, Tex.

SN..... Office of Education (DHEW), Washington, D.C. (RMQ66000)

LG..... Spanish

AV..... National Dissemination and Assessment Center, 7703 North Lamar Boulevard, Austin, Texas 78752 ($1.00); ERIC Document Reproduction Service, P.O. Box 190, Arlington, Virginia 22210 ($2.06; microfiche $0.83; ED127823)

NT..... 36 p.
For related readers, see 000567-569.

DE..... Childrens Literature; Cultural Context; Cultural Traits; Elementary Education; *Spanish; *Instructional Materials; *Reading Materials; Vocabulary; Grade 1; Grade 2; Grade 3; Grade 4; Grade 5; *Supplementary Reading Materials

AB..... This is the fourth in a series of four reading books written in Spanish and designed for use in elementary bilingual education programs. The supplement may be used in first through fifth grades. It contains five stories: four relate the adventures of various animals, and the last concerns a wedding. Each story is followed by a list of new vocabulary, and the reader is illustrated with black-and-white and color drawings. (DS)

CP..... N

AN..... 000571

TI..... Things to Do: Activities for a Bilingual Classroom.

YR..... 74

AU..... Baker, Jean M.; Ross, Joy; Walters, Barbara

IN..... San Bernardino County Schools, Calif. Regional Project Office. (BBB07971)

SN..... Office of Education (DHEW), Washington, D.C. (RMQ66000)

AV..... National Dissemination and Assessment Center, 7703 North Lamar Boulevard, Austin, Texas 78752 ($3.00)

NT..... ix, 38 p.
Rev. ed.

DE..... *Small Group Instruction; Art; Communication Skills; *Learning Activities; Manuals; Mathematics; Music; *Primary Grades; Schedule Modules; Social Studies; *Spanish; *Teaching Guides

AB..... This manual was prepared for teachers who are using or wish to use small-group organization in bilingual bicultural programs at the primary grade level. The manual includes several daily schedules and a series of activities appropriate for small groups of children. The activities described are of varying levels of complexity in Spanish and English and are organized around the content of several learning or interest centers, including a communications center (language arts, reading, writing); a math center; a science and social studies center; an art center; and a music and listening center. (Author/DS)

CP..... N

AN..... 000572

ER..... ED087210

TI..... Escucho, digo, y aprendo (I Listen, I Say, and I Learn): Spanish Reading Readiness Program for Primary Grades.

YR..... 77

AU..... Pérez, Carlos E., ed.; Perkins, Carolita, ill.

IN..... Edgewood Independent School District, San Antonio, Tex. (XPT23584); National Dissemination and Assessment Center, Austin, Tex.

SN..... Office of Education (DHEW), Washington, D.C. (RMQ66000)

LG..... Spanish

AV..... National Dissemination and Assessment Center, 7703 North Lamar Boulevard, Austin, Texas 78752 ($4.50); ERIC Document Reproduction Service, P.O. Box 190, Arlington, Virginia 22210 ($17.13; microfiche $0.76; ED087210)

NT..... viii, 261 p., [44] leaves.

DE..... Primary Education; Lesson Plans; *Basic Reading; Consonants; Elementary School Students; *Instructional Materials; Language Instruction; Phonemics; Phonetics; Reading; *Reading Instruction; Reading Materials; *Spanish; *Textbooks; Vowels; *Reading Readiness

AB..... This reading manual was prepared for Spanish-speaking children in the first grade. It consists of a diagnostic exam, a scale to evaluate the reading readiness of each child, 39 lessons, and 12 tests. Also included is a series of drawings designed to elicit conversation and stimulate the child to make specific phonemes. The program has been designed to be completed in 8 to 10 weeks, with each of the lessons requiring a 15- to 20-minute presentation. (DS)

CP..... N

AN..... 000573

ER..... ED127824

TI..... Alaskan Folktales (Dinjii zhuu gwandak).

YR..... Jun76

AU..... Peter, Katherine; Pope, Mary L.; Hanson, J. Leslie, ill.

IN..... Alaska State-Operated Schools, Anchorage. (APE00627); National Dissemination and Assessment Center, Austin, Tex.

SN..... Office of Education (DHEW), Washington, D.C. (RMQ66000)

LG..... English; Gwich'in

AV..... ERIC Document Reproduction Service, P.O. Box 190, Arlington, Virginia 22210 ($3.50; microfiche $0.83; ED127824)

NT..... 73 p.

DE..... Alaska Natives; *American Indian Culture; American Indian Languages; American Indians; Athapascan Languages; Cultural Context; *Folk Culture; *Instructional Materials; *Reading Materials; Legends; *Short Stories

ID..... *Gwich'in

AB..... This volume of Alaskan folktales contains eight stories written in English and Gwich'in. The book is designed with the English and Gwich'in versions on opposite pages and is illustrated with line drawings. (DS)

CP..... N

AN..... 000574

ER..... ED148163

TI..... Gracejo em leitura (Fun in Reading).

YR..... Dec76

IN..... ABC Unified School District, Cerritos, Calif. (BBB03110); National Dissemination and Assessment Center, Austin, Tex.

SN..... Office of Education (DHEW), Washington, D.C. (RMQ66000)

LG..... Portuguese

AV..... National Dissemination and Assessment Center, 7703 North Lamar Boulevard, Austin, Texas 78752 (ISBN 0-89417-049-X; $1.50); ERIC Document Reproduction Service, P.O. Box 190, Arlington, Virginia 22210 ($4.67; microfiche $0.83; ED148163)

NT..... 80 p.
For companion workbook, see 000575.

DE..... Basic Reading; Elementary Education; *Instructional Materials; *Language Instruction; *Portuguese; Primary Education; Pronunciation; *Reading Instruction; *Reading Materials; Vocabulary; Childrens Books

AB..... This is a primary-level Portuguese reader for use in a bilingual education program. Three illustrated stories provide elementary vocabulary and reading practice. A vocabulary list follows each story. (AM)

CP..... N

AN..... 000575

ER..... ED148164

TI..... Gracejo em leitura (Fun in Reading).

YR..... Dec76

IN..... ABC Unified School District, Cerritos, Calif. (BBB03110); National Dissemination and Assessment Center, Austin, Tex.

SN..... Office of Education (DHEW), Washington, D.C. (RMQ66000)

LG..... Portuguese

AV..... National Dissemination and Assessment Center, 7703 North Lamar Boulevard, Austin, Texas 78752 (ISBN 0-89417-050-3; $1.50); ERIC Document Reproduction Service, P.O. Box 190, Arlington, Virginia 22210 ($6.01; microfiche $0.83; ED148164)

NT..... 66 p.
For companion reader, see 000574.

DE..... Basic Reading; Childrens Games; Elementary Education; Freehand Drawing; Illustrations; *Instructional Materials; *Language Instruction; *Learning Activities; *Portuguese; Primary Education; Printing; *Reading Instruction; Spelling; Vocabulary; *Workbooks; Writing Exercises

ID..... *Coloring Books

AB..... This workbook is designed to accompany a primary-level Portuguese reader for use in a bilingual education program. The workbook consists of illustrations with writing, drawing, and coloring exercises, in addition to some games. (AM)

CP..... N

AN..... 000576

ER..... ED151139

TI..... Seven Constitutions (Anumpa vlhpisa un tuklo): Government of the Choctaw Republic, 1826-1906.

YR..... Feb78

AU..... Morrison, James D.

IN..... Southeastern Oklahoma State Univ., Durant. Choctaw Education Program.

SN..... Office of Education (DHEW), Washington, D.C. (RMQ66000)

AV..... ERIC Document Reproduction Service, P.O. Box 190, Arlington, Virginia 22210 ($7.35; microfiche $0.83; ED151139)

NT..... x, 127 p.

DE..... American Indians; Civil Liberties; Community Control; Conflict; *Constitutional History; *Constitutional Law; *Government (Administrative Body); *Governmental Structure; Government Role; Individual Power; Justice; Policy Formation; Power Structure; Reservations (Indian); Tribes; *American History

ID..... *Choctaw (Tribe)

AB..... The pressure of removal of all Indians from the Eastern States and territories to the underdeveloped West caused the Indians of the Five Civilized Tribes to reframe their basic institutions, including their governments, in an attempt to conform with Anglo-American ideas of what was "civilized." Both the Choctaws and Cherokees established

governments under written constitutions before removal to
Oklahoma from the East, and both wrote new instruments of
government soon after their arrival in the West. Between
1826 and 1860, the Choctaws wrote seven constitutions;
each succeeding constitution was an amendment and
improvement over its predecessor. The final document in
1860 served as their constitution for 46 years, until the
end of the existence of the Choctaw Republic. The
government thus created, although using the basic
political forms of the Anglo-American tradition, was
successful in retaining Indian concepts; e.g., the
conviction that a government was designed to serve the
people's needs, not to oppress them. Great care was
taken, by means of frequent elections, short terms, and a
minimum of appointive offices, to insure that the actions
of the government and its officials were constantly
subject to check by the voters. The Choctaw bill of
rights was included as Article I in the main body of all
their constitutions. Appended are the text of the
Constitution of 1860, a listing of the chiefs of the
Choctaw Nation from 1802 to 1977, and a 32-item
bibliography on the government and laws of the Choctaw
Nation. (Author/DS)

CP..... N

AN..... 000577

TI..... Cufe horkopv (Why the Rabbit Steals).

YR..... Sep78

AU..... Davis, Lorene; Factor, Susannah, trans.; Chuleewah, Quannah, ill.

IN..... East Central University, Ada, Okla. Seminole Bilingual Education Project.

SN..... Office of Education (DHEW), Washington, D.C. (RMQ66000)

LG..... English; Seminole

AV..... National Dissemination and Assessment Center, 7703 North Lamar Boulevard, Austin, Texas 78752 (ISBN 0-89417-303-0)

NT..... [16] p.
Rev. ed.

DE..... *Childrens Books; *Reading Materials; *American Indian Languages; American Indian Culture; Primary Education; Primary Grades; Folklore Books; *Instructional Materials

ID..... *Coloring Books; *Seminole

AB..... This reader and coloring book is intended for Seminole language instruction on the elementary level. Each page consists of a large black-and-white illustration plus a caption in Seminole. English translations of the captions appear at the end of the book. (SH)

CP..... N

AN..... 000578

TI..... Sciences: Biology, English-Spanish.

SE..... Learning Achievement Packages (Series).

YR..... Feb76

AU..... Rendón, René; Rosenblum, Mark

IN..... Calexico Intercultural Design, Calif.; National Dissemination and Assessment Center, Austin, Tex.

SN..... Office of Education (DHEW), Washington, D.C. (RMQ66000)

LG..... English; Spanish

AV..... National Dissemination and Assessment Center, 7703 North Lamar Boulevard, Austin, Texas 78752 ($3.00)

NT..... vi, 91 p.
Rev. ed.

DE..... Adult Education; *Biology Instruction; *Curriculum Guides; Lesson Plans; Secondary Education; *Spanish; Spanish Speaking; *Teaching Guides; Cell Theory; Magnification Methods; First Aid; *Sciences; *Instructional Materials

AB..... Four suggested science curriculum units are presented which were developed to deal with the learning problems of students with special language difficulties in grade 7 through 12, in addition to classes in adult education. The units, which are presented in both English and Spanish, deal with cell theory, mitosis, magnification, and wounds. Information for the teacher and student, exercises or activities, and a pretest and posttest are included. An eight-item bibliography is provided. (DS)

CP..... N

AN..... 000579

TI..... Driver Education: English-Spanish.

SE..... Learning Achievement Packages (Series).

YR..... Feb76

AU..... Rendón, René

IN..... Calexico Intercultural Design, Calif.; National Dissemination and Assessment Center, Austin, Tex.

SN..... Office of Education (DHEW), Washington, D.C. (RMQ66000)

LG..... English; Spanish

AV..... National Dissemination and Assessment Center, 7703 North Lamar Boulevard, Austin, Texas 78752 ($3.50)

NT..... viii, 185 p.

DE.....	*Curriculum Guides; *Driver Education; Language Instruction; Secondary Grades; Adult Education; *Social Studies; *Spanish; *Teaching Guides; *Instructional Materials
AB.....	This publication presents three suggested social studies curriculum units designed for use in the bilingual Spanish-English classroom or in advanced Spanish language classes for English speakers. The units, originally developed for grades 7-11, are entitled "Procedures for Driving, " "Maintenance of Automobile," and "Tires," and are to be used for driver education instruction. Each unit contains explanatory information and lesson plans for the teacher, background information and diagrams for the student, and tests. Three bibliographic references are provided. (DS)
CP.....	N

AN.....	000580
ER.....	ED123896
TI.....	Language Arts: Spanish Grammar.
SE.....	Learning Achievement Packages (Series).
YR.....	Oct75
AU.....	Andrade, Magdalena; Sones, Mary
IN.....	Calexico Intercultural Design, Calif.; National Dissemination and Assessment Center, Austin, Tex.
SN.....	Office of Education (DHEW), Washington, D.C. (RMQ66000)
LG.....	English; Spanish
AV.....	National Dissemination and Assessment Center, 7703 North Lamar Boulevard, Austin, Texas 78752 ($3.00); ERIC Document Reproduction Service, P.O. Box 190, Arlington, Virginia 22210 ($6.01; microfiche $0.83; ED123896)
NT.....	v, 129 p.
DE.....	Capitalization (Alphabetic); *Curriculum Guides; Dictionaries; *Language Arts; *Language Instruction; Lesson Plans; *Spanish; Spelling Instruction; *Teaching Guides; Grammar; Secondary Education; *Instructional Materials
AB.....	This set of 3 Spanish curriculum units was developed to deal with special language difficulties in grade 7-12 and adult education classes. These units are intended to aid the first- or second-year student in specific problem areas: capital letters, dictionary use, and orthographic eccentricities of the letter "g". Each unit contains basic grammatical information for the teacher, guidelines and remarks, exercises, general review, and prelesson and postlesson tests. A 12-item bibliography is included. (DS)
CP.....	N

AN..... 000581

ER..... ED148168

TI..... Mexican American Studies: The Gateway and the Barrier.

SE..... Learning Achievement Packages (Series).

YR..... Jun77

AU..... Iruegas, Efraín; Rendón, René

IN..... Calexico Intercultural Design, Calif.; National Dissemination and Assessment Center, Austin, Tex.

SN..... Office of Education (DHEW), Washington, D.C. (RMQ66000)

LG..... English; Spanish

AV..... National Dissemination and Assessment Center, 7703 North Lamar Boulevard, Austin, Texas 78752 (ISBN 0-89417-097-X; $3.00); ERIC Document Reproduction Service, P.O. Box 190, Arlington, Virginia 22210 ($7.35; microfiche $0.83; ED148168)

NT..... vii, 155 p.

DE..... Cultural Education; *Curriculum Guides; English; Ethnic Studies; Geography; High School Curriculum; Illegal Immigrants; *Immigrants; Instructional Materials; Learning Activities; *Mexican Americans; Migrant Problems; Migrants; Secondary Education; Social Problems; Social Studies; Sociocultural Patterns; *Spanish; Vocabulary; *Teaching Guides; Cultural Education

ID..... *California (Imperial Valley)

AB..... This publication presents two suggested Mexican American studies curriculum units developed to deal with the learning problems of students with special language difficulties. Originally developed for grades 7 through 12, these units may be adapted for use in adult education or at any other grade level. The units are entitled "Mexican Immigrants in the United States" and "Imperial Valley" and appear in an English and a Spanish version. A series of reading passages, a glossary of relevant vocabulary, suggestions for extended activities, and worksheets to accompany the readings are included. The units are followed by seven-item and nine-item bibliographies, suggestions for teachers using the units, and answer sheets for the worksheets. (DS)

CP..... N

AN..... 000582

ER..... ED127826

TI..... Language Arts: English Grammar.

SE..... Learning Achievement Packages (Series).

YR..... 77

AU..... Réndon, Clara; Rodríguez, Mary Jane; Sones, Mary

IN..... Calexico Intercultural Design, Calif.; National Dissemination and Assessment Center, Austin, Tex.

SN..... Office of Education (DHEW), Washington, D.C. (RMQ66000)

AV..... National Dissemination and Assessment Center, 7703 North Lamar Boulevard, Austin, Texas 78752 (ISBN 0-89417-090-2; $3.00); ERIC Document Reproduction Service, P.O. Box 190, Arlington, Virginia 22210 ($7.35; microfiche $0.83; ED127826)

NT..... v, 127 p.

DE..... *Curriculum Guides; *Teaching Guides; Dictionaries; *English (Second Language); *Grammar; Instructional Materials; *Language Arts; Language Handicaps; Language Patterns; Language Proficiency; Morphology (Languages); Nominals; Secondary Education; *Spanish

AB..... This publication presents four suggested language arts curriculum units developed to deal with the learning problems of students with special language difficulties. Originally designed for grades 7-12, these units may be adapted for use in adult education or at other grade levels. They are primarily intended for use with students learning English as a second language, to develop habits of proper usage in English. The four units cover common and proper nouns, homonyms, singular and plural nouns, and the use of the dictionary. Each unit includes: (1) information for the teacher in the form of the principal idea to be communicated, behavioral objectives, and the rationale of the unit; (2) an information sheet which outlines the main points to be taught; (3) exercises; (4) a pretest and a posttest; and (5) an answer key. An eight-item bibliography follows the units. (DS)

CP..... N

AN..... 000583

TI..... El Osito (The Little Bear).

SE..... Qué bonito es leer: Libros de lectura (How Nice It is to Read: Readers) (Series).

YR..... 76

IN..... Curriculum Adaptation Network for Bilingual/Bicultural Education, San Antonio, Tex. Southwest Regional Adaptation Center. (BBB11923); Edgewood Independent School District, San Antonio, Tex. (XPT23584); National Dissemination and Assessment Center, Austin, Tex.

SN..... Office of Education (DHEW), Washington, D.C. (RMQ66000)

LG..... Spanish

AV..... National Dissemination and Assessment Center, 7703 North
Lamar Boulevard, Austin, Texas 78752 (set of 12 $3.50)

NT..... 13 p.
Rev. ed.
For related documents, see 000584-598.

DE..... *Spanish; *Reading Materials; Primary Education;
*Instructional Materials; *Reading Instruction; Teacher
Developed Materials; Childrens Books; Grade 1

AB..... Illustrated in black and white, this Spanish reader is
designed for use in a first grade bilingual program. It
is accompanied by 11 other readers, a teacher's guide, a
workbook, and a set of cards. (CO)

CP..... N

AN..... 000584

TI..... Paca.

SE..... Qué bonito es leer: Libros de lectura (How Nice It Is to
Read: Readers) (Series).

YR..... 76

IN..... Curriculum Adaption Network for Bilingual/Bicultural
Education, San Antonio, Tex. Southwest Regional
Adaptation Center. (BBB11923); Edgewood Independent
School District, San Antonio, Tex. (XPT23584); National
Dissemination and Assessment Center, Austin, Tex.

SN..... Office of Education (DHEW), Washington, D.C. (RMQ66000)

LG..... Spanish

AV..... National Dissemination and Assessment Center, 7703 North
Lamar Boulevard, Austin, Texas 78752 (set of 12 $3.50)

NT..... 14 p.
Rev. ed.
For related documents, see 000583 and 585-598.

DE..... *Spanish; *Reading Materials: Primary Education;
*Instructional Materials; *Reading Instruction; Teacher
Developed Materials; Childrens Books; Grade 1

AB..... This Spanish reader, illustrated in black and white, is
designed for use in a first grade bilingual program. It
is accompanied by 11 other readers, a teacher's guide, a
workbook, and a set of cards. (CO)

CP..... N

AN..... 000585

TI..... La Carrera (The Race).

SE..... Qué bonito es leer: Libros de lectura (How Nice It Is to
Read: Readers) (Series).

YR..... 76

IN..... Curriculum Adaptation Network for Bilingual/Bicultural Education, San Antonio, Tex. Southwest Regional Adaptation Center. (BBB11923); Edgewood Independent School District, San Antonio, Tex. (XPT23584); National Dissemination and Assessment Center, Austin, Tex.

SN..... Office of Education (DHEW), Washington, D.C. (RMQ66000)

LG..... Spanish

AV..... National Dissemination and Assessment Center, 7703 North Lamar Boulevard, Austin, Texas 78752 (set of 12 $3.50)

NT..... 12 p.
Rev. ed.
For related documents, see 000583-584 and 586-598.

DE..... *Spanish; *Reading Materials; Primary Education; *Instructional Materials; Reading Instruction; Teacher Developed Materials; Childrens Books; Grade 1

AB..... This Spanish reader, illustrated in black and white, is designed for use in a first grade bilingual program. It is accompanied by 11 other readers, a teacher's guide, a workbook, and a set of cards. (CO)

CP..... N

AN..... 000586

TI..... La Casita de Lobo (Lobo's Little House).

SE..... Qué bonito es leer: Libros de lectura (How Nice It Is to Read: Readers) (Series).

YR..... 76

IN..... Curriculum Adaptation Network for Bilingual/Bicultural Education, San Antonio, Tex. Southwest Regional Adaptation Center. (BBB11923); Edgewood Independent School District, San Antonio, Tex. (XPT23584); National Dissemination and Assessment Center, Austin, Tex.

SN..... Office of Education (DHEW), Washington, D.C. (RMQ66000)

LG..... Spanish

AV..... National Dissemination and Assessment Center, 7703 North Lamar Boulevard, Austin, Texas 78752 (set of 12 $3.50)

NT..... 12 p.
Rev. ed.
For related documents, see 000583-585 and 587-598.

DE..... *Spanish; *Reading Materials; Primary Education; *Instructional Materials; *Reading Instruction; Teacher Developed Materials; Childrens Books; Grade 1

AB..... This Spanish reader, illustrated in black and white, is
designed for use in a first grade bilingual program. It
is accompanied by 11 other readers, a teacher's guide, a
workbook, and a set of cards. (CO)

CP..... N

AN..... 000587

TI..... La Rata de Rico (Rico's Mouse).

SE..... Qué bonito es leer: Libros de lectura (How Nice It Is to
Read: Readers) (Series).

YR..... 76

IN..... Curriculum Adaptation Network for Bilingual/Bicultural
Education, San Antonio, Tex. Southwest Regional
Adaptation Center. (BBB11923); Edgewood Independent
School District, San Antonio, Tex. (XPT23584); National
Dissemination and Assessment Center, Austin, Tex.

SN..... Office of Education (DHEW), Washington, D.C. (RMQ66000)

LG..... Spanish

AV..... National Dissemination and Assessment Center, 7703 North
Lamar Boulevard, Austin, Texas 78752 (set of 12 $3.50)

NT..... 13 p.
Rev. ed.
For related documents, see 000583-586 and 588-598.

DE..... *Spanish; *Reading Materials; Primary Education;
*Instructional Materials; *Reading Instruction; Teacher
Developed Materials; Childrens Books; Grade 1

AB..... Illustrated in black and white, this Spanish reader is
designed for use in a first grade bilingual program. It
is accompanied by 11 other readers, a teacher's guide, a
workbook, and a set of cards. (CO)

CP..... N

AN..... 000588

TI..... Como Tú (Like You).

SE..... Qué bonito es leer: Libros de lectura (How Nice It Is to
Read: Readers) (Series).

YR..... 76

IN..... Curriculum Adaptation Network for Bilingual/Bicultural
Education, San Antonio, Tex. Southwest Regional
Adaptation Center. (BBB11923); Edgewood Independent
School District, San Antonio, Tex. (XPT23584); National
Dissemination and Assessment Center, Austin, Tex.

SN..... Office of Education (DHEW), Washington, D.C. (RMQ66000)

LG..... Spanish

AV..... National Dissemination and Assessment Center, 7703 North Lamar Boulevard, Austin, Texas 78752 (set of 12 $3.50)

NT..... 17 p.
Rev. ed.
For related documents, see 00583-587 and 589-598.

DE..... *Spanish; *Reading Materials; Primary Education; *Instructional Materials; Reading Instruction; Teacher Developed Materials; Childrens Books; Grade 1

AB..... Designed for use in a first grade bilingual program, this Spanish reader is illustrated in black and white. It is accompanied by 11 other readers, a teacher's guide, a workbook, and a set of cards. (CO)

CP..... N

AN..... 000589

TI..... Es un fantasma? (Is It a Ghost?)

SE..... Qué bonito es leer: Libros de lectura (How Nice It Is to Read: Readers) (Series).

YR..... 76

IN..... Curriculum Adaptation Network for Bilingual/Bicultural Education, San Antonio, Tex. Southwest Regional Adaptation Center. (BBB11923); Edgewood Independent School District, San Antonio, Tex. (XPT23584); National Dissemination and Assessment Center, Austin, Tex.

SN..... Office of Education (DHEW), Washington, D.C. (RMQ66000)

LG..... Spanish

AV..... National Dissemination and Assessment Center, 7703 North Lamar Boulevard, Austin, Texas 78752 (set of 12 $3.50)

NT..... 13 p.
Rev. ed.
For related documents, see 00583-588 and 590-598.

DE..... *Spanish; *Reading Materials; Primary Education; *Instructional Materials; Reading Instruction; Teacher Developed Materials; Childrens Books; Grade 1

AB..... This Spanish reader, illustrated in black and white, is designed for use in a first grade bilingual program. It is accompanied by a teacher's guide, a workbook, a set of cards, and 11 other readers. (CO)

CP..... N

AN..... 000590

TI..... Los Niños (The Children).

SE..... Qué bonito es leer: Libros de lectura (How Nice It Is to Read: Readers) (Series).

YR..... 76

IN..... Curriculum Adaptation Network for Bilingual/Bicultural Education, San Antonio, Tex. Southwest Regional Adaptation Center. (BBB11923); Edgewood Independent School District, San Antonio, Tex. (XPT23584); National Dissemination and Assessment Center, Austin, Tex.

SN..... Office of Education (DHEW), Washington, D.C. (RMQ66000)

LG..... Spanish

AV..... National Dissemination and Assessment Center, 7703 North Lamar Boulevard, Austin, Texas 78752 (set of 12 $3.50)

NT..... 16 p.
Rev. ed.
For related documents, see 000583-589 and 591-598.

DE..... *Spanish; *Reading Materials; Primary Education; *Instructional Materials; *Reading Instruction; Teacher Developed Materials; Childrens Books; Grade 1

AB..... This Spanish reader, illustrated in black and white, is designed for use in a first grade bilingual program. It is accompanied by 11 other readers, a teacher's guide, a workbook, and a set of cards. (CO)

CP..... N

AN..... 000591

TI..... El Elefante y la tortuga (The Elephant and the Turtle).

SE..... Qué bonito es leer: Libros de lectura (How Nice It Is to Read: Readers) (Series).

YR..... 76

IN..... Curriculum Adaptation Network for Bilingual/Bicultural Education, San Antonio, Tex. Southwest Regional Adaptation Center. (BBB11923); Edgewood Independent School District, San Antonio, Tex. (XPT23584); National Dissemination and Assessment Center, Austin, Tex.

SN..... Office of Education (DHEW), Washington, D.C. (RMQ66000)

LG..... Spanish

AV..... National Dissemination and Assessment Center, 7703 North Lamar Boulevard, Austin, Texas 78752 (set of 12 $3.50)

NT..... 19 p.
Rev. ed.
For related documents, see 000583-590 and 592-598.

DE..... *Spanish; *Reading Materials; Primary Education;
*Instructional Materials; *Reading Instruction; Teacher
Developed Materials; Childrens Books; Grade 1

AB..... Designed for use in a first grade bilingual program, this
Spanish reader is illustrated in black and white. It is
accompanied by 11 other readers, a teacher's guide, a
workbook, and a set of cards. (CO)

CP..... N

AN..... 000592

TI..... Vina, la víbora (Vina, the Viper).

SE..... Qué bonito es leer: Libros de lectura (How Nice It Is To
Read: Readers) (Series).

YR..... 76

IN..... Curriculum Adaptation Network for Bilingual/Bicultural
Education, San Antonio, Tex. Southwest Regional
Adaptation Center. (BBB11923); Edgewood Independent
School District, San Antonio, Tex. (XPT23584); National
Dissemination and Assessment Center, Austin, Tex.

SN..... Office of Education (DHEW), Washington, D.C. (RMQ66000)

LG..... Spanish

AV..... National Dissemination and Assessment Center, 7703 North
Lamar Boulevard, Austin, Texas 78752 (set of 12 $3.50)

NT..... 16 p.
Rev. ed.
For related documents, see 000583-591 and 593-598.

DE..... *Spanish; *Reading Materials; Primary Education;
*Instructional Materials; *Reading Instruction; Teacher
Developed Materials; Childrens Books; Grade 1

AB..... Designed for use in a first grade bilingual program, this
Spanish reader is illustrated in black and white. It is
accompanied by 11 other readers, a teacher's guide, a
workbook, and a set of cards. (CO)

CP..... N

AN..... 000593

TI..... Chiquita.

SE..... Qué bonito es leer: Libros de lectura (How Nice It Is to
Read: Readers) (Series).

YR..... 76

IN..... Curriculum Adaptation Network for Bilingual/Bicultural
Education, San Antonio, Tex. Southwest Regional
Adaptation Center. (BBB11923); Edgewood Independent
School District, San Antonio, Tex. (XPT23584); National
Dissemination and Assessment Center, Austin, Tex.

SN..... Office of Education (DHEW), Washington, D.C. (RMQ66000)

LG..... Spanish

AV..... National Dissemination and Assessment Center, 7703 North
Lamar Boulevard, Austin, Texas 78752 (set of 12 $3.50)

NT..... 16 p.
Rev. ed.
For related documents, see 000583-592 and 594-598.

DE..... *Spanish; *Reading Materials; Primary Education;
*Instructional Materials; *Reading Instruction; Teacher
Developed Materials; Childrens Books; Grade 1

AB..... This Spanish reader, illustrated in black and white, is
designed for use in a first grade bilingual program. It
is accompanied by 11 other readers, a workbook, a
teacher's guide, and a set of cards. (CO)

CP..... N

AN..... 000594

TI..... La Tos de René (René's Cough).

SE..... Qué bonito es leer: Libros de lectura (How Nice It Is to
Read: Readers) (Series).

YR..... 76

IN..... Curriculum Adaptation Network for Bilingual/Bicultural
Education, San Antonio, Tex. Southwest Regional
Adaptation Center. (BBB11923); Edgewood Independent
School District, San Antonio, Tex. (XPT23584); National
Dissemination and Assessment Center, Austin, Tex.

SN..... Office of Education (DHEW), Washington, D.C. (RMQ66000)

LG..... Spanish

AV..... National Dissemination and Assessment Center, 7703 North
Lamar Boulevard, Austin, Texas 78752 (set of 12 $3.50)

NT..... 13 p.
Rev. ed.
For related documents, see 000583-593 and 595-598.

DE..... *Spanish; *Reading Materials; Primary Education;
*Instructional Materials; *Reading Instruction; Teacher
Developed Materials; Childrens Books; Grade 1

AB..... This Spanish reader, illustrated in black and white, is
designed for use in a first grade bilingual program. It
is accompanied by 11 other readers, a workbook, a
teacher's guide, and a set of cards. (CO)

CP..... N

AN..... 000595

TI..... Guía para el maestro (Teacher's Guide).

SE..... Qué bonito es leer (How Nice It Is to Read) (Series).

YR..... Feb74

AU..... Villarreal, Abelardo; Peña, Becky de la; Nichols, Lucille; Flores, Salvador; Hoeflich, Carmen; Rivera, Lina R.; Morales, Oscar, ill.; Becerril, Diana, ill.

IN..... Curriculum Adaptation Network for Bilingual/Bicultural Education, San Antonio, Tex. Southwest Regional Adaptation Center. (BBB11923); Edgewood Independent School District, San Antonio, Tex. (XPT23584); National Dissemination and Assessment Center, Austin, Tex.

SN..... Office of Education (DHEW), Washington, D.C. (RMQ66000)

LG..... Spanish

AV..... National Dissemination and Assessment Center, 7703 North Lamar Boulevard, Austin, Texas 78752 ($4.50)

NT..... xxvi, 221 p.
For related documents, see 000583-594 and 596-598.

DE..... *Teaching Guides; *Spanish; *Instructional Materials; Comprehension Development; Decoding (Reading); Language Arts; Primary Education; *Reading Instruction; Reading Materials; Reading Skills; Teacher Developed Materials; Vocabulary Development

AB..... This Spanish-language supplementary language arts program focuses on the development of decoding, encoding, comprehension, and interpretation skills, and is oriented toward the Mexican American child's experience. It is designed for first grade bilingual programs and as a resource for instruction in Spanish as a second language up to the third grade. The program consists of a teacher's manual, an exercise workbook for the student, 65 flashcards color-coded to match the workbook, and 12 readers which can be used separately or as part of the program. The vocabulary is sequenced to parallel the reading lessons, building from a line or two of text on a page in the first to about eight lines per page in the last of the series. (Author/AM)

CP..... N

AN..... 000596

TI..... Cuaderno de ejercicios (Workbook).

SE..... Qué bonito es leer (How Nice It Is to Read) (Series).

YR..... 74

AU..... Villarreal, Abelardo; Peña, Becky de la; Nichols, Lucille; Flores, Salvador; Hoeflich, Carmen; Rivera, Lina R.; Morales, Oscar, ill.; Becerril, Diana, ill.

IN..... Curriculum Adaptation Network for Bilingual/Bicultural Education, San Antonio, Tex. Southwest Regional Adaptation Center. (BBB11923); Edgewood Independent School District, San Antonio, Tex. (XPT23584); National Dissemination and Assessment Center, Austin, Tex.

SN..... Office of Education (DHEW), Washington, D.C. (RMQ66000)

LG..... Spanish

AV..... National Dissemination and Assessment Center, 7703 North Lamar Boulevard, Austin, Texas 78752 ($3.50)

NT..... iv, 220 p.
For related documents, see 000583-595 and 597-598.

DE..... *Workbooks; *Spanish; *Instructional Materials; Language Arts; Comprehension Development; Decoding (Reading); Primary Education; *Reading Instruction; Reading Materials; Reading Skills; Vocabulary Development; Teacher Developed Materials

AB..... This workbook is part of a Spanish-language supplementary language arts program focusing on the development of decoding, encoding, comprehension, and interpretation skills. Oriented toward the Mexican American child's experience, it is designed for first grade bilingual programs and as a resource for instruction in Spanish as a second language up to the third grade. The vocabulary is sequenced to parallel the reading lessons, building from a line or two of text on a page in the first to about eight lines per page in the last of the series. The workbook is accompanied by a teacher's guide, 12 readers, and 65 flashcards color-coded to match the workbook. (CO)

CP..... N

AN..... 000597

TI..... Tarjetas relámpago (Flashcards).

SE..... Qué bonito es leer (How Nice It Is to Read) (Series).

YR..... 74

AU..... Villarreal, Abelardo; Peña, Becky de la; Nichols, Lucille; Flores, Salvador; Hoeflich, Carmen; Rivera, Lina R.; Morales, Oscar, ill.; Becerril, Diana, ill.

IN..... Curriculum Adaptation Network for Bilingual/Bicultural Education, San Antonio, Tex. Southwest Regional Adaptation Center. (BBB11923); Edgewood Independent School District, San Antonio, Tex. (XPT23584)

SN..... Office of Education (DHEW), Washington, D.C. (RMQ66000)

LG..... Spanish

AV..... National Dissemination and Assessment Center, 7703 North Lamar Boulevard, Austin, Texas 78752 ($3.50)

NT..... 65 flashcards.
For related documents, see 000583-596 and 598.

DE..... *Cues; Primary Education; *Spanish; Auditory
Discrimination; Auditory Perception; Comprehension
Development; Instructional Materials; *Language Arts;
Language Skills; *Visual Aids

ID..... *Flashcards

AB..... These 65 flashcards are color-coded to match the
accompanying workbooks and numbered to correspond to the
units in the accompanying teacher's guide. Each
flashcard contains four pictures which reinforce the
learning of the initial alphabet letter. The material is
intended to develop language comprehension, hearing, and
interpreting skills at the primary level. (CO)

CP..... N

AN..... 000598

TI..... Escuchando y participando aprendo (I Learn by Listening
and Participating).

YR..... Jul77

AU..... Villarreal, Abelardo; Peña, Becky de la; Nichols,
Lucille; Flores, Salvador; Rivera, Lina R.; Hoeflich,
Carmen, ed.; Morales, Oscar, ill.; Becerril, Diana, ill.

IN..... National Dissemination and Assessment Center, Austin,
Tex.; Curriculum Adaptation Network for
Bilingual/Bicultural Education, San Antonio, Tex.
Southwest Regional Adaptation Center. (BBB11923)

SN..... Office of Education (DHEW), Washington, D.C. (RMQ66000)

LG..... Spanish

AV..... National Dissemination and Assessment Center, 7703 North
Lamar Boulevard, Austin, Texas 78752 ($3.00)

NT..... 39 cards, 10"x13".

DE..... Primary Education; *Spanish; Alphabets; *Auditory
Discrimination; Auditory Perception; Comprehension
Development; *Instructional Materials; *Language Arts;
Language Skills; *Letters (Alphabet); Listening
Comprehension; Visual Aids

ID..... *Alphabet Cards

AB..... This series of color-illustrated alphabet cards contains
all the letters of the Spanish alphabet with
illustrations to show their sounds. On the reverse of
each card, or series of related cards, is a short story,
along with some activities and games designed to
reinforce the sound of the letter. The material is
intended to develop language comprehension, hearing, and
interpreting skills at the primary level and may be used

as a supplement to the series "Qué bonito es leer" or
correlated with the Spanish Curricula Development
Center's Language Arts Strand, Kits 2-9. Instructional
notes for the teacher are included. (CO)

CP..... N

AN..... 000599

TI..... Daily Curriculum Guide: Spanish Dame Program: Songs.

YR..... [7?]

IN..... Spanish Dame Bilingual Bicultural Project, San Jose,
Calif. (BBB11959); National Dissemination and Assessment
Center, Austin, Tex.

SN..... Office of Education (DHEW), Washington, D.C. (RMQ66000)

LG..... English; Spanish

AV..... National Dissemination and Assessment Center, 7703 North
Lamar Boulevard, Austin, Texas 78752 ($1.50)

NT..... 45-min. cassette
For related documents, see 000600-602 and 621-628.

DE..... *Magnetic Tape Cassettes; *Spanish; *Songs; Learning
Activities; *Preschool Education; Instructional Media

AB..... This cassette contains songs in both Spanish and English
which supplement the Daily Curriculum Guide, a program
for paraprofessionals working with preschool
Mexican-American children in a home setting.
Accompanying materials include two teaching guides, two
three-volume curriculum guide sets, and supplements to
the curriculum guides. (CO)

CP..... N

AN..... 000600

TI..... Daily Curriculum Supplement: Part I.

YR..... 76

IN..... Spanish Dame Bilingual Bicultural Project, San Jose,
Calif. (BBB11959); National Dissemination and Assessment
Center, Austin, Tex.

SN..... Office of Education (DHEW), Washington, D.C. (RMQ66000)

LG..... English; Spanish

AV..... National Dissemination and Assessment Center, 7703 North
Lamar Boulevard, Austin, Texas 78752 ($5.00 with ditto
patterns and flannel patterns)

NT..... 137 p.
Rev. ed.
For related documents, see 000599, 601-602, and 621-628.

DE..... Curriculum Guides; English (Second Language); *Home Instruction; *Instructional Materials; Language Instruction; *Preschool Education; *Spanish; Teaching Guides; Tutorial Programs; Tutoring; Educational Games; Songs; Learning Activities

AB..... This guide is designed to supplement a program for paraprofessionals (or home tutors) working with preschool Mexican-American children in a home setting. The program's aims are to improve the child's Spanish language skills; develop basic listening and verbal skills in English; assure basic concept development in the child's primary language, Spanish; and train the mothers of project children in new methods for working with their children. The material is adaptable also to other early childhood bilingual programs. The supplement contains class preparation instructions; a chart of materials needed for each day; stories, songs, rhymes, poems, finger plays, and other games, and is tab-indexed for easy use. Accompanying materials include ditto and flannel masters, two teaching guides, two 3-volume curriculum guide sets, and a cassette of songs. (AM)

CP..... N

AN..... 000601

TI..... Daily Curriculum Supplement: Part III, Flannel Patterns.

YR..... 76

IN..... Spanish Dame Bilingual Bicultural Project, San Jose, Calif. (BBB11959); National Dissemination and Assessment Center, Austin, Tex.

SN..... Office of Education (DHEW), Washington, D.C. (RMQ66000)

LG..... English; Spanish

AV..... National Dissemination and Assessment Center, 7703 North Lamar Boulevard, Austin, Texas 78752 ($5.00 with ditto patterns and guide.)

NT..... 181 leaves
Rev. ed.
For related documents, see 000599-600, 602, and 621-628.

DE..... Educational Games; Songs; *Learning Activities; *Spanish; *Preschool Education; Language Instruction; *Visual Aids; Instructional Media; Realia

AB..... These 179 flannel patterns are part of a set of supplements to the curriculum guides in a series intended for paraprofessionals working with preschool Mexican-American children in a home setting. The program is adaptable to other early childhood programs and is based on a language maintenance model in which Spanish is used as a means to develop basic concepts, skills, and attitudes. Accompanying materials include ditto patterns, a curriculum supplement, two three-volume curriculum guide sets, teaching guides, and a cassette of songs. (CO)

CP..... N

AN..... 000602

TI..... Daily Curriculum Supplement: Part II, Ditto Patterns.

YR..... 76

IN..... Spanish Dame Bilingual Bicultural Project, San Jose, Calif. (BBB11959); National Assessment and Dissemination Center, Cambridge, Mass.

SN..... Office of Education (DHEW), Washington, D.C. (RMQ66000)

AV..... National Dissemination and Assessment Center, 7703 North Lamar Boulevard, Austin, Texas 78752 ($5.00 with flannel patterns and guide)

NT..... Rev. ed.
For related documents, see 000599-601 and 621-628.

DE..... *Visual Aids; Learning Activities; *Spanish; *Preschool Education; Language Instruction; Instructional Media

ID..... *Dittos

AB..... These 115 ditto masters are part of a set of supplements to the curriculum guides in a series intended for paraprofessionals working with preschool Mexican-American children in a home setting. The program is adaptable to other early childhood programs and is based on a language maintenance model in which Spanish is used as a means to develop basic concepts, skills, and attitudes. Accompanying materials include flannel masters, a curriculum supplement, two three-volume curriculum guide sets, teaching guides, and a cassette of songs. (CO)

CP..... N

AN..... 000608

TI..... Diné bikéyah (Navajo Lands).

YR..... Aug76

IN..... Native American Materials Development Center, Albuquerque, N. Mex.

SN..... Office of Education (DHEW), Washington, D.C. (RMQ66000)

LG..... Navajo

AV..... National Dissemination and Assessment Center, 7703 North Lamar Boulevard, Austin, Texas 78752 ($1.50)

NT..... 22 p.

DE..... Grade 7; Grade 8; Grade 9; Grade 10; Grade 11; Grade 12; *Land Acquisition; Land Settlement; *American Indians; Reservations (Indian); *American History; *Navajo; High Schools; *Maps

ID..... *Navajos; Arizona; New Mexico; United States (Southwest)

AB..... This book, intended for native Navajo-speaking students in grades 7 through 12, contains a series of black-and-white maps which illustrate the territorial growth of the Navajo Nation from 1868 to 1962. The captions explaining the historical data are in Navajo. (SH)

CP..... N

AN..... 000609

TI..... Ha'át'íísh áté? (What Is That?).

YR..... Jul76

IN..... Native American Materials Development Center, Albuquerque, N. Mex.

SN..... Office of Education (DHEW), Washington, D.C. (RMQ66000)

LG..... Navajo

AV..... National Dissemination and Assessment Center, 7703 North Lamar Boulevard, Austin, Texas 78752 ($1.00)

NT..... 11 leaves.

DE..... Grade 1; Grade 2; Kindergarten; Primary Education; *Mathematical Concepts; Athapascan Languages; Mathematical Enrichment; Mathematics; Elementary School Mathematics; *Navajo; Mathematics Curriculum; *Mathematics Materials; Arithmetic Curriculum; *Instructional Materials; *Reading Materials

AB..... This illustrated reader contains vocabulary designed to introduce a few premathematical concepts before presenting the Navajo child with mathematical concepts in a classroom situation. Terms like "least," "most," "many," and "few" are introduced, first individually and then on the same page so that the child can identify differences among concepts. The book is intended for children in kindergarten through second grade. (Author/SH)

CP..... N

AN.....	000610
TI.....	Ch'al (Frog).
SE.....	Diné k'ejí naaltsoos wólta' bóhó'aa'ígíí (Learning Written Navajo): Book 1.
YR.....	Dec77
AU.....	Rosier, Helen Cody; Singer, Ed, ill.; Kinsman, Carolyn, ill.
IN.....	Native American Materials Development Center, Albuqerque, N. Mex.; Rock Point Community School, Chinle, Ariz.
SN.....	Office of Education (DHEW), Washington, D.C. (RMQ66000)
LG.....	Navajo
AV.....	National Dissemination and Assessment Center, 7703 North Lamar Boulevard, Austin, Texas 78752 (ISBN 0-89417-305-7; $2.25)
NT.....	81 p. For Books 2 and 3 in this series, see 000611-612.
DE.....	Kindergarten; Grade 1; Primary Education; *Navajo; *Reading Readiness; Reading Materials; *Instructional Materials; *Language Instruction; *Phonics; *Workbooks; Childrens Books; Athapascan Languages
ID.....	Language Exercises
AB.....	This color-illustrated reader and workbook is designed to teach decoding skills to kindergarten and first grade children whose dominant language is Navajo. It introduces 14 consonant symbol/sound associations and 16 vowel environments. All words in the book are one syllable except for two recurring two-syllable verbs. (SH)
CP.....	N

AN.....	000611
TI.....	Chaá (Beaver).
SE.....	Diné k'ejí naaltsoos wóltá bóhóaa'ígíí (Learning Written Navajo): Book 2.
YR.....	Apr78
AU.....	Rosier, Helen Cody; Whitethorne, Billy, ill.; Kinsman, Carolyn, ill.

IN..... Native American Materials Development Center,
       Albuquerque, N. Mex.; Rock Point Community School,
       Chinle, Ariz.

SN..... Office of Education (DHEW), Washington, D.C. (RMQ66000)

LG..... Navajo

AV..... National Dissemination and Assessment Center, 7703 North
       Lamar Boulevard, Austin, Texas 78752 (ISBN
       0-89417-484-3; $2.25)

NT..... 84 p.
       For Books 1 and 3 in this series, see 000610 and 612.

DE..... Kindergarten; Grade 1; Primary Education; *Navajo;
       Athapascan Languages; Childrens Books; *Instructional
       Materials; Language Instruction; Reading Instruction;
       *Reading Materials; Reading Readiness; *Phonics;
       *Workbooks; *Decoding (Reading)

ID..... Language Exercises

AB..... This color-illustrated workbook is designed to teach
       decoding skills to kindergarten and first grade children
       whose dominant language is Navajo. It introduces
       consonant symbol and sound associations, 11 vowel
       environments, and 6 diphthong environments. Most
       vocabulary in the book is two-syllable. (SH)

CP..... N

AN..... 000612

TI..... Náshdóí (Bobcat).

SE..... Diné k'ejí naaltsoos wóltá bóhó 'aa'ígíí
       (Learning Written Navajo): Book 3.

YR..... Oct78

AU..... Rosier, Helen Cody; Whitethorne, Billy, ill.

IN..... Native American Materials Development Center,
       Albuquerque, N. Mex.; Rock Point Community School,
       Chinle, Ariz.

SN..... Office of Education (DHEW), Washington, D.C. (RMQ66000)

LG..... Navajo

AV..... National Dissemination and Assessment Center, 7703 North
       Lamar Boulevard, Austin, Texas 78752 (ISBN
       0-89417-517-3)

NT..... 74 p.
       For Books 1 and 2 in this series, see 000610-611.

DE..... Childrens Books; Athapascan Languages; *Navajo;
       Kindergarten; Grade 1; Primary Education; *Instructional
       Materials; *Language Instruction; Reading Readiness;
       *Phonics; *Workbooks; Reading Instruction; Reading
       Materials; *Decoding (Reading)

ID..... Language Exercises

AB..... This color-illustrated reader and workbook is designed to teach decoding skills to kindergarten and first grade children whose dominant language is Navajo. It introduces the consonant x, 13 vowel environments, and most of the diphthongs not covered in Books 1 and 2 of this series. Words are usually composed of three syllables or less. (SH)

CP..... N

AN..... 000613

TI..... Ma'ii Wáshindoongóó deeyá (Coyote Goes to Washington).

YR..... Jul76

IN..... Native American Materials Development Center, Albuquerque, N. Mex.

SN..... Office of Education (DHEW), Washington, D.C. (RMQ66000)

LG..... Navajo

AV..... National Dissemination and Assessment Center, 7703 North Lamar Boulevard, Austin, Texas 78752 ($1.50)

NT..... 12 p.

DE..... *Navajo; Kindergarten; Grade 1; Grade 2; Grade 3; Primary Education; Athapascan Languages; Childrens Books; *Instructional Materials; *Language Instruction; *Reading Instruction; *Reading Materials

ID..... District of Columbia

AB..... This color-illustrated story written in Navajo relates the experiences of the main character, Coyote, as he leaves home to go on a business trip to Washington, D.C. The reader is intended for native Navajo-speaking children in kindergarten through third grade. (SH)

CP..... N

AN..... 000614

TI..... Tsék'ina'asdzooí: Tse deiízheshigií baa hane' (Inscription Rock: Eroding of a Rock Formation).

YR..... Sep76

AU..... Chatto, John; Henio, Clyde; Rafaelito, Johnson

IN..... Native American Materials Development Center, Albuquerque, N. Mex.

SN..... Office of Education (DHEW), Washington, D.C. (RMQ66000)

LG..... Navajo

AV..... National Dissemination and Assessment Center, 7703 North
       Lamar Boulevard, Austin, Texas 78752 ($1.00)

NT..... 18 p.

DE..... Grade 7; Grade 8; Grade 9; Grade 10; Grade 11; Grade 12;
       High Schools; Geology; *Physical Geography; High School
       Curriculum; Science Curriculum; *Instructional Materials;
       *Photographs; *Navajo; *Language Instruction; *Reading
       Materials

ID..... New Mexico

AB..... Black-and-white photographs supplement the text in this
       book dealing with Inscription Rock at El Morro National
       Monument in New Mexico, which contains more than 500
       inscriptions made during and after the Coronado
       expedition. The material is aimed at Navajo high school
       students in the 7th through 12th grades. (SH)

CP..... N

AN..... 000615

TI..... Ólta' (School).

YR..... Jul76

IN..... Native American Materials Development Center,
       Albuquerque, N. Mex.

SN..... Office of Education (DHEW), Washington, D.C. (RMQ66000)

LG..... Navajo

AV..... National Dissemination and Assessment Center, 7703 North
       Lamar Boulevard, Austin, Texas 78752 ($1.50)

NT..... 8 p.

DE..... Kindergarten; Grade 1; Grade 2; Grade 3; Primary
       Education; *Navajo; Athapascan Languages; Childrens
       Books; *Instructional Materials; *Language Instruction;
       *Reading Instruction; *Reading Materials

AB..... The experiences of the main character, Coyote, as he
       attempts to teach a group of active boys and girls are
       related in this reader. The story, illustrated in color,
       is written for children at the kindergarten through third
       grade level whose native language is Navajo. (SH)

CP..... N

AN..... 000616

TI..... Tsé' ádó'ii (Fly).

YR..... Aug76

IN..... Native American Materials Development Center, Albuquerque, N. Mex.

SN..... Office of Education (DHEW), Washington, D.C. (RMQ66000)

LG..... Navajo

AV..... National Dissemination and Assessment Center, 7703 North Lamar Boulevard, Austin, Texas 78752 ($1.50)

NT..... 11 p.

DE..... Kindergarten; Grade 1; Grade 2; Grade 3; Primary Education; *Navajo; Athapascan Languages; Childrens Books; *Instructional Materials; *Language Instruction; *Reading Instruction; *Reading Materials; *Health Education

AB..... This descriptive reader for native Navajo-speaking students in the primary grades presents health concepts, such as germ transmission, through the use of color illustrations and text depicting the daily activities of a fly. (SH)

CP..... N

AN..... 000617

TI..... Hualapai misid mispo (Learn to Read Hualapai): Book 1.

YR..... May78

IN..... Peach Springs School District 8, Ariz. Hualapai Bilingual Education Program.

SN..... Office of Education (DHEW), Washington, D.C. (RMQ66000)

LG..... Hualapai

AV..... National Dissemination and Assessment Center, 7703 North Lamar Boulevard, Austin, Texas 78752 (ISBN 0-89417-495-9; $1.00)

NT..... 14 p.
For Book 2 and primers, see 000618-620.

DE..... Kindergarten; Grade 1; Primary Education; Reading Instruction; Reading Materials; *Phonics; *Instructional Materials; Language Instruction; American Indian Languages; *Reading Readiness; *Workbooks; Phonology

ID..... *Language Exercises; *Hualapai

AB..... Using an analytical approach, this book introduces half the sounds of the Hualapai language to children at the kindergarten or first grade level. Each page presents one lesson, consisting of a black-and-white picture, a word or sentence printed below it, and the words broken down. Exercises at the end of the book require the child to match the same printed words with the pictures and to identify other pictures with similar sounds. (SH)

CP..... N

AN..... 000618

TI..... Hamsi and Joker (Bright Star and Joker).

YR..... May78

IN..... Peach Springs School District 8, Ariz. Hualapai Bilingual Education Program.

SN..... Office of Education (DHEW), Washington, D.C. (RMQ66000)

LG..... Hualapai

AV..... National Dissemination and Assessment Center, 7703 North Lamar Boulevard, Austin, Texas 78752 (ISBN 0-89417-497-5; $1.00)

NT..... 8 p.
For companion workbooks and primer, see 000617 and 619-620.

DE..... Kindergarten; Grade 1; Primary Education; *Reading Instruction; *Reading Materials; Phonics; *Instructional Materials; *Language Instruction; American Indian Languages; Childrens Books

ID..... *Hualapai

AB..... Native Hualapai-speaking children at the kindergarten and first grade levels read this book after mastering the sounds and vocabulary presented in the workbook entitled "Hualapai misid mispo, Book 1." The black-and-white illustrations and captions which appear on each page tell the story of a wild horse. (SH)

CP..... N

AN..... 000619

TI..... Hualapai misid mispó (Learn to Read Hualapai): Book 2.

YR..... May78

IN..... Peach Springs School District 8, Ariz. Hualapai Bilingual Education Program.

SN..... Office of Education (DHEW), Washington, D.C. (RMQ66000)

LG..... Hualapai

AV..... National Dissemination and Assessment Center, 7703 North Lamar Boulevard, Austin, Texas 78752 (ISBN 0-89417-496-7; $1.00)

NT..... 22 p.
For Book 1 and primers, see 000617-618 and 620.

DE..... Kindergarten; Grade 1; Primary Education; American Indian Languages; Reading Instruction; Reading Materials; *Phonics; *Instructional Materials; Language Instruction; *Reading Readiness; *Workbooks; Phonology

ID..... *Hualapai

AB..... This black-and-white illustrated workbook for native
Hualapai-speaking children introduces the second half of
the sounds of that language. Each page constitutes one
lesson, consisting of a picture, a sentence below it, and
words broken down. (SH)

CP..... N

AN..... 000620

TI..... Iyas iyasma:viyam ma:k (Eating Turkey During
Thanksgiving).

YR..... May78

IN..... Peach Springs School District 8, Peach Springs, Ariz.
Hualapai Bilingual Education Program.

SN..... Office of Education (DHEW), Washington, D.C. (RMQ66000)

LG..... Hualapai

AV..... National Dissemination and Assessment Center, 7703 North
Lamar Boulevard, Austin, Texas 78752 (ISBN
0-89417-498-3; $1.00)

NT..... 12 p.
For companion workbooks and primer, see 000617-619.

DE..... Kindergarten; Grade 1; Primary Education; American Indian
Languages; *Reading Instruction; *Reading Materials;
*Instructional Materials; *Language Instruction;
Childrens Books

ID..... *Hualapai

AB..... This primer is to be read by native Hualapai-speaking
children at the kindergarten and first grade level once
they have mastered the sounds and vocabulary introduced
in the workbook entitled "Hualapai misid mispo, Book 2."
The black-and-white illustrations and captions appearing
on each page tell the story of a boy who goes turkey
shooting. (SH)

CP..... N

AN..... 000621

TI..... The Daily Curriculum Guide: Year I, Weeks 1-10. A
Preschool Program for the Spanish-Speaking Child.

YR..... Oct74

IN..... Spanish Dame Bilingual Bicultural Project, San Jose,
Calif. (BBB11959); National Dissemination and Assessment
Center, Austin, Tex.

SN..... Office of Education (DHEW), Washington, D.C. (RMQ66000)

LG..... English; Spanish

AV..... National Dissemination and Assessment Center, 7703 North
Lamar Boulevard, Austin, Texas 78752 ($5.00); ERIC
Document Reproduction Service, P.O. Box 190, Arlington,
Virginia 22210 (set of 3 volumes $71.74; microfiche
$2.34; ED108507)

NT..... vii, 269 p.
For related documents, see 000599-602 and 622-628.

DE..... Preschool Programs; *Preschool Curriculum; *Spanish;
Language Maintenance; Preschool Education; *Instructional
Materials; Home Instruction; Paraprofessional Personnel;
*Teaching Guides; Educational Games; Songs; Learning
Activities

AB..... This curriculum guide, adaptable to other early childhood
programs, is designed for use with 3-year-olds primarily
by paraprofessionals working with the parents in
children's homes. It is one volume of a three-volume set
covering Year I. The curriculum is based on a language
maintenance model in which Spanish is used as a means to
develop basic concepts, skills, and attitudes. Daily
lessons are outlined in detail in both English and
Spanish. Each lesson plan includes a list of objectives,
activities, and necessary materials. Activities are then
outlined step by step with suggested songs and games.
Other materials in the program include volumes 2 and 3 of
this set, a 3-volume curriculum guide for Year II,
supplements to the curriculum guides, a cassette tape of
songs, and training materials for the home tutor. (SH)

CP..... N

AN..... 000622

TI..... The Daily Curriculum Guide: Year I, Weeks 11-20. A
Preschool Program for the Spanish-Speaking Child.

YR..... Dec74

IN..... Spanish Dame Bilingual Bicultural Project, San Jose,
Calif. (BBB11959); National Dissemination and Assessment
Center, Austin, Tex.

SN..... Office of Education (DHEW), Washington, D.C. (RMQ66000)

LG..... English; Spanish

AV..... National Dissemination and Assessment Center, 7703 North
Lamar Boulevard, Austin, Texas 78752 ($5.00); ERIC
Document Reproduction Service, P.O. Box 190, Arlington,
Virginia 22210 (set of 3 volumes $71.74; microfiche
$2.34; ED108507)

NT..... 229 p.
For related documents, see 000599-602, 621, and
623-628.

DE..... Preschool Programs; *Preschool Curriculum; *Spanish;
Language Maintenance; *Preschool Education;

           *Instructional Materials; *Home Instruction;
           Paraprofessional Personnel; *Teaching Guides; Educational
           Games; Songs; Learning Activities

AB..... This curriculum guide, adaptable to other early childhood
           programs, is designed for use with 3-year-olds primarily
           by paraprofessionals working with the parents in
           children's homes. It is one volume of a 3-volume set
           covering Year I. The curriculum is based on a language
           maintenance model in which Spanish is used as a means to
           develop basic concepts, skills, and attitudes. Daily
           lessons are outlined in detail in both English and
           Spanish. Each lesson plan includes a list of objectives,
           activities, and necessary materials. Activities are then
           outlined step by step with suggested songs and games.
           Other materials in the program include volumes 1 and 3 of
           this set, a 3-volume curriculum guide for Year II,
           supplements to the curriculum guides, a cassette tape of
           songs, and training materials for the home tutor. (SH)

CP..... N

AN..... 000623

TI..... The Daily Curriculum Guide: Year I, Weeks 21-30. A
           Preschool Program for the Spanish-Speaking Child.

YR..... Mar75

IN..... Spanish Dame Bilingual Project, San Jose, Calif.
           (BBB11959); National Dissemination and Assessment Center,
           Austin, Tex.

SN..... Office of Education (DHEW), Washington, D.C. (RMQ66000)

LG..... English; Spanish

AV..... National Dissemination and Assessment Center, 7703 North
           Lamar Boulevard, Austin, Texas 78752 ($5.00); ERIC
           Document Reproduction Service, P.O. Box 190, Arlington,
           Virginia 22210 (set of 3 volumes $71.74; microfiche
           $2.34; ED108507)

NT..... 204 p.
           For related documents, see 000599-602, 621-622, and 624-628.

DE..... Preschool Programs; *Preschool Curriculum; *Spanish;
           Language Maintenance; *Preschool Education;
           *Instructional Materials; *Home Instruction;
           Paraprofessional Personnel; *Teaching Guides; Educational
           Games; Songs; Learning Activities

AB..... This curriculum guide, adaptable to other early childhood
           programs, is designed for use with 3-year-olds primarily
           by paraprofessionals working with the parents in
           children's homes. It is one volume of a three-volume set
           covering Year I. The curriculum is based on a language
           maintenance model in which Spanish is used as a means to
           develop basic concepts, skills, and attitudes. Daily
           lessons are outlined in detail in both English and

Spanish. Each lesson plan includes a list of objectives, activities, and necessary materials. Activities are then outlined step by step with suggested songs and games. Other materials in the program include volume 1 and 2 of this set, a 3-volume curriculum guide for Year II, supplements to the curriculum guides, a cassette tape of songs, and training materials for the home tutor. (SH)

CP..... N

AN..... 000624

TI..... The Daily Curriculum Guide: Year II, Weeks 1-10. A Preschool Program for the Spanish-Speaking Child.

YR..... Jul76

IN..... Spanish Dame Bilingual Bicultural Project, San Jose, Calif. (BBB11959); National Dissemination and Assessment Center, Austin, Tex.

SN..... Office of Education (DHEW), Washington, D.C. (RMQ66000)

LG..... English; Spanish

AV..... National Dissemination and Assessment Center, 7703 North Lamar Boulevard, Austin, Texas 78752 ($5.00)

NT..... 321 p.
For related documents, see 000599-602, 621-623, and 625-628.

DE..... Preschool Programs; *Preschool Curriculum; Spanish Speaking; Language Maintenance; Preschool Education; *Instructional Materials; Home Instruction; Paraprofessional Personnel; *Spanish; *Teaching Guides; Educational Games; Songs; Learning Activities

AB..... This curriculum guide, adaptable to other early childhood programs, is designed for use with 4-year-olds primarily by paraprofessionals working with the parents in children's homes. The 3-volume set of curriculum guides for Year II is designed for use over a 34-week period. The curriculum is based on a language maintenance model in which Spanish is used as a means to develop basic concepts, skills, and attitudes. Daily lessons are outlined in detail in both English and Spanish. Each lesson plan includes a list of objectives, activities, and necessary materials. Activities are then outlined step by step with suggested songs and games. Other materials in the program include three guides for Year I, supplements to the curriculum guides, a cassette tape of songs, and training materials for the home tutor. (SH)

CP..... N

AN..... 000625

TI..... The Daily Curriculum Guide: Year II, Weeks 11-20. A Preschool Program for the Spanish-Speaking Child.

YR..... Feb77

IN..... Spanish Dame Bilingual Bicultural Project, San Jose,
Calif. (BBB11959); National Dissemination and Assessment
Center, Austin, Tex.

SN..... Office of Education (DHEW), Washington, D.C. (RMQ66000)

LG..... English; Spanish

AV..... National Dissemination and Assessment Center, 7703 North
Lamar Boulevard, Austin, Texas 78752 (ISBN
0-89417-004-X; $5.00)

NT..... 245 p.
For related documents, see 000599-602, 621-624, and 626-628.

DE..... Preschool Programs; *Preschool Curriculum; *Spanish;
Language Maintenance; Preschool Education; *Instructional
Materials; Home Instruction; Paraprofessional Personnel;
*Teaching Guides; Educational Games; Songs; Learning
Activities

AB..... This curriculum guide, adaptable to other early childhood
programs, is designed for use with 4-year-olds primarily
by paraprofessionals working with the parents in
children's homes. The 3-volume set of curriculum guides
for Year II is designed for use over a 34-week period.
The curriculum is based on a language maintenance model
in which Spanish is used as a means to develop basic
concepts, skills, and attitudes. Daily lessons are
outlined in detail in both English and Spanish. Each
lesson plan includes a list of objectives, activities,
and necessary materials. Activities are then outlined
step by step with suggested songs and games. Other
materials in the program include three guides for Year I,
supplements to the curriculum guides, a cassette tape of
songs, and training materials for the home tutor. (SH)

CP..... N

AN..... 000626

TI..... The Daily Curriculum Guide: Year II, Weeks 21-34. A
Preschool Program for the Spanish-Speaking Child.

YR..... Feb78

IN..... Spanish Dame Bilingual Bicultural Project, San Jose,
Calif. (BBB11959); National Dissemination and Assessment
Center, Austin, Tex.

SN..... Office of Education (DHEW), Washington, D.C. (RMQ66000)

LG..... English; Spanish

AV..... National Dissemination and Assessment Center, 7703 North
Lamar Boulevard, Austin, Texas 78752 (ISBN 0-89417-338-3;
$5.00)

NT..... 321 p.
For related documents, see 000599-602, 621-625,
and 627-628.

DE..... Preschool Programs; *Preschool Curriculum; *Spanish; Language Maintenance; Preschool Education; *Instructional Materials; *Home Instruction; Paraprofessional Personnel; *Teaching Guides; Educational Games; Songs; Learning Activities

AB..... This curriculum guide, adaptable to other early childhood programs, is designed for use with 4-year-olds primarily by paraprofessionals working with the parents in children's homes. The 3-volume set of curriculum guides for Year II is designed for use over a 34-week period. The curriculum is based on a language maintenance model in which Spanish is used as a means to develop basic concepts, skills, and attitudes. Daily lessons are outlined in detail in both English and Spanish. Each lesson plan includes a list of objectives, activities, and necessary materials. Activities are then outlined step by step with suggested songs and games. Other materials in the program include three guides for Year I, supplements to the curriculum guides, a cassette tape of songs, and training materials for the home tutor. (SH)

CP..... N

AN..... 000627

ER..... ED109899

TI..... Instructional Guide for the Home Tutor.

YR..... Dec74

IN..... Spanish Dame Bilingual Bicultural Project, San Jose, Calif. (BBB11959); National Dissemination and Assessment Center, Austin, Tex.

SN..... Office of Education (DHEW), Washington, D.C. (RMQ66000)

AV..... National Dissemination and Assessment Center, 7703 North Lamar Boulevard, Austin, Texas 78752 ($2.00); ERIC Document Reproduction Service, P.O. Box 190, Arlington, Virginia 22210 ($3.32; microfiche $0.76)

NT..... v, 59 p.
For related documents, see 000599-602, 621-626 and 628.

DE..... Curriculum Guides, Instructional Materials; Learning Activities; *Preschool Education; *Spanish; *Teaching Guides; *Tutorial Programs; Tutoring; Tutors; Home Instruction

AB..... This guide is part of a series intended as a basic reference tool for the paraprofessional working in a preschool Spanish/English bilingual program in a home setting. Characteristics of 3- and 4-year-olds are discussed, followed by procedures for working with parents and with children. Understanding and interpersonal rapport are stressed. A sample home interview form is included in the section on parents. A general lesson plan is also provided, and guidelines are given for preparing daily lesson plans, conducting class activities, and evaluating lessons. Concluding the guide is a chart giving detailed instructional objectives and activities designed to meet them. Accompanying materials include a planning guide, two 3-volume curriculum guide sets, supplements to the curriculum guides, and a cassette of songs. (Author/AM)

CP..... N

AN..... 000628

ER..... ED108493

TI..... Planning the Program with the Home Tutor.

YR..... Apr75

IN..... Spanish Dame Bilingual Bicultural Project, San Jose, Calif. (BBB11959); National Dissemination and Assessment Center, Austin, Tex.

SN..... Office of Education (DHEW), Washington, D.C. (RMQ66000)

LG..... English; Spanish

AV..... National Dissemination and Assessment Center, 7703 North Lamar Boulevard, Austin, Texas 78752 ($2.00); ERIC Document Reproduction Service, P.O. Box 190, Arlington, Virginia 22210 ($8.24; microfiche $0.76)

NT..... ix, 151 p.
For related documents, see 000599-602 and 621-627.

DE..... Audiovisual Aids; Bibliographies; Criterion Referenced Tests; Diagnostic Tests; Educational Games; Home Instruction; Home Programs; Individual Instruction; Instructional Materials; Language Instruction; Measurement Instruments; *Preschool Education; Program Descriptions; Programed Tutoring; Program Guides; Program Planning; *Resource Materials; *Spanish; Testing; *Tutorial Programs; Tutoring

AB..... This guide is part of a series intended as a basic resource for preschool Spanish/English bilingual home training. It presents an overview of the bilingual project of which it is an outgrowth and offers guidelines for setting up similar programs. The guidelines cover such topics as: (1) tutor selection, training, and evaluation; (2) recommended materials for preservice and inservice training (consisting of an extensive list of U.S. Government Reports, bilingual education resource guides, and films); (3) suggested distributors of educational materials in Spanish; and (4) evaluation instruments (including diagnostic and criterion-referenced tests; vocabulary, grammar, and concept tests; and child information reports). In addition, parent involvement is discussed, and suggestions are given regarding the setting up of a bilingual program. Accompanying materials include a teaching guide, two three-volume curriculum guide sets, supplements to the curriculum guides, and a cassette of songs. (Author/AM)

CP..... N

AN..... 000629

TI..... The Mexican Experience: A Social Studies Approach to Art and Architecture. Teacher's Guide.

YR..... Oct75

AU..... Finer, Neal B.

IN..... National Dissemination and Assessment Center, Austin, Tex.; Education Service Center Region 13, Austin, Tex. (XPT82322)

SN..... Office of Education (DHEW), Washington, D.C. (RMQ66000)

AV..... National Dissemination and Assessment Center, 7703 North Lamar Boulevard, Austin, Texas 78752 ($2.00); ERIC Document Reproduction Service, P.O. Box 190, Arlington, Virginia 22210 (with resource material $8.69; microfiche $0.83; ED122633)

NT..... vii, 110 p.
For accompanying resource material, see 000630.

DE..... *Architecture; *Art; Cultural Awareness; *Cultural Education; Higher Education; Humanities Instruction; Instructional Materials; Learning Activities; Senior High Schools; *Mexicans; *Teaching Guides; *Social Studies; Adult Education; Lesson Plans

ID..... *Mexico

AB..... This manual is designed to be used as part of a social studies program on Mexican culture at the senior high school, college, or adult levels. It stresses an art-architecture perspective, wth content areas applicable to classes in Spanish, English as a second language, art history, and humanities. The volume contains a course overview, suggested course presentation, materials criteria, literature review, suggested structure for instruction, and eight lesson samples. Each lesson includes a statement of the key idea, objectives to be developed, suggested materials, recommended activities, and sources of information for students and teachers. A 93-item bibliography is appended. (JB)

CP..... N

AN..... 000630

TI..... The Mexican Experience: A Social Studies Approach to Art and Architecture. Resource Material.

YR..... Oct75

AU..... Finer, Neal B.

IN..... National Dissemination and Assessment Center, Austin, Tex.; Education Service Center Region 13, Austin, Tex. (XPT82322)

SN..... Office of Education (DHEW), Washington, D.C. (RMQ66000)

AV..... National Dissemination and Assessment Center, 7703 North
Lamar Boulevard, Austin, Texas 78752 ($2.00); ERIC
Document Reproduction Service, P.O. Box 190, Arlington,
Virginia 22210 (with teacher's guide $8.69; microfiche
$0.83; ED122633)

NT..... 64 p.
For accompanying teacher's guide, see 000629.

DE..... *Architecture; *Art; Cultural Awareness; *Cultural
Education; Higher Education; Humanities Instruction;
Instructional Materials; Learning Activities; Senior High
Schools; *Mexicans; *Resource Materials; *Social Studies;
Illustrations; Adult Education

ID..... *Mexico; Dittos

AB..... The materials in this volume accompany a social studies
program on Mexican culture for use at the senior high
school, college, or adult levels. It stresses an
art-architecture perspective with content areas
applicable to classes in Spanish, English as a second
language, art history, and humanities. Resources include
transparency masters, content outlines, charts, maps,
illustrations, timelines, projects, and a pupil
evaluation form. (JB)

CP..... N

AN..... 000639

ER..... ED107580

TI..... Struggle for Independence: Mexico's Rebellion Against
Spain. Social Studies. A Teacher's Guide for Grades
1-9.

YR..... Mar79

AU..... Crespín, Emil; Rodríguez, Robert; Crespín, Lila, ill.;
Frey, Sarah, ill.; León, José de, ill.

IN..... National Dissemination and Assessment Center, Austin,
Tex.; Curriculum Adaptation Network for
Bilingual/Bicultural Education, San Diego, Calif. Far
West Regional Adaptation Center. (BBB11920)

SN..... Office of Education (DHEW), Washington, D.C. (RMQ66000);
William Randolph Hearst Foundation, Los Angeles, Calif.
(BBB11728)

AV..... National Dissemination and Assessment Center, 7703 North
Lamar Boulevard, Austin, Texas 78752 (ISBN
0-89417-0-79-1; $1.50); ERIC Document Reproduction
Service, P.O. Box 190, Arlington, Virginia 22210
(microfiche $0.76)

NT..... ix, 57 p.

DE..... Biculturalism; Cultural Awareness; *Mexican American
History; Elementary Secondary Education; Ethnic Studies;
Learning Activities; Mexicans; *Revolution; *Social
Studies; *Teaching Guides; History; *History Instruction;

```
           Instructional Materials; *American History; Grade 1;
           Grade 2; Grade 3; Grade 4; Grade 5; Grade 6; Grade 7;
           Grade 8; Grade 9
```

ID..... *Mexico

AB..... This resource guide is designed for teaching the history
and culture of the Mexican American child. This unit,
for grades one through nine, focuses on Mexico's revolt
against Spanish rule and highlights famous persons and
events of the period. The materials can serve as a
reference on Mexican historical events and patriotic
commemorations in order that the teacher may have some
information readily available for classroom use.
Historical facts are included, as well as activities for
use in the classroom, in the school, or for community
presentation. The unit is arranged in nine sections
according to either famous persons or events. Each
section includes presentation of facts, a list of reasons
for remembering the day, vocabulary, ways for teachers to
highlight the facts, ideas for discussion, and
activities. Suggestions for classroom activities
include role playing, bulletin boards, reports, and
timelines. The listing of commemoration dates is
sequenced to allow teachers to plan the school calendar
accordingly. (Author/CO)

CP..... N

AN..... 000640

ER..... ED108489

TI..... Presentaciones escolares: Serie de programas para
conmemorar acontecimientos de valor cultural para el
México Americano (School Assembly Presentations: Series
of Programs to Commemorate Events of Cultural Value to
the Mexican American).

YR..... 76

AU..... Villarreal, Abelardo; Escamilla, Valentina; Flores,
Salvador; Serna, Leonila; Hoeflich, Carmen, ed.; Morales,
Oscar, ill.

IN..... National Dissemination and Assessment Center, Austin,
Tex.; Curriculum Adaptation Network for
Bilingual/Bicultural Education, San Antonio, Tex.
Southwest Regional Adaptation Center. (BBB11923)

SN..... Office of Education (DHEW), Washington, D.C. (RMQ66000);
William Randolph Hearst Foundation, Los Angeles, Calif.
(BBB11728)

LG..... Spanish

AV..... National Dissemination and Assessment Center, 7703 North
Lamar Boulevard, Austin, Texas 78752 ($3.00); ERIC
Document Reproduction Service, P.O. Box 190, Arlington,
Virginia 22210 ($3.32; microfiche $0.76; ED108489)

NT..... vii, 78 p.
Rev. ed.

DE..... *Assembly Programs; Biculturalism; Cultural Awareness; Cultural Enrichment; Curriculum Guides; Elementary Education; *Enrichment Activities; Latin American Culture; Mexican American History; *Mexican Americans; Spanish; *Cultural Education; *Cultural Background

AB..... This material consists of a series of cultural presentations designed for elementary school assemblies or special programs. The activities are intended to strengthen Mexican American children's awareness of their cultural heritage. Program scripts, poems, songs, historical narratives, and skits are included to illustrate and celebrate Mexican and American holidays such as Mexican Independence Day, Columbus Day, Thanksgiving, Christmas and the New Year, the Fifth of May, and Mother's Day. (CO)

CP..... N

AN..... 000641

ER..... ED108492

TI..... Guías para los carteles puertorriqueños (Guides for the Puerto Rican Posters).

YR..... Aug74

AU..... Colón, Luisa; Rivera, Carlos; Maldonado, Juan, ill.

IN..... National Dissemination and Assessment Center, Austin, Tex.; Curriculum Adaptation Network for Bilingual/Bicultural Education, Bronx, N.Y. Northeast Regional Adaptation Center (BBB11922)

SN..... Office of Education (DHEW), Washington, D.C. (RMQ66000); William Randolph Hearst Foundation, Los Angeles, Calif. (BBB11728)

LG..... Spanish

AV..... National Dissemination and Assessment Center, 7703 North Lamar Boulevard, Austin, Texas 78752 ($1.50, plus $5.00 for 4 posters); ERIC Document Reproduction Service, P.O. Box 190, Arlington, Virginia 22210 ($4.43; microfiche $0.76)

NT..... ix, 85 p.
Four accompanying color posters, 21"x29".

DE..... Biculturalism; Bilingual Students; Elementary Secondary Education; Instructional Materials; *Puerto Rican Culture; *Puerto Ricans; *Spanish; Spanish Speaking; *Teaching Guides; Social Studies; Visual Aids

ID..... *Puerto Rico; *Posters

AB..... The four teacher's guides and corresponding Puerto Rican posters in this set cover the following: (1) "My Race," origins and history of the Indian, African, and Spanish strains which make up the Puerto Rican people; (2) "Distinguished Puerto Ricans," a painter, patriots, and a composer; (3) "Distinguished Women," poets, a mayor, a patriot, and an educator; and (4) "Puerto Rican Governors," five governors of the Commonwealth. Each narrative or biographical sketch in the guides is followed by lists of suggested learning objectives, materials needed for the lesson, instructions for presentation to the students, vocabulary, and classroom learning activities. (DS)

CP..... N

AN..... 000642

ER..... ED108500

TI..... Serie de rimas illustradas (Series of Illustrated Rhymes).

YR..... Mar74

AU..... Escamilla, Valentina

IN..... National Dissemination and Assessment Center, Austin, Tex.; Curriculum Adaptation Network for Bilingual/Bicultural Education, San Antonio, Tex. Southwest Regional Adaptation Center. (BBB11923)

SN..... Office of Education (DHEW), Washington, D.C. (RMQ66000); William Randolph Hearst Foundation, Los Angeles, Calif. (BBB11728)

LG..... Spanish

AV..... National Dissemination and Assessment Center, 7703 North Lamar Boulevard, Austin, Texas 78752 ($2.00); ERIC Document Reproduction Service, P.O. Box 190, Arlington, Virginia 22210 ($4.43; microfiche $0.76)

NT..... 79 p.

DE..... Classroom Games; Classrooms; Community; *Educational Games; Family Life; Family Relationship; Individual Activities; *Instructional Materials; Learning Activities; Mexican Americans; Neighborhood; *Poetry; Primary Education; Puzzles; *Spanish; *Workbooks

AB..... This workbook for children in the primary grades contains three sections of rhymes and activities about family members; the community's houses, shops, and streets; and the schoolroom and its equipment. An individual activity accompanies each rhyme. The workbook is designed to strengthen children's knowledge of their environment and language by emphasizing ideas that interest them and activities corresponding to their aptitudes. The book is fully illustrated, and learning activities include questions and answers, follow-the-dots, picture puzzles, coloring, and drawing. The material has been classroom tested and revised accordingly. (DS)

CP..... N

AN..... 000643

ER..... ED108499

TI..... Cantando y aprendiendo (Singing and Learning): Primary Song Book.

YR..... Mar74

AU..... Badías, Bertha, mus.; Guardarramas, Eduardo, mus.; Martí, Osvaldo R., ill.

IN..... National Dissemination and Assessment Center, Austin, Tex.; Curriculum Adaptation Network for Bilingual/Bicultural Education, Bronx, N.Y. Northeast Regional Adaptation Center. (BBB11922)

SN..... Office of Education (DHEW), Washington, D.C. (RMQ66000); William Randolph Hearst Foundation, Los Angeles, Calif. (BBB11728)

LG..... Spanish

AV..... National Dissemination and Assessment Center, 7703 North Lamar Boulevard, Austin, Texas 78752 (ISBN 0-89417-033-3; $1.20); ERIC Document Reproduction Service, P.O. Box 190, Arlington, Virginia 22210 ($3.32; microfiche $0.76)

NT..... vii, 44 p.

DE..... Curriculum Guides; Elementary Education; *Instructional Materials; Music; *Music Activities; Music Education; *Puerto Rican Culture; Puerto Ricans; Second Language Learning; *Singing; Skill Development; *Spanish; *Vocal Music; Listening Comprehension

ID..... *Song Books

AB..... This illustrated teacher's songbook contains 18 songs and game songs to be used with the Spanish Curricula Development Center (SCDC) publications or with other bilingual instructional materials. The songs are based on the SCDC Reading Series for the Language Arts strand, Kits 2-11. The objective of the book is to develop children's listening and comprehension skills, music appreciation, and rhythmic expression. Various songs are culturally relevant to the Puerto Rican child. (DS)

CP..... N

AN..... 000644

TI..... Crucigramas: Crossword Puzzles for Primary Grades.

YR..... 74

AU..... García, María H.; Mendoza, Ricardo, ill.; Nuñez, Armando, ill.

IN..... National Dissemination and Assessment Center, Austin, Tex.; Curriculum Adaptation Network for Bilingual/Bicultural Education, San Diego, Calif. Far West Regional Adaptation Center. (BBB11920)

SN..... Office of Education (DHEW), Washington, D.C. (RMQ66000); William Randolph Hearst Foundation, Los Angeles, Calif. (BBB11728)

LG..... English; Spanish

AV..... National Dissemination and Assessment Center, 7703 North Lamar Boulevard, Austin, Texas 78752 ($3.00)

NT..... vii, 79 p.
Rev. ed.

DE..... Basic Reading; *Classroom Games; Educational Games; Instructional Aids; *Instructional Materials; Primary Education; Puzzles; *Spanish; Spelling; Teacher Developed Materials; *Word Recognition; Word Study Skills; *Workbooks

ID..... *Crossword Puzzles

AB..... This workbook is intended as an aid to the teacher of a bilingual bicultural Spanish-English program in the primary grades. It contains modified crossword puzzles in Spanish. The puzzles are intended to reinforce reading words and to familiarize the student with a modified method of working crossword puzzles. Some of the letters found in the words are supplied to aid the student; in some instances, the entire word may be supplied if a picture would not adequately portray the word. An answer key is provided for each puzzle. (Author/AM)

CP..... N

AN..... 000645

TI..... New Approaches to Bilingual, Bicultural Education.

YR..... Aug75

AU..... Harper, Pam, ed.; Frey, Sarah, ill.

IN..... National Dissemination and Assessment Center, Austin, Tex.

SN..... Office of Education (DHEW), Washington, D.C. (RMQ66000)

NO..... G OEG-9-72-0154(280)

AV..... National Dissemination and Assessment Center, 7703 North Lamar Boulevard, Austin, Texas 78752 (ISBN 0-89417-021-X; $3.50)

NT..... vii, 127 p.
For individual manuals and set of assessment units, see 000646-653.

DE..... *Bilingual Education; *Teaching Guides; Teaching Methods; *Teacher Education; *Educational Philosophy; Bilingualism; Biculturalism; Bilingual Students; Bilingual Teachers; Educational Innovations; Educational Improvements; Cultural Differences; Mexican Americans; Educational Planning; Learning Characteristics; *Teacher Education Curriculum; Cognitive Development; Cognitive Style; Cognitive Tests; Individualized Instruction; Programed Materials; Teacher Evaluation; *Instructional Materials

AB..... This series of teacher training materials consists of seven teaching manuals and a set of self-assessment units. The manuals, designed for use in bilingual bicultural programs, cover a wide range of topics, including educational philosophy, cultural values, learning styles, teaching styles, and curriculum. The self-assessment units, designed both as a review and as a means of emphasizing important concepts, may be used to conclude the study of each manual. (CO)

CP..... N

AN..... 000646

ER..... ED108497

TI..... New Approaches to Bilingual, Bicultural Education, Manual 3: Introduction to Cognitive Styles.

YR..... Aug75

AU..... Ramírez, Manuel; Herold, P. Leslie; Castañeda, Alfredo

IN..... National Dissemination and Assessment Center, Austin, Tex.

SN..... Office of Education (DHEW), Washington, D.C. (RMQ66000)

NO..... G OEG-9-72-0154(280)

AV..... National Dissemination and Assessment Center, 7703 North Lamar Boulevard, Austin, Texas 78752 (set of 7 $3.50); ERIC Document Reproduction Service, P.O. Box 190, Arlington, Virginia 22210 ($1.58; microfiche $0.76; ED108497)

NT..... p. 35-48.

DE..... Bilingual Education; Bilingualism; *Biculturalism; Bilingual Students; Bilingual Teachers; *Cognitive Processes; Conceptual Tempo; *Cultural Pluralism; Cultural Differences; Culturally Disadvantaged; Educational Improvement; Educationally Disadvantaged; Educational Planning; Individualized Instruction; *Learning Characteristics; Mexican Americans; Programed Materials; Teacher Education; Teacher Education Curriculum; *Teaching Guides; *Cognitive Style

AB..... This teaching manual is one in a set of seven designed for use in bilingual bicultural programs. The subject discussed here is the influence of socialization

practices on children's cognitive styles, and in
particular children's learning styles, and the resulting
implications for bilingual bicultural education. The
characteristics of field sensitive and field independent
cognitive styles are described, followed by a discussion
of the relationship between cognitive style and culture
and socialization styles. An illustration of this
relationship is drawn from the situation of Mexican
American children, who typically score in a field
sensitive direction on tests of cognitive style. Such
scores are thought to result from the traditional Mexican
American emphasis on family loyalty and a close
interpersonal relationship between mother and children,
values that encourage field sensitivity. It is concluded
that an appreciation of the diversity of cognitive and
socialization styles must precede the planning of
culturally democratic educational environments. A manual
of self-assessment units accompanies this series. (AM)

CP..... N

AN..... 000647

ER..... ED108496

TI..... New Approaches to Bilingual, Bicultural Education, Manual 2: Mexican American Values and Culturally Democratic Educational Environments.

YR..... Aug75

AU..... Ramírez, Manuel; Herold, P. Leslie; Castañeda, Alfredo

IN..... National Dissemination and Assessment Center, Austin, Tex.

SN..... Office of Education (DHEW), Washington, D.C. (RMQ66000)

NO..... G OEG-9-72-0154(280)

AV..... National Dissemination and Assessment Center, 7703 North Lamar Boulevard, Austin, Texas 78752 (set of 7 $3.50); ERIC Document Reproduction Service, P.O. Box 190, Arlington, Virginia 22210 ($1.95; microfiche $0.76; ED108496)

NT..... p. 15-33.

DE..... Bilingual Education; Bilingualism; *Biculturalism; Bilingual Students; Bilingual Teachers; *Cultural Differences; Cultural Pluralism; Culture Conflict; Democratic Values; Educational Planning; Ethnic Groups; *Mexican Americans; Minority Groups; *Social Values; Sociocultural Patterns; *Teaching Guides; Teacher Education; Teacher Education Curriculum

AB..... This teaching manual is one in a set of seven (accompanied by a manual of self-assessment units) designed for use in bilingual bicultural programs. It outlines some features of culturally democratic educational environments and illustrates ways in which the schools can take positive steps to assure that children preserve pride and loyalty toward the culture represented by their family and community. Examples are given of the conflicts that children can experience when schools undermine cultural loyalties and of their consequences; e.g., tensions between parents and children; alienation of children from the school, teachers, and peer groups; and antagonism between school and community. In spite of the diversity in values, there are recurrent themes in what is taken seriously and emphasized in most Mexican American communities. These fall into the categories of identification with family, community, and ethnic group; personalization of interpersonal relationships; status and role definition in family and community; and Mexican Catholic ideology. The manual examines these value areas in detail and offers a 10-point set of guideliness suggesting ways to create educational environments in which Mexican American values are afforded dignity and respect. (AM)

CP..... N

AN..... 000648

ER..... ED111181

TI..... New Approaches to Bilingual, Bicultural Education, Manual 1: A New Philosophy of Education.

YR..... Aug75

AU..... Castañeda, Alfredo; Herold, P. Leslie; Ramírez, Manuel

IN..... National Dissemination and Assessment Center, Austin, Tex.

SN..... Office of Education (DHEW), Washington, D.C. (RMQ66000)

NO..... G OEG-9-72-0154(280)

AV..... National Dissemination and Assessment Center, 7703 North Lamar Boulevard, Austin, Texas 78752 (set of 7 $3.50); ERIC Document Reproduction Service, P.O. Box 190, Arlington, Virginia 22210 ($1.58; microfiche $0.76)

NT..... p. 1-13.

DE..... Bilingual Education; Bilingualism; Biculturalism; *Acculturation; Bilingual Students; Bilingual Teachers; *Compensatory Education; Cultural Differences; Cultural Pluralism; Educational Improvement; Educational Innovation; Educationally Disadvantaged; *Educational Philosophy; *Mexican Americans; Public Education; Teacher Education; *Teaching Guides

AB..... This teaching manual is one in a set of seven (accompanied by a manual of self-assessment units) that have been designed for use in bilingual bicultural programs. The components of the series may be used either individually or together. This manual explores the many issues concerning the responsibilities of public education to the Mexican American child. A critical examination is made of assumptions about compensatory education. The melting pot theory, or enforced acculturation, is contrasted to cultural democracy or acculturation assistance. The latter view goes beyond recognition and respect to use and reinforcement of culture as an integral part of the majority culture. (AM)

CP..... N

AN..... 000649

ER..... ED111180

TI..... New Approaches to Bilingual, Bicultural Education, Manual 4: Field Sensitivity and Field Independence in Children.

YR..... Aug75

AU..... Ramírez, Manuel; Herold, P. Leslie; Castañeda, Alfredo

IN..... National Dissemination and Assessment Center, Austin, Tex.

SN..... Office of Education (DHEW), Washington, D.C. (RMQ66000)

NO..... G OEG-9-72-0154(280)

AV..... National Dissemination and Assessment Center, 7703 North Lamar Boulevard, Austin, Texas 78752 (set of 7 $3.50); ERIC Document Reproduction Service, P.O. Box 190, Arlington, Virginia 22210 ($1.58; microfiche $0.76; ED111180)

NT..... p. 49-62.

DE..... Bilingual Education; Bilingualism; Biculturalism; Bilingual Students; Bilingual Teachers; Cognitive Development; *Cognitive Measurement; *Cognitive Processes; Measurement Instruments; Observation; Programed Materials; Teacher Education; *Teaching Guides; Teaching Methods; *Cognitive Tests; Cultural Differences; Learning Characteristics; Teacher Education Curriculum; *Cognitive Style

ID..... Child Embedded Figures Test; Field Independence; Field Sensitivity; Portable Rod and Frame Test

AB..... This teaching manual is one in a set of seven (accompanied by a manual of self-assessment units) that have been designed for use in bilingual bicultural programs. The components of the series may be used either individually or together. This manual is intended to familiarize the teacher with ways of measuring cognitive styles in children. The teacher's objective is to determine whether a particular child is field sensitive, field independent, or "bicognitive." Two techniques of measuring cognitive style in children, the Portable Rod and Frame Test and the Child Embedded Figures Test, are described, along with their shortcomings. Most of the manual describes how the teacher can determine cognitive styles by observing children in the school setting, with the aid of "Child

Rating Forms." These observations are used in assigning children to one of three instruction groups, and a different teaching strategy is used with each group. (AM)

CP..... N

AN..... 000650

ER..... ED108495

TI..... New Approaches to Bilingual, Bicultural Education, Manual 5: Field Sensitive and Field Independent Teaching Strategies.

YR..... Aug75

AU..... Herold, P. Leslie; Ramírez, Manuel; Castañeda, Alfredo

IN..... National Dissemination and Assessment Center, Austin, Tex.

SN..... Office of Education (DHEW), Washington, D.C. (RMQ66000)

NO..... G OEG-9-72-0154(280)

AV..... National Dissemination and Assessment Center, 7703 North Lamar Boulevard, Austin, Texas 78752 (set of 7 $3.50); ERIC Document Reproduction Service, P.O. Box 190, Arlington, Virginia 22210 ($1.58; microfiche $0.76; ED108495)

NT..... p. 63-82.

DE..... Bilingual Education; *Bilingual Teachers; Cognitive Processes; Cultural Differences; Cultural Pluralism; Curriculum Planning; Educational Change; Educational Planning; Individualized Instruction; *Teaching Guides; *Teaching Methods; *Teaching Styles; *Cognitive Style; Teacher Education Curriculum

ID..... Field Independence; Field Sensitivity

AB..... This teaching manual is one in a set of seven designed for use in bilingual bicultural programs. The purpose of the manual is to acquaint teachers with both field sensitive and field independent teaching strategies and to help them adjust their teaching styles to the learning styles of their students. This objective is considered very important in creating culturally democratic educational environments. The manual begins with a number of exercises which indicate how easily the two teaching strategies can be mastered. Instructions for using field sensitive and field independent teaching strategies are explained, and a rating form for determining success in using either of the two strategies is included. Finally, a discussion of curriculum indicates how the "style" of instructional materials can be identified and, when necessary, altered for use in

field sensitive or field independent teaching.
Observation checklists for both types of strategies are
appended. A manual of self-assessment units accompanies
this series. (AM)

CP..... N

AN..... 000651

ER..... ED111179

TI..... New Approaches to Bilingual, Bicultural Education, Manual 6: Developing Cognitive Flexibility.

YR..... Aug75

AU..... Ramírez, Manuel; Herold, P. Leslie; Castañeda, Alfredo

IN..... National Dissemination and Assessment Center, Austin, Tex.

SN..... Office of Education (DHEW), Washington, D.C. (RMQ66000)

NO..... G OEG-9-72-0154(280)

AV..... National Dissemination and Assessment Center, 7703 North Lamar Boulevard, Austin, Texas 78752 (set of 7 $3.50); ERIC Document Reproduction Service, P.O. Box 190, Arlington, Virginia 22210 ($1.58; microfiche $0.76; ED111179)

NT..... p. 83-91.

DE..... Bilingual Education; Bilingualism; *Biculturalism; *Bilingual Students; Bilingual Teachers; *Cognitive Development; Cognitive Processes; Cultural Differences; Cultural Pluralism; Educational Improvement; Educationally Disadvantaged; Individualized Instruction; Learning Characteristics; Mexican Americans; Programed Materials; Teacher Education; *Teaching Guides; Cognitive Style; Teacher Education Curriculum

AB..... This teaching manual is one in a set of seven (accompanied by a manual of self-assessment units) that have been designed for use in bilingual bicultural programs. The components of the series may be used either individually or together. The subject discussed in this manual is a frontier area of cultural democracy that has far-reaching implications: promoting "bicognitive" development, that is, addressing education to children's potentials for cognitive flexibility as well as linguistic and cultural flexibility. Bicognitive development is held to be an asset for all children, but a necessity for culturally different children in the U.S. public school system, especially Mexican American children. (AM)

CP..... N

AN..... 000652

ER..... ED108494

TI..... New Approaches to Bilingual, Bicultural Education, Manual 7: Concepts and Strategies for Teaching the Mexican American Experience.

YR..... Aug75

AU..... Cortes, Carlos E.

IN..... National Dissemination and Assessment Center, Austin, Tex.

SN..... Office of Education (DHEW), Washington, D.C. (RMQ66000)

NO..... G OEG-9-72-0154(280)

AV..... National Dissemination and Assessment Center, 7703 North Lamar Boulevard, Austin, Texas 78752 (set of 7 $3.50); ERIC Document Reproduction Service, P.O. Box 190, Arlington, Virginia 22210 ($1.58; microfiche $0.76)

NT..... p. 93-103.

DE..... Bilingual Education; *Biculturalism; Bilingual Students; Bilingual Teachers; *Cultural Awareness; Cultural Differences; Cultural Pluralism; Curriculum Development; Curriculum Enrichment; Educational Planning; Ethnic Groups; *Ethnic Studies; *Mexican Americans; Programed Materials; Social Attitudes; Sociocultural Patterns; *Teaching Guides; Teaching Methods; Teacher Education; Teacher Education Curriculum

AB..... This teaching manual is one in a set designed for use in bilingual bicultural programs. The manual discusses ideas for applying the concept of cultural democracy to the school curriculum by incorporating the study of the Mexican American. Six alternative exploratory concepts are suggested as ways of escaping the traditional frames of reference for the Chicano experience and helping to eradicate common misconceptions. The concepts are: (1) a recognition of the influences of the American cultures that existed prior to the arrival of the Europeans on the development of the "Greater America"; (2) the comparative analysis of ethnic experiences; (3) the diversity among Chicanos; (4) the view of society as a problem for Chicanos, rather than Chicanos as a problem for society; (5) an awareness of the history of Mexican Americans; and (6) a recognition of the Chicano people as a whole, not through isolated individual success stories. Teaching strategies and techniques, the use of community resources, and supplementary materials related to these concepts are also suggested. These concepts and strategies can also be adapted to the study of other ethnic groups. A manual of self-assessment units accompanies this series. (AM)

CP..... N

AN..... 000653

ER..... ED111178

TI..... New Approaches to Bilingual, Bicultural Education: Self-Assessment Units.

YR..... Aug75

AU..... Cox, Barbara G.; Ramírez, Manuel; Herold, P. Leslie; Castañeda, Alfredo

IN..... National Dissemination and Assessment Center, Austin, Tex.

SN..... Office of Education (DHEW), Washington, D.C. (RMQ66000)

NO..... G OEG-9-72-0154(280)

AV..... National Dissemination and Assessment Center, 7703 North Lamar Boulevard, Austin, Texas 78752 (set of 7 $3.50); ERIC Document Reproduction Service, P.O. Box 190, Arlington, Virginia 22210 ($3.32; microfiche $0.76; ED111178)

NT..... p. 105-127.

DE..... Bilingual Education; *Bilingual Teachers; Instructional Aids; Measurement Instruments; Multiple Choice Tests; *Programed Materials; *Self Evaluation; Teacher Education; Teacher Evaluation; *Teaching Guides; Tests

AB..... These 21 self-assessment units are intended to accompany the 7 teaching manuals in the set "New Approaches to Bilingual, Bicultural Education." The units consist of three self-administered evaluation instruments for each manual. They are designed both as a review and as a means of emphasizing the important concepts found in the teaching manuals. (AM)

CP..... N

AN..... 000654

TI..... El Camino hacia la buena salud: Guía para el maestro (The Road to Good Health: Teacher s Guide).

YR..... Aug75

AU..... Villarreal, Abelardo; Flores, Salvador; Nichols, Lucille; Sáenz Esther; Lazos, Héctor; De la Peña, Becky; Rivera, Lina R.; Serna, Leonila; Morales, Oscar, ill.; Hill, Patti, ill.

IN..... National Dissemination and Assessment Center, Austin, Tex.; Curriculum Adaptation Network for Bilingual/Bicultural Education, San Antonio, Tex. Southwest Regional Adaptation Center. (BBB11923)

SN..... Office of Education (DHEW), Washington, D.C. (RMQ66000)

LG..... Spanish

AV..... National Dissemination and Assessment Center, 7703 North Lamar Boulevard, Austin, Texas 78752 ($3.00)

NT..... xiv, 143 p.
For accompanying workbook, see 000655.

DE..... *Curriculum Guides; Elementary Education; *Hygiene; Language Instruction; Lesson Plans; Second Language Learning; *Spanish; *Teaching Guides; *Instructional Materials; Health Education; Illustrations

AB..... This Spanish-language teacher's guide consists of eight units: "An Adequate Diet," "Brushing Your Teeth," "A Visit to the Dentist," "Is It Necessary to Sleep?," "Who Can Do Better?," "A Visit to the Doctor," "Resting," and "Bathing." Among the concepts introduced are ideas on why we need to keep our bodies healthy and how we go about doing this. Various lessons and activities are contained within each unit, and a supplement of pertinent black-and-white illustrations is appended. The material is intended for use with children in the primary grades. (DS)

CP..... N

AN..... 000655

TI..... El Camino hacia la buena salud: Cuaderno de ejercicios (The Road to Good Health: Workbook) and Posters.

YR..... Aug75

AU..... Villarreal, Abelardo; Flores, Salvador; Nichols, Lucille; Sáenz, Esther; Lazos, Héctor; Peña, Becky de la; Rivera, Lina R.; Serna, Leonila; Hill, Patti, ill.

IN..... National Dissemination and Assessment Center, Austin, Tex.; Curriculum Adaptation Network for Bilingual/Bicultural Education, San Antonio, Tex. Southwest Regional Adaptation Center. (BBB11923)

SN..... Office of Education (DHEW), Washington, D.C. (RMQ66000)

LG..... Spanish

AV..... National Dissemination and Assessment Center, 7703 North Lamar Boulevard, Austin, Texas 78752 ($1.50)

NT..... 51 p.; 8 posters, color, 14-1/2"x18".
For accompanying teacher's guide, see 000654.

DE..... *Workbooks; Elementary Education; *Hygiene; Language Instruction; Second Language Learning; *Spanish; *Health Education; *Instructional Materials; Illustrations

AB..... The exercises in this illustrated Spanish workbook correspond to the eight units in the accompanying teacher's guide: "An Adequate Diet," "Brushing Your Teeth," "A Visit to the Dentist," "Is It Necessary to Sleep?," "Who Can Do Better?," "A Visit to the Doctor," "Resting," and "Bathing." Eight poster-sized photographs corresponding to the units are also included. (CO)

CP..... N

AN..... 000656

ER..... ED081516

TI..... Information and Materials to Teach the Cultural Heritage of the Mexican-American Child: Grades K-9.

YR..... Feb74

AU..... Gorena, Minerva, comp.; León, José de, ill.

IN..... National Dissemination and Assessment Center, Austin, Tex.; Education Service Center Region 13, Austin, Tex. Title VII Region 13 Bilingual Classroom Project.

SN..... Office of Education (DHEW), Washington, D.C. (RMQ66000)

AV..... National Dissemination and Assessment Center, 7703 North Lamar Boulevard, Austin, Texas 78752 ($7.50); ERIC Document Reproduction Service, P.O. Box 190, Arlington, Virginia 22210 ($14.59; microfiche $0.76; ED081516)

NT..... xiv, 263 p.
Rev. ed.

DE..... Biculturalism; Class Activities; Cultural Background; *Instructional Materials; *Mexican American History; *Mexican Americans; *Resource Guides; Supplementary Reading Materials; Elementary Secondary Education; *Resource Materials; *Cultural Education; Kindergarten; Grade 1; Grade 2; Grade 3; Grade 4; Grade 5; Grade 6; Grade 7; Grade 8; Grade 9

ID..... Texas; Mexico

AB..... Information in this resource guide was gathered in response to teacher requests for supplemental historical and cultural materials for the bilingual classroom. Major sections are: (1) "Historical Background"; (2) "Overview of Mexico"; (3) "Places to See"; (4) "Important Celebrations"; (5) "Arts and Crafts"; (6) "Foods of Mexico"; (7) "Poems, Songs, and Games"; (8) "Dances"; (9) "Legends, Fables, and Stories"; (10) "Mexican Histo-Wall"; (11) "Simple Spanish Vocabulary and Sentences"; and (12) "Units for Teaching Mexican American Cultural Heritage." A bibliography of 14 references, a list of materials used by the Region XIII Bilingual Program, and sources for these materials are also included. (CO)

CP..... N

AN..... 000657

ER..... ED111177

TI..... Resource Material for Bilingual Education.

YR..... Jan73

AU..... Garza, Beatríz de la, ed.

IN..... National Dissemination and Assessment Center, Austin, Tex.; Fort Worth Public Schools, Tex. (XPT27340)

SN..... Office of Education (DHEW), Washington, D.C. (RMQ66000)

LG..... English; Spanish

AV..... National Dissemination and Assessment Center, 7703 North Lamar Boulevard, Austin, Texas 78752 ($5.50); ERIC Document Reproduction Service, P.O. Box 190, Arlington, Virginia 22210 ($8.24; microfiche $0.76)

NT..... v, 164 p.
Rev. ed.

DE..... Classroom Games; Clothing; Color; Food; Health Education; History; Instructional Aids; *Instructional Materials; *Language Enrichment; Letters (Alphabet); Mathematics; Numbers; Plant Identification; Primary Education; *Resource Materials; Safety Education; Science Education; Social Studies; *Spanish; Teacher Developed Materials; *Vocabulary; *Teaching Guides

AB..... This handbook for primary school teachers and aides incorporates a variety of classroom ideas and materials related to bilingual instruction. Written in English and Spanish, the handbook can be used for language enrichment purposes. The material is presented in nine broad areas: (1) days, months, and seasons; (2) colors, letters, and numbers; (3) plants and animals; (4) self, family, and community; (5) food and clothing; (6) holidays and special events; (7) classroom terms and expressions; (8) biographies; and (9) games and stories. Terminology for mathematics, science, social studies, and health and safety has been included to supplement each area of the curriculum. Although no grade-level limitations have been placed on the use of the material, it is suggested that teachers adapt the ideas and activities suitable for their grade level to the curriculum for that grade. (Author/DS)

CP..... N

AN..... 000658

TI..... Au Coeur du vent (Heart of the Wind).

YR..... 78

AU..... Dubé, Normand; Jalbert, Paul, ill.

IN..... National Assessment and Dissemination Center, Cambridge, Mass.

SN..... Office of Education (DHEW), Washington, D.C. (RMQ66000)

LG..... French

AV..... National Assessment and Dissemination Center, 49 Washington Avenue, Cambridge, Massachusetts 02140 ($2.50)

NT..... vi, 96 p.

DE..... *French; *Poetry; Folk Culture; French Literature; *Instructional Materials; Curriculum Enrichment; Modern Language Curriculum; Secondary Education; *Reading Materials

ID..... *Franco Americans

AB..... This collection of 54 French poems focuses on the Franco-American experience in New England. Black-and-white illustrations supplement the text. French-speaking junior or senior high school students are the intended audience, but this volume could also be used by English-speaking students studying French at the advanced level. (SH)

CP..... N

AN..... 000659

TI..... Un Niño llamado Manuel: Lectura en español, educación primaria (A Boy Named Manuel: Reading in Spanish, Primary Education).

YR..... Mar74

AU..... Zayas, Madeline; Canals, Dhoel, photo.

IN..... National Dissemination and Assessment Center, Austin, Tex.; Curriculum Adaptation Network for Bilingual/Bicultural Education, Bronx, N.Y. Northeast Regional Adaptation Center. (BBB11922)

SN..... Office of Education (DHEW), Washington, D.C. (RMQ66000); William Randolph Hearst Foundation, Los Angeles, Calif. (BBB11728)

LG..... Spanish

AV..... National Dissemination and Assessment Center, 7703 North Lamar Boulevard, Austin, Texas 78752 (set of English and Spanish versions $1.75); ERIC Document Reproduction Service, P.O. Box 190, Arlington, Virginia 22210 (set of English and Spanish versions $5.70; microfiche $0.76; ED108485)

NT..... ii, 54 p.

DE..... *Instructional Materials; Language Instruction; Primary Education; *Reading Instruction; *Reading Materials; *Spanish; Puerto Ricans; Childrens Books

AB..... This Spanish reader, designed for use in bilingual education programs, tells the story of a young Puerto Rican boy who lives in New York. The story, illustrated with full-page black-and-white photographs, is designed for oral activities with first graders and for reading and comprehension with second and third graders. Bilingual education, nostalgia for one's home country, and community pride are touched on in the story. (CO)

CP..... N

AN..... 000660

ER..... ED084924

TI..... Estudio cultural de Puerto Rico. A Cultural Study of Puerto Rico.

YR..... Sep74

AU..... Santiago, Jorge; Torres, Francisco; Maldonado, Sonia; Deane, Minerva

IN..... National Dissemination and Assessment Center, Austin, Tex.

SN..... Office of Education (DHEW), Washington, D.C. (RMQ66000)

LG..... Spanish

AV..... National Dissemination and Assessment Center, 7703 North Lamar Boulevard, Austin, Texas 78752 ($2.00); ERIC Document Reproduction Service, P.O. Box 190, Arlington, Virginia 22210 ($4.43; microfiche $0.76)

NT..... viii, 83 p.

DE..... Bibliographies; Biculturalism; Educational Resources; Ethnic Groups; Geography; History; *Instructional Materials; Minority Groups; Poetry; *Puerto Rican Culture; Puerto Ricans; *Spanish; Supplementary Textbooks; Secondary Education; *Cultural Education; Cultural Awareness

ID..... *Puerto Rico

AB..... This book presents resource materials for teaching the cultural heritage of the Puerto Rican student. It includes biographical sketches of outstanding figures in Puerto Rican history from colonial times to the 20th century. It also contains descriptions of national festivities and holidays, as well as poetry representative of Puerto Rican literature. A list of evaluation exercises for the student follows each reading selection. A bibliography of six citations is included. (CO)

CP..... N

AN..... 000664

ER..... ED109903

TI..... Handbook on Mexico for Elementary and Secondary Teachers.

YR..... Aug73

AU..... Gill, Clark C.; Mellenbruch, Julia K.; Finer, Neal, ill.

IN..... National Dissemination and Assessment Center, Austin, Tex.

SN..... Office of Education (DHEW), Washington, D.C. (RMQ66000)

NO..... G OEG-0-70-0402(824)

AV..... National Dissemination and Assessment Center, 7703 North Lamar Boulevard, Austin, Texas 78752 (ISBN 0-89417-071-6; $2.50)

NT..... viii, 110 p.
Rev. ed.

DE..... Cultural Awareness; Bibliographies; Biculturalism; Social Studies; *Cultural Education; Cultural Background; Curriculum Development; *Curriculum Guides; Elementary Secondary Education; *Instructional Materials; History; Mexican Americans; Mexicans; Resource Materials; Social Studies; *Teaching Guides; *Latin American Culture; Cross Cultural Studies; Comparative Analysis

ID..... *Mexico

AB..... This guide presents a rationale for the study of the Mexican culture and develops ways of fitting this cultural education into the elementary and secondary curriculum. Mexico is chosen because: (1) it is a neighboring country representing the Latin America cultural area, (2) it is an emerging nation with many descendants in the U.S., and (3) much up-to-date material on Mexico is available. Key ideas about Mexico are developed around the topics of physical environment, historical background, contemporary culture, society, and the political and economic situation. Teaching suggestions for the implementation of each of these key ideas are provided, including: comparative discussions of a particular aspect of Spanish and English American culture; debates on historical issues and social and political problems; and studies of the literature, folklore, and music of Mexico. A list is provided of bibliographies, Spanish books, materials sources, and curriculum guide materials. Geographical information and some important dates are supplied in an appendix. (Author/DS)

CP..... N

AN..... 000665

ER..... ED108483

TI..... Forming an Estudiantina and Symbols of Music Notation.

YR..... Jul73

AU..... Horne, Anne

IN..... National Dissemination and Assessment Center, Austin, Tex.; Calexico Intercultural Design, Calif.

SN..... Office of Education (DHEW), Washington, D.C. (RMQ66000)

LG..... English; Spanish

AV..... National Dissemination and Assessment Center, 7703 North
Lamar Boulevard, Austin, Texas 78752 ($3.00); ERIC
Document Reproduction Service, Box 190, Arlington,
Virginia 22210 ($4.43; microfiche $0.76)

NT..... vi, 95 p.

DE..... *Curriculum Guides; *Instructional Materials; Learning
Activities; *Music Activities; *Music Education; Music
Reading; Resource Materials; *Spanish; *Teaching Guides;
Teaching Methods; Vocabulary; Singing; Musical
Instruments

AB..... This guide for music teachers in Spanish/English
bilingual education presents the basic musical vocabulary
in English and Spanish and is adaptable to all levels.
The units cover: forming a student musical group, or
estudiantina, including costs and method of instruction;
symbols of musical notation and definition of musical
terms in English and Spanish; simple songs for beginners,
also in both languages; and costume sketches. (Author/AM)

CP..... N

AN..... 000666

TI..... La Música del sol: Un Cuento náhuatl y una obra de
teatro (The Music of the Sun: A Nahuatl Story and Play).

YR..... 75

AU..... González, Josué M.; Pérez, Mary L.; Santiago, Nick M.;
González, Josué M., ill.; Pérez, Mary L., ill.

IN..... National Dissemination and Assessment Center, Austin,
Tex.; Curriculum Adaptation Network for
Bilingual/Bicultural Education. San Diego, Calif. Far
West Regional Adaptation Center. (BBB11920)

SN..... Office of Education (DHEW), Washington, D.C. (RMQ66000);
William Randolph Hearst Foundation, Los Angeles, Calif.
(BBB11728)

LG..... English; Spanish

AV..... National Dissemination and Assessment Center, 7703 North
Lamar Boulevard, Austin, Texas 78752 (ISBN 0-89417-035-X;
$1.30 with teacher's guide); ERIC Document Reproduction
Service, P.O. Box 190, Arlington, Virginia 22210 (with
teacher's guide $3.32; microfiche $0.76; ED108491)

NT..... 32 p.
Rev. ed.
For accompanying teacher's guide, see 000667.

DE..... Beginning Reading; *Drama; Elementary Education;
*Legends; Mexican Americans; *Reading Materials;
*Spanish; Story Reading; *Folk Culture

ID..... Nahuatl

AB..... An Aztec legend about the bringing of music to the earth is presented as a story and as a play. The story version is offered in Spanish; the play is in Spanish and English. The material contained in the story and the play may be presented to prekindergarten through sixth grade students. (CO)

CP..... N

AN..... 000667

TI..... La Música del sol (The Music of the Sun): Teacher's Guide.

YR..... Jul/5

AU..... Santiago, Nick M.; Sánchez de la Vega-Lockler, Elsa, ed.

IN..... National Dissemination and Assessment Center, Austin, Tex.; Curriculum Adaptation Network for Bilingual/Bicultural Education, San Diego, Calif. Far West Regional Adaptation Center. (BBB11920)

SN..... Office of Education (DHEW), Washington, D.C. (RMQ66000); William Randolph Hearst Foundation, Los Angeles, Calif. (BBB11728)

AV..... National Dissemination and Assessment Center, 7703 North Lamar Boulevard, Austin, Texas 78752 ($1.30 with reader); ERIC Document Reproduction Service, P.O. Box 190, Arlington, Virginia 22210 (with reader $3.32; microfiche $0.76; ED108491)

NT..... 5 p.
Rev. ed.
For accompanying reader, see 000666.

DE... *Teaching Guides; *Folk Culture; Beginning Reading; *Drama; Elementary Education; *Legends; Reading Materials; Story Reading; *Spanish

ID..... Nahuatl

AB..... This teacher's guide accompanies a reader which contains an Aztec legend about the bringing of music to the earth. The legend is presented as a story (in Spanish) and as a play (in Spanish and English). The teacher's guide suggests activities and teaching methods for presenting the material to prekindergarten through sixth grade students. (CO)

CP..... N

AN..... 000668

ER..... ED123899

TI..... Spanish as a Second Language Units, Grade 6.

YR..... Feb76

AU..... Galindo, Angelina; Sánchez de la Vega-Lockler, Elsa, ed.; Harper, Pam, ed.; Appleby, Larry, ill.

IN..... National Dissemination and Assessment Center, Austin, Tex.; Fort Worth Independent School District, Tex. Bilingual Education Program. (BBB13287)

SN..... Office of Education (DHEW), Washington, D.C. (RMQ66000)

AV..... National Dissemination and Assessment Center, 7703 North Lamar Boulevard, Austin, Texas 78752 ($3.00); ERIC Document Reproduction Service, P.O. Box 190, Arlington, Virginia 22210 ($6.01; microfiche $0.83)

NT..... 115 p.

DE..... Cultural Awareness; Curriculum Guides; Elementary Education; Grade 6; *Fles Materials; *Instructional Materials; *Language Instruction; Language Skills; Learning Activities; *Lesson Plans; Second Language Learning; *Spanish; Teaching Guides; Teaching Methods; Vocabulary; Learning Activities

AB..... This guide provides 11 basic lessons for the English-monolingual and English-dominant 6th grader. It may also be adapted for other grade levels. The guide may be used independently as introductory material or as a supplement to other Spanish-as-a-second-language programs. The units are designed to develop first the listening and speaking skills, then the reading and writing skills, by utilizing a culturally relevant approach. The activities are intended to develop an understanding in English-speaking students of the major patterns, traditions, and values of many of the Spanish-speaking people around them. A lesson may take from 1 to 3 weeks. A typical lesson includes: notes to the teacher, concept, objective stated in behavioral terms, vocabulary, a list of materials needed and directions for their use, activities, evaluation, and optional activities. (Author/DS)

CP..... N

AN..... 000669

TI..... Manual de pronunciación del español para personas de habla inglesa (Spanish Pronunciation Manual for Speakers of English).

YR..... 77

AU..... Curt, Carmen Judith Nine

IN..... Northeast Center for Curriculum Development, Bronx, N.Y.

SN..... Office of Education (DHEW), Washington, D.C. (RMQ66000)

LG..... Spanish

AV..... National Assessment and Dissemination Center, 49 Washington Avenue, Cambridge, Massachusetts 02140

NT..... ix, 77 p.

DE..... *Spanish; *Pronunciation; *Pronunciation Instruction;
*Instructional Materials; Language Instruction; Phonemes;
Consonants; Vowels; Intonation; Stress (Phonology);
Pattern Drills (Language)

AB..... This manual is designed for use with learners of Spanish
at the elementary or advanced level who need help with
pronunciation. It can be used as a semester course by
itself or to supplement existing courses in Spanish
grammar. Puerto Rican Spanish is the specific variety
covered. The 18 lessons cover the sounds of individual
letters, accent, and intonation. The final lesson
provides special exercises for Puerto Rican students. A
bibliography of eight citations is included. (CO)

CP..... Y

AN..... 000670

TI..... Le Bois maudit (The Haunted Woods).

YR..... [7?]

AU..... Pipyn, Michel; Ganim, Barbara, ill.; Aqua, Karen, ill.

IN..... National Materials Development Center for French,
Bedford, N.H.

SN..... Office of Education (DHEW), Washington, D.C. (RMQ66000)

LG..... French

AV..... National Dissemination and Assessment Center, 7703 North
Lamar Boulevard, Austin, Texas 78752 ($7.00)

NT..... 52 p.

DE..... *French; Elementary Education; *Reading Materials;
*Reading Instruction; *Instructional Materials; Childrens
Literature; Grade 5; Grade 6; *Childrens Books

AB..... Designed for use in a bilingual program at the elementary
level, this French reader is divided into two parts: the
story and a dictionary of pictures. Color illustrations
are used in the dictionary and fill each page of the
story. (CO)

CP..... N

AN..... 000671

TI..... Ti-Jean et Colette (Ti-Jean and Colette).

YR..... 78

AU..... Dugas, Donald; Jackson, Kris, ill.

IN..... National Materials Development Center for French,
Bedford, N.H.

SN..... Office of Education (DHEW), Washington, D.C. (RMQ66000)

LG..... French

AV..... National Assessment and Dissemination Center, 49
Washington Avenue, Cambridge, Massachusetts 02140 ($1.25)

NT..... [20] p.

DE..... Primary Education; *French; *Reading Materials;
*Instructional Materials; *Reading Instruction; Childrens
Literature; Grade 2; Grade 3; *Childrens Books

AB..... Designed for use in a bilingual program at the primary
level, this French reader about two frogs emphasises
positive aspects of being bilingual. The text is
illustrated with black-and-white drawings. (CO)

CP..... N

AN..... 000672

TI..... La Gocciolina (The Little Drop of Water).

YR..... [7?]

AU..... Palandra, Maria; Ramos Nieves, Ernesto, ill.

IN..... Northeast Center for Curriculum Development, Bronx, N.Y.
(BBB17015)

SN..... Office of Education (DHEW), Washington, D.C. (RMQ66000)

LG..... Italian

AV..... National Assessment and Dissemination Center, 49
Washington Avenue, Cambridge, Massachusetts 02140 ($1.50)

NT..... 23 p.
For Spanish and Greek versions, see 000673-674.

DE..... Primary Education; *Italian; *Reading Materials; *Reading
Instruction; *Instructional Materials; Childrens
Literature; Grade 1; Grade 2; Grade 3; *Childrens Books

AB..... Color illustrations accompany this story about a "drop of
water" which comes to life and travels through the water
cycle of evaporation, condensation, and rain. It is
designed for use in Italian bilingual classes at the
primary level. (CO)

CP..... N

AN..... 000673

TI..... La Gotita de agua (The Little Drop of Water).

YR..... [7?]

AU..... Palandra, Maria; Puigdollers, Carmen, trans.; Ramos
Nieves, Ernesto, ill.

IN..... Northeast Center for Curriculum Development, Bronx, N.Y.
       (BBB17015)

SN..... Office of Education (DHEW), Washington, D.C. (RMQ66000)

LG..... Spanish

AV..... National Assessment and Dissemination Center, 49
       Washington Avenue, Cambridge, Massachusetts 02140 ($1.50)

NT..... 23 p.
       For Italian and Greek versions, see 000672 and 674.

DE..... Primary Education; *Spanish; *Reading Materials; *Reading
       Instruction; *Instructional Materials; Childrens
       Literature; Grade 1; Grade 2; Grade 3; *Childrens Books

AB..... Color illustrations accompany this story about a "drop of
       water" which comes to life and travels through the water
       cycle of evaporation, condensation, and rain. It is
       designed for use in Spanish bilingual classes at the
       primary level. (CO)

CP..... N

AN..... 000674

TI..... Mia mikre stagona (The Little Drop of Water).

YR..... [7?]

AU..... Palandra, Maria; Spiridakis, Eugenia, trans.; Ramos
       Nieves, Ernesto J., ill.

IN..... Northeast Center for Curriculum Development, Bronx, N.Y.
       (BBB17015)

SN..... Office of Education (DHEW), Washington, D.C. (RMQ66000)

LG..... Greek

AV..... National Assessment and Dissemination Center, 49
       Washington Avenue, Cambridge, Massachusetts 02140 ($1.50)

NT..... 23 p.
       For Spanish and Italian versions, see 000672-673.

DE..... Primary Education; *Greek; *Reading Materials; *Reading
       Instruction; *Instructional Materials; Childrens
       Literature; Grade 1; Grade 2; Grade 3; *Childrens Books

AB..... Color illustrations accompany this story about a "drop of
       water" which comes to life and travels through the water
       cycle of evaporation, condensation, and rain. It is
       designed for use in Greek bilingual classes at the
       primary level. (CO)

CP..... N

AN..... 000675

TI..... Taxidi gyro ston cosmo (Trip Around the World).

YR..... 78

AU..... Spiridakis, Eugenia; Marinos, Giorgos, ill.

IN..... Northeast Center for Curriculum Development, Bronx, N.Y. (BBB17015)

SN..... Office of Education (DHEW), Washington, D.C. (RMQ66000)

LG..... Greek

AV..... National Assessment and Dissemination Center, 49 Washington Avenue, Cambridge, Massachusetts 02140 ($1.00)

NT..... 11 p.

DE..... *Greek; *Reading Materials; *Reading Instruction; *Instructional Materials; Primary Education; *Childrens Books; Childrens Literature; Grade 1; Grade 2; Grade 3; Kindergarten

AB..... Children in other lands figure prominently in the Greek lyrics included in this reader designed for use in bilingual classes at the primary level. Black-and-white illustrations accompany the text. (CO)

CP..... Y

AN..... 000676

TI..... Phengaraki moi lampro (My Bright Moon).

YR..... 78

AU..... Spiridakis, Eugenia; Marinos, Giorgos, ill.

IN..... Northeast Center for Curriculum Development, Bronx, N.Y. (BBB17015)

SN..... Office of Education (DHEW), Washington, D.C. (RMQ66000)

LG..... Greek

AV..... National Assessment and Dissemination Center, 49 Washington Avenue, Cambridge, Massachusetts 02140 ($1.25)

NT..... 15 p.

DE..... *Greek; *Reading Materials; *Reading Instruction; *Instructional Materials; Primary Education; *Childrens Books; Childrens Literature; Grade 1; Kindergarten

AB..... The Greek nursery rhyme "My Bright Moon," about a young Greek boy's determination to attend night school, is retold here in story form. The black-and-white illustrated reader is designed for use in bilingual classes at the primary level. (CO)

CP..... Y

AN..... 000677

TI..... Kathe proi (Every Morning).

YR..... 78

AU..... Spiridakis, Eugenia; Marinos, Giorgos, ill.

IN..... Northeast Center for Curriculum Development, Bronx, N.Y. (BBB17015)

SN..... Office of Education (DHEW), Washington, D.C. (RMQ66000)

LG..... Greek

AV..... National Assessment and Dissemination Center, 49 Washington Avenue, Cambridge, Massachusetts 02140 ($1.25)

NT..... 16 p.

DE..... *Greek; *Reading Materials; *Reading Instruction; *Instructional Materials; Primary Education; *Childrens Books; Childrens Literature; Grade 1; Kindergarten

AB..... Rhymes describe early morning routines from first awakening to arrival at school in this Greek reader designed for use in bilingual classes at the primary level. Black-and-white illustrations complement the story. (CO)

CP..... Y

AN..... 000678

TI..... Tesoros de mi raza (Treasures of My Race).

SE..... Programa de lectura y enseñanza del lenguaje, Unidad A (Reading and Teaching Program for Language, Unit A) (Series).

YR..... Aug75

IN..... Edgewood Independent School District, San Antonio, Tex. (XPT23584); National Dissemination and Assessment Center, Austin, Tex.

SN..... Office of Education (DHEW), Washington, D.C. (RMQ66000)

LG..... Spanish

AV..... National Dissemination and Assessment Center, 7703 North Lamar Boulevard, Austin, Texas 78752 ($3.50)

NT..... 87 p.
For accompanying teacher's guide and workbook, see 000679-680.

DE..... Childrens Literature; *Spanish; *Reading Materials; Cultural Education; Biculturalism; *Language Arts; *Reading Instruction; Cultural Awareness; Elementary Secondary Education; *Instructional Materials; Language Skills; Language Proficiency; Mexican Americans; Spanish Americans; Vocabulary; Grammar; Punctuation; Sentences; Verbs; Form Classes (Language); Ungraded Curriculum; Childrens Books; *Short Stories

ID..... Songs

AB..... Part of an 8-unit, ungraded Spanish language arts and reading program that can be used in grades 4 through 12, this black-and-white illustrated reader contains 12 stories and 2 songs in Spanish which present aspects of history, culture, and contemporary experiences of special relevance to the Mexican American student. Among the grammatical concepts presented or reviewed in this unit are: (1) conjugation of present, past, and future verbs; (2) punctuation; (3) declarative, interrogative, and exclamatory sentences; (4) possessive and demonstrative adjectives and pronouns; and (5) antonyms and synonyms. A Spanish-Spanish vocabulary is appended. (CO)

CP..... N

AN..... 000679

TI..... Tesoros de mi raza: Guía para el maestro (Treasures of My Race: Teacher's Guide).

SE..... Programa de lectura y enseñanza del lenguaje, Unidad A (Reading and Teaching Program for Language, Unit A) (Series).

YR..... Aug76

IN..... Edgewood Independent School District, San Antonio, Tex. (XPT23584); National Dissemination and Assessment Center, Austin, Tex.

SN..... Office of Education (DHEW), Washington, D.C. (RMQ66000)

LG..... Spanish

AV..... National Dissemination and Assessment Center, 7703 North Lamar Boulevard, Austin, Texas 78752 (ISBN 0-89417-062-7; $3.00)

NT..... 88 p.
Rev. ed.
For accompanying reader and workbook, see 000678 and 680.

DE..... Biculturalism; Cultural Awareness; Cultural Education; Elementary Secondary Education; Grammar; *Instructional Materials; *Language Arts; Language Proficiency; Language Skills; Learning Activities; Mexican Americans; *Reading Instruction; Sociocultural Patterns; *Spanish; Student Evaluation; *Teaching Guides; Teaching Methods; Vocabulary; Ungraded Curriculum

AB..... Part of an 8-unit, ungraded Spanish language arts and reading program that can be used in grades 4 through 12, this teacher's manual is matched to a reader containing 12 stories and 2 songs in Spanish which present aspects of history, culture, and contemporary experiences of special relevance to the Mexican American student. Among the grammatical concepts presented or reviewed in this unit are: (1) conjugation of verbs in the present, past, and future tense; (2) the use of punctuation signs; (3) declarative, interrogative, and exclamatory sentences; (4) possessive and demonstrative adjectives and pronouns; and (5) antonyms and synonyms. For each story/lesson, the teacher's guide discusses theme, objectives, materials, preparation, directed study, language skills exercises and enrichment activities, and evaluation. A glossary of grammatical terms, a list of new words, and a subject index are appended. (CO)

CP..... N

AN..... 000680

TI..... Tesoros de mi raza: Cuaderno de trabajo (Treasures of My Race: Workbook).

SE..... Programa de lectura y enseñanza del lenguaje, Unidad A (Reading and Teaching Program for Language, Unit A) (Series).

YR..... Aug76

IN..... Edgewood Independent School District, San Antonio, Tex. (XPT23584); National Dissemination and Assessment Center, Austin, Tex.

SN..... Office of Education (DHEW), Washington, D.C. (RMQ66000)

LG..... Spanish

AV..... National Dissemination and Assessment Center, 7703 North Lamar Boulevard, Austin, Texas 78752 (ISBN 0-89417-063-5; $2.00)

NT..... 88 p.
Rev. ed.
For accompanying reader and teacher's guide, see 000678-679.

DE..... Elementary Secondary Education; Grammar; *Instructional Materials; *Language Arts; Language Patterns; Language Proficiency; Language Skills; Reading Comprehension; Reading Instruction; Semantics; *Spanish; Vocabulary; *Workbooks; Ungraded Curriculum; *Pattern Drills (Language)

AB..... Part of an 8-unit, ungraded Spanish language arts and reading program that can be used in grades 4 through 12, this workbook contains ditto masters for exercises, tests, and activities to be completed by the student and is organized according to the 12 stories and 2 songs found in the companion reader. Workbook lessons include questions about the stories and exercises in vocabulary, spelling, composition, and grammar. (CO)

CP..... N

AN..... 000681

ER..... ED148165

TI..... Raza de tesoros (Race of Treasures).

SE..... Programa de lectura y enseñanza del lenguaje, Unidad B (Reading and Teaching Program for Language, Unit B) (Series).

YR..... Apr76

IN..... Edgewood Independent School District, San Antonio, Tex. (XPT23584); National Dissemination and Assessment Center, Austin, Tex.

SN..... Office of Education (DHEW), Washington, D.C. (RMQ66000)

LG..... Spanish

AV..... National Dissemination and Assessment Center, 7703 North Lamar Boulevard, Austin, Texas 78752 ($3.50); ERIC Document Reproduction Service, P.O. Box 190, Arlington, Virginia 22210 ($4.67; microfiche $0.83; ED148165)

NT..... 83 p.
For accompanying teacher's guide and workbook, see 000682-683.

DE..... Biculturalism; Childrens Literature; Cultural Awareness; Cultural Education; Elementary Secondary Education; *Instructional Materials; *Language Arts; Language Proficiency; Language Skills; Mexican American History; Mexican Americans; *Reading Instruction; *Reading Materials; Sociocultural Patterns; *Spanish; Spanish Americans; Vocabulary; *Short Stories; Grammar; Verbs; Form Classes (Language); Diacritical Marking; Paragraph Composition; Sentences; Creative Writing; Ungraded Curriculum; Childrens Books

AB..... This Spanish reader is part of an ungraded language arts and reading program that can be used in classes from upper elementary through high school. The program is designed around 11 stories which present aspects of history, culture, and experiences of special relevance to the Mexican American student. Among the grammatical concepts presented or reviewed in the unit are: (1) conjugation of verbs in the present, past, and future; (2) antonyms and synonyms; (3) diphthongs; (4) orthographic and prosodic accents; (5) prefixes and suffixes; (6) compound words; (7) the organization of a paragraph; (8) topic sentences; (9) cause and effect; (10) simile; and (11) personification. The reader contains a Spanish-Spanish vocabulary list and is illustrated with black-and-white line drawings. (CO)

CP..... N

AN..... 000682

ER..... ED148166

TI..... Raza de tesoros: Guía para el maestro (Race of Treasures: Teacher's Guide).

SE..... Programa de lectura y enseñanza del lenguaje, Unidad B (Reading and Teaching Program for Language, Unit B) (Series).

YR..... Aug76

IN..... Edgewood Independent School District, San Antonio, Tex. (XPT23584); National Dissemination and Assessment Center, Austin, Tex.

SN..... Office of Education (DHEW), Washington, D.C. (RMQ66000)

LG..... Spanish

AV..... National Dissemination and Assessment Center, 7703 North Lamar Boulevard, Austin, Texas 78752 ($3.00); ERIC Document Reproduction Service, P.O. Box 190, Arlington, Virginia 22210 ($4.67; microfiche $0.83)

NT..... 86 p.
For accompanying reader and workbook, see 000681 and 683.

DE..... Biculturalism; Cultural Awareness; Cultural Education; Elementary Secondary Education; Grammar; *Instructional Materials; *Language Arts; Language Proficiency; Language Skills; Learning Activities; Mexican Americans; *Reading Instruction; Sociocultural Patterns; *Spanish; Student Evaluation; *Teaching Guides; Teaching Methods; Vocabulary; Ungraded Curriculum

AB..... This teacher's guide is part of an ungraded language arts and reading program that can be used in classes from upper elementary through high school. The program is designed around 11 stories contained in the companion reader which present aspects of history, culture, and present-day experiences of special relevance to the Mexican American student. Among the grammatical concepts presented or reviewed in the unit are: (1) conjugation of verbs in the present, past, and future; (2) antonyms and synonyms; (3) diphthongs; (4) orthographic and prosodic accents; (5) prefixes and suffixes; (6) compound words; (7) paragraph organization; (8) topic sentences; (9) cause and effect; (10) simile; and (11) personification. The teacher's guide contains instructional suggestions for each lesson relating to materials, preparing students for reading, directed reading (both silent and oral), language skills, exercises, enrichment activities, and evaluation. The guide also contains suggestions for games, as well as a glossary of grammatical terms and a list of the new vocabulary presented in the stories. (CO)

CP..... N

AN.....	000683
ER.....	ED148167
TI.....	Raza de tesoros: Cuaderno de trabajo (Race of Treasures: Workbook).
SE.....	Programa de lectura y enseñanza del lenguaje, Unidad B (Reading and Teaching Program for Language, Unit B) (Series).
YR.....	Aug76
IN.....	Edgewood Independent School District, San Antonio, Tex. (XPT23584); National Dissemination and Assessment Center, Austin, Tex.
SN.....	Office of Education (DHEW), Washington, D.C. (RMQ66000)
LG.....	Spanish
AV.....	National Dissemination and Assessment Center, 7703 North Lamar Boulevard, Austin, Texas 78752 ($2.00); ERIC Document Reproduction Service, P.O. Box 190, Arlington, Virginia 22210 ($4.67; microfiche $0.83)
NT.....	72 p. For accompanying reader and teacher's guide, see 000681-682.
DE.....	Elementary Secondary Education; Grammar; *Instructional Materials; *Language Arts; Language Patterns; Language Proficiency; Language Skills; Reading Comprehension; Reading Instruction; Semantics; *Spanish; Vocabulary; *Workbooks; Ungraded Curriculum; *Pattern Drills (Language)
AB.....	Part of un ungraded Spanish language arts and reading program that can be used in classes from upper elementary through high school, this workbook contains ditto masters for exercises, tests, and activities to be completed by the student. The 11 workbook lessons, each corresponding to a story in the companion reader, include questions about the stories and exercises in vocabulary, spelling, composition, and grammar. (CO)
CP.....	N

AN.....	000684
TI.....	Escaparate (Showcase).
SE.....	Programa de lectura y enseñanza del lenguaje, Unidad C (Reading and Teaching Program for Language, Unit C) (Series).
YR.....	Apr78

AU..... Santos, Richard, comp.; Pérez, Jimmy, ill.

IN..... Edgewood Independent School District, San Antonio, Tex.
(XPT23584); National Dissemination and Assessment Center,
Austin, Tex.

SN..... Office of Education (DHEW), Washington, D.C. (RMQ66000)

LG..... Spanish

AV..... National Dissemination and Assessment Center, 7703 North
Lamar Boulevard, Austin, Texas 78752 (ISBN
0-89417-351-0; $3.50)

NT..... 154 p.
For accompanying teacher's guide and workbook, see 000685-686.

DE..... Biculturalism; Childrens Literature; Cultural Awareness;
Cultural Education; Elementary Secondary Education;
*Instructional Materials; *Language Arts; Language
Proficiency; Language Skills; Mexican American History;
Mexican Americans; *Reading Instruction; *Reading
Materials; Sociocultural Patterns; *Spanish; Spanish
Americans; Spelling; Diacritical Marking; Form Classes
(Language); Paragraph Composition; Sentences; Creative
Writing; Letters (Correspondence); Adverbs; Literary
Conventions; Vocabulary; Grammar; Ungraded Curriculum

AB..... Part of an 8-unit, ungraded Spanish language arts and
reading program that can be used in grades 4-12, this
black-and-white illustrated reader contains 11 stories in
Spanish which present aspects of history, culture, and
contemporary experience of special relevance to the
Mexican American student. Among the grammatical concepts
presented or reviewed in this unit are: (1) consonant
clusters, (2) diphthongs, (3) orthographic and prosodic
accents, (4) prefixes and suffixes, (5) compound words,
(6) paragraph organization, (7) topic sentences, (8)
cause and effect, (9) simile, (10) personification, (11)
letter writing, (12) adverbs, and (13) literary forms. A
Spanish-Spanish vocabulary is appended. (CO)

CP..... N

AN..... 000685

TI..... Escaparate: Guía para el maestro (Showcase: Teacher's
Guide).

SE..... Programa de lectura y enseñanza del lenguaje, Unidad C
(Reading and Teaching Program for Language, Unit C)
(Series).

YR..... Apr78

IN..... Edgewood Independent School District, San Antonio, Tex.
(XPT23584); National Dissemination and Assessment Center,
Austin, Tex.

SN..... Office of Education (DHEW), Washington, D.C. (RMQ66000)

LG..... Spanish

AV..... National Dissemination and Assessment Center, 7703 North Lamar Boulevard, Austin, Texas 78752 (ISBN 0-89417-349-9; $3.00)

NT..... 88 p.
For accompanying reader and workbook, see 000684 and 686.

DE..... Biculturalism; Cultural Awareness; Cultural Education; Elementary Secondary Education; Grammar; *Instructional Materials; *Language Arts; Language Proficiency; Language Skills; Learning Activities; Mexican Americans; *Reading Instruction; Sociocultural Patterns; *Spanish; Student Evaluation; *Teaching Guides; Teaching Methods; Vocabulary; Ungraded Curriculum

AB..... Part of an 8-unit, ungraded Spanish language arts and reading program that can be used in grades 4 through 12, this teacher's manual is matched to a reader containing 11 stories in Spanish which present aspects of history, culture, and contemporary experience of special relevance to the Mexican American student. Among the grammatical concepts presented or reviewed in this unit are: (1) consonant clusters, (2) diphthongs, (3) orthographic and prosodic accents, (4) prefixes and suffixes, (5) compound words, (6) paragraph organization, (7) topic sentences, (8) cause and effect, (9) simile, (10) personification, (11) letter writing, (12) adverbs, and (13) literary forms. For each story/lesson, the teacher's guide discusses themes, objectives, materials, preparation, directed study, language skills exercises and enrichment activities, and evaluation. A glossary, a Spanish-Spanish vocabulary, and a subject index are appended. (CO)

CP..... N

AN..... 000686

TI..... Escaparate: Cuaderno de trabajo (Showcase: Workbook).

SE..... Programa de lectura y enseñanza del lenguaje, Unidad C (Reading and Teaching Program for Language, Unit C) (Series).

YR..... Apr78

IN..... Edgewood Independent School District, San Antonio, Tex. (XPT23584); National Dissemination and Assessment Center, Austin, Tex.

SN..... Office of Education (DHEW), Washington, D.C. (RMQ66000)

LG..... Spanish

AV..... National Dissemination and Assessment Center, 7703 North Lamar Boulevard, Austin, Texas 78752 (ISBN 0-89417-350-2; $2.00)

NT..... 80 p.
For accompanying reader and teacher's guide, see 000684-685.

DE..... Elementary Secondary Education; Grammar; *Instructional Materials; *Language Arts; Language Patterns; Language

Proficiency; Language Skills; Reading Comprehension;
Reading Instruction; Semantics; *Spanish; Vocabulary;
Ungraded Curriculum; *Workbooks; *Pattern Drills
(Language)

AB..... Part of an 8-unit, ungraded Spanish language arts and
reading program that can be used in grades 4 through 12,
this workbook contains ditto masters for exercises,
tests, and activities to be completed by the student and
is organized according to the 11 Spanish stories found in
the companion reader. Workbook lessons include questions
about the stories and exercises in vocabulary, spelling,
composition, and grammar. (CO)

CP..... N

AN..... 000687

TI..... Gennarino il pizzaiolo (Gennarino the Pizza Maker).

YR..... 78

AU..... Cardone, Romolo; Impiglia, Giancarlo, ill.

IN..... Northeast Center for Curriculum Development, Bronx, N.Y.;
National Assessment and Dissemination Center, Cambridge,
Mass.

SN..... Office of Education (DHEW), Washington, D.C. (RMQ66000)

LG..... Italian

AV..... National Assessment and Dissemination Center, 49
Washington Avenue, Cambridge, Massachusetts 02140
($1.25)

NT..... 16 p.

DE..... *Italian; *Reading Materials; Reading Instruction;
*Instructional Materials; Primary Education; Grade 1;
Kindergarten; *Childrens Books; *Language Instruction

AB..... The story of how pizza was invented is told in this
Italian reader designed for use in a bilingual class at
the primary level. Black-and-white illustrations
accompany the text. (CO)

CP..... Y

AN..... 000688

TI..... Dalla a alla z: L'alfabeto dei bambini (From A to Z:
Children's Alphabet).

YR..... 78

AU..... Palandra, Maria; Cardone, Romolo; Impiglia, Giancarlo,
ill.

IN..... Northeast Center for Curriculum Development, Bronx, N.Y.; National Assessment and Dissemination Center, Cambridge, Mass.

SN..... Office of Education (DHEW), Washington, D.C. (RMQ66000)

LG..... Italian

AV..... National Assessment and Dissemination Center, 49 Washington Avenue, Cambridge, Massachusetts 02140 ($1.25)

NT..... iii, 43 p.

DE..... *Italian; *Reading Instruction; *Instructional Materials; Primary Education; Grade 1; Kindergarten; Childrens Books; *Letters (Alphabet); *Language Instruction

AB..... Each letter of the Italian alphabet is presented in upper and lower case and accompanied by a black-and-white illustration and a single-sentence caption. Designed for use in bilingual Italian classes at the primary level, this alphabet book includes a teacher's introduction in Italian. (CO)

CP..... Y

AN..... 000689

TI..... Girotondo dei numeri (Ring of Numbers).

YR..... 78

AU..... Palandra, Maria; Impiglia, Giancarlo, ill.; Esposito, Antonio, mus.

IN..... Northeast Center For Curriculum Development, Bronx, N.Y.; National Assessment and Dissemination Center, Cambridge, Mass.

SN..... Office of Education (DHEW), Washington, D.C. (RMQ66000)

LG..... Italian

AV..... National Assessment and Dissemination Center, 49 Washington Avenue, Cambridge, Massachusetts 02140 ($1.25)

NT..... 24 p.

DE..... *Italian; *Instructional Materials; Primary Education; Grade 1; Kindergarten; Childrens Books; *Numbers; Mathematics Instruction; *Singing

AB..... A song is used in this Italian textbook to introduce students to numbers 1 to 10. Each numeral is pictured as part of a black-and-white illustration, and a verse links each number to its pictorially associated object. These verses are intended to be sung in substitution for the last line of the song that appears at the beginning of the book. The text is designed to be used in bilingual classes at the primary level. (CO)

CP..... Y

AN..... 000690

TI..... Vestiti femminili di un tempo (Traditional Women's Costumes).

YR..... 78

AU..... Impiglia, Giancarlo, ill.

IN..... Northeast Center for Curriculum Development, Bronx, N.Y.; National Assessment and Dissemination Center, Cambridge, Mass.

SN..... Office of Education (DHEW), Washington, D.C. (RMQ66000)

LG..... Italian

AV..... National Assessment and Dissemination Center, 49 Washington Avenue, Cambridge, Massachusetts 02140 ($2.50)

NT..... 20 cards, 8-1/2"x11".

DE..... *Italian; *Instructional Materials; Kindergarten; Grade 1; Grade 2; Grade 3; Primary Education; *Illustrations; *Visual Aids; *Folk Culture; *Clothing

AB..... These 20 cards containing pen-and-ink illustrations of traditional women's costumes from the regions of Italy are designed to be copied for use in bilingual Italian classes at the primary level. A teacher's introduction in both English and Italian is included. (CO)

CP..... Y

AN..... 000691

TI..... Un po' d'Italia (A Bit of Italy).

YR..... 78

AU..... Impiglia, Giancarlo, ill.

IN..... Northeast Center for Curriculum Development, Bronx, N.Y.; National Assessment and Dissemination Center, Cambridge, Mass.

SN..... Office of Education (DHEW), Washington, D.C. (RMQ66000)

LG..... Italian

AV..... National Assessment and Dissemination Center, 49 Washington Avenue, Cambridge, Massachusetts 02140 ($2.50)

NT..... 10 cards, 8-1/2"x11".

DE..... *Italian; Kindergarten; Grade 1; Grade 2; Grade 3; Primary Education; *Illustrations; *Visual Aids; *Instructional Materials

AB..... These 10 picture cards are designed to be copied and used in bilingual Italian classes at the primary level. Illustrations in the portfolio include objects and characters which form a part of the Italian cultural heritage. A brief introduction in both English and Italian accompanies the black-and-white illustrations. (CO)

CP..... Y

AN..... 000692

TI..... L'Apprendimento della lettura e della scrittura (Learning Reading and Writing).

YR..... 78

AU..... Fallone, Nino

IN..... Northeast Center for Curriculum Development, Bronx, N.Y.; National Assessment and Dissemination Center, Cambridge, Mass.

SN..... Office of Education (DHEW), Washington, D.C. (RMQ66000)

LG..... Italian

AV..... National Assessment and Dissemination Center, 49 Washington Avenue, Cambridge, Massachusetts 02140 ($2.00)

NT..... v, 41 p. Cover title: Lettura e scrittura: Come? Quando? (Reading and Writing: How? When?).

DE..... *Italian; *Teaching Guides; Language Arts; Language Skills; *Reading Skills; Reading Comprehension; Reading Instruction; Handwriting; Spelling; *Writing Skills; Communication Skills; Speech Communication; Phonetic Transcription; Primary Education; Kindergarten; Grade 1; Perceptual Development; Psychomotor Skills

AB..... The principal theoretical tenet of this teacher's manual is that reading and writing, like listening and speaking, are forms of linguistic communication that open up new possibilities for the child and are major motivational building blocks. The manual presents the underlying method and theory of activities for teaching reading and writing in the Italian bilingual curriculum for kindergarten and first grade. Topics covered include: (1) development of perceptual and psychomotor abilities needed for reading and writing, (2) spoken and written languages as symbolic systems for communication, (3) encoding spoken language in phonetic script, (4) teaching cursive writing, and (5) handling spelling difficulties in Italian. The manual is written in Italian. (CO)

CP..... Y

AN..... 000693

TI..... A cada paso: Lengua, lectura y cultura (At Each Step: Language, Reading and Culture). Level 1.

YR..... 78

AU..... Schmitt, Conrad J.; Saslow, Joan, ed.; Weaver, Jack, ill.

IN..... McGraw-Hill Book Co., New York, N.Y. (BBB11014)

LG..... Spanish

AV..... McGraw-Hill Book Co., 1221 Ave. of the Americas, New York, New York 10020 (ISBN 0-07-055489-7; $6.72)

NT..... 78 p.
For accompanying teacher's manual and workbook, see 000694-695

DE..... Grade 1; Primary Education; *Spanish; *Language Arts; *Instructional Materials; Reading Materials; *Reading Skills; *Textbooks; Speech Skills; *Social Studies

AB..... This first grade textbook for the bilingual classroom presents Spanish language development and basic social studies concepts. The reading selections, which reinforce decoding and encoding skills and develop comprehension skills, present content related to the social sciences. Color illustrations, photographs, and discussion questions are included to develop speaking skills. (JB)

CP..... Y

AN..... 000694

TI..... A cada paso: Lengua, lectura y cultura (At Each Step: Language, Reading and Culture). Teacher's Manual. Level 1.

YR..... 78

AU..... Schmitt, Conrad J.; Saslow, Joan, ed.

IN..... McGraw-Hill Book Co., New York, N.Y. (BBB11014)

LG..... Spanish

AV..... McGraw-Hill Book Co., 1221 Avenue of the Americas, New York, New York 10020 (ISBN 0-07-055490-0)

NT..... 71 p.
For accompanying textbook and workbook, see 000693 and 695.

DE..... Grade 1; Primary Education; *Spanish; *Language Arts;
        *Instructional Materials; *Reading Skills; Speech Skills;
        *Teaching Guides; *Social Studies

AB..... This teacher's manual is part of a unit for developing
        Spanish language and basic social studies concepts for
        first grade bilingual classrooms. It follows the lessons
        presented in the textbook. Answers to workbook exercises
        are appended. (JB)

CP..... N

AN..... 000695

TI..... A cada paso: Lengua, lectura y cultura. Cuaderno de
        ejercicios (At Each Step: Language, Reading and Culture.
        Workbook). Level 1.

YR..... 78

AU..... Schmitt, Conrad J.

IN..... McGraw-Hill Book Co., New York, N.Y. (BBB11014)

LG..... Spanish

AV..... McGraw-Hill Book Co., 1221 Avenue of the Americas, New
        York, New York 10020 (ISBN 0-07-055491-9)

NT..... 120 p.
        For accompanying textbook and teacher's manual, see 000693-694.

DE..... Grade 1; Primary Education; *Spanish; *Workbooks;
        *Language Arts; *Instructional Materials; *Writing
        Exercises; Pattern Drills (Language); *Social Studies;
        Spelling

AB..... This illustrated workbook for first grade bilingual
        classrooms is part of a unit for developing Spanish
        language and basic social studies concepts. It includes
        writing and spelling exercises which follow the lessons
        in the textbook. (JB)

CP..... Y

AN..... 000696

TI..... A cada paso: Lengua, lectura y cultura (At Each Step:
        Language, Reading and Culture). Level 2.

YR..... 78

AU..... Schmitt, Conrad J.; Saslow, Joan, ed.; Taylor, Katrina,
        ill.

IN..... McGraw-Hill Book Co., New York, N.Y. (BBB11014)

LG..... Spanish

AV..... McGraw-Hill Book Co., 1221 Avenue of the Americas, New
        York, New York 10020 (ISBN 0-07-055492-7; $7.32)

NT..... 124 p.
        For accompanying teacher's edition and workbook, see 000697-69

DE..... Grade 2; Primary Education; *Spanish; *Language Arts;
        *Instructional Materials; Reading Materials; *Reading
        Skills; *Textbooks; Speech Skills; *Social Studies

AB..... This second grade textbook for the bilingual classroom
        presents Spanish language development and basic social
        studies concepts. The reading selections, which reinforce
        decoding and encoding skills and develop comprehension
        skills, present content related to the social sciences.
        Color illustrations, photographs, and discussion
        questions are included to develop reading skills. (JB)

CP..... N

AN..... 000697

TI..... A cada paso: Lengua, lectura y cultura (At Each Step:
        Language, Reading and Culture). Teacher's Edition,
        Annotated. Level 2.

YR..... 78

AU..... Schmitt, Conrad J.; Saslow, Joan, ed.; Taylor, Katrina,
        ill.

IN..... McGraw-Hill Book Co., New York, N.Y. (BBB11014)

LG..... Spanish

AV..... McGraw-Hill Book Co., 1221 Ave. of the Americas, New
        York, New York 10020 (ISBN 0-07-055493-5; $7.32)

NT..... 124 p.
        For accompanying textbook and workbook, see 000696 and 698.

DE..... Grade 2; Primary Education; *Spanish; *Language Arts;
        *Instructional Materials; Reading Materials; Reading
        Skills; *Textbooks; Speech Skills; *Social Studies;
        *Teaching Guides

AB..... This second grade textbook for the bilingual classroom
        presents Spanish language development and basic social
        studies concepts. The reading selections, which
        reinforce decoding and encoding skills and develop
        comprehension skills, present content related to the
        social sciences. Color illustrations, photographs, and
        discussion questions are included to develop speaking
        skills. (JB)

CP..... Y

AN..... 000698

TI..... A cada paso: Lengua, lectura y cultura. Cuaderno de ejercicios (At Each Step: Language, Reading and Culture. Workbook). Level 2.

YR..... 78

AU..... Schmitt, Conrad J.

IN..... McGraw-Hill Book Co., New York, N.Y. (BBB11014)

LG..... Spanish

AV..... McGraw-Hill Book Co., 1221 Avenue of the Americas, New York, New York 10020 (ISBN 0-07-055494-3)

NT..... 86 p.
For accompanying textbook and teacher's edition, see 000696-697.

DE..... Grade 2; Primary Education; *Spanish; *Workbooks; *Language Arts; *Instructional Materials; *Writing Exercises; Pattern Drills (Language); *Social Studies; Spelling

AB..... This illustrated workbook for second grade bilingual classrooms is part of a unit for developing Spanish language and basic social studies concepts. It includes writing and spelling exercises which follow the lessons in the textbook. (JB)

CP..... Y

AN..... 000699

TI..... A cada paso: Lengua, lectura y cultura (At Each Step: Language, Reading and Culture). Level 3.

YR..... 78

AU..... Schmitt, Conrad J.; Saslow, Joan, ed.; Banek, Yvette Santiago, ill.

IN..... McGraw-Hill Book Co., New York, N.Y. (BBB11014)

LG..... Spanish

AV..... McGraw-Hill Book Co., 1221 Avenue of the Americas, New York, New York 10020 (ISBN 0-07-055495-1; $7.32)

NT..... 151 p.
For accompanying teacher's edition and workbook, see 000700-701.

DE..... Grade 3; Primary Education; *Spanish; Language Arts; *Instructional Materials; Reading Materials; *Reading Skills; *Textbooks; Speech Skills; *Social Studies

AB..... This third grade textbook for the bilingual classroom
       presents Spanish language development and basic social
       studies concepts. The reading selections, which reinforce
       decoding and encoding skills and develop comprehension
       skills, present content related to the social sciences.
       Color illustrations, photographs, and discussion
       questions are included to develop reading skills. (JB)

CP..... Y

AN..... 000700

TI..... A cada paso: Lengua, lectura y cultura (At Each Step:
       Language, Reading and Culture). Teacher's Edition,
       Annotated. Level 3.

YR..... 78

AU..... Schmitt, Conrad J.; Saslow, Joan, ed.; Banek, Yvette
       Santiago, ill.

IN..... McGraw-Hill Book Co., New York, N.Y. (BBB11014)

LG..... Spanish

AV..... McGraw-Hill Book Co., 1221 Avenue of the Americas, New
       York, New York 10020 (ISBN 0-07-055496-X)

NT..... 151 p.
       For accompanying textbook and workbook, see 000699 and 701.

DE..... Grade 3; Primary Education; *Spanish; *Language Arts;
       *Instructional Materials; Reading Materials; Reading
       Skills; *Textbooks; Speech Skills; *Social Studies;
       *Teaching Guides

AB..... This third grade textbook for the bilingual classroom
       presents Spanish language development and basic social
       studies concepts. The reading selections, which reinforce
       decoding and encoding skills and develop comprehension
       skills, present content related to the social sciences.
       Color illustrations, photographs, and discussion
       questions are included to develop speaking skills. (JB)

CP..... Y

AN..... 000701

TI..... A cada paso: Lengua, lectura y cultura. Cuaderno de
       ejercicios (At Each Step: Language, Reading and Culture.
       Workbook). Level 3.

YR..... 78

AU..... Schmitt, Conrad J.

IN..... McGraw-Hill Book Co., New York, N.Y. (BBB11014)

LG..... Spanish

AV..... McGraw-Hill Book Co., 1121 Ave. of the Americas, New York, New York 10020 (ISBN 0-07-055497-8)

NT..... 112 p.
For accompanying textbook and teacher's edition, see 000699-700.

DE..... Grade 3; Primary Education; *Spanish; *Language Arts; *Instructional Materials; Reading Materials; Pattern Drills (Language); *Writing Exercises; *Workbooks; Spelling; *Social Studies

AB..... This workbook for third grade bilingual classrooms is part of a unit for developing Spanish language development and basic social studies concepts. It includes writing and spelling exercises which follow the lessons in the textbook. (JB)

CP..... Y

AN..... 000702

TI..... A cada paso: Lengua, lectura y cultura (At Each Step: Language, Reading and Culture). Level 4.

YR..... 78

AU..... Schmitt, Conrad J.; Saslow, Joan, ed.; Snyder, Joel, ill.

IN..... McGraw-Hill Book Co., New York, N.Y. (BBB11014)

LG..... Spanish

AV..... McGraw-Hill Book Co., 1221 Ave. of the Americas, New York, New York 10020 (ISBN 0-07-055499-4; $7.32)

NT..... 150 p.
For accompanying teacher's edition and workbook, see 000703-704.

DE..... Grade 4; Intermediate Grades; *Spanish; *Language Arts; *Instructional Materials; *Reading Skills; *Textbooks; Speech Skills; *Social Studies

AB..... This fourth grade textbook for the bilingual classroom presents Spanish language development and basic social studies concepts. The reading selections, which reinforce decoding and encoding skills and develop comprehension skills, present content related to the social sciences. Color illustrations, photographs, and discussion questions are included to develop speaking skills. (JB)

CP..... Y

AN..... 000703

TI..... A cada paso: Lengua, lectura y cultura (At Each Step: Language, Reading and Culture). Teacher's Edition, Annotated. Level 4.

YR..... 78

AU..... Schmitt, Conrad J.; Saslow, Joan, ed.; Snyder, Joel, ill.

IN..... McGraw-Hill Book Co., New York, N.Y. (BBB11014)

LG..... Spanish

AV..... McGraw-Hill Book Co., 1221 Ave. of the Americas, New York, New York 10020 (ISBN 0-07-055499-4; $7.32)

NT..... 150 p.
For accompanying textbook and workbook, see 000702 and 704.

DE..... Grade 4; Intermediate Grades; *Spanish; *Language Arts; *Instructional Materials; Reading Materials; *Reading Skills; *Textbooks; Speech Skills; *Teaching Guides; *Social Studies

AB..... This fourth grade textbook for the bilingual classroom presents Spanish language development and basic social studies concepts. The reading selections, which reinforce decoding and encoding skills and develop comprehension skills, present content related to the social sciences. Color illustrations, photographs, and discussion questions are included to develop speaking skills. (JB)

CP..... Y

AN..... 000704

TI..... A cada paso: Lengua, lectura y cultura. Cuaderno de ejercicios (At Each Step: Language, Reading and Culture. Workbook). Level 4.

YR..... 78

AU..... Schmitt, Conrad J.

IN..... McGraw-Hill Book Co., New York, N.Y. (BBB11014)

LG..... Spanish

AV..... McGraw-Hill Book Co., 1221 Avenue of the Americas, New York, New York 10020 (ISBN 0-07-055500-1)

NT..... 136 p.
For accompanying textbook and teacher's edition, see 000702-703.

DE..... Grade 4; Intermediate Grades; *Spanish; *Language Arts; Reading Materials; *Workbooks; *Writing Exercises; *Instructional Materials; *Social Studies; Spelling; Pattern Drills (Language)

AB..... This workbook for fourth grade bilingual classrooms is
part of a unit for developing Spanish language and social
studies concepts. It includes writing and spelling
exercises which follow the lessons in the textbook. (JB)

CP..... Y

AN..... 000705

TI..... Maskoke (Muskokee) onvkuce cokv enhvteceskv (Beginning
Muskogee Story Book).

YR..... Sep78

AU..... Factor, Susannah, trans.; Scott, Chester, ill.;
Chuleewah, Quannah, ill.

IN..... National Dissemination and Assessment Center, Austin,
Tex.

SN..... Office of Education (DHEW), Washington, D.C. (RMQ66000)

LG..... Creek

AV..... National Dissemination and Assessment Center, 7703 North
Lamar Boulevard, Austin, Texas 78752 (ISBN
0-89417-377-4; $1.00)

NT..... 12 p.

DE..... Childrens Literature; Childrens Books; *Reading
Materials; American Indian Languages; American Indian
Culture; Elementary Education; *Folklore Books; *Legends;
*Instructional Materials

ID..... *Coloring Books; *Creek

AB..... The legends in this storybook are for use by
Creek-speaking children at the elementary level.
Full-page black-and-white illustrations appear facing
each page of text. (JB)

CP..... N

AN..... 000706

TI..... Sebechem el menguiu? Hong er a kot el skuul (Can You
Read? Book for First Grade).

YR..... 77

AU..... Ramarui, Hermana; Faustino, Theodosia; Bravo, Ray, ill.

IN..... Palauan Reading Program.

SN..... Office of Education (DHEW), Washington, D.C. (RMQ66000)

LG..... Palauan

AV..... National Dissemination and Assessment Center, California
State University, 5151 State University Drive, Los
Angeles, California 90032 (supplies are limited)

NT..... 50 p.
Cover title: Ng sebechem el menguiu?

DE..... Uncommonly Taught Languages; Filipino Americans; Asian
Americans; Reading Instruction; *Reading Materials;
Primary Education; *Instructional Materials; *Short
Stories; *Childrens Literature; Language Instruction;
Childrens Books

ID..... *Palauan

AB..... This reader contains 10 short stories for use in a
primary level bilingual education program. Each page
contains a black-and-white illustration and a text in
Palauan. The illustrations are also available in poster
form. (AM)

CP..... N

AN..... 000707

TI..... Ke medengei a omonguiu? (Do You Know What You Read?).

YR..... 78

AU..... Ramarui, Hermana; Rechetaoch, Maech; Ruluked, Toyoko;
Faustino, Theodosia; Besedes, Akemi; Katase, Linda, ill.;
Imetuker, Joselita, ill.

IN..... Palauan Reading Program.

SN..... Office of Education (DHEW), Washington, D.C. (RMQ66000)

LG..... Palauan

AV..... National Dissemination and Assessment Center, California
State ($2.65)

NT..... 46 p.

DE..... *Instructional Materials; Malayo Polynesian Languages;
Reading Development; Reading; Elementary Education;
*Reading Materials; Childrens Literature; *Childrens
Books

ID..... *Palauan

AB..... This Palauan reader contains six stories illustrated in
black and white for students at the elementary level.
(SH)

CP..... N

AN.....	000708
ER.....	ED062174
TI.....	Diagnostic Mathematics Form A, Form B, and Test Manual.
YR.....	76
AU.....	Harsh, J. Richard
IN.....	National Dissemination and Assessment Center, Austin, Tex.; Education Service Center Region 13, Austin, Tex. (XPT82322)
SN.....	Office of Education (DHEW), Washington, D.C. (RMQ66000)
AV.....	ERIC Document Reproduction Service, P.O. Box 190, Arlington, Virginia 22210 ($1.95; microfiche $0.76; ED062174)
NT.....	[30] p.
DE.....	Grade 9; Grade 10; *Achievement Tests; *Arithmetic; *Secondary School Mathematics; *Diagnostic Tests; Student Evaluation Tests
AB.....	These materials consist of a test manual and two forms of the mathematics test with corresponding answer keys. The tests, designed to be used at the 9th and 10th grade level, provide a measure of the conventional sequence of arithmetic computation and selected application problems. The test requires students to show their work and reduces the guessing effect. Each form consists of 44 completion items with space for figuring and requires 30-45 minutes for completion. (JB)
CP.....	N

AN.....	000710
TI.....	Ann ang gusto mo? Ano ang ginagawa mo? (What Do You Like? What Are You Doing?).
SE.....	Pag-aaral ng wika (Units in Language Learning) (Series).
YR.....	77
AU.....	Casalucan, Ernest; Boffa, J. Leslie, ill.
IN.....	Alaska Univ., Anchorage. National Bilingual Materials Development Center.
SN.....	Office of Education (DHEW), Washington, D.C. (RMQ66000)
NO.....	G G007605457

LG..... Tagalog

AV..... National Bilingual Materials Development Center,
University of Alaska, 2223 Spenard Road, Anchorage,
Alaska 99503 ($1.50; supplies are limited)

NT..... 42 p.

DE..... *Childrens Books; *Instructional Materials; *Reading
Materials; Elementary Education; *Language Instruction;
Uncommonly Taught Languages; Indonesian Languages;
*Alaska Natives; *Tagalog

AB..... This illustrated reader, written in Tagalog, is intended
for use at the elementary school level. It uses a
question-and-answer approach with content relevant to
daily activities in the Alaskan villages. A vocabulary
list is appended. (JB)

CP..... N

AN..... 000711

TI..... Ano ang gagawin niya? Ano ang ginawa niya? (What Will
He Do? What Did He Do?).

SE..... Pag-aaral ng wika (Units in Language Learning) (Series).

YR..... 77

AU..... Casalucan, Ernest; Boffa, J. Leslie, ill.

IN..... Alaska Univ., Anchorage. National Bilingual Materials
Development Center.

SN..... Office of Education (DHEW), Washington, D.C. (RMQ66000)

NO..... G G007605457

LG..... Tagalog

AV..... National Bilingual Materials Development Center,
University of Alaska, 2223 Spenard Road, Anchorage,
Alaska 99503 ($1.25; supplies are limited)

NT..... 24 p.

DE..... *Childrens Books; *Instructional Materials; *Reading
Materials; Elementary Education; *Language Instruction;
Uncommonly Taught Languages; Indonesian Languages;
*Alaska Natives; *Tagalog

AB..... This illustrated reader, written in Tagalog, is intended
for use at the elementary level. A question-and-answer
approach is used to present information about daily
activities in the Alaskan villages. A vocabulary list is
appended. (JB)

CP..... N

AN..... 000712

TI..... Ano iyon? Ano ang magagawa mo diyan? (What Is It? What Can You Do With It?).

SE..... Pag-aaral ng wika (Units in Language Learning) (Series).

YR..... 77

AU..... Casalucan, Ernest; Boffa, J. Leslie, ill.

IN..... Alaska Univ., Anchorage. National Bilingual Materials Development Center.

SN..... Office of Education (DHEW), Washington, D.C. (RMQ66000)

NO..... G G007605457

LG..... Tagalog

AV..... National Bilingual Materials Development Center, University of Alaska, 2223 Spenard Road, Anchorage, Alaska 99503 ($1.30; supplies are limited)

NT..... 28 p.

DE..... *Childrens Books; *Instructional Materials; *Reading Materials; Elementary Education; *Language Instruction; Uncommonly Taught Languages; Indonesian Languages; *Alaska Natives; *Tagalog

AB..... This illustrated reader, written in Tagalog, is intended for use at the elementary level. A question-and-answer approach is used to present information about daily activities in the Alaskan villages. (JB)

CP..... N

AN..... 000713

TI..... Bakit? Sapagka't (Why? Because).

SE..... Pag-aaral ng wika (Units in Language Learning) (Series).

YR..... 77

AU..... Casalucan, Ernest; Boffa, J. Leslie, ill.

IN..... Alaska Univ., Anchorage. National Bilingual Materials Development Center.

SN..... Office of Education (DHEW), Washington, D.C. (RMQ66000)

NO..... G G007605457

LG..... Tagalog

AV..... National Bilingual Materials Development Center, University of Alaska, 2223 Spenard Road, Anchorage, Alaska 99503 ($1.40; supplies are limited)

NT..... 30 p.

DE..... *Childrens Books; *Instructional Materials; *Reading Materials; Elementary Education; *Language Instruction; Uncommonly Taught Languages; Indonesian Languages; *Alaska Natives; *Tagalog

AB..... This illustrated reader, written in Tagalog, is intended for use at the elementary level. A question-and-answer approach is used to present information about daily activities in the Alaskan villages. (JB)

CP..... N

AN..... 000714

TI..... Ang aking bahay (My House).

YR..... 77

AU..... Casalucan, Ernest; Boffa, J. Leslie, ill.

IN..... Alaska Univ., Anchorage. National Bilingual Materials Development Center.

SN..... Office of Education (DHEW), Washington, D.C. (RMQ66000)

NO..... G G007605457

LG..... Tagalog

AV..... National Bilingual Materials Development Center, University of Alaska, 2223 Spenard Road, Anchorage, Alaska 99503 ($1.25; supplies are limited)

NT..... 25 p.

DE..... *Childrens Books; *Instructional Materials; *Reading Materials; Elementary Education; *Language Instruction; Uncommonly Taught Languages; Indonesian Languages; *Alaska Natives; *Tagalog

AB..... This illustrated reader, written in Tagalog, is intended for use at the elementary level. In it, a young Alaskan girl describes her house. A vocabulary list is appended. (JB)

CP..... N

AN..... 000715

TI..... Ako ay nagtatrabaho (Work in the Home).

YR..... 78

AU..... Casalucan, Ernest; Boffa, J. Leslie, ill.

IN..... Alaska Univ., Anchorage. National Bilingual Materials Development Center.

LG..... Tagalog

AV..... National Bilingual Materials Development Center, University of Alaska, 2223 Spenard Road, Anchorage, Alaska 99503 ($1.25; supplies are limited)

NT..... 26 p.

DE..... *Childrens Books; *Instructional Materials; *Reading Materials; Elementary Education; *Language Instruction; Uncommonly Taught Languages; Indonesian Languages; *Alaska Natives; *Tagalog

AB..... This illustrated reader, written in Tagalog, is intended for use in the elementary grades. It describes a young Alaskan girl's work in her home. (JB)

CP..... N

AN..... 000716

TI..... Sammy.

YR..... 78

AU..... Casalucan, Ernest; Boffa, J. Leslie, ill.

IN..... Alaska Univ., Anchorage. National Bilingual Materials Development Center.

LG..... Tagalog

AV..... National Bilingual Materials Development Center, University of Alaska, 2223 Spenard Road, Anchorage, Alaska 99503 ($1.00; supplies are limited)

NT..... 17 p.

DE..... *Childrens Books; *Instructional Materials; *Reading Materials; Elementary Education; *Language Instruction; Uncommonly Taught Languages; Indonesian Languages; *Alaska Natives; *Tagalog

AB..... This illustrated reader, written in Tagalog, is intended for use in the elementary grades. In it, a young Alaskan boy goes shopping for his family. A vocabulary list is appended. (JB)

CP..... N

AN..... 000717

TI..... Mga pangalan ng aking pamilya (My Family).

YR..... 77

AU..... Casalucan, Ernest; Boffa, J. Leslie, ill.

IN..... Alaska Univ., Anchorage. National Bilingual Materials Development Center.

SN..... Office of Education (DHEW), Washington, D.C. (RMQ66000)

NO..... G G007605457

LG..... Tagalog

AV..... National Bilingual Materials Development Center, University of Alaska, 2223 Spenard Road, Anchorage, Alaska 99503 ($1.00; supplies are limited)

NT..... 16 p.

DE..... *Childrens Books; *Instructional Materials; *Reading Materials; Elementary Education; *Language Instruction; Uncommonly Taught Languages; Indonesian Languages; *Alaska Natives; *Tagalog

AB..... This illustrated reader, written in Tagalog, is intended for use at the elementary level. Family members are introduced, and blanks are left to be filled in by each child. (JB)

CP..... N

AN..... 000718

TI..... Papunta sa tindahan (Going to the Store).

YR..... 77

AU..... Casalucan, Ernest; Boffa, J. Leslie, ill.

IN..... Alaska Univ., Anchorage. National Bilingual Materials Development Center.

SN..... Office of Education (DHEW), Washington, D.C. (RMQ66000)

NO..... G G007605457

LG..... Tagalog

AV..... National Bilingual Materials Development Center, University of Alaska, 2223 Spenard Road, Anchorage, Alaska 99503 ($1.00; supplies are limited)

NT..... 21 p.

DE..... *Childrens Books; *Instructional Materials; *Reading Materials; Elementary Education; *Language Instruction; Uncommonly Taught Languages; Indonesian Languages; *Alaska Natives; *Tagalog

AB..... This illustrated reader, written in Tagalog, is intended for use at the elementary level. It tells the story of a young Alaskan boy who goes shopping. (JB)

CP..... N

AN.....	000719
TI.....	Pag-aaral tungkol sa oras (Learning About Time).
YR.....	77
AU.....	Casalucan, Ernest; Boffa, J. Leslie, ill.
IN.....	Alaska Univ., Anchorage. National Bilingual Materials Development Center.
LG.....	Tagalog
AV.....	National Bilingual Materials Development Center, University of Alaska, 2223 Spenard Road, Anchorage, Alaska 99503 ($1.00; supplies are limited)
NT.....	22 p.
DE.....	*Childrens Books; *Instructional Materials; *Reading Materials; Elementary Education; *Language Instruction; Uncommonly Taught Languages; Indonesian Languages; *Alaska Natives; *Tagalog
AB.....	This illustrated reader, written in Tagalog, is intended for use in the elementary grades. Periods of the day -- morning, noon, and night -- are illustrated by a variety of daily activities. (JB)
CP.....	N

AN.....	000720
TI.....	Gin kk'aa da-eent'aa? Dont'aanh? (What Do You Like? What Are You Doing?).
SE.....	Dinaakk'a bidots'uhdil-eeghee (Units in Language Learning) (Series).
YR.....	77
AU.....	Jones, Eliza; Boffa, J. Leslie, ill.
IN.....	Alaska Univ., Anchorage. National Bilingual Materials Development Center.
SN.....	Office of Education (DHEW), Washington, D.C. (RMQ66000)
NO.....	G G007605457
LG.....	Koyukon Athapascan
AV.....	National Bilingual Materials Development Center, University of Alaska, 2223 Spenard Road, Anchorage, Alaska 99503 ($1.50; supplies are limited)
NT.....	42 p.

```
DE..... *Athapascan Languages; Alaska Natives; Uncommonly Taught
        Languages; Elementary Education; *Reading Materials;
        *Instructional Materials; *Childrens Books; *Language
        Instruction; *American Indians

ID..... Alaska (Koyukon)

AB..... This illustrated reader in Central Koyukon Athapascan,
        like others in the same series, uses a
        question-and-answer approach to teach language to Alaskan
        children at the elementary level.  Content is relevant to
        daily activities in Alaskan villages.  A vocabulary list
        is included.  (SH)

CP..... N
```

```
AN..... 000721

TI..... Dotot´eek?  Daaghat´eek?  (What Will He Do?  What Did He
        Do?).

SE..... Dinaakk´a bidots´uhdil-eeghee (Units in Language
        Learning) (Series).

YR..... 77

AU..... Jones, Eliza; Boffa, J. Leslie; ill.

IN..... Alaska Univ., Anchorage. National Bilingual Materials
        Development Center.

SN..... Office of Education (DHEW), Washington, D.C. (RMQ66000)

NO..... G G007605457

LG..... Koyukon Athapascan

AV..... Alaska Univ., Anchorage. National Bilingual Materials
        Development Center. ($1.25; supplies are limited)

NT..... 24 p.

DE..... *Athapascan Languages; Alaska Natives; Uncommonly Taught
        Languages; Elementary Education; *Reading Materials;
        *Instructional Materials; *Childrens Books; *Language
        Instruction; *American Indians

ID..... Alaska (Koyukon)

AB..... This illustrated reader in Central Koyukon Athapascan,
        like others in the same series, uses a
        question-and-answer approach to teach language to Alaskan
        children at the elementary level.  Content is relevant to
        daily activities in Alaskan villages.  A vocabulary list
        is included.  (SH)

CP..... N
```

AN.....	000722
TI.....	Ginghunh ginghu? ...Ts'ahagha-ana (Why? Because).
SE.....	Dinaakk'a bidots'uhdil-eeghee (Units in Language Learning) (Series).
YR.....	77
AU.....	Jones, Eliza; Boffa, J. Leslie, ill.
IN.....	Alaska Univ., Anchorage. National Bilingual Materials Development Center.
SN.....	Office of Education (DHEW), Washington, D.C. (RMQ66000)
NO.....	G G007605457
LG.....	Koyukon Athapascan
AV.....	National Bilingual Materials Development Center, University of Alaska, 2223 Spenard Road, Anchorage, Alaska 99503 ($1.40; supplies are limited)
NT.....	30 p.
DE.....	*Athapascan Languages; Alaska Natives; Uncommonly Taught Languages; Elementary Education; *Reading Materials; *Instructional Materials; *Childrens Books; *Language Instruction; *American Indians
ID.....	Alaska (Koyukon)
AB.....	This illustrated reader in Central Koyukon Athapascan, like others in the same series, uses a question-and-answer approach to teach language to Alaskan children at the elementary level. Content is relevant to daily activities in Alaskan villages. A vocabulary list is included. (SH)
CP.....	N

AN.....	000723
TI.....	Yah hukk'o-eeneeya' (Work in the Home).
YR.....	78
AU.....	Jones, Eliza; Boffa, J. Leslie; ill.
IN.....	Alaska Univ., Anchorage. National Bilingual Materials Development Center.
LG.....	Koyukon Athapascan
AV.....	National Bilingual Materials Development Center, University of Alaska, 2223 Spenard Road, Anchorage, Alaska 99503 ($1.25; supplies are limited)

NT..... 26 p.

DE..... *Athapascan Languages; Alaska Natives; Uncommonly Taught Languages; Elementary Education; *Reading Materials; *Instructional Materials; *Childrens Books; *American Indians; *Language Instruction

ID..... Alaska (Koyukon)

AB..... An Alaskan girl who likes to help at home tells of her household chores in this illustrated reader. The text is in Central Koyukon Athapascan and is intended for use at the elementary level. (SH)

CP..... N

AN..... 000724

TI..... Sidilnakkaa siyilniyookkaa ooza' (My Family).

YR..... 77

AU..... Jones, Eliza; Boffa, J. Leslie, ill.

IN..... Alaska Univ., Anchorage. National Bilingual Materials Development Center.

SN..... Office of Education (DHEW), Washington, D.C. (RMQ66000)

NO..... G G007605457

LG..... Koyukon Athapascan

AV..... National Bilingual Materials Development Center, University of Alaska, 2223 Spenard Road, Anchorage, Alaska 99503 ($1.00; supplies are limited)

NT..... 20 p.

DE..... *Athapascan Languages; Alaska Natives; Uncommonly Taught Languages; Elementary Education; *Reading Materials; *Instructional Materials; *Childrens Books; *American Indians; *Language Instruction

ID..... Alaska (Koyukon)

AB..... Members of the immediate family are introduced in this illustrated reader. Blanks are left in the sentences for children to fill in with the appropriate names from their own families. The text is in Central Koyukon Athapascan, and the intended grade level is elementary. (SH)

CP..... N

AN..... 000725

TI..... Dii eh saanaih xaah iilii? Nts'at diidi'? (What Do You Like? What Are You Doing?).

SE..... Nee'aaneegn' uudeldii (Units in Language Learning) (Series).

YR..... 77

AU..... John, Alfred; Milanowski, Paul; Boffa, J. Leslie, ill.

IN..... Alaska Univ., Anchorage. National Bilingual Materials Development Center.

SN..... Office of Education (DHEW), Washington, D.C. (RMQ66000)

NO..... G G007605457

LG..... Upper Tanana Athapascan

AV..... National Bilingual Materials Development Center, University of Alaska, 2223 Spenard Road, Anchorage, Alaska 99503 ($1.50; supplies are limited)

NT..... 42 p.

DE..... *Childrens Books; Alaska Natives; *Athapascan Languages; *Instructional Materials; *Reading Materials; Elementary Education; *Language Instruction; Uncommonly Taught Languages; *American Indians

ID..... Alaska (Upper Tanana)

AB..... This illustrated reader in Upper Tanana Athapascan, like others in the same series, uses a question-and-answer approach to teach language to Alaskan children at the elementary level. Content is relevant to daily activities in Alaskan villages. (SH)

CP..... N

AN..... 000726

TI..... Nts'at taadiil? Nts'at diidii'? (What Will He Do? What Did He Do?).

SE..... Nee'aaneegn' uudeldii (Units in Language Learning) (Series).

YR..... 77

AU..... John, Alfred; Milanowski, Paul; Boffa, J. Leslie, ill.

IN..... Alaska Univ., Anchorage. National Bilingual Materials Development Center.

SN..... Office of Education (DHEW), Washington, D.C. (RMQ66000)

NO..... G G007605457

LG..... Upper Tanana Athapascan

AV..... National Bilingual Materials Development Center, University of Alaska, 2223 Spenard Road, Anchorage, Alaska 99503 ($1.25; supplies are limited)

NT..... 24 p.

DE..... *Childrens Books; Alaska Natives; *Athapascan Languages; *Instructional Materials; *Reading Materials; Elementary

Education; *Language Instruction; Uncommonly Taught
Languages; *American Indians

ID..... Alaska (Upper Tanana)

AB..... This illustrated reader in Upper Tanana Athapascan, like
others in the same series, uses a question-and-answer
approach to teach language to Alaskan children at the
elementary level. Content is relevant to daily
activities in Alaskan villages. A vocabulary list is
included. (SH)

CP..... N

AN..... 000727

TI..... Dii ch'ant'aiy? Nts'at dih'ih? (What Is It? What Can
You Do With It?).

SE..... Nee'aaneegn' uudeldii (Units in Language Learning)
(Series).

YR..... 77

AU..... John, Alfred; Milanowski, Paul; Boffa, J. Leslie, ill.

IN..... Alaska Univ., Anchorage. National Bilingual Materials
Development Center.

SN..... Office of Education (DHEW), Washington, D.C. (RMQ66000)

NO..... G G007605457

LG..... Upper Tanana Athapascan

AV..... National Bilingual Materials Development Center,
University of Alaska, 2223 Spenard Road, Anchorage,
Alaska 99503

NT..... 28 p.

DE..... *Childrens Books; Alaska Natives; *Instructional
Materials; *Reading Materials; Elementary Education;
*Language Instruction; Uncommonly Taught Languages;
*Athapascan Languages; *American Indians

ID..... Alaska (Upper Tanana)

AB..... This illustrated reader in Upper Tanana Athapascan, like
others in its series, uses a question-and-answer approach
to teach language to Alaskan children at the elementary
level. Content is relevant to daily activities in
Alaskan villages. (SH)

CP..... N

AN..... 000728

TI..... Dii xaah? ...eh (Why? Because).

SE..... Nee'aaneegn' uudeldii (Units in Language Learning)
(Series).

YR..... 77

AU..... John, Alfred; Milanowski, Paul; Boffa, J. Leslie, ill.

IN..... Alaska Univ., Anchorage. National Bilingual Materials Development Center.

SN..... Office of Education (DHEW), Washington, D.C. (RMQ66000)

NO..... G G007605457

LG..... Upper Tanana Athapascan

AV..... National Bilingual Materials Development Center, University of Alaska, 2223 Spenard Road, Anchorage, Alaska 99503 ($1.40; supplies are limited)

NT..... 30 p.

DE..... *Childrens Books; Alaska Natives; *Athapascan Languages; *Instructional Materials; *Reading Materials; Elementary Education; *Language Instruction; Uncommonly Taught Languages; *American Indians

ID..... Alaska (Upper Tanana)

AB..... This illustrated reader in Upper Tanana Athapascan, like others in the same series, uses a question-and-answer approach to teach language to Alaskan children at the elementary level. Content is relevant to daily activities in Alaskan villages. (SH)

CP..... N

AN..... 000729

TI..... Doo? Nts'at di'? (What Are They Doing? Where Are They Doing It?).

SE..... Nee'aaneegn' uudeldii (Units in Language Learning) (Series).

YR..... 77

AU..... John, Alfred; Milanowski, Paul; Boffa, J. Leslie, ill.

IN..... Alaska Univ., Anchorage. National Bilingual Materials Development Center.

LG..... Upper Tanana Athapascan

AV..... National Bilingual Materials Development Center, University of Alaska, 2223 Spenard Road, Anchorage, Alaska 99503 ($1.50; supplies are limited)

NT..... 40 p.

DE..... *Childrens Books; Alaska Natives; *Athapascan Languages; *Instructional Materials; *Reading Materials; Elementary Education; *Language Instruction; Uncommonly Taught Languages; *American Indians

ID..... Alaska (Upper Tanana)

AB..... This illustrated reader in Upper Tanana Athapascan, like
others in the same series, uses a question-and-answer
approach to teach language to Alaskan children at the
elementary level. Content is relevant to daily
activities in Alaskan villages. (SH)

CP..... N

AN..... 000730

TI..... Nts'aa' eedlah? Nts'aa ihdlaan? (How Much? How Many?).

SE..... Nee'aaneegn' uudeldii (Units in Language Learning)
(Series).

YR..... 77

AU..... John, Alfred; Milanowski, Paul; Boffa, J. Leslie, ill.

IN..... Alaska Univ., Anchorage. National Bilingual Materials
Development Center.

LG..... Upper Tanana Athapascan

AV..... National Bilingual Materials Development Center,
University of Alaska, 2223 Spenard Road, Anchorage,
Alaska 99503 ($1.50; supplies are limited)

NT..... 40 p.

DE..... *Childrens Books; Alaska Natives; *Athapascan Languages;
*Instructional Materials; *Reading Materials; Elementary
Education; *Language Instruction; Uncommonly Taught
Languages; Number Concepts; Concept Formation; *American
Indians

ID..... Alaska (Upper Tanana)

AB..... This illustrated reader in Upper Tanana Athapascan, like
others in the same series, uses a question-and-answer
approach to teach language to Alaskan children at the
elementary level. Content is relevant to daily
activities in Alaskan villages. (SH)

CP..... N

AN..... 000731

TI..... Doo ts'an ch'ant'aiy? Ndee ch'adadiinaiy? (Which?
Whose?).

SE..... Nee'aaneegn' uudeldii (Units in Language Learning)
(Series).

YR..... 77

AU..... John, Alfred; Milanowski, Paul; Boffa, J. Leslie, ill.

IN..... Alaska Univ., Anchorage. National Bilingual Materials
Development Center.

SN..... Office of Education (DHEW), Washington, D.C. (RMQ66000)

NO..... G G007605457

LG..... Upper Tanana Athapascan

AV..... National Bilingual Materials Development Center, University of Alaska, 2223 Spenard Road, Anchorage, Alaska 99503 ($1.00; supplies are limited)

NT..... 20 p.

DE..... *Childrens Books; Alaska Natives; *Athapascan Languages; *Instructional Materials; *Reading Materials; Elementary Education; *Language Instruction; Uncommonly Taught Languages; *American Indians

ID..... Alaska (Upper Tanana)

AB..... This illustrated reader in Upper Tanana Athapascan, like others in the same series, uses a question-and-answer approach to teach language to Alaskan children at the elementary level. Content is relevant to daily activities in Alaskan villages. (SH)

CP..... N

AN..... 000732

TI..... Shyah (My House).

YR..... 77

AU..... John, Alfred; Milanowski, Paul; Boffa, J. Leslie, ill.

IN..... Alaska Univ., Anchorage. National Bilingual Materials Development Center.

SN..... Office of Education (DHEW), Washington, D.C. (RMQ66000)

NO..... G G007605457

LG..... Upper Tanana Athapascan

AV..... National Bilingual Materials Development Center, University of Alaska, 2223 Spenard Road, Anchorage, Alaska 99503 ($1.25; supplies are limited)

NT..... 25 p.

DE..... *Childrens Books; Alaska Natives; *Athapascan Languages; *Instructional Materials; *Reading Materials; Elementary Education; *Language Instruction; Uncommonly Taught Languages; *American Indians

ID..... Alaska (Upper Tanana)

AB..... An Alaskan girl proudly shows you through her house in this illustrated reader. The text is in Upper Tanana Athapascan and is intended for children at the elementary level. (SH)

CP..... N

AN..... 000733

TI..... Sammy.

YR..... 77

AU..... John, Alfred; Milanowski, Paul; Boffa, J. Leslie, ill.

IN..... Alaska Univ., Anchorage. National Bilingual Materials Development Center.

SN..... Office of Education (DHEW), Washington, D.C. (RMQ66000)

NO..... G G007605457

LG..... Upper Tanana Athapascan

AV..... National Bilingual Materials Development Center, University of Alaska, 2223 Spenard Road, Anchorage, Alaska 99503 ($1.00; supplies are limited)

NT..... 17 p.

DE..... *Childrens Books; Alaska Natives; *Instructional Materials; *Reading Materials; Elementary Education; *Language Instruction; Uncommonly Taught Languages; *Athapascan Languages; *American Indians

ID..... Alaska (Upper Tanana)

AB..... This illustrated reader incorporates items commonly found in an Alaskan store into its story line. It is written in Upper Tanana Athapascan and is intended for use at the elementary level. A vocabulary list is included. (SH)

CP..... N

AN..... 000734

TI..... Ch'utkeedn shyah ts'a' teeshyah (Going to the Store).

YR..... 77

AU..... John, Alfred; Milanowski, Paul; Boffa, J. Leslie, ill.

IN..... Alaska Univ., Anchorage. National Bilingual Materials Development Center.

SN..... Office of Education (DHEW), Washington, D.C. (RMQ66000)

NO..... G G007605457

LG..... Upper Tanana Athapascan

AV..... National Bilingual Materials Development Center, University of Alaska, 2223 Spenard Road, Anchorage, Alaska 99503 ($1.00; supplies are limited)

NT..... 21 p.

DE..... *Childrens Books; Alaska Natives; *Athapascan Languages; *Instructional Materials; *Reading Materials; Elementary

Education; *Language Instruction; Uncommonly Taught Languages; *American Indians

ID..... Alaska (Upper Tanana)

AB..... A trip to an Alaskan store is described in this reader. The illustrated story, written in Upper Tanana Athapascan, is intended for use at the elementary level. (SH)

CP..... N

AN..... 000735

TI..... Xa' dakthan iin huu'oosi' (My Family).

YR..... 77

AU..... John, Alfred; Milanowski, Paul; Boffa, J. Leslie, ill.

IN..... Alaska Univ., Anchorage. National Bilingual Materials Development Center.

SN..... Office of Education (DHEW), Washington, D.C. (RMQ66000)

NO..... G G007605457

LG..... Upper Tanana Athapascan

AV..... National Bilingual Materials Development Center, University of Alaska, 2223 Spenard Road, Anchorage, Alaska 99503 ($1.00; supplies are limited)

NT..... 20 p.

DE..... *Childrens Books; Alaska Natives; *Athapascan Languages; *Instructional Materials; *Reading Materials; Elementary Education; *Language Instruction; Uncommonly Taught Languages; *American Indians

ID..... Alaska (Upper Tanana)

AB..... Members of the immediate family are introduced in this illustrated reader. Blanks are left for the name of the family member to be written in by each child. The text, intended for use at the elementary level, is in Upper Tanana Athapascan. (SH)

CP..... N

AN..... 000736

TI..... Jidii eet'indhan? Deeni'in? (What Do You Like? What Are You Doing?).

SE..... Gwich'in ginjik agwaraa'ee (Units in Language Learning) (Series).

YR..... 77

AU..... Peter, Katherine; Boffa, J. Leslie, ill.

IN..... Alaska Univ., Anchorage. National Bilingual Materials Development Center.

SN..... Office of Education (DHEW), Washington, D.C. (RMQ66000)

NO..... G G007605457

LG..... Gwich'in

AV..... National Bilingual Materials Development Center, University of Alaska, 2223 Spenard Road, Anchorage, Alaska 99503 ($1.50; supplies are limited)

NT..... 42 p.

DE..... *Childrens Books; *Instructional Materials; *Reading Materials; Elementary Education; *Language Instruction; Uncommonly Taught Languages; Athapascan Languages; *American Indians; Alaska Natives

ID..... *Gwich'in

AB..... This illustrated reader is one of a series designed for use by elementary school children who speak Gwich'in. It uses a question-and-answer approach with content relevant to the daily activities in Alaskan villages. A vocabulary list is included. (JB)

CP..... N

AN..... 000737

TI..... Deehee'yaa? Deezhik? (What Will He Do? What Did He Do?).

SE..... Gwich'in ginjik agwaraa'ee (Units in Language Learning) (Series).

YR..... 77

AU..... Peter, Katherine; Boffa, J. Leslie, ill.

IN..... Alaska Univ., Anchorage. National Bilingual Materials Development Center.

SN..... Office of Education (DHEW), Washington, D.C. (RMQ66000)

NO..... G G007605457

LG..... Gwich'in

AV..... National Bilingual Materials Development Center, University of Alaska, 2223 Spenard Road, Anchorage, Alaska 99503 ($1.25; supplies are limited)

NT..... 24 p.

DE..... *Childrens Books; *Instructional Materials; *Reading Materials; Elementary Education; *Language Instruction; Uncommonly Taught Languages; Athapascan Languages; Alaska Natives; *American Indians

ID..... *Gwich'in

AB..... This illustrated reader is one of a series intended for use by elementary school children who speak Gwich'in. It uses a question-and-answer approach to illustrate daily activities relevant to life in Alaskan villages such as dogsledding, boating, and snowmobiling. A vocabulary list is included. (JB)

CP..... N

AN..... 000738

TI..... Jidii? Vaa deehini'yaa? (What Is It? What Can You Do With It?).

SE..... Gwich'in ginjik agwaraa'ee (Units in Language Learning) (Series).

YR..... 77

AU..... Peter, Katherine; Boffa, J. Leslie, ill.

IN..... Alaska Univ., Anchorage. National Bilingual Materials Development Center.

SN..... Office of Education (DHEW), Washington, D.C. (RMQ66000)

NO..... G G007605457

LG..... Gwich'in

AV..... National Bilingual Materials Development Center, University of Alaska, 2223 Spenard Road, Anchorage, Alaska 99503 ($1.30; supplies are limited)

NT..... 28 p.

DE..... *Childrens Books; *Instructional Materials; *Reading Materials; Elementary Education; *Language Instruction; Uncommonly Taught Languages; Athapascan Languages; Alaska Natives; *American Indians

ID..... *Gwich'in

AB..... This illustated reader is one of a series designed for use by elementary school children who speak Gwich'in. It uses a question-and-answer approach with content relevant to daily life in Alaskan villages. (JB)

CP..... N

AN..... 000739

TI..... Jaghaii? Geh'an (Why? Because).

SE..... Gwich'in ginjik agwaraa'ee (Units in Language Learning) (Series).

YR..... 77

AU..... Peter, Katherine; Boffa, J. Leslie, ill.

IN..... Alaska Univ., Anchorage. National Bilingual Materials Development Center.

SN..... Office of Education (DHEW), Washington, D.C. (RMQ66000)

NO..... G G007605457

LG..... Gwich'in

AV..... National Bilingual Materials Development Center, University of Alaska, 2223 Spenard Road, Anchorage, Alaska 99503 ($1.40; supplies are limited)

NT..... 30 p.

DE..... *Childrens Books; *Instructional Materials; *Reading Materials; Elementary Education; *Language Instruction; Uncommonly Taught Languages; Athapascan Languages; Alaska Natives; *American Indians

ID..... *Gwich'in

AB..... This illustrated reader is intended for use by elementary school children who speak Gwich'in. It is part of a series that uses a question-and-answer style with content relevant to daily activities in the Alaskan villages. (JB)

CP..... N

AN..... 000740

TI..... Juu'? Dee'in? (What Are They Doing? Where Are They Doing It?).

SE..... Gwich'in ginjik agwaraa'ee (Units in Language Learning) (Series).

YR..... 77

AU..... Peter, Katherine; Boffa, J. Leslie, ill.

IN..... Alaska Univ., Anchorage. National Bilingual Materials Development Center.

SN..... Office of Education (DHEW), Washington, D.C. (RMQ66000)

NO..... G G007605457

LG..... Gwich'in

AV..... National Bilingual Materials Development Center, University of Alaska, 2223 Spenard Road, Anchorage, Alaska 99503 ($1.50; supplies are limited)

NT..... 40 p.

DE..... *Childrens Books; *Instructional Materials; *Reading Materials; Elementary Education; *Language Instruction; Uncommonly Taught Languages; Athapascan Languages; Alaska Natives; *American Indians

ID..... *Gwich'in

AB..... This illustrated reader is one of a series intended for use by elementary school children who speak Gwich'in. It uses a question-and-answer approach to illustrate a variety of daily activities such as eating, sports, and school. (JB)

CP..... N

AN..... 000741

TI..... Deeghwahtsii? Daahchy'aa? (How Much? How Many?).

SE..... Gwich'in ginjik agwaraa'ee (Units in Language Learning) (Series).

YR..... 77

AU..... Peter, Katherine; Boffa, J. Leslie, ill.

IN..... Alaska Univ., Anchorage. National Bilingual Materials Development Center.

LG..... Gwich'in

AV..... National Bilingual Materials Development Center, University of Alaska, 2223 Spenard Road, Anchorage, Alaska 99503 ($1.50; supplies are limited)

NT..... 40 p.

DE..... *Childrens Books; *Instructional Materials; *Reading Materials; Elementary Education; *Language Instruction; Uncommonly Taught Languages; Athapascan Languages; Alaska Natives; *American Indians

ID..... *Gwich'in

AB..... This illustrated reader is one of a series designed for elementary school children who speak Gwich'in. A question-and-answer approach is used to cover content relevant to daily activities in Alaskan villages. (JB)

CP..... N

AN..... 000742

TI..... Jidii? Juu vats'an? (Which? Whose?).

SE..... Gwich'in ginjik agwaraa'ee (Units in Language Learning) (Series).

YR..... 77

AU..... Peter, Katherine; Boffa, J. Leslie, ill.

IN..... Alaska Univ., Anchorage. National Bilingual Materials Development Center.

SN..... Office of Education (DHEW), Washington, D.C. (RMQ66000)

NO..... G G007605457

LG..... Gwich'in

AV..... National Bilingual Materials Development Center, University of Alaska, 2223 Spenard Road, Anchorage, Alaska 99503 ($1.00; supplies are limited)

NT..... 20 p.

DE..... *Childrens Books; *Instructional Materials; *Reading Materials; Elementary Education; *Language Instruction; Uncommonly Taught Languages; Athapascan Languages; Alaska Natives; *American Indians

ID..... *Gwich'in

AB..... This illustrated reader, written in a question-and-answer style, is intended for use by elementary school children who speak Gwich'in. The items discussed are relevant to daily activities in the Alaskan villages. (JB)

CP..... N

AN..... 000743

TI..... Shizheh (My House).

YR..... 77

AU..... Peter, Katherine; Boffa, J. Leslie, ill.

IN..... Alaska Univ., Anchorage. National Bilingual Materials Development Center.

SN..... Office of Education (DHEW), Washington, D.C. (RMQ66000)

NO..... G G007605457

LG..... Gwich'in

AV..... National Bilingual Materials Development Center, University of Alaska, 2223 Spenard Road, Anchorage, Alaska 99503 ($1.25; supplies are limited)

NT..... 25 p.

DE..... *Childrens Books; *Instructional Materials; *Reading Materials; Elementary Education; *Language Instruction; Uncommonly Taught Languages; Athapascan Languages; Alaska Natives; *American Indians

ID..... *Gwich'in

AB..... An Alaskan girl gives a tour of her house in this illustrated reader intended for use by elementary school children who speak Gwich'in. (JB)

CP..... N

AN..... 000744

TI..... Ch'ookwat zheh gwats'a' hihshyaa (Going to the Store).

YR..... 77

AU..... Peter, Katherine; Boffa, J. Leslie, ill.

IN..... Alaska Univ., Anchorage. National Bilingual Materials Development Center.

SN..... Office of Education (DHEW), Washington, D.C. (RMQ66000)

NO..... G G007605457

LG..... Gwich'in

AV..... National Bilingual Materials Development Center, University of Alaska, 2223 Spenard Road, Anchorage, Alaska 99503 ($1.00; supplies are limited)

NT..... 21 p.

DE..... *Childrens Books; *Instructional Materials; *Reading Materials; Elementary Education; *Language Instruction; Uncommonly Taught Languages; Athapascan Languages; Alaska Natives; *American Indians

ID..... *Gwich'in

AB..... This illustrated reader, intended for use at the elementary level by children who speak Gwich'in, is about a boy who goes shopping in an Alaskan store. (JB)

CP..... N

AN..... 000745

TI..... Sammy.

YR..... 77

AU..... Peter, Katherine; Boffa, J. Leslie, ill.

IN..... Alaska Univ., Anchorage. National Bilingual Materials Development Center.

SN..... Office of Education (DHEW), Washington, D.C. (RMQ66000)

NO..... G G007605457

LG..... Gwich'in

AV..... National Bilingual Materials Development Center, University of Alaska, 2223 Spenard Road, Anchorage, Alaska 99503 ($1.00; supplies are limited)

NT..... 17 p.

DE..... *Childrens Books; *Instructional Materials; *Reading Materials; Elementary Education; *Language Instruction; Uncommonly Taught Languages; Athapascan Languages; Alaska Natives; *American Indians

ID..... *Gwich'in

AB..... This illustrated reader, intended for use by elementary school children who speak Qwich'in, tells the story of a boy who goes shopping. (JB)

CP..... N

AN..... 000746

TI..... Gweedhaa garagwaa'ee (Learning About Time).

YR..... Feb78

AU..... Peter, Katherine; Boffa, J. Leslie, ill.

IN..... Alaska Univ., Anchorage. National Bilingual Materials Development Center.

LG..... Qwich'in

AV..... National Bilingual Materials Development Center, University of Alaska, 2223 Spenard Road, Anchorage, Alaska 99503 ($1.00; supplies are limited)

NT..... 22 p.

DE..... *Childrens Books; *Instructional Materials; *Reading Materials; Elementary Education; *Language Instruction; Uncommonly Taught Languages; Athapascan Languages; Alaska Natives; *American Indians

ID..... *Gwich'in

AB..... This illustrated reader, intended for use by elementary school children who speak Gwich'in, is about the activities that occur at different times of the day. (JB)

CP..... N

AN..... 000747

TI..... Shizhehk'aa eenjit ch'oozhri' (My Family).

YR..... 77

AU..... Peter, Katherine; Boffa, J. Leslie, ill.

IN..... Alaska Univ., Anchorage. National Bilingual Materials Development Center.

SN..... Office of Education (DHEW), Washington, D.C. (RMQ66000)

NO..... G G007605457

LG..... Gwich'in

AV..... National Bilingual Materials Development Center, University of Alaska, 2223 Spenard Road, Anchorage, Alaska 99503 ($1.00; supplies are limited)

NT..... 16 p.

DE..... *Childrens Books; *Instructional Materials; *Reading Materials; Elementary Education; *Language Instruction; Uncommonly Taught Languages; Athapascan Languages; Alaska Natives; *American Indians

ID..... *Gwich'in

AB..... This illustrated booklet, intended for use by elementary school children who speak Gwich'in, introduces members of the family with blanks left to be filled in by the child. (JB)

CP..... N

AN..... 000748

TI..... Mada? Dot'an? (What Are They Doing? Where Are They Doing It?).

SE..... Dinakinaja' ik'ats'itolnish (Units In Language Learning) (Series).

YR..... 77

AU..... Petruska, Betty; Boffa, J. Leslie, ill.

IN..... Alaska Univ., Anchorage. National Bilingual Materials Development Center.

LG..... Upper Kuskokwim Athapascan

AV..... National Bilingual Materials Development Center, University of Alaska, 2223 Spenard Road, Anchorage, Alaska 99503 ($1.50; supplies are limited)

NT..... 40 p.

DE..... *Childrens Books; *Instructional Materials; *Reading Materials; Elementary Education; *Language Instruction; Uncommonly Taught Languages; Alaska Natives; *Athapascan Languages; *American Indians

ID..... Alaska (Upper Kuskokwim)

AB..... This illustrated reader, written in Upper Kuskokwim Athapascan, is intended for use at the elementary level. It uses a question-and-answer approach with content relevant to daily activities in Alaskan villages. (JB)

CP..... N

AN.....	000749
TI.....	Nidots´o hikogh? Nidots´o dinogholt´aye? (How Much? How Many?).
SE.....	Dinakinaja´ ik´ats´itolnish (Units in Language Learning) (Series).
YR.....	77
AU.....	Petruska, Betty; Boffa, J. Leslie, ill.
IN.....	Alaska Univ., Anchorage. National Bilingual Materials Development Center.
LG.....	Upper Kuskokwim Athapascan
AV.....	National Bilingual Materials Development Center, University of Alaska, 2223 Spenard Road, Anchorage, Alaska 99503 ($1.50; supplies are limited)
NT.....	40 p.
DE.....	*Childrens Books; *Instructional Materials; *Reading Materials; Elementary Education; *Language Instruction; Uncommonly Taught Languages; Alaska Natives; *Athapascan Languages; *American Indians
ID.....	Alaska (Upper Kuskokwim)
AB.....	This illustrated reader, written in Upper Kuskokwim Athapascan, is intended for use at the elementary level. It uses a question-and-answer approach with content relevant to daily activities in Alaskan villages. (JB)
CP.....	N

AN.....	000750
TI.....	Mada heye? Hondo heye? (Which? Whose?).
SE.....	Dinakinaja´ ik´ats´olnish (Units in Language Learning) (Series).
YR.....	77
AU.....	Petruska, Betty; Boffa, J. Leslie, ill.
IN.....	Alaska Univ., Anchorage. National Bilingual Materials Development Center.
SN.....	Office of Education (DHEW), Washington, D.C. (RMQ66000)
NO.....	G G007605457
LG.....	Upper Kuskokwim Athapascan
AV.....	National Bilingual Materials Development Center, University of Alaska, 2223 Spenard Road, Anchorage, Alaska 99503 ($1.00; supplies are limited)
NT.....	20 p.

DE..... *Childrens Books; *Instructional Materials; *Reading
       Materials; Elementary Education; *Language Instruction;
       Uncommonly Taught Languages; Alaska Natives; *Athapascan
       Languages; *American Indians

ID..... Alaska (Upper Kuskokwim)

AB..... This illustrated reader, written in Upper Kuskokwim
       Athapascan, is intended for use at the elementary level.
       It uses a question-and-answer approach with content
       relevant to daily activities in Alaskan villages. (JB)

CP..... N

AN..... 000751

TI..... Sikayih (My House).

YR..... 77

AU..... Petruska, Betty; Boffa, J. Leslie, ill.

IN..... Alaska Univ., Anchorage. National Bilingual Materials
       Development Center.

SN..... Office of Education (DHEW), Washington, D.C. (RMQ66000)

NO..... G G007605457

LG..... Upper Kuskokwim Athapascan

AV..... National Bilingual Materials Development Center,
       University of Alaska, 2223 Spenard Road, Anchorage,
       Alaska 99503 ($1.25; supplies are limited)

NT..... 25 p.

DE..... *Childrens Books; *Instructional Materials; *Reading
       Materials; Elementary Education; *Language Instruction;
       Uncommonly Taught Languages; Alaska Natives; *Athapascan
       Languages; *American Indians

ID..... Alaska (Upper Kuskokwim)

AB..... This illustrated reader, written in Upper Kuskokwim
       Athapascan, is intended for use at the elementary level.
       In the story, an Alaskan girl describes her house. A
       vocabulary list is appended. (JB)

CP..... N

AN..... 000752

TI..... Hi'il time ghots'idelt'a ts'e' (Learning About Time).

YR..... 77

AU..... Petruska, Betty; Boffa, J. Leslie, ill.

IN..... Alaska Univ., Anchorage. National Bilingual Materials Development Center.

SN..... Office of Education (DHEW), Washington, D.C. (RMQ66000)

NO..... G G007605457

LG..... Upper Kuskokwim Athapascan

AV..... National Bilingual Materials Development Center, University of Alaska, 2223 Spenard Road, Anchorage, Alaska 99503 ($1.00; supplies are limited)

NT..... 22 p.

DE..... *Childrens Books; *Instructional Materials; *Reading Materials; Elementary Education; *Language Instruction; Uncommonly Taught Languages; Alaska Natives; *Athapascan Languages; *American Indians

ID..... Alaska (Upper Kuskokwim)

AB..... This illustrated reader, written in Upper Kuskokwim Athapascan, is intended for use at the elementary level. The times of the day, such as morning, noon, and night, are presented with their corresponding daily activities. (JB)

CP..... N

AN..... 000753

TI..... Sammy.

YR..... 77

AU..... Petruska, Betty; Boffa, J. Leslie, ill.

IN..... Alaska Univ., Anchorage. National Bilingual Materials Development Center.

SN..... Office of Education (DHEW), Washington, D.C. (RMQ66000)

NO..... G G007605457

LG..... Upper Kuskokwim Athapascan

AV..... National Bilingual Materials Development Center, University of Alaska, 2223 Spenard Road, Anchorage, Alaska 99503 ($1.00; supplies are limited)

NT..... 17 p.

DE..... *Childrens Books; *Instructional Materials; *Reading Materials; Elementary Education; *Language Instruction; Uncommonly Taught Languages; Alaska Natives; *Athapascan Languages; *American Indians

ID..... Alaska (Upper Kuskokwim)

AB..... This illustrated reader, written in Upper Kuskokwim Athapascan, is intended for use at the elementary level.

In the story, an Alaskan boy goes shopping for his family. A vocabulary list is appended. (JB)

CP..... N

AN..... 000754

TI..... Ch'ukayih hits'e' (Going to the Store).

YR..... 77

AU..... Petruska, Betty; Boffa, J. Leslie, ill.

IN..... Alaska Univ., Anchorage. National Bilingual Materials Development Center.

SN..... Office of Education (DHEW), Washington, D.C. (RMQ66000)

NO..... G G007605457

LG..... Upper Kuskokwim Athapascan

AV..... National Bilingual Materials Development Center, University of Alaska, 2223 Spenard Road, Anchorage, Alaska 99503 ($1.00; supplies are limited)

NT..... 21 p.

DE..... *Childrens Books; *Instructional Materials; *Reading Materials; Elementary Education; *Language Instruction; Uncommonly Taught Languages; Alaska Natives; *Athapascan Languages; *American Indians

ID..... Alaska (Upper Kuskokwim)

AB..... This illustrated reader, written in Upper Kuskokwim Athapascan, is intended for use at the elementary level. In the story, an Alaskan boy goes shopping. (JB)

CP..... N

AN..... 000755

TI..... Sutalya na udizre ts'e' (My Family).

YR..... 77

AU..... Petruska, Betty; Boffa, J. Leslie, ill.

IN..... Alaska Univ., Anchorage. National Bilingual Materials Development Center.

SN..... Office of Education (DHEW), Washington, D.C. (RMQ66000)

NO..... G G007605457

LG..... Upper Kuskokwim Athapascan

AV..... National Bilingual Materials Development Center,
University of Alaska, 2223 Spenard Road, Anchorage,
Alaska 99503 ($1.00; supplies are limited)

NT..... 20 p.

DE..... *Childrens Books; *Instructional Materials; *Reading
Materials; Elementary Education; *Language Instruction;
Uncommonly Taught Languages; Alaska Natives; *Athapascan
Languages; *American Indians

ID..... Alaska (Upper Kuskokwim)

AB..... This illustrated reader, written in Upper Kuskokwim
Athapascan, is intended for use at the elementary level.
Family members are presented with spaces left to be
filled in by the child. (JB)

CP..... N

AN..... 000756

TI..... Gin k'aa da-eent'aa? Dont'aan? (What Do You Like? What
Are You Doing?).

SE..... Dinaakanaaga' (Units in Language Learning) (Series).

YR..... 77

AU..... Jones, Eliza; Boffa, J. Leslie, ill.

IN..... Alaska Univ., Anchorage. National Bilingual Materials
Development Center.

SN..... Office of Education (DHEW), Washington, D.C. (RMQ66000)

NO..... G G007605457

LG..... Koyukon Athapascan

AV..... National Bilingual Materials Development Center,
University of Alaska, 2223 Spenard Road, Anchorage,
Alaska 99503; ($1.50; supplies are limited)

NT..... 42 p.

DE..... *Childrens Books; *Instructional Materials; *Reading
Materials; Elementary Education; *Language Instruction;
Uncommonly Taught Languages; Alaska Natives; *Athapascan
Languages; *American Indians

ID..... Alaska (Lower Koyukon)

AB..... This illustrated reader, written in Lower Koyukon
Athapascan, is intended for use at the elementary level.
A question-and-answer approach is used with content
relevant to daily activities in Alaskan villages. A
vocabulary list is appended. (JB)

CP..... N

AN..... 000757

TI..... Dotot'eek? Daaghat'eek? (What Will He Do? What Did He Do?).

SE..... Dinaakanaaga' (Units in Language Learning) (Series).

YR..... 77

AU..... Jones, Eliza; Boffa, J. Leslie, ill.

IN..... Alaska Univ., Anchorage. National Bilingual Materials Development Center.

SN..... Office of Education (DHEW), Washington, D.C. (RMQ66000)

NO..... G G007605457

LG..... Koyukon Athapascan

AV..... National Bilingual Materials Development Center, University of Alaska, 2223 Spenard Road, Anchorage, Alaska 99503; ($1.25; supplies are limited)

NT..... 24 p.

DE..... *Childrens Books; *Instructional Materials; *Reading Materials; Elementary Education; *Language Instruction; Uncommonly Taught Languages; Alaska Natives; *Athapascan Languages; *American Indians

ID..... Alaska (Lower Koyukon)

AB..... This illustrated reader, written in Lower Koyukon Athapascan, is intended for use at the elementary level. A question-and-answer approach is used with content relevant to daily activities in Alaskan villages. A vocabulary list is appended. (JB)

CP..... N

AN..... 000758

TI..... Gin ghun? Ts'i haa-an (Why? Because).

SE..... Dinaakanaaga' (Units in Language Learning) (Series).

YR..... 77

AU..... Jones, Eliza; Boffa, J. Leslie, ill.

IN..... Alaska Univ., Anchorage. National Bilingual Materials Development Center.

SN..... Office of Education (DHEW), Washington, D.C. (RMQ66000)

NO..... G G007605457

LG..... Koyukon Athapascan

AV..... National Bilingual Materials Development Center,
University of Alaska, 2223 Spenard Road, Anchorage,
Alaska 99503; ($1.25; supplies are limited)

NT..... 30 p.

DE..... *Childrens Books; *Instructional Materials; *Reading
Materials; Elementary Education; *Language Instruction;
Uncommonly Taught Languages; Alaska Natives; *Athapascan
Languages; *American Indians

ID..... Alaska (Lower Koyukon)

AB..... This illustrated reader, written in Lower Koyukon
Athapascan, is intended for use at the elementary level.
A question-and-answer approach is used with content
relevant to daily activities in Alaskan villages. (JB)

CP..... N

AN..... 000759

TI..... Nidaats'uh kk'a? Donaalt'aayee? (How Much? How Many?).

SE..... Dinaakanaaga' (Units in Language Learning) (Series).

YR..... 77

AU..... Mountain, Josephine; Stickman, Paulina; Jones, Eliza;
Boffa, J. Leslie, ill.

IN..... Alaska Univ., Anchorage. National Bilingual Materials
Development Center.

LG..... Koyukon Athapascan

AV..... National Bilingual Materials Development Center,
University of Alaska, 2223 Spenard Road, Anchorage,
Alaska 99503; ($1.50; supplies are limited)

NT..... 40 p.

DE..... *Childrens Books; *Instructional Materials; *Reading
Materials; Elementary Education; *Language Instruction;
Uncommonly Taught Languages; Alaska Natives; *Athapascan
Languages; *American Indians

ID..... Alaska (Lower Koyukon)

AB..... This illustrated reader, written in Lower Koyukon
Athapascan, is intended for use at the elementary level.
A question-and-answer approach is used with content
relevant to daily activities in Alaskan villages. (JB)

CP..... N

AN..... 000760

TI..... Dimaa? Dot'aanh? (What Are They Doing? Where Are They Doing It?).

SE..... Dinaakanaaga' (Units in Language Learning) (Series).

YR..... 77

AU..... Mountain, Josephine; Stickman, Paulina; Jones, Eliza; Boffa, J. Leslie, ill.

IN..... Alaska Univ., Anchorage. National Bilingual Materials Development Center.

LG..... Koyukon Athapascan

AV..... National Bilingual Materials Development Center, University of Alaska, 2223 Spenard Road, Anchorage, Alaska 99503; ($1.50; supplies are limited)

NT..... 40 p.

DE..... *Childrens Books; *Instructional Materials; *Reading Materials; Elementary Education; *Language Instruction; Uncommonly Taught Languages; Alaska Natives; *Athapascan Languages; *American Indians

ID..... Alaska (Lower Koyukon)

AB..... This illustrated reader, written in Lower Koyukon Athapascan, is intended for use at the elementary level. A question-and-answer approach is used with content relevant to daily activities in Alaskan villages. (JB)

CP..... N

AN..... 000761

TI..... Tom k'ookkaayah nitaalyo (Going to the Store).

YR..... 77

AU..... Mountain, Josephine; Stickman, Paulina; Jones, Eliza; Boffa, J. Leslie, ill.

IN..... Alaska Univ., Anchorage. National Bilingual Materials Development Center.

SN..... Office of Education (DHEW), Washington, D.C. (RMQ66000)

NO..... G G007605457

LG..... Koyukon Athapascan

AV..... National Bilingual Materials Development Center,
University of Alaska, 2223 Spenard Road, Anchorage,
Alaska 99503; ($1.00; supplies are limited)

NT..... 21 p.

DE..... *Childrens Books; *Instructional Materials; *Reading
Materials; Elementary Education; *Language Instruction;
Uncommonly Taught Languages; Alaska Natives; *Athapascan
Languages; *American Indians

ID..... Alaska (Lower Koyukon)

AB..... This illustrated reader, written in Lower Koyukon
Athapascan, is intended for use in the elementary grades.
In it, an Alaskan boy goes shopping. (JB)

CP..... N

AN..... 000762

TI..... Sammy.

YR..... 77

AU..... Mountain, Josephine; Stickman, Paulina; Jones, Eliza;
Boffa, J. Leslie, ill.

IN..... Alaska Univ., Anchorage. National Bilingual Materials
Development Center.

SN..... Office of Education (DHEW), Washington, D.C. (RMQ66000)

NO..... G G007605457

LG..... Koyukon Athapascan

AV..... National Bilingual Materials Development Center,
University of Alaska, 2223 Spenard Road, Anchorage,
Alaska 99503; ($1.00; supplies are limited)

NT..... 17 p.

DE..... *Childrens Books; *Instructional Materials; *Reading
Materials; Elementary Education; *Language Instruction;
Uncommonly Taught Languages; Alaska Natives; *Athapascan
Languages; *American Indians

ID..... Alaska (Lower Koyukon)

AB..... This illustrated reader, written in Lower Koyukon
Athapascan, is intended for use at the elementary level.
In the story, an Alaskan boy goes shopping for his
family. A vocabulary list is appended. (JB)

CP..... N

AN..... 000763

TI..... Yada q'u nel yagheli? Yada q'u t'enl'an? (What Do You Like? What Are You Doing?).

SE..... Naqenaga duch'deldih (Units in Language Learning) (Series).

YR..... 77

AU..... Wassillie, Albert; Boffa, J. Leslie, ill.

IN..... Alaska Univ., Anchorage. National Bilingual Materials Development Center.

SN..... Office of Education (DHEW), Washington, D.C. (RMQ66000)

NO..... G G007605457

LG..... Dena'ina Athapascan

AV..... National Bilingual Materials Development Center, University of Alaska, 2223 Spenard Road, Anchorage, Alaska 99503 ($1.50; supplies are limited)

NT..... 42 p.

DE..... *Athapascan Languages; Alaska Natives; Uncommonly Taught Languages; Elementary Education; *Reading Materials; *Instructional Materials; *Childrens Books; *American Indians; *Language Instruction

AB..... This illustrated reader, written in Dena'ina Athapascan, uses a question-and-answer approach to teach language to children at the elementary level. Content is relevant to daily activities in Alaskan villages. (SH)

CP..... N

AN..... 000764

TI..... Yada q'u tul'il? Yada q'u tghil'an? (What Will He Do? What Did He Do?).

SE..... Naqenaga duch'deldih (Units in Language Learning) (Series).

YR..... 77

AU..... Wassillie, Albert; Boffa, J. Leslie, ill.

IN..... Alaska Univ., Anchorage. National Bilingual Materials Development Center.

SN..... Office of Education (DHEW), Washington, D.C. (RMQ66000)

NO..... G G007605457

LG..... Dena'ina Athapascan

AV..... National Bilingual Materials Development Center, University of Alaska, 2223 Spenard Road, Anchorage, Alaska 99503 ($1.25; supplies are limited)

NT..... 24 p.

DE..... *Athapascan Languages; Alaska Natives; Uncommonly Taught Languages; Elementary Education; *Reading Materials; *Instructional Materials; *Childrens Books; *American Indians; *Language Instruction

AB..... This illustrated reader, written in Dena'ina Athapascan, uses a question-and-answer approach to teach language to children at the elementary level. Content is relevant to daily activities in Alaskan villages. (SH)

CP..... N

AN..... 000765

TI..... Yada di? Nda'ich' q'u vel tghit'il? (What Is It? What Can You Do With It?).

SE..... Naqenaga duch'deldih (Units in Language Learning) (Series).

YR..... 77

AU..... Wassillie, Albert; Boffa, J. Leslie, ill.

IN..... Alaska Univ., Anchorage. National Bilingual Materials Development Center.

SN..... Office of Education (DHEW), Washington, D.C. (RMQ66000)

NO..... G G007605457

LG..... Dena'ina Athapascan

AV..... National Bilingual Materials Development Center, University of Alaska, 2223 Spenard Road, Anchorage, Alaska 99503 ($1.30; supplies are limited)

NT..... 28 p.

DE..... *Athapascan Languages; Alaska Natives; Uncommonly Taught Languages; Elementary Education; *Reading Materials; *Instructional Materials; *Childrens Books; *American Indians; *Language Instruction

AB..... This illustrated reader, written in Dena'ina Athapascan, uses a question-and-answer approach to teach language to children at the elementary level. Content is relevant to daily activities in Alaskan villages. (SH)

CP..... N

AN.....	000766

TI.....	Nda'ihdu? Ent'i (Why? Because).
SE.....	Naqenaga duch'deldih (Units in Language Learning) (Series).
YR.....	77
AU.....	Wassillie, Albert; Boffa, J. Leslie, ill.
IN.....	Alaska Univ., Anchorage. National Bilingual Materials Development Center.
SN.....	Office of Education (DHEW), Washington, D.C. (RMQ66000)
NO.....	G G007605457
LG.....	Dena'ina Athapascan
AV.....	National Bilingual Materials Development Center, University of Alaska, 2223 Spenard Road, Anchorage, Alaska 99503 ($1.40; supplies are limited)
NT.....	30 p.
DE.....	*Athapascan Languages; Alaska Natives; Uncommonly Taught Languages; Elementary Education; *Reading Materials; *Instructional Materials; *Childrens Books; *American Indians; *Language Instruction
AB.....	This illustrated reader, written in Dena'ina Athapascan, uses a question-and-answer approach to teach language to children at the elementary level. Content is relevant to daily activities in Alaskan villages. (SH)
CP.....	N

AN.....	000767

TI.....	Vada? Yada tul'il? (What Are They Doing? Where Are They Doing It?).
SE.....	Naqenaga duch'deldih (Units in Language Learning) (Series).
YR.....	Oct77
AU.....	Wassillie, Albert; Boffa, J. Leslie, ill.
IN.....	Alaska Univ., Anchorage. National Bilingual Materials Development Center.
LG.....	Dena'ina Athapascan
AV.....	National Bilingual Materials Development Center, University of Alaska, 2223 Spenard Road, Anchorage, Alaska 99503 ($1.50; supplies are limited)

NT..... 40 p.

DE..... *Athapascan Languages; Alaska Natives; Uncommonly Taught Languages; Elementary Education; *Reading Materials; *Instructional Materials; *Childrens Books; *American Indians; *Language Instruction

AB..... This illustrated reader in Dena'ina Athapascan, like others in the same series, uses a question-and-answer approach to teach language to children at the elementary level. Content is relevant to daily activities in Alaskan villages. (SH)

CP..... N

AN..... 000768

TI..... Ndahqugh? Ndahdi? (How Much? How Many?).

SE..... Naqenaga duch'deldih (Units in Language Learning) (Series).

YR..... [77]

AU..... Wassillie, Albert; Boffa, J. Leslie, ill.

IN..... Alaska Univ., Anchorage. National Bilingual Materials Development Center.

LG..... Dena'ina Athapascan

AV..... National Bilingual Materials Development Center, University of Alaska, 2223 Spenard Road, Anchorage, Alaska 99503 ($1.50; supplies are limited)

NT..... 40 p.

DE..... *Athapascan Languages; Alaska Natives; Uncommonly Taught Languages; Elementary Education; *Reading Materials; *Instructional Materials; *Childrens Books; *American Indians; Number Concepts; Concept Formation; *Language Instruction

AB..... This illustrated reader in Dena'ina Athapascan, like others in the same series, uses a question-and-answer approach to teach language to children at the elementary level. Content is relevant to daily activities in Alaskan villages. (SH)

CP..... N

AN..... 000769

TI..... Vada idi? Ndan'i? (Which? Whose?).

SE..... Naqenaga duch'deldih (Units in Language Learning) (Series).

YR..... 77

AU.....	Wassillie, Albert; Boffa, J. Leslie, ill.
IN.....	Alaska Univ., Anchorage. National Bilingual Materials Development Center.
SN.....	Office of Education (DHEW), Washington, D.C. (RMQ66000)
NO.....	G G007605457
LG.....	Dena'ina Athapascan
AV.....	National Bilingual Materials Development Center, University of Alaska, 2223 Spenard Road, Anchorage, Alaska 99503 ($1.00; supplies are limited)
NT.....	20 p.
DE.....	*Athapascan Languages; Alaska Natives; Uncommonly Taught Languages; Elementary Education; *Reading Materials; *Instructional Materials; *Childrens Books; *American Indians; *Language Instruction
AB.....	This illustrated reader in Dena'ina Athapascan, like others in the same series, uses a question-and-answer approach to teach language to children at the elementary level. Content is relevant to daily activities in Alaskan villages. (SH)
CP.....	N

AN.....	000770
TI.....	Shqenq'a (My House).
YR.....	77
AU.....	Wassillie, Albert; Boffa, J. Leslie, ill.
IN.....	Alaska Univ., Anchorage. National Bilingual Materials Development Center.
NO.....	Office of Education (DHEW), Washington, D.C. (RMQ66000)
LG.....	Dena'ina Athapascan
AV.....	National Bilingual Materials Development Center, University of Alaska, 2223 Spenard Road, Anchorage, Alaska 99503 ($1.25; supplies are limited)
NT.....	25 p.
DE.....	*Athapascan Languages; Alaska Natives; Uncommonly Taught Languages; Elementary Education; *Reading Materials; *Instructional Materials; *Childrens Books; *American Indians; *Language Instruction
AB.....	An Alaskan girl shows you proudly through her house in this illustrated reader. Intended for use at the elementary level, the text is in Dena'ina Athapascan. (SH)
CP.....	N

AN..... 000771

TI..... Shdesnaqa izhi'a (My Family).

YR..... 77

AU..... Wassillie, Albert; Boffa, J. Leslie, ill.

IN..... Alaska Univ., Anchorage. National Bilingual Materials Development Center.

SN..... Office of Education (DHEW), Washington, D.C. (RMQ66000)

NO..... G G007605457

LG..... Dena'ina Athapascan

AV..... National Bilingual Materials Development Center, University of Alaska, 2223 Spenard Road, Anchorage, Alaska 99503 ($1.00; supplies are limited)

NT..... 20 p.

DE..... *Athapascan Languages; Alaska Natives; Uncommonly Taught Languages; Elementary Education; *Reading Materials; *Instructional Materials; *Childrens Books; *American Indians; *Language Instruction

AB..... This illustrated reader introduces members of the immediate family in sentence form, leaving blanks which each child can fill in with the names of family members. The text is in Dena'ina Athapascan and is intended for use at the elementary grade level. (SH)

CP..... N

AN..... 000772

TI..... Tets qilan (Learning About Time).

YR..... 77

AU..... Wassillie, Albert; Boffa, J. Leslie, ill.

IN..... Alaska Univ., Anchorage. National Bilingual Materials Development Center.

SN..... Office of Education (DHEW), Washington, D.C. (RMQ66000)

NO..... G G007605457

LG..... Dena'ina Athapascan

AV..... National Bilingual Materials Development Center, University of Alaska, 2223 Spenard Road, Anchorage, Alaska 99503 ($1.00; supplies are limited)

NT..... 22 p.

DE..... *Athapascan Languages; Alaska Natives; Uncommonly Taught Languages; Elementary Education; *Reading Materials; *Instructional Materials; *Childrens Books; *American Indians; Time; *Language Instruction

AB..... This illustrated reader introduces blocks of time, such as morning, noon, and night, and depicts activities which take place during each block. The text is in Dena'ina Athapascan and is intended for the elementary level. (SH)

CP..... N

AN..... 000773

Tl..... Lahgagh ch'tuyul (Going to the Store).

YR..... 77

AU..... Wassillie, Albert; Boffa, J. Leslie, ill.

IN..... Alaska Univ., Anchorage. National Bilingual Materials Development Center.

SN..... Office of Education (DHEW), Washington, D.C. (RMQ66000)

NO..... G G007605457

LG..... Dena'ina Athapascan

AV..... National Bilingual Materials Development Center, University of Alaska, 2223 Spenard Road, Anchorage, Alaska 99503 ($1.00; supplies are limited)

NT..... 21 p.

DE..... *Athapascan Languages; Alaska Natives; Uncommonly Taught Languages; Elementary Education; *Reading Materials; *Instructional Materials; *Childrens Books; *American Indians; *Language Instruction

AB..... This illustrated reader is about an Alaskan boy who goes to the store. It is written in Dena'ina Athapascan and is intended for the elementary level. (SH)

CP..... N

AN..... 000774

Tl..... Sammy.

YR..... 77

AU..... Wassillie, Albert; Boffa, J. Leslie, ill.

IN..... Alaska Univ., Anchorage. National Bilingual Materials Development Center.

SN..... Office of Education (DHEW), Washington, D.C. (RMQ66000)

NO..... G G007605457

LG..... Dena'ina Athapascan

AV..... National Bilingual Materials Development Center,
University of Alaska, 2223 Spenard Road, Anchorage,
Alaska 99503 ($1.00; supplies are limited)

NT..... 17 p.

DE..... *Athapascan Languages; Alaska Natives; Uncommonly Taught
Languages; Elementary Education;*Reading Materials;
*Instructional Materials; *Childrens Books; *American
Indians; *Language Instruction

AB..... An Alaskan boy goes to the store for members of his
family in this illustrated reader. Written in Dena'ina
Athapascan, the reader is intended for use at the
elementary level. A vocabulary list is included. (SH)

CP..... N

AN..... 000775

TI..... K'qizaghetnu ht'ana (Lime Village).

YR..... Apr78

AU..... Kari, James; Boffa, J. Leslie, ill.

IN..... Alaska Univ., Anchorage. National Bilingual Materials
Development Center.

SN..... Office of Bilingual Education (DHEW/OE), Washington, D.C.
(BBB12883)

NO..... G G007605457

LG..... Dena'ina Athapascan; English

AV..... National Bilingual Materials Development Center,
University of Alaska, 2223 Spenard Road, Anchorage,
Alaska 99503 ($1.50; supplies are limited)

NT..... 31 p.

DE..... *Athapascan Languages; Alaska Natives; Uncommonly Taught
Languages; Elementary Education; *Reading Materials;
*Instructional Materials; *Childrens Books; *American
Indians; *Language Instruction

ID..... Alaska (Lime Village)

AB..... This illustrated reader is composed of incidents from
around Lime Village which are related in English and
Dena'ina Athapascan for use at the elementary level.
(SH)

CP..... N

AN..... 000777

TI..... Alqutax̂ maduukalix inga? Alqutax̂ malix ingaya? (What Will He Do? What Did He Do?).

SE..... Tunum achigaasingin (Units in Language Learning) (Series).

YR..... 77

AU..... Mensoff, Olga; Boffa, J. Leslie, ill.

IN..... Alaska Univ., Anchorage. National Bilingual Materials Development Center.

LG..... Aleut

AV..... National Bilingual Materials Development Center, University of Alaska, 2223 Spenard Road, Anchorage, Alaska 99503 ($1.25; supplies are limited)

NT..... 24 p.

DE..... Eskimo Aleut Languages; *Childrens Books; Alaska Natives; *Eskimos; *Instructional Materials; *Reading Materials; Elementary Education; *Language Instruction; Uncommonly Taught Languages

ID..... *Aleut

AB..... This illustrated book in Eastern Aleut, like others in the same series, uses a question-and-answer approach to teach language to children at the elementary level. Content is relevant to daily activities in Alaskan villages. (SH)

CP..... N

AN..... 000778

TI..... Alqutax̂ amaya? Alqutax̂ maasdukatxin? (What Is It? What Can You Do With It?).

SE..... Tunum achigaasingin (Units in Language Learning) (Series).

YR..... 77

AU..... Mensoff, Olga; Boffa, J. Leslie, ill.

IN..... Alaska Univ., Anchorage. National Bilingual Materials Development Center.

SN..... Office of Education (DHEW), Washington, D.C. (RMQ66000)

LG..... Aleut

AV..... National Bilingual Materials Development Center,
University of Alaska, 2223 Spenard Road, Anchorage,
Alaska 99503 ($1.30; supplies are limited)

NT..... 28 p.

DE..... Eskimo Aleut Languages; *Childrens Books; Alaska Natives;
Eskimos; *Instructional Materials; *Reading Materials;
Elementary Education; *Language Instruction; Uncommonly
Taught Languages

ID..... *Aleut

AB..... This illustrated book in Eastern Aleut, like others in
the same series, uses a question-and-answer approach to
teach language to children at the elementary level.
Content is relevant to daily activities in Alaskan
villages. (SH)

CP..... N

AN..... 000779

TI..... Alix waya? Aaĝan (Why? Because).

SE..... Tunum achigaasingin (Units in Language Learning)
(Series).

YR..... 77

AU..... Mensoff, Olga; Boffa, J. Leslie, ill.

IN..... Alaska Univ., Anchorage. National Bilingual Materials
Development Center.

SN..... Office of Education (DHEW), Washington, D.C. (RMQ66000)

NO..... G G007605457

LG..... Aleut

AV..... National Bilingual Materials Development Center,
University of Alaska, 2223 Spenard Road, Anchorage,
Alaska 99503 ($1.40; supplies are limited)

NT..... 30 p.

DE..... Eskimo Aleut Languages; *Childrens Books; Alaska Natives;
*Eskimos; *Instructional Materials; *Reading Materials;
Elementary Education; *Language Instruction; Uncommonly
Taught Languages

ID..... *Aleut

AB..... This illustrated book in Eastern Aleut, like others in
the same series, uses a question-and-answer approach to
teach language to children at the elementary level.
Content is relevant to daily activities in Alaskan
villages. (SH)

CP..... N

AN..... 000780

TI..... Qanasanax̂? Qanaangasax̂? (How Much? How Many?).

SE..... Tunum achigaasingin (Units in Language Learning) (Series).

YR..... May77

AU..... Mensoff, Olga; Boffa, J. Leslie, ill.

IN..... Alaska Univ., Anchorage. National Bilingual Materials Development Center.

LG..... Aleut

AV..... National Bilingual Materials Development Center, University of Alaska, 2223 Spenard Road, Anchorage, Alaska 99503 ($1.50; supplies are limited)

NT..... 40 p.

DE..... Eskimo Aleut Languages; *Childrens Books; Alaska Natives; *Eskimos; *Instructional Materials; *Reading Materials; Elementary Education; *Language Instruction; Uncommonly Taught Languages; Number Concepts; Concept Formation.

ID..... *Aleut

AB..... This illustrated book in Eastern Aleut, like others in the same series, uses a question-and-answer approach to teach language to children at the elementary level. Content is relevant to daily activities in Alaskan villages. (SH)

CP..... N

AN..... 000781

TI..... Kiin? Alqutax̂ malix? (What Are They doing? Where Are They Doing It?).

SE..... Tunum achigaasingin (Units in Language Learning) (Series).

YR..... Aug77

AU..... Mensoff, Olga; Boffa, J. Leslie, ill.

IN..... Alaska Univ., Anchorage. National Bilingual Materials Development Center.

LG..... Aleut

AV..... National Dissemination and Assessment Center, 7703 North Lamar Boulevard, Austin, Texas 78752 ($1.50; supplies are limited)

NT..... 40 p.

DE..... *Eskimos; *Instructional Materials; *Reading Materials; Elementary Education; *Language Instruction; Uncommonly Taught Languages; Eskimo Aleut Languages; *Childrens Books; Alaska Natives

ID..... *Aleut

AB..... This illustrated book in Eastern Aleut, like others in the same series, uses a question-and-answer approach to teach the Aleut language to children at the elementary level. Content is relevant to daily activities in Alaskan villages. (SH)

CP..... N

AN..... 000782

TI..... Kiin? Qanan? (Which? Whose?).

SE..... Tunum achigaasingin (Units in Language Learning) (Series).

YR..... 77

AU..... Mensoff, Olga; Boffa, J. Leslie, ill.

IN..... Alaska Univ., Anchorage. National Bilingual Materials Development Center.

SN..... Office of Education (DHEW), Washington, D.C. (RMQ66000)

LG..... Aleut

AV..... National Bilingual Materials Development Center, University of Alaska, 2223 Spenard Road, Anchorage, Alaska 99503 ($1.50; supplies are limited)

NT..... 20 p.

DE..... Eskimo Aleut Languages; *Childrens Books; Alaska Natives; *Eskimos; *Instructional Materials; *Reading Materials; Elementary Education; *Language Instruction; Uncommonly Taught Languages

ID..... *Aleut

AB..... This illustrated book in Eastern Aleut, like others in the same series, uses a question-and-answer approach to teach language to children at the elementary level. Content is relevant to daily activities in Alaskan villages. (SH)

CP..... N

AN..... 000783

TI..... Ting ulang (My House).

YR..... 77

AU..... Mensoff, Olga; Boffa, J. Leslie, ill.

IN..... Alaska Univ., Anchorage. National Bilingual Materials Development Center.

SN..... Office of Education (DHEW), Washington, D.C. (RMQ66000)

NO..... G G007605457

LG..... Aleut

AV..... National Bilingual Materials Development Center, University of Alaska, 2223 Spenard Road, Anchorage, Alaska 99503 ($1.25; supplies are limited)

NT..... 25 p.

DE..... Eskimo Aleut Languages; *Childrens Books; Alaska Natives; *Eskimos; *Instructional Materials; *Reading Materials; Elementary Education; *Language Instruction; Uncommonly Taught Languages

ID..... *Aleut

AB..... An Alaskan girl shows you proudly through her house in this illustrated reader. The text is in Eastern Aleut and is intended for use at the elementary level. (SH)

CP..... N

AN..... 000784

TI..... Akutanax̂ (Akutan).

YR..... 77

AU..... Mensoff, Olga; Dirks, Moses; Mensoff, John, ill.; Boffa, J. Leslie, ill.

IN..... Alaska Univ., Anchorage. National Bilingual Materials Development Center. (BBB16750)

SN..... Office of Education (DHEW), Washington, D.C. (RMQ66000)

NO..... G G007605457

LG..... Aleut

AV..... National Bilingual Materials Development Center, University of Alaska, 2223 Spenard Road, Anchorage, Alaska 99503 ($1.50; supplies are limited)

NT.   32 p.

DE..... Eskimo Aleut Languages; Childrens Books; Alaska Natives; *Eskimos; *Instructional Materials; *Reading Materials; Elementary Education; *Language Instruction; Uncommonly Taught Languages

ID..... *Aleut; *Alaska (Akutan)

AB..... Simple happenings from Akutan, Alaska, are related by a
lifelong resident in both Eastern Aleut and English.
Black-and-white illustrations accompany the text. The
reader is intended for use at the elementary level. (SH)

CP..... N

AN..... 000785

TI..... Samayilax̂ (Sammy).

YR..... 77

AU..... Mensoff, Olga; Boffa, J. Leslie, ill.

IN..... Alaska Univ., Anchorage. National Bilingual Materials
Development Center.

SN..... Office of Education (DHEW), Washington, D.C. (RMQ66000)

NO..... G G007605457

LG..... Aleut

AV..... National Bilingual Materials Development Center,
University of Alaska, 2223 Spenard Road, Anchorage,
Alaska 99503 ($1.00; supplies are limited)

NT..... 17 p.

DE..... Eskimo Aleut Languages; *Childrens Books; Alaska Natives;
*Eskimos; *Instructional Materials; *Reading Materials;
Elementary Education; *Language Instruction; Uncommonly
Taught Languages

ID..... *Aleut

AB..... This illustrated reader relates the story of a boy who
goes to the store for members of his family. The text is
in Eastern Aleut and is directed at the elementary level.
A vocabulary list is included. (SH)

CP..... N

AN..... 000786

TI..... Laavkam adan uyakux̂ (Going to the Store).

YR..... 77

AU..... Mensoff, Olga; Boffa, J. Leslie, ill.

IN..... Alaska Univ., Anchorage. National Bilingual Materials
Development Center.

SN..... Office of Education (DHEW), Washington, D.C. (RMQ66000)

NO..... G G007605457

LG..... Aleut

AV..... National Bilingual Materials Development Center, University of Alaska, 2223 Spenard Road, Anchorage, Alaska 99503 ($1.00; supplies are limited)

NT..... 21 p.

DE..... Eskimo Aleut Languages; *Childrens Books; Alaska Natives; *Eskimos; *Instructional Materials; *Reading Materials; Elementary Education; *Language Instruction; Uncommonly Taught Languages

ID..... *Aleut

AB..... This illustrated reader relates the story of an Alaskan boy who goes to the store. The text is in Eastern Aleut and is intended for use at the elementary level. (SH)

CP..... N

AN..... 000787

TI..... Chasam adaan achigalix (Learning About Time).

YR..... 77

AU..... Mensoff, Olga; Boffa, J. Leslie, ill.

IN..... Alaska Univ., Anchorage. National Bilingual Materials Development Center.

SN..... Office of Education (DHEW), Washington, D.C. (RMQ66000)

NO..... G G007605457

LG..... Aleut

AV..... National Bilingual Materials Development Center, University of Alaska, 2223 Spenard Road, Anchorage, Alaska 99503 ($1.00; supplies are limited)

NT..... 22 p.

DE..... Eskimo Aleut Languages; *Childrens Books; Alaska Natives; *Eskimos; *Instructional Materials; *Reading Materials; Elementary Education; *Language Instruction; Uncommonly Taught Languages; Time

ID..... *Aleut

AB..... This illustrated book in Eastern Aleut introduces blocks of time like morning, noon, night, summer, and winter. It is intended for use at the elementary level. (SH)

CP..... N

AN..... 000789

TI..... Alqus iĝamax̂t azax̂t? Alqus max̂t? (What Do You Like? What Are You Doing?).

SE..... Achixaasis (Units in Language Learning) (Series).

YR..... 77

AU..... Dirks, Moses; Golley, Nadesta; Boffa, J. Leslie, ill.

IN..... Alaska Univ., Anchorage. National Bilingual Materials Development Center.

SN..... Office of Education (DHEW), Washington, D.C. (RMQ66000)

NO..... G G007605457

LG..... Aleut

AV..... National Bilingual Materials Development Center, University of Alaska, 2223 Spenard Road, Anchorage, Alaska 99503 ($1.50; supplies are limited)

NT..... 42 p.

DE..... Eskimo Aleut Languages; *Childrens Books; Alaska Natives; *Eskimos; *Instructional Materials; *Reading Materials; Elementary Education; *Language Instruction; Uncommonly Taught Languages

ID..... *Aleut

AB..... This illustrated reader in Western Aleut, like others in the same series, uses a question-and-answer approach to teach language to children at the elementary level. Content is relevant to daily activities in Alaskan villages. A vocabulary list is included. (SH)

CP..... N

AN..... 000790

TI..... Alqus maaĝan axs? Alqus manax̂? (What Will He Do? What Did He Do?).

SE..... Achixaasis (Units in Language Learning) (Series).

YR..... 77

AU..... Dirks, Moses; Golley, Nadesta; Boffa, J. Leslie, ill.

IN..... Alaska Univ., Anchorage. National Bilingual Materials Development Center.

SN..... Office of Education (DHEW), Washington, D.C. (RMQ66000)

NO..... G G007605457

LG..... Aleut

AV..... National Bilingual Materials Development Center, University of Alaska, 2223 Spenard Road, Anchorage, Alaska 99503 ($1.25; supplies are limited)

NT..... 24 p.

DE..... Eskimo Aleut Languages; *Childrens Books; Alaska Natives; *Eskimos; *Instructional Materials; *Reading Materials; Elementary Education; *Language Instruction; Uncommonly Taught Languages

ID..... *Aleut

AB..... This illustrated reader in Western Aleut, like others in the same series, uses a question-and-answer approach to teach language to children at the elementary level. Content is relevant to daily activities in Alaskan villages. A vocabulary list is included. (SH)

CP..... N

AN..... 000791

TI..... Alqul? Mal (Why? Because).

SE..... Achixaasis (Units in Language Learning) (Series).

YR..... 77

AU..... Dirks, Moses; Golley, Nadesta; Boffa, J. Leslie, ill.

IN..... Alaska Univ., Anchorage. National Bilingual Materials Development Center.

SN..... Office of Education (DHEW), Washington, D.C. (RMQ66000)

NO..... G G007605457

LG..... Aleut

AV..... National Bilingual Materials Development Center, University of Alaska, 2223 Spenard Road, Anchorage, Alaska 99503 ($1.40; supplies are limited)

NT..... 30 p.

DE..... Eskimo Aleut Languages; *Childrens Books; Alaska Natives; *Eskimos; *Instructional Materials; *Reading Materials; Elementary Education; *Language Instruction; Uncommonly Taught Languages

ID..... *Aleut

AB..... This illustrated reader in Western Aleut, like others in the same series, uses a question-and-answer approach to teach language to children at the elementary level. Content is relevant to daily activities in Alaskan villages. (SH)

CP..... N

AN..... 000792

TI..... Kiin? Alqus mal? (Which? Whose?).

SE..... Achixaasis (Units in Language Learning) (Series).

YR..... 77

AU..... Dirks, Moses; Golley, Nadesta; Boffa, J. Leslie, ill.

IN..... Alaska Univ., Anchorage. National Bilingual Materials Development Center.

SN..... Office of Education (DHEW), Washington, D.C. (RMQ66000)

NO..... G G007605457

LG..... Aleut

AV..... National Bilingual Materials Development Center, University of Alaska, 2223 Spenard Road, Anchorage, Alaska 99503 ($1.00; supplies are limited)

NT..... 20 p.

DE..... Eskimo Aleut Languages; *Childrens Books; Alaska Natives; *Eskimos; *Instructional Materials; *Reading Materials; Elementary Education; *Language Instruction; Uncommonly Taught Languages

ID..... *Aleut

AB..... This illustrated reader in Western Aleut, like others in the same series, uses a question-and-answer approach to teach language to children at the elementary level. Content is relevant to daily activities in Alaskan villages. (SH)

CP..... N

AN..... 000793

TI..... Qanan sanax̂? Qanaang azax̂? (How Much? How Many?).

SE..... Achixaasis (Units in Language Learning) (Series).

YR..... 77

AU..... Dirks, Moses; Golley, Nadesta; Boffa, J. Leslie, ill.

IN..... Alaska Univ., Anchorage. National Bilingual Materials Development Center.

SN..... Office of Education (DHEW), Washington, D.C. (RMQ66000)

NO..... G G007605457

LG..... Aleut

AV..... National Bilingual Materials Development Center, University of Alaska, 2223 Spenard Road, Anchorage, Alaska 99503 ($1.50; supplies are limited)

NT..... 40 p.

DE..... Eskimo Aleut Languages; *Childrens Books; Alaska Natives; *Eskimos; *Instructional Materials; *Reading Materials; Elementary Education; Number Concepts; Concept Formation

ID..... *Aleut

AB..... This illustrated reader in Western Aleut, like others in the same series, uses a question-and-answer approach to teach language to children at the elementary level. Content is relevant to daily activities in Alaskan villages. (SH)

CP..... N

AN..... 000794

TI..... Kdam ilan hunax̂ (The Hole in the Ice).

YR..... Feb78

AU..... Dirks, Moses; Boffa, J. Leslie, ill.

IN..... Alaska Univ., Anchorage. National Bilingual Materials Development Center.

LG..... Aleut

AV..... National Bilingual Materials Development Center, University of Alaska, 2223 Spenard Road, Anchorage, Alaska 99503 ($2.00; supplies are limited)

NT..... 42 p.

DE..... Eskimo Aleut Languages; *Childrens Books; Alaska Natives; *Eskimos; *Instructional Materials; *Reading Materials; Elementary Education; *Language Instruction; Uncommonly Taught Languages; *Science Fiction

ID..... *Aleut

AB..... This illustrated science fiction story set in Alaska is written in Western Aleut for use at the elementary level. (SH)

CP..... N

AN..... 000795

TI..... Niiĝuĝim qalgadangis (Atkan Food).

YR..... Jun78

AU..... Dirks, Moses; Boffa, J. Leslie, ill.; Dirks, Mike, ill.

IN..... Alaska Univ., Anchorage. National Bilingual Materials Development Center.

SN..... Office of Education (DHEW), Washington, D.C. (RMQ66000)

NO..... G G007605457

LG..... Aleut; English

AV..... National Bilingual Materials Development Center, University of Alaska, 2223 Spenard Road, Anchorage, Alaska 99503 ($2.00; supplies are limited)

NT..... 46 p.

DE..... Eskimo Aleut Languages; Childrens Books; Alaska Natives; *Eskimos; *Instructional Materials; *Reading Materials; Elementary Secondary Education; Language Instruction; Uncommonly Taught Languages; Cooking Instruction; *Recipes

ID..... *Aleut; *Cookbooks; Alaska (Atka)

AB..... This illustrated cookbook provides recipes in both Western Aleut and English for food common to Atka in the Aleutian Islands. (SH)

CP..... N

AN..... 000796

TI..... Strumiintas Piitram ayx̂aasii (Peter's Boat/Tools).

YR..... 77

AU..... Dirks, Moses; Golley, Nadesta; Nevzoroff, Vera S.; Nevzoroff, John L.; Golodoff, Dennis A.; Boffa, J. Leslie, ill.

IN..... Alaska Univ., Anchorage. National Bilingual Materials Development Center.

SN..... Office of Education (DHEW), Washington, D.C. (RMQ66000)

NO..... G G007605457

LG..... Aleut

AV..... National Bilingual Materials Development Center, University of Alaska, 2223 Spenard Road, Anchorage, Alaska 99503 ($1.25; supplies are limited)

NT..... 19 p.

DE..... Eskimo Aleut Languages; *Childrens Books; Alaska Natives; *Eskimos; *Instructional Materials; *Reading Materials; Elementary Education; *Language Instruction; Uncommonly Taught Languages

ID..... *Aleut

AB..... Two subjects, boats and tools, are presented in this illustrated reader for Western Aleut-speaking children at the elementary level. (SH)

CP..... N

AN..... 000797

TI..... Atx̂ax̂ (Atka).

YR..... Apr78

AU..... Dirks, Moses; Boffa, J. Leslie, ill.

IN..... Alaska Univ., Anchorage. National Bilingual Materials Development Center.

SN..... Office of Education (DHEW), Washington, D.C. (RMQ66000)

NO..... G G007605457

LG..... Aleut; English

AV..... National Bilingual Materials Development Center, University of Alaska, 2223 Spenard Road, Anchorage, Alaska 99503 ($1.50; supplies are limited)

NT..... 31 p.

DE..... Eskimo Aleut Languages; Childrens Books; Alaska Natives; *Eskimos; *Instructional Materials; *Reading Materials; Elementary Education; *Language Instruction; Uncommonly Taught Languages

ID..... *Aleut; *Alaska (Atka)

AB..... A lifetime resident of Atka in the Aleutian Islands relates simple happenings from years past in this illustrated reader for Western Aleut-speaking elementary school children. The text appears in both Western Aleut and English. (SH)

CP..... N

AN..... 000798

TI..... Saamii (Sammy).

YR..... 77

AU..... Dirks, Moses; Boffa, J. Leslie, ill.

IN..... Alaska Univ., Anchorage. National Bilingual Materials Development Center.

SN..... Office of Education (DHEW), Washington, D.C. (RMQ66000)

NO..... G G007605457

LG..... Aleut

AV..... National Bilingual Materials Development Center, University of Alaska, 2223 Spenard Road, Anchorage, Alaska 99503 ($1.00; supplies are limited)

NT..... 17 p.

DE..... Eskimo Aleut Languages; *Childrens Books; Alaska Natives; *Eskimos; *Instructional Materials; *Reading Materials; Elementary Education; *Language Instruction; Uncommonly Taught Languages

ID..... *Aleut

AB..... This reader relates the story of an Alaskan boy who goes to the store for members of his family. It is illustrated and written in Western Aleut for children at the elementary level. (SH)

CP..... N

AN..... 000799

TI..... Angalim ama amgim ilan malganas (Learning About Time).

YR..... 77

AU..... Mensoff, Olga; Boffa, J. Leslie, ill.

IN..... Alaska Univ., Anchorage. National Bilingual Materials Development Center.

SN..... Office of Education (DHEW), Washington, D.C. (RMQ66000)

NO..... G G007605457

LG..... Aleut

AV..... National Bilingual Materials Development Center, University of Alaska, 2223 Spenard Road, Anchorage, Alaska 99503 ($1.00; supplies are limited)

NT..... 22 p.

DE..... Eskimo Aleut Languages; *Childrens Books; Alaska Natives; *Eskimos; *Instructional Materials; Reading Materials; Elementary Education; *Language Instruction; Uncommonly Taught Languages; Time

ID..... *Aleut

AB..... This illustrated reader in Western Aleut for children at the elementary level examines time in blocks, such as morning, noon, and night, and depicts activities associated with them. (SH)

CP..... N

AN..... 000800

TI..... Niiĝuĝim tunugan ilakuchangis. Introduction to Atkan Grammar and Lexicon.

YR..... May78

AU..... Bergsland, Knut, comp.; Dirks, Moses, comp.; Boffa, J. Leslie, ill.

IN..... Alaska Univ., Anchorage. National Bilingual Materials
        Development Center.

SN..... Office of Education (DHEW), Washington, D.C. (RMQ66000)

NO..... G G007605457

LG..... Aleut; English

AV..... National Bilingual Materials Development Center,
        University of Alaska, 2223 Spenard Road, Anchorage,
        Alaska 99503 ($5.00; supplies are limited)

NT..... 237 p.

DE..... Eskimo Aleut Languages; Alaska Natives; Eskimos;
        *Instructional Materials; Elementary Education; *Language
        Instruction; Uncommonly Taught Languages; Instructional
        Aids; Vocabulary Development; *Dictionaries; *Grammar;
        Vocabulary; Reference Books

ID..... *Aleut

AB..... This publication in Atkan Aleut, commonly referred to as
        Western Aleut, consists of two major sections: the
        elements of Atkan Aleut grammar and a Western
        Aleut-English dictionary. The grammar portion was
        designed more as a teacher's aid rather than a complete
        grammar. The illustrated dictionary contains 1,500 main
        entries plus derivative forms, all of which are commonly
        used by the young people of Atka today. English
        translations are provided next to the words. A
        pronunciation guide is also included. (SH)

CP..... N

AN..... 000801

TI..... Cacaq ai? Cacamen aturnayarciu? (What Is It? What Can
        You Do With It?).

SE..... Alutiicestun litnaurluta (Units in Language Learning)
        (Series).

YR..... 77

AU..... Anahonak, Carl; Anahonak, Dan; Moonin, Arthur; Johnson,
        Ralph; Leer, Jeff; Boffa, J. Leslie, ill.

IN..... Alaska Univ., Anchorage. National Bilingual Materials
        Development Center.

SN..... Office of Education (DHEW), Washington, D.C. (RMQ66000)

NO..... G G007605457

LG..... Yupik

AV..... National Bilingual Materials Development Center,
        University of Alaska, 2223 Spenard Road, Anchorage,
        Alaska 99503 ($1.30; supplies are limited)

NT..... 28 p.

DE..... Eskimo Aleut Languages; *Childrens Books; Alaska Natives;
        *Eskimos; *Instructional Materials; *Reading Materials;
        Elementary Education; *Language Instruction; Uncommonly
        Taught Languages

ID..... *Yupik

AB..... This illustrated book in Alutiiq, like others in the same
        series, uses a question-and-answer approach to teach
        language to children at the elementary level. Content is
        relevant to daily activities in Alaskan villages. (SH)

CP..... N

AN..... 000802

TI..... Enka (My House).

YR..... 77

AU..... Anahonak, Carl; Anahonak, Dan; Moonin, Arthur; Johnson,
        Ralph; Leer, Jeff; Boffa, J. Leslie, ill.

IN..... Alaska Univ., Anchorage. National Bilingual Materials
        Development Center.

SN..... Office of Education (DHEW), Washington, D.C. (RMQ66000)

NO..... G G007605457

LG..... Yupik

AV..... National Bilingual Materials Development Center,
        University of Alaska, 2223 Spenard Road, Anchorage,
        Alaska 99503 ($1.25; supplies are limited)

NT..... 25 p.

DE..... Eskimo Aleut Languages; *Childrens Books; Alaska Natives;
        *Eskimos; *Instructional Materials; *Reading Materials;
        Elementary Education; *Language Instruction; Uncommonly
        Taught Languages

ID..... *Yupik

AB..... An Alaskan girl shows you proudly through her house in
        this illustrated book for Alutiiq-speaking children at
        the elementary level. (SH)

CP..... N

AN..... 000803

TI..... Sam.

YR..... 77

AU..... Anahonak, Carl; Anahonak, Dan; Moonin, Arthur; Johnson, Ralph; Leer, Jeff; Boffa, J. Leslie, ill.

IN..... Alaska Univ., Anchorage. National Bilingual Materials Development Center.

SN..... Office of Education (DHEW), Washington, D.C. (RMQ66000)

NO..... G G007605457

LG..... Yupik

AV..... National Bilingual Materials Development Center, University of Alaska, 2223 Spenard Road, Anchorage, Alaska 99503 ($1.00; supplies are limited)

NT..... 17 p.

DE..... Eskimo Aleut Languages; *Childrens Books; Alaska Natives; *Eskimos; *Instructional Materials; *Reading Materials; Elementary Education; *Language Instruction; Uncommonly Taught Languages

ID..... *Yupik

AB..... This reader, written for Alutiiq-speaking children at the elementary level, tells the story of an Alaskan boy who goes to the store for his family. A vocabulary list is included. (SH)

CP..... N

AN..... 000804

TI..... Erenret casaa'it (Learning About Time).

YR..... 77

AU..... Anahonak, Carl; Anahonak, Dan; Moonin, Arthur; Johnson, Ralph; Leer, Jeff; Boffa, J. Leslie, ill.

IN..... Alaska Univ., Anchorage. National Bilingual Materials Development Center.

SN..... Office of Education (DHEW), Washington, D.C. (RMQ66000)

NO..... G G007605457

LG..... Yupik

AV..... National Bilingual Materials Development Center, University of Alaska, 2223 Spenard Road, Anchorage, Alaska 99503 ($1.00; supplies are limited)

NT..... 22 p.

DE..... Eskimo Aleut Languages; *Childrens Books; Alaska Natives; *Eskimos; *Instructional Materials; *Reading Materials; Elementary Education; *Language Instruction; Uncommonly Taught Languages; *Time

ID..... *Yupik

AB..... This illustrated reader introduces time in blocks, such
as morning, noon, and night, and depicts activities
associated with them. The text is in Alutiiq and is
intended for use at the elementary level. (SH)

CP..... N

AN..... 000805

TI..... Ilama atrit (My Family).

YR..... 77

AU..... Anahonak, Carl; Anahonak, Dan; Moonin, Arthur; Johnson,
Ralph; Leer, Jeff; Boffa, J. Leslie, ill.

IN..... Alaska Univ., Anchorage. National Bilingual Materials
Development Center.

SN..... Office of Education (DHEW), Washington, D.C. (RMQ66000)

NO..... G G007605457

LG..... Yupik

AV..... National Bilingual Materials Development Center,
University of Alaska, 2223 Spenard Road, Anchorage,
Alaska 99503 ($1.00; supplies are limited)

NT..... 20 p.

DE..... Eskimo Aleut Languages; *Childrens Books; Alaska Natives;
*Eskimos; *Instructional Materials: *Reading Materials;
Elementary Education; *Language Instruction; Uncommonly
Taught Languages

ID..... *Yupik

AB..... Members of the immediate family are introduced in
sentence form with blanks left for children to write in
the names of their own family members. The intended
audience of this illustrated reader is Alutiq-speaking
children at the elementary level. (SH)

CP..... N

AN..... 000806

TI..... Suluq (Sammy).

YR..... 77.

AU..... Satre, Sharon; Boffa, J. Leslie, ill.

IN..... Alaska Univ., Anchorage. National Bilingual Materials
Development Center.

SN..... Office of Education (DHEW), Washington, D.C. (RMQ66000)

NO..... G G007605457

LG..... Yupik

AV..... National Bilingual Materials Development Center, University of Alaska, 2223 Spenard Road, Anchorage, Alaska 99503 ($1.00; supplies are limited)

NT..... 17 p.

DE..... Eskimo Aleut Languages; *Childrens Books; Alaska Natives; *Eskimos; *Instructional Materials; *Reading Materials; Elementary Education; *Language Instruction; Uncommonly Taught Languages

ID..... *Yupik

AB..... This book, written for Siberian Yupik-speaking children at the elementary level, tells the story of an Alaskan boy who goes to the store for his family. (SH)

CP..... N

AN..... 000807

TI..... Naten akitutkaa? Qafsinat? (How Much? How Many?).

SE..... Naraqelleq yupigestun (Units in Language Learning) (Series).

YR..... 77

AU..... Oozeea, Eleanor; Boffa, J. Leslie, ill.

IN..... Alaska Univ., Anchorage. National Bilingual Materials Development Center.

LG..... Yupik

AV..... National Bilingual Materials Development Center, University of Alaska, 2223 Spenard Road, Anchorage, Alaska 99503 ($1.50; supplies are limited)

NT..... 40 p.

DE..... Eskimo Aleut Languages; *Childrens Books; Alaska Natives; *Eskimos; *Instructional Materials; *Reading Materials; Elementary Education; *Language Instruction; Uncommonly Taught Languages; Daily Living Skills

ID..... *Yupik; Alaska (St. Lawrence Island)

AB..... This illustrated reader is one of a series intended for use by elementary school children who speak St. Lawrence Island Yupik. It uses a question-and-answer approach to teach concepts relevant to the daily life in Alaskan villages. (JB)

CP..... N

AN..... 000808

TI..... Mangteghaqa (My House).

YR..... 77

AU..... Oozeea, Eleanor; Boffa, J. Leslie, ill.

IN..... Alaska Univ., Anchorage. National Bilingual Materials Development Center.

SN..... Office of Education (DHEW), Washington, D.C. (RMQ66000)

NO..... G G007605457

LG..... Yupik

AV..... National Bilingual Materials Development Center, University of Alaska, 2223 Spenard Road, Anchorage, Alaska 99503 ($1.25; supplies are limited)

NT..... 25 p.

DE..... Eskimo Aleut Languages; *Childrens Books; Alaska Natives; *Eskimos; *Instructional Materials; *Reading Materials; Elementary Education; *Language Instruction; Uncommonly Taught Languages

ID..... *Yupik; Alaska (St. Lawrence Island)

AB..... This illustrated reader, written in St. Lawrence Island Yupik, is intended for use in the elementary grades. In it a young girl describes her house. A brief vocabulary list is appended. (JB)

CP..... N

AN..... 000809

TI..... Sivuqam ungipaghaatangi. St. Lawrence Island Legends.

YR..... 77

AU..... Slwooko, Grace; Boffa, J. Leslie, ill.

IN..... Alaska Univ., Anchorage. National Bilingual Materials Development Center.

SN..... Office of Education (DHEW), Washington, D.C. (RMQ66000)

NO..... G G007605457

LG..... English; Yupik

AV..... National Bilingual Materials Development Center, University of Alaska, 2223 Spenard Road, Anchorage, Alaska 99503 ($5.00; supplies are limited)

NT..... 79 p.

DE..... Secondary Education; Eskimo Aleut Languages; Alaska Natives; *Eskimos; *Reading Materials; Uncommonly Taught Languages; *Legends; *Folk Culture; *Instructional Materials; High Schools

ID..... *Yupik; Alaska (St. Lawrence Island)

AB..... Eleven illustrated legends written in both St. Lawrence Island Yupik and English are included in this book designed for secondary and high school students. (JB)

CP..... N

AN..... 000810

TI..... Ca assiksiu? Calisit? (What Do You Like? What Are You Doing?).

SE..... Caliarkat qaneryaramek elicalriani (Units in Language Learning) (Series).

YR..... 77

AU..... Paukan, Andy; Boffa, J. Leslie, ill.

IN..... Alaska Univ., Anchorage. National Bilingual Materials Development Center.

SN..... Office of Education (DHEW), Washington, D.C. (RMQ66000)

NO..... G G007605457

LG..... Yupik

AV..... National Bilingual Materials Development Center, University of Alaska, 2223 Spenard Road, Anchorage, Alaska 99503 ($1.50; supplies are limited)

NT..... 42 p.

DE..... *Childrens Books; Alaska Natives; Eskimo Aleut Languages; *Eskimos; *Instructional Materials; *Reading Materials; Elementary Education; *Language Instruction; Uncommonly Taught Languages

ID..... *Yupik

AB..... This illustrated reader is part of a series which
attempts to teach language, oral and written, through a
question-and-answer approach. The content centers around
activities and objects familiar to Alaskan children at
the elementary level who speak Central Yupik. (SH)

CP..... N

AN..... 000811

TI..... Caciqa? Callrua? (What Will He Do? What Did He Do?).

SE..... Caliarkat qaneryaramek elicalriani (Units in Language Learning) (Series).

YR..... 77

AU..... Paukan, Andy; Boffa, J. Leslie, ill.

IN..... Alaska Univ., Anchorage. National Bilingual Materials Development Center.

SN..... Office of Education (DHEW), Washington, D.C. (RMQ66000)

NO..... G G007605457

LG..... Yupik

AV..... National Bilingual Materials Development Center, University of Alaska, 2223 Spenard Road, Anchorage, Alaska 99503 ($1.25; supplies are limited)

NT..... 24 p.

DE..... *Childrens Books; Alaska Natives; Eskimo Aleut Languages; *Eskimos; *Reading Materials; Elementary Education; *Language Instruction; Uncommonly Taught Languages; *Instructional Materials

ID..... *Yupik

AB..... This illustrated reader is part of a series which uses a question-and-answer format to teach oral and written Central Yupik to children at the elementary level. Content is relevant to daily activities in the Alaskan villages. (SH)

CP..... N

AN..... 000812

TI..... Una cauga? Caksuumasiu? (What Is It? What Can You Do With It?).

SE..... Caliarkat qaneryaramek elicalriani (Units in Language Learning) (Series).

YR..... 77

AU..... Paukan, Andy; Boffa, J. Leslie, ill.

IN..... Alaska Univ., Anchorage. National Bilingual Materials
Development Center.

SN..... Office of Education (DHEW), Washington, D.C. (RMQ66000)

NO..... G G007605457

LG..... Yupik

AV..... National Bilingual Materials Development Center,
University of Alaska, 2223 Spenard Road, Anchorage,
Alaska 99503 ($1.30; supplies are limited)

NT..... 30 p.

DE..... *Childrens Books; Alaska Natives; *Instructional
Materials; *Reading Materials; Elementary Education;
*Language Instruction; Eskimo Aleut Languages; Uncommonly
Taught Languages; *Eskimos

ID..... *Yupik

AB..... Using a question-and-answer approach, this illustrated
reader, like others in the same series, teaches oral and
written Central Yupik to children at the elementary
level. Content is relevant to daily activities in the
Alaskan villages. (SH)

CP..... N

AN..... 000813

TI..... Ciin? Tua-wa (Why? Because).

SE..... Caliarkat qaneryaramek elicàlriani (Units in Language
Learning) (Series).

YR..... 77

AU..... Paukan, Andy; Boffa, J. Leslie, ill.

IN..... Alaska Univ., Anchorage. National Bilingual Materials
Development Center.

SN..... Office of Education (DHEW), Washington, D.C. (RMQ66000)

NO..... G G007605457

LG..... Yupik

AV..... National Bilingual Materials Development Center,
University of Alaska, 2223 Spenard Road, Anchorage,
Alaska 99503 ($1.40; supplies are limited)

NT..... 30 p.

DE..... *Childrens Books; Alaska Natives; Eskimo Aleut Languages;
*Eskimos; *Instructional Materials; *Reading Materials;
Elementary Education; *Language Instruction; Uncommonly
Taught Languages

ID..... *Yupik

AB..... This illustrated reader, like others in the same series,
uses a question-and-answer approach to teach Central
Yupik to children at the elementary level. Content is
relevant to daily activities in the Alaskan villages.
(SH)

CP..... N

AN..... 000814

TI..... Kina? Calria? (What Are They Doing? Where Are They
Doing It?).

SE..... Caliarkat qaneryaramek elicalriani (Units in Language
Learning) (Series).

YR..... Apr78

AU..... Paukan, Andy; Boffa, J. Leslie, ill.

IN..... Alaska Univ., Anchorage. National Bilingual Materials
Development Center.

LG..... Yupik

AV..... National Bilingual Materials Development Center,
University of Alaska, 2223 Spenard Road, Anchorage,
Alaska 99503 ($1.50; supplies are limited)

NT..... 40 p.

DE..... *Childrens Books; Alaska Natives; Eskimo Aleut Languages;
*Eskimos; *Instructional Materials; *Reading Materials;
Elementary Education; *Language Instruction; Uncommonly
Taught Languages

ID..... *Yupik

AB..... Using a question-and-answer approach, this reader, like
others in the same series, teaches oral and written
Central Yupik to children at the elementary level.
Content is relevant to daily activities in the Alaskan
villages. (SH)

CP..... N

AN..... 000815

TI..... Qayutun? Qavcinek? (How Much? How Many?).

SE..... Caliarkat qaneryaramek elicalriani (Units in Language
Learning) (Series).

YR..... Apr78

AU..... Paukan, Andy; Boffa, J. Leslie, ill.

IN..... Alaska Univ., Anchorage. National Bilingual Materials Development Center.

LG..... Yupik

AV..... National Bilingual Materials Development Center, University of Alaska, 2223 Spenard Road, Anchorage, Alaska 99503 ($1.50; supplies are limited)

NT..... 40 p.

DE..... *Childrens Books; Alaska Natives; Eskimo Aleut Languages; *Eskimos; *Instructional Materials; *Reading Materials; Elementary Education; Number Concepts; Concept Formations; *Language Instruction; Uncommonly Taught Languages

ID..... *Yupik

AB..... This illustrated reader, like others in the same series, uses a question-and-answer approach to teach oral and written Central Yupik to children at the elementary level. The text and illustrations in this book introduce the concept of quantity and are relevant to daily activities in the Alaskan villages. (SH)

CP..... N

AN..... 000816

TI..... Kia? Naliat? (Which? Whose?).

SE..... Caliarkat qaneryaramek elicalriani (Units in Language Learning) (Series).

YR..... 77

AU..... Paukan, Andy; Boffa, J. Leslie, ill.

IN..... Alaska Univ., Anchorage. National Bilingual Materials Development Center.

SN..... Office of Education (DHEW), Washington, D.C. (RMQ66000)

NO..... G G007605457

LG..... Yupik

AV..... National Bilingual Materials Development Center, University of Alaska, 2223 Spenard Road, Anchorage, Alaska 99503 ($1.00; supplies are limited)

NT..... 20 p.

DE..... *Childrens Books; Alaska Natives; Eskimo Aleut Languages; *Eskimos; *Reading Materials; Elementary Education; *Language Instruction; Uncommonly Taught Languages; Pronouns; *Instructional Materials

ID..... *Yupik

AB..... This reader, like others in the same series, uses a question-and-answer format to teach Central Yupik to children at the elementary level. The illustrations and text of this book emphasize the use of interrogative pronouns and are relevant to daily activities in the Alaskan villages. (SH)

CP..... N

AN..... 000817

TI..... Nek'a (My House).

YR..... 77

AU..... Paukan, Andy; Boffa, J. Leslie, ill.

IN..... Alaska Univ., Anchorage. National Bilingual Materials Development Center.

SN..... Office of Education (DHEW), Washington, D.C. (RMQ66000)

NO..... G G007605457

LG..... Yupik

AV..... National Bilingual Materials Development Center, University of Alaska, 2223 Spenard Road, Anchorage, Alaska 99503 ($1.25; supplies are limited)

NT..... 25 p.

DE..... *Childrens Books; Alaska Natives; Eskimo Aleut Languages; *Eskimos; *Instructional Materials; *Reading Materials; Elementary Education; *Language Instruction; Uncommonly Taught Languages

ID..... *Yupik

AB..... An Alaskan girl shows you proudly through her house in this illustrated book for Central Yupik-speaking elementary school children. (SH)

CP..... N

AN..... 000818

TI..... Caliaq kingunermi (Work in the Home).

YR..... Apr78

AU..... Paukan, Andy; Boffa, J. Leslie, ill.

IN..... Alaska Univ., Anchorage. National Bilingual Materials Development Center.

LG..... Yupik

AV..... National Bilingual Materials Development Center, University of Alaska, 2223 Spenard Road, Anchorage, Alaska 99503 ($1.25; supplies are limited)

NT..... 26 p.

DE..... *Childrens Books; Alaska Natives; Eskimo Aleut Languages; *Eskimos; *Reading Materials; Elementary Education; *Language Instruction; Uncommonly Taught Languages; *Instructional Materials

ID..... *Yupik

AB..... This illustrated reader, designed for Central Yupik-speaking children at the elementary level, tells the story of an Alaskan girl who likes to help at home. (SH)

CP..... N

AN..... 000819

TI..... Laavkaartelleq (Going to the Store).

YR..... 77

AU..... Paukan, Andy; Boffa, J. Leslie, ill.

IN..... Alaska Univ., Anchorage. National Bilingual Materials Development Center.

SN..... Office of Education (DHEW), Washington, D.C. (RMQ66000)

NO..... G G007605457

LG..... Yupik

AV..... National Bilingual Materials Development Center, University of Alaska, 2223 Spenard Road, Anchorage, Alaska 99503 ($1.00; supplies are limited)

NT..... 21 p.

DE..... *Childrens Books; Alaska Natives; Eskimo Aleut Languages; *Eskimos; *Instructional Materials; *Reading Materials; Elementary Education; *Language Instruction; Uncommonly Taught Languages

ID..... *Yupik

AB..... This illustrated reader for Central Yupik-speaking children at the elementary level tells the story of an Alaskan boy who goes to the store. (SH)

CP..... N

AN..... 000820

TI..... Elitelleq taimamek (Learning About Time).

YR..... 77

AU..... Paukan, Andy; Boffa, J. Leslie,, ill.

IN..... Alaska Univ., Anchorage. National Bilingual Materials Development Center.

SN..... Office of Education (DHEW), Washington, D.C. (RMQ66000)

NO..... G G007605457

AV..... National Bilingual Materials Development Center, University of Alaska, 2223 Spenard Road, Anchorage, Alaska 99503 ($1.00; supplies are limited)

NT..... 22 p.

DE..... *Childrens Books; Alaska Natives; Eskimo Aleut Languages; *Eskimos; *Instructional Materials; *Reading Materials; Elementary Education; *Language Instruction; Uncommonly Taught Languages; Time

ID..... *Yupik

AB..... This illustrated reader teaches about time in large blocks, like morning, noon, and night, by relating them to different activities. It is written for Central Yupik-speaking children at the elementary level. (SH)

CP..... N

AN..... 000821

TI..... Atrit ilama (My Family).

YR..... 77

AU..... Paukan, Andy; Boffa, J. Leslie, ill.

IN..... Alaska Univ., Anchorage. National Bilingual Materials Development Center.

SN..... Office of Education (DHEW), Washington, D.C. (RMQ66000)

NO..... G G007605457

AV..... National Bilingual Materials Development Center, University of Alaska, 2223 Spenard Road, Anchorage, Alaska 99503 ($1.00; supplies are limited)

NT..... 20 p.

DE..... *Childrens Books; Alaska Natives; Eskimo Aleut Languages; *Eskimos; *Instructional Materials; *Reading Materials; Elementary Education; *Language Instruction; Uncommonly Taught Languages

ID..... *Yupik

AB..... This illustrated reader introduces members of the immediate family in sentence form with blanks left for the name of the family member to be written in for each child. It is intended for use with Central Yupik-speaking children at the elementary level. (SH)

CP..... N

AN..... 000822

TI..... Suvaata? Takku (Why? Because).

SE..... Sulhich uqayusriliksrakun (Units in Language Learning) (Series).

YR..... 77

AU..... Sun, Susie; Boffa, J. Leslie, ill.

IN..... Alaska Univ., Anchorage. National Bilingual Materials Development Center.

SN..... Office of Education (DHEW), Washington, D.C. (RMQ66000)

NO..... G G007605457

LG..... Inupiat

AV..... National Bilingual Materials Development Center, University of Alaska, 2223 Spenard Road, Anchorage, Alaska 99503 ($1.40; supplies are limited)

NT..... 30 p.

DE..... *Childrens Books; *Instructional Materials; *Reading Materials; Elementary Education; *Language Instruction; Uncommonly Taught Languages; Alaska Natives; *Eskimos; Eskimo Aleut Languages

ID..... Inupiat; Alaska (Upper Kobuk)

AB..... This illustrated reader, written in Upper Kobuk Inupiat, is intended for use at the elementary level. It uses a question-and-answer approach with content relevant to daily activities in Alaskan villages. (JB)

CP..... N

AN..... 000823

TI..... Kiapia? Naliak? (Which? Whose?).

SE..... Sulhich uqayusriliksrakun (Units in Language Learning) (Series).

YR..... 77

AU..... Sun, Susie; Boffa, J. Leslie, ill.

IN..... Alaska Univ., Anchorage. National Bilingual Materials Development Center.

SN..... Office of Education (DHEW), Washington, D.C. (RMQ66000)

NO..... G G007605457

LG..... Inupiat

AV..... National Bilingual Materials Development Center,
       University of Alaska, 2223 Spenard Road, Anchorage,
       Alaska 99503 ($1.00; supplies are limited)

NT..... 20 p.

DE..... *Childrens Books; *Instructional Materials; *Reading
       Materials; Elementary Education; *Language Instruction;
       Uncommonly Taught Languages; Alaska Natives; *Eskimos;
       Eskimo Aleut Languages

ID..... *Inupiat; Alaska (Upper Kobuk)

AB..... This illustrated reader, written in Upper Kobuk Inupiat,
       is intended for use at the elementary level. It uses a
       question-and-answer approach with content relevant to
       daily activities in Alaskan villages. (JB)

CP..... N

AN..... 000824

TI..... Tuaqsigñiaqtilialiq (Going to the Store).

YR..... 77

AU..... Sun, Susie; Boffa, J. Leslie, ill.

IN..... Alaska Univ., Anchorage. National Bilingual Materials
       Development Center.

SN..... Office of Education (DHEW), Washington, D.C. (RMQ66000)

NO..... G G007605457

LG..... Inupiat

AV..... National Bilingual Materials Development Center,
       University of Alaska, 2223 Spenard Road, Anchorage,
       Alaska 99503 ($1.00; supplies are limited)

NT..... 21 p.

DE..... *Childrens Books; *Instructional Materials; *Reading
       Materials; Elementary Education; *Language Instruction;
       Uncommonly Taught Languages; Alaska Natives; *Eskimos;
       Eskimo Aleut Languages

ID..... *Inupiat; Alaska (Upper Kobuk)

AB..... This illustrated reader, written in Upper Kobuk Inupiat,
       is intended for use at the elementary level. It tells
       the story of a boy who goes shopping. (JB)

CP..... N

AN..... 000825

TI..... Atinich ilama (My Family).

YR..... 77

AU..... Sun, Susie; Boffa, J. Leslie, ill.

IN..... Alaska Univ., Anchorage. National Bilingual Materials Development Center.

SN..... Office of Education (DHEW), Washington, D.C. (RMQ66000)

NO..... G G007605457

LG..... Inupiat

AV..... National Bilingual Materials Development Center, University of Alaska, 2223 Spenard Road, Anchorage, Alaska 99503 ($1.00; supplies are limited)

NT..... 16 p.

DE..... *Childrens Books; *Instructional Materials; *Reading Materials; Elementary Education; *Language Instruction; Uncommonly Taught Languages; Alaska Natives; *Eskimos; Eskimo Aleut Languages

ID..... *Inupiat; Alaska (Upper Kobuk)

AB..... This illustrated reader, written in Upper Kobuk Inupiat, is intended for use at the elementary level. Members of the family are presented in sentence form with blanks left to be filled in by the child. (JB)

CP..... N

AN..... 000826

TI..... Ilinniaqpaaluktuni (Learning About Time).

YR..... 77

AU..... Sun, Susie; Boffa, J. Leslie, ill.

IN..... Alaska Univ., Anchorage. National Bilingual Materials Development Center.

SN..... Office of Education (DHEW), Washington, D.C. (RMQ66000)

NO..... G G007605457

LG..... Inupiat

AV..... National Bilingual Materials Development Center, University of Alaska, 2223 Spenard Road, Anchorage, Alaska 99503 ($1.00; supplies are limited)

NT..... 22 p.

DE..... *Childrens Books; *Instructional Materials; *Reading Materials; Elementary Education; *Language Instruction; Uncommonly Taught Languages; *Alaska Natives; *Eskimos; Eskimo Aleut Languages

ID..... *Inupiat; Alaska (Upper Kobuk)

AB..... This illustrated reader, written in Upper Kobuk Inupiat, is intended for use at the elementary level. The times of the day, morning, noon, and night, are presented with accompanying daily activities. (JB)

CP..... N

AN..... 000827

TI..... Sua nakuagiviun? Suvit? (What Do You Like? What Are You Doing?).

SE..... Units in Language Learning (Series).

YR..... 77

AU..... Swanson, Elvina; Boffa, J. Leslie, ill.

IN..... Alaska Univ., Anchorage. National Bilingual Materials Development Center.

SN..... Office of Education (DHEW), Washington, D.C. (RMQ66000)

NO..... G G007605457

LG..... Inupiat

AV..... National Bilingual Materials Development Center, University of Alaska, 2223 Spenard Road, Anchorage, Alaska 99503 ($1.50; supplies are limited)

NT..... 42 p.

DE..... *Childrens Books; Alaska Natives; Eskimo Aleut Languages; *Eskimos; *Instructional Materials; Elementary Education; *Reading Materials; *Language Instruction; Uncommonly Taught Languages

ID..... *Inupiat

AB..... Part of a series designed for use at the elementary level, this illustrated reader written in Koyuk Inupiat uses a question-and-answer format to teach language. Content is relevant to life in the Alaskan villages. A vocabulary list is included. (CO)

CP..... N

AN..... 000828

TI..... Sugisiva? Suva? (What Will He Do? What Did He Do?).

SE..... Units in Language Learning (Series).

YR..... 77

AU..... Nassuk, Loleta; Boffa, J. Leslie, ill.

IN..... Alaska Univ., Anchorage. National Bilingual Materials Development Center.

SN..... Office of Education (DHEW), Washington, D.C. (RMQ66000)

NO..... G G007605457

LG..... Inupiat

AV..... National Bilingual Materials Development Center, University of Alaska, 2223 Spenard Road, Anchorage, Alaska 99503 ($1.25; supplies are limited)

NT..... 24 p.

DE..... *Childrens Books; Alaska Natives; Eskimo Aleut Languages; *Eskimos; *Instructional Materials; *Reading Materials; Elementary Education; *Language Instruction; Uncommonly Taught Languages

ID..... *Inupiat

AB..... Part of a series designed for use at the elementary level, this illustrated reader written in Koyuk Inupiat uses a question-and-answer format to teach language. Content is relevant to life in the Alaskan villages. A vocabulary list is included. (CO)

CP..... N

AN..... 000829

TI..... Sua una? Sugisiniqpiun? (What Is It? What Can You Do With It?).

SE..... Units in Language Learning (Series).

YR..... 77

AU..... Nassuk, Loleta; Boffa, J. Leslie, ill.

IN..... Alaska Univ., Anchorage. National Bilingual Materials Development Center.

SN..... Office of Education (DHEW), Washington, D.C. (RMQ66000)

NO..... G G007605457

LG..... Inupiat

AV..... National Bilingual Materials Development Center, University of Alaska, 2223 Spenard Road, Anchorage, Alaska 99503 ($1.30; supplies are limited)

NT..... 28 p.

DE..... *Childrens Books; Alaska Natives; Eskimo Aleut Languages; *Eskimos; *Instructional Materials; *Reading Materials; Elementary Education; *Language Instruction; Uncommonly Taught Languages

ID..... *Inupiat

AB..... Part of a series designed for use at the elementary
level, this illustrated reader written in Koyuk Inupiat
uses a question-and-answer format to teach language.
Content is relevant to life in the Alaskan villages.
(CO)

CP..... N

AN..... 000830

TI..... Suva? Tavra (Why? Because).

SE..... Units in language Learning (Series).

YR..... 77

AU..... Nassuk, Loleta; Boffa, J. Leslie, ill.

IN..... Alaska Univ., Anchorage. National Bilingual Materials
Development Center.

SN..... Office of Education (DHEW), Washington, D.C. (RMQ66000)

NO..... G G007605457

LG..... Inupiat

AV..... National Bilingual Materials Development Center,
University of Alaska, 2223 Spenard Road, Anchorage,
Alaska 99503 ($1.40; supplies are limited)

NT..... 30 p.

DE..... *Childrens Books; Alaska Natives; Eskimo Aleut Languages;
*Eskimos; *Instructional Materials; *Reading Materials;
Elementary Education; *Language Instruction; Uncommonly
Taught Languages

ID..... *Inupiat

AB..... Part of a series designed for use at the elementary
level, this illustrated reader written in Koyuk uses a
question-and-answer format to teach language. Content is
relevant to life in the Alaskan villages. (CO)

CP..... N

AN..... 000831

TI..... Kina? Nani? (What Are They Doing? Where Are They Doing
It?).

SE..... Units in Language Learning (Series).

YR..... 77

AU..... Pulu, Tupou L.; Pope, Mary L.; Nassuk, Loleta; Swanson,
Elvina; Boffa, J. Leslie, ill.

IN..... Alaska Univ., Anchorage. National Bilingual Materials Development Center.

SN..... Office of Education (DHEW), Washington, D.C. (RMQ66000)

NO..... G G007605457

LG..... Inupiat

AV..... National Bilingual Materials Development Center, University of Alaska, 2223 Spenard Road, Anchorage, Alaska 99503 ($1.50; supplies are limited)

NT..... 40 p.

DE..... *Childrens Books; Alaska Natives; *Eskimo Aleut Languages; *Eskimos; *Instructional Materials; *Reading Materials; Elementary Education; *Language Instruction; Uncommonly Taught Languages

ID..... *Inupiat

AB..... Part of a series designed for use at the elementary level, this illustrated reader written in Koyuk uses a question-and-answer format to teach language. Content is relevant to life in the Alaskan villages. (CO)

CP..... N

AN..... 000832

TI..... Qanutun? Qapsinik? (How Much? How Many?).

SE..... Units in Language Learning (Series).

YR..... Feb78

AU..... Nassuk, Loleta; Boffa, J. Leslie, ill.

IN..... Alaska Univ., Anchorage. National Bilingual Materials Development Center.

LG..... Inupiat

AV..... National Bilingual Materials Development Center, University of Alaska, 2223 Spenard Road, Anchorage, Alaska 99503 ($1.50; supplies are limited)

NT..... 40 p.

DE..... *Childrens Books; Alaska Natives; Eskimo Aleut Languages; *Eskimos; *Instructional Materials; *Reading Materials; Elementary Education; *Language Instruction; Uncommonly Taught Languages

ID..... *Inupiat

AB..... Part of a series designed for use at the elementary level, this illustrated reader written in Koyuk Inupiat uses a question-and-answer format to teach language. Content is relevant to life in the Alaskan villages. (CO)

CP..... N

AN.....	000833
TI.....	Kiapia? Nalliak? (Which? Whose?).
SE.....	Units in Language Learning (Series).
YR.....	77
AU.....	Nassuk, Loleta; Boffa, J. Leslie, ill.
IN.....	Alaska Univ., Anchorage. National Bilingual Materials Development Center.
SN.....	Office of Education (DHEW), Washington, D.C. (RMQ66000)
NO.....	G G007605457
LG.....	Inupiat
AV.....	National Bilingual Materials Development Center, University of Alaska, 2223 Spenard Road, Anchorage, Alaska 99503 ($1.00; supplies are limited)
NT.....	20 p.
DE.....	*Childrens Books; Alaska Natives; Eskimo Aleut Languages; *Eskimos; *Instructional Materials; *Reading Materials; Elementary Education; *Language Instruction; Uncommonly Taught Languages
ID.....	*Inupiat
AB.....	Part of a series designed for use at the elementary level, this illustrated reader written in Koyuk Inupiat uses a question-and-answer format to teach language. Content is relevant to life in the Alaskan villages. (CO)
CP.....	N

AN.....	000834
TI.....	Tupiga (My House).
YR.....	77
AU.....	Nassuk, Loleta; Boffa, J. Leslie, ill.
IN.....	Alaska Univ., Anchorage. National Bilingual Materials Development Center.
SN.....	Office of Education (DHEW), Washington, D.C. (RMQ66000)
NO.....	G G007605457
LG.....	Inupiat
AV.....	National Bilingual Materials Development Center, University of Alaska, 2223 Spenard Road, Anchorage, Alaska 99503 ($1.25; supplies are limited)
NT.....	25 p.

DE..... *Childrens Books; Alaska Native; Eskimo Aleut Languages;
*Eskimos; *Instructional Materials; *Reading Materials;
Elementary Education; *Language Instruction; Uncommonly
Taught Languages

ID..... *Inupiat

AB..... In this illustrated reader, written in Koyuk Inupiat, an
Alaskan girl gives a tour of her house. The reader is
intended for use at the elementary level. A vocabulary
list is included. (CO)

CP..... N

AN..... 000835

TI..... Atinit ilama (My Family).

YR..... 77

AU..... Nassuk, Loleta; Boffa, J. Leslie, ill.

IN..... Alaska Univ., Anchorage. National Bilingual Materials
Development Center.

SN..... Office of Education (DHEW), Washington, D.C. (RMQ66000)

NO..... G G007605457

LG..... Inupiat

AV..... National Bilingual Materials Development Center,
University of Alaska, 2223 Spenard Road, Anchorage,
Alaska 99503 ($1.00; supplies are limited)

NT..... 16 p.

DE..... *Childrens Books; Alaska Natives; Eskimo Aleut Languages;
*Eskimos; *Instructional Materials; *Reading Materials;
Elementary Education; *Language Instruction; Uncommonly
Taught Languages

ID..... *Inupiat

AB..... This illustrated reader is designed for use at the
elementary level. The booklet introduces the members of
the immediate family with blanks left in sentences so
that the student can fill in the names of family members.
The text is in Koyuk Inupiat. (CO)

CP..... N

AN..... 000836

TI..... Tauqsignialiq (Going to the Store).

YR..... 77

AU..... Swanson, Elvina; Boffa, J. Leslie, ill.

IN..... Alaska Univ., Anchorage. National Bilingual Materials
       Development Center.

SN..... Office of Education (DHEW), Washington, D.C. (RMQ66000)

NO..... G G007605457

LG..... Inupiat

AV..... National Bilingual Materials Development Center,
       University of Alaska, 2223 Spenard Road, Anchorage,
       Alaska 99503 ($1.00; supplies are limited)

NT..... 21 p.

DE..... *Childrens Books; Alaska Natives; Eskimo Aleut Languages;
       *Eskimos; *Instructional Materials; *Reading Materials;
       Elementary Education; *Language Instruction; Uncommonly
       Taught Languages

ID..... *Inupiat

AB..... This illustrated reader for the elementary grades tells
       the story of an Alaskan boy who goes shopping. The text
       is in Koyuk Inupiat. (CO)

CP..... N

AN..... 000837

TI..... Ilitchuksaliq piliksramik   (Learning About Time).

YR..... Feb78

AU..... Nassuk, Loleta; Boffa, J. Leslie, ill.

IN..... Alaska Univ., Anchorage. National Bilingual Materials
       Development Center.

LG..... Inupiat

AV..... National Bilingual Materials Development Center,
       University of Alaska, 2223 Spenard Road, Anchorage,
       Alaska 99503 ($1.00; supplies are limited)

NT..... 22 p.

DE..... *Childrens Books; Alaska Natives; Eskimo Aleut Languages;
       *Eskimos; *Instructional Materials; *Reading Materials;
       Elementary Education; *Language Instruction; Uncommonly
       Taught Languages

ID..... *Inupiat

AB..... Blocks of time, such as morning, noon, and night, and
       activities associated with them are presented in this
       illustrated reader. Written in Koyuk Inupiat, it is
       designed for use at the elementary level. (CO)

CP..... N

AN..... 000838

TI..... Qanusiq naguaguwiun? Sulivin? (What Do You Like? What Are You doing?).

SE..... Ilisaaksrat qannuziqtuni (Units in Language Learning) (Series).

YR..... [77]

AU..... Sinnok, John; Eningowuk, Johnson; Boffa, J. Leslie, ill.

IN..... Alaska Univ., Anchorage. National Bilingual Materials Development Center.

LG..... Inupiat

AV..... National Bilingual Materials Development Center, University of Alaska, 2223 Spenard Road, Anchorage, Alaska 99503 ($1.50; supplies are limited)

NT..... 42 p.

DE..... *Childrens Books; Alaska Natives; Eskimo Aleut Languages; *Eskimos; *Instructional Materials; *Reading Materials; Elementary Education; *Language Instruction; Uncommonly Taught Languages

ID..... Alaska (Shishmaref); *Inupiat

AB..... A question-and-answer format is used to teach language to elementary school children in this illustrated reader written in Shishmaref Inupiat. Content is relevant to daily living in Alaskan villages. A vocabulary list is included. (CO)

CP..... N

AN..... 000839

TI..... Suliuqpa? Suzruaq? (What Will He Do? What Did He Do?).

SE..... Ilisaaksrat qannuziqtuni (Units in Language Learning) (Series).

YR..... 77

AU..... Sinnok, John; Eningowuk, Johnson; Boffa, J. Leslie, ill.

IN..... Alaska Univ., Anchorage. National Bilingual Materials Development Center.

SN..... Office of Education (DHEW), Washington, D.C. (RMQ66000)

NO..... G G007605457

LG..... Inupiat

AV..... National Bilingual Materials Development Center, University of Alaska, 2223 Spenard Road, Anchorage, Alaska 99503 ($1.25; supplies are limited)

NT..... 24 p.

DE..... *Childrens Books; Alaska Natives; Eskimo Aleut Languages; *Eskimos; *Instructional Materials; *Reading Materials; Elementary Education; *Language Instruction; Uncommonly Taught Languages

ID..... Alaska (Shishmaref); *Inupiat

AB..... A question-and-answer format is used to teach language to elementary school children in this illustrated reader written in Shishmaref Inupiat. Content is relevant to daily living in Alaskan villages. A vocabulary list is included. (CO)

CP..... N

AN..... 000840

TI..... Qanusiuva? Sulguwiun? (What Is It? What Can You Do With It?).

SE..... Ilisaaksrat qannuziqtuni (Units in Language Learning) (Series).

YR..... 77

AU..... Sinnok, John; Eningowuk, Johnson; Boffa, J. Leslie, ill.

IN..... Alaska Univ., Anchorage. National Bilingual Materials Development Center.

SN..... Office of Education (DHEW), Washington, D.C. (RMQ66000)

NO..... G G007605457

LG..... Inupiat

AV..... National Bilingual Materials Development Center, University of Alaska, 2223 Spenard Road, Anchorage, Alaska 99503 ($1.30; supplies are limited)

NT..... 28 p.

DE..... *Childrens Books; Alaska Natives; Eskimo Aleut Languages; *Eskimos; *Instructional Materials; *Reading Materials; Elementary Education; *Language Instruction; Uncommonly Taught Languages

ID..... Alaska (Shishmaref); *Inupiat

AB..... A question-and-answer format is used to teach language to elementary school children in this illustrated reader written in Shishmaref Inupiat. Content is relevant to daily living in Alaskan villages. (CO)

CP..... N

AN..... 000841

TI..... Suami? Qanu-ataa (Why? Because).

SE..... Ilisaaksrat qannuziqtuni (Units in Language Learning) (Series).

YR..... 77

AU..... Sinnok, John; Eningowuk, Johnson; Boffa, J. Leslie, ill.

IN..... Alaska Univ., Anchorage. National Bilingual Materials Development Center.

SN..... Office of Education (DHEW), Washington, D.C. (RMQ66000)

NO..... G G007605457

LG..... Inupiat

AV..... National Bilingual Materials Development Center, University of Alaska, 2223 Spenard Road, Anchorage, Alaska 99503 ($1.40; supplies are limited)

NT..... 30 p.

DE..... *Childrens Books; Alaska Natives; Eskimo Aleut Languages; *Eskimos; *Instructional Materials; *Reading Materials; Elementary Education; *Language Instruction; Uncommonly Taught Languages

ID..... Alaska (Shishmaref); *Inupiat

AB..... A question-and-answer format is used to teach language to elementary school children in this illustrated reader written in Shishmaref Inupiat. Content is relevant to daily living in Alaskan villages. (CO)

CP..... N

AN..... 000842

TI..... Kina? Suzruaq? (What Are They Doing? Where Are They Doing It?).

SE..... Ilisaaksrat qannuziqtuni (Units in Language Learning) (Series).

YR..... [77]

AU..... Sinnok, John; Eningowuk, Johnson; Boffa, J. Leslie, ill.

IN..... Alaska Univ., Anchorage. National Bilingual Materials Development Center.

LG..... Inupiat

AV..... National Bilingual Materials Development Center, University of Alaska, 2223 Spenard Road, Anchorage, Alaska 99503 ($1.50; supplies are limited)

NT..... 40 p.

DE..... *Childrens Books; Alaska Natives; Eskimo Aleut Languages; *Eskimos; *Instructional Materials; *Reading Materials; Elementary Education; *Language Instruction; Uncommonly Taught Languages

ID..... Alaska (Shishmaref); *Inupiat

AB..... A question-and-answer format is used to teach language to elementary school children in this illustrated reader written in Shishmaref Inupiat. Content is relevant to daily living in Alaskan villages. (CO)

CP..... N

AN..... 000844

TI..... Qanutun? Qapsinik? (How Much? How Many?).

SE..... Ilisaaksrat qannuziqtuni (Units in Language Learning) (Series).

YR..... [77]

AU..... Sinnok, John; Eningowuk, Johnson; Boffa, J. Leslie, ill.

IN..... Alaska Univ., Anchorage. National Bilingual Materials Development Center.

LG..... Inupiat

AV..... National Bilingual Materials Development Center, University of Alaska, 2223 Spenard Road, Anchorage, Alaska 99503 ($1.50; supplies are limited)

NT..... 40 p.

DE..... *Childrens Books; Alaska Natives; Eskimo Aleut Languages; *Eskimos; *Instructional Materials; *Reading Materials; Elementary Education; *Language Instruction; Uncommonly Taught Languages

ID..... Alaska (Shishmaref); *Inupiat

AB..... A question-and-answer format is used to teach language to elementary school children in this illustrated reader written in Shishmaref Inupiat. Content is relevant to daily living in Alaskan villages. (CO)

CP..... N

AN..... 000845

TI..... Kia? Naliak? (Which? Whose?).

SE..... Ilisaaksrat qannuziqtuni (Units in Language Learning) (Series).

YR..... 77

AU..... Sinnok, John; Eningowuk, Johnson; Boffa, J. Leslie, ill.

IN..... Alaska Univ., Anchorage. National Bilingual Materials Development Center.

SN..... Office of Education (DHEW), Washington, D.C. (RMQ66000)

NO..... G G007605457

LG..... Inupiat

AV..... National Bilingual Materials Development Center, University of Alaska, 2223 Spenard Road, Anchorage, Alaska 99503 ($1.00; supplies are limited)

NT..... 20 p.

DE..... *Childrens Books; Alaska Natives; Eskimo Aleut Languages; *Eskimos; *Instructional Materials; *Reading Materials; Elementary Education; *Language Instruction; Uncommonly Taught Languages

ID..... Alaska (Shishmaref); *Inupiat

AB..... A question-and-answer format is used to teach language to elementary school children in this illustrated reader written in Shishmaref Inupiat. Content is relevant to daily living in Alaskan villages. (CO)

CP..... N

AN..... 000846

TI..... Ilisaatuni sassaanigmik (Learning About Time).

YR..... Apr78

AU..... Sinnok, John; Eningowuk, Johnson; Boffa, J. Leslie, ill.

IN..... Alaska Univ., Anchorage. National Bilingual Materials Development Center.

LG..... Inupiat

AV..... National Bilingual Materials Development Center, University of Alaska, 2223 Spenard Road, Anchorage, Alaska 99503 ($1.00; supplies are limited)

NT..... 22 p.

DE..... *Childrens Books; Alaska Natives; Eskimo Aleut Languages; *Eskimos; *Instructional Materials; *Reading Materials; Elementary Education; *Language Instruction; Uncommonly Taught Languages

ID..... Alaska (Shishmaref); *Inupiat

AB..... This illustrated reader, written in Shishmaref Inupiat, presents blocks of time, such as morning, noon, and night, and depicts activities associated with them. It is designed for use at the elementary level. (CO)

CP..... N

AN..... 000847

TI..... Ilama atqit (My Family).

YR..... 77

AU..... Sinnok, John; Eningowuk, Johnson; Boffa, J. Leslie, ill.

IN..... Alaska Univ., Anchorage. National Bilingual Materials Development Center.

SN..... Office of Education (DHEW), Washington, D.C. (RMQ66000)

NO..... G G007605457

LG..... Inupiat

AV..... National Bilingual Materials Development Center, University of Alaska, 2223 Spenard Road, Anchorage, Alaska 99503 ($1.00; supplies are limited)

NT..... 16 p.

DE..... *Childrens Books; Alaska Natives; Eskimo Aleut Languages; *Eskimos; *Instructional Materials; *Reading Materials; Elementary Education; *Language Instruction; Uncommonly Taught Languages

ID..... Alaska (Shishmaref); *Inupiat

AB..... This illustrated reader introduces members of the immediate family; blanks are left for the names of family members to be written in by each child. The text is in Shishmaref Inupiat and is designed for use at the elementary level. (CO)

CP..... N

AN..... 000848

TI..... Niivaniagvilialiq (Going to the Store).

YR..... 77

AU..... Sinnok, John; Eningowuk, Johnson; Boffa, J. Leslie, ill.

IN..... Alaska Univ., Anchorage. National Bilingual Materials Development Center.

SN..... Office of Education (DHEW), Washington, D.C. (RMQ66000)

NO..... G G007605457

LG..... Inupiat

AV..... National Bilingual Materials Development Center, University of Alaska, 2223 Spenard Road, Anchorage, Alaska 99503 ($1.00; supplies are limited)

NT..... 21 p.

DE..... *Childrens Books; Alaska Natives; Eskimo Aleut Languages; *Eskimos; *Instructional Materials; *Reading Materials; Elementary Education; *Language Instruction; Uncommonly Taught Languages

ID..... Alaska (Shishmaref); *Inupiat

AB..... This illustrated reader tells the story of an Alaskan boy who goes shopping. Written in Shishmaref Inupiat, the text is intended for use at the elementary level. (CO)

CP..... N

AN..... 000850

TI..... Qanusit naguaguwii nigikhavgi? (What Do You Like to Eat?).

YR..... 77

AU..... Pulu, Tupou L.; Pope, Mary L.; Ongtowasruk, Faye; Eningowuk, Johnson; Boffa, J. Leslie, ill.

IN..... Alaska Univ., Anchorage. National Bilingual Materials Development Center.; Bering Strait Regional School District, Alaska.

SN..... Office of Education (DHEW), Washington, D.C. (RMQ66000)

NO..... G G007605457

LG..... Inupiat

AV..... National Bilingual Materials Development Center, University of Alaska, 2223 Spenard Road, Anchorage, Alaska 99503 ($1.00; supplies are limited)

NT..... 32 p.

DE..... Eskimo Aleut Languages; *Eskimos; Alaska Natives; Uncommonly Taught Languages; Preschool Education; *Reading Materials; *Instructional Materials; *Childrens Books; *Language Instruction

ID..... *Inupiat; Alaska (Teller); Alaska (Wales); Alaska (Shishmaref); Coloring Books

AB..... This illustrated reader in Inupiat is for use with
children at the preschool level who live in the Teller,
Wales, or Shishmaref areas of Alaska. It describes kinds
of food likely to be served in the villages. Foods are
pictured in both their raw and cooked forms. The reader
may also be used as a coloring book. (SH)

CP..... N

AN..... 000851

TI..... Suna naguaqqhayun? Suwin? (What Do You Like? What Are
You Doing?).

SE..... Units in Language Learning (Series).

YR..... 77

AU..... Seeganna, Margaret; Boffa, J. Leslie, ill.

IN..... Alaska Univ., Anchorage. National Bilingual Materials
Development Center.; Nome Public Schools, Alaska.

SN..... Office of Education (DHEW), Washington, D.C. (RMQ66000)

NO..... G G007605457

LG..... Inupiat

AV..... National Bilingual Materials Development Center,
University of Alaska, 2223 Spenard Road, Anchorage,
Alaska 99503 ($1.50; supplies are limited)

NT..... 42 p.

DE..... Eskimo Aleut Languages; *Eskimos; Alaska Natives;
Uncommonly Taught Languages; Elementary Education;
*Reading Materials; *Instructional Materials; *Childrens
Books; *Language Instruction

ID..... *Inupiat; Alaska (King Island)

AB..... This illustrated reader, written in King Island Inupiat,
uses a question-and-answer approach to teach language to
Alaskan children at the elementary level. Content is
relevant to daily activities in Alaskan villages. (SH)

CP..... N

AN..... 000852

TI..... Suluq (Sammy).

YR..... 77

AU..... Seeganna, Margaret; Boffa, J. Leslie, ill.

IN..... Alaska Univ., Anchorage. National Bilingual Materials
Development Center.; Nome Public Schools, Alaska.

SN..... Office of Education (DHEW), Washington, D.C. (RMQ66000)

NO..... G G007605457

LG..... Inupiat

AV..... National Bilingual Materials Development Center, University of Alaska, 2223 Spenard Road, Anchorage, Alaska 99503 ($1.00; supplies are limited)

NT..... 17 p.

DE..... Eskimo Aleut Languages; *Eskimos; Alaska Natives; Uncommonly Taught Languages; Elementary Education; *Reading Materials; *Instructional Materials; *Childrens Books; *Language Instruction

ID..... *Inupiat; Alaska (King Island)

AB..... This illustrated reader is written in King Island Inupiat and is intended for use on the elementary level. It tells the story of a boy who goes shopping. (SH)

CP..... N

AN..... 000853

TI..... Kiuva una? (My Family).

YR..... 77

AU..... Seeganna, Margaret; Boffa, J. Leslie, ill.

IN..... Alaska Univ., Anchorage. National Bilingual Materials Development Center.; Nome Public Schools, Alaska.

SN..... Office of Education (DHEW), Washington, D.C. (RMQ66000)

NO..... G G007605457

LG..... Inupiat

AV..... National Bilingual Materials Development Center, University of Alaska, 2223 Spenard Road, Anchorage, Alaska 99503 ($1.00; supplies are limited)

NT..... 20 p.

DE..... Eskimo Aleut Languages; *Eskimos; Alaska Natives, Uncommonly Taught Languages; Elementary Education; *Reading Materials; *Instructional Materials; *Childrens Books; *Language Instruction

ID..... *Inupiat; Alaska (King Island)

AB..... This illustrated reader introduces members of an Alaskan family. Blanks are left for names of family members to be written in by each child. The text is in King Island Inupiat and intended for use at the elementary level. (SH)

CP..... N

AN..... 000854

TI..... Sua nakuagiviun? Suliqivich? (What Do You Like? What Are You Doing?).

SE..... Sulhich uqayusiliksrakun (Units in Language Learning) (Series).

YR..... 77

AU..... Thomas, Evans; Sun, Susie; Boffa, J. Leslie, ill.

IN..... Alaska Univ., Anchorage. National Bilingual Materials Development Center.; Northwest Arctic School District, Alaska.

SN..... Office of Education (DHEW), Washington, D.C. (RMQ66000)

NO..... G G007605457

LG..... Inupiat

AV..... National Bilingual Materials Development Center, University of Alaska, 2223 Spenard Road, Anchorage, Alaska 99503 ($1.50; supplies are limited)

NT..... 42 p.

DE..... *Childrens Books; *Instructional Materials; *Reading Materials; Elementary Education; *Language Instruction; Uncommonly Taught Languages; Alaska Natives; *Eskimos; Eskimo Aleut Languages

ID..... *Inupiat; Alaska (Buckland); Alaska (Deering)

AB..... This illustrated reader, written in Buckland and Deering Inupiat, is intended for use at the elementary school level. It uses a question-and-answer approach with content relevant to daily activities in Alaskan villages. A vocabulary list is appended. (JB)

CP..... N

AN..... 000855

TI..... Sugisiva? Suliqiva? (What Will He Do? What Did He Do?).

SE..... Sulhich uqayusiliksrakun (Units in Language Learning) (Series).

YR..... 77

AU..... Thomas, Evans; Sun, Susie; Boffa, J. Leslie, ill.

IN..... Alaska Univ., Anchorage. National Bilingual Materials Development Center.; Northwest Arctic School District, Alaska.

SN..... Office of Education (DHEW), Washington, D.C. (RMQ66000)

NO..... G G007605457

LG..... Inupiat

AV..... National Bilingual Materials Development Center,
University of Alaska, 2223 Spenard Road, Anchorage,
Alaska 99503 ($1.25; supplies are limited)

NT..... 24 p.

DE..... *Childrens Books; *Instructional Materials; *Reading
Materials; Elementary Education; *Language Instruction;
Uncommonly Taught Languages; Alaska Natives; *Eskimos;
Eskimo Aleut Languages

ID..... *Inupiat; Alaska (Buckland); Alaska (Deering)

AB..... This illustrated reader, written in Buckland and Deering
Inupiat, is intended for use at the elementary school
level. It uses a question-and-answer approach with
content relevant to daily activities in Alaskan villages.
A vocabulary list is appended. (JB)

CP..... N

AN..... 000856

TI..... Sua una? Sutlanayaqpiun? (What Is It? What Can You Do
With It?).

SE..... Sulhich uqayusiliksrakun (Units in Language Learning)
(Series).

YR..... 77

AU..... Thomas, Evans; Sun, Susie; Boffa, J. Leslie, ill.

IN..... Alaska Univ., Anchorage. National Bilingual Materials
Development Center.; Northwest Arctic School District,
Alaska.

SN..... Office of Education (DHEW), Washington, D.C. (RMQ66000)

NO..... G G007605457

LG..... Inupiat

AV..... National Bilingual Materials Development Center,
University of Alaska, 2223 Spenard Road, Anchorage,
Alaska 99503 ($1.30; supplies are limited)

NT..... 28 p.

DE..... *Childrens Books; *Instructional Materials; *Reading
Materials; Elementary Education; *Language Instruction;
Uncommonly Taught Languages; Alaska Natives; *Eskimos;
Eskimo Aleut Languages

ID..... *Inupiat; Alaska (Buckland); Alaska (Deering)

AB..... This illustrated reader, written in Buckland and Deering
Inupiat, is intended for use at the elementary school
level. It uses a question-and-answer approach with
content relevant to daily activities in Alaskan villages.
(JB)

CP..... N

AN..... 000857

TI..... Suvaata? Atakkii (Why? Because).

SE..... Sulhich uqayusiliksrakun (Units in Language Learning)
       (Series).

YR..... 77

AU..... Thomas, Evans; Sun, Susie; Boffa, J. Leslie, ill.

IN..... Alaska Univ., Anchorage. National Bilingual Materials
       Development Center.; Northwest Arctic School District,
       Alaska.

SN..... Office of Education (DHEW), Washington, D.C. (RMQ66000)

NO..... G G007605457

LG..... Inupiat

AV..... National Bilingual Materials Development Center,
       University of Alaska, 2223 Spenard Road, Anchorage,
       Alaska 99503 ($1.40; supplies are limited)

NT..... 30 p.

DE..... *Childrens Books; *Instructional Materials; *Reading
       Materials; Elementary Education; *Language Instruction;
       Uncommonly Taught Languages; Alaska Natives; *Eskimos;
       Eskimo Aleut Languages

ID..... *Inupiat; Alaska (Buckland); Alaska (Deering)

AB..... This illustrated reader, written in Buckland and Deering
       Inupiat, is intended for use at the elementary school
       level. It uses a question-and-answer approach with
       content relevant to daily activities in Alaskan villages.
       (JB)

CP..... N

AN..... 000858

TI..... Kiña? Sugisiva? (What Are They Doing? Where Are They
       Doing It?).

SE..... Sulhich uqayusiliksrakun (Units in Language Learning)
       (Series).

YR..... 77

AU..... Thomas, Evans; Sun, Susie; Boffa, J. Leslie, ill.

IN..... Alaska Univ., Anchorage. National Bilingual Materials
       Development Center.; Northwest Arctic School District,
       Alaska.

LG..... Inupiat

AV..... National Bilingual Materials Development Center,
University of Alaska, 2223 Spenard Road, Anchorage,
Alaska 99503 ($1.50; supplies are limited)

NT..... 40 p.

DE..... *Childrens Books; *Instructional Materials; *Reading
Materials; Elementary Education; *Language Instruction;
Uncommonly Taught Languages; Alaska Natives; *Eskimos;
Eskimo Aleut Languages

ID..... *Inupiat; Alaska (Buckland); Alaska (Deering)

AB..... This illustrated reader, written in Buckland and Deering
Inupiat, is intended for use at the elementary school
level. It uses a question-and-answer approach with
content relevant to daily activities in Alaskan villages.
(JB)

CP..... N

AN..... 000859

TI..... Qanutun? Qapsich? (How Much? How Many?).

SE..... Sulhich uqayusiliksrakun (Units in Language Learning)
(Series).

YR..... 77

AU..... Thomas, Evans; Sun, Susie; Boffa, J. Leslie, ill.

IN..... Alaska Univ., Anchorage. National Bilingual Materials
Development Center.; Northwest Arctic School District,
Alaska.

LG..... Inupiat

AV..... National Bilingual Materials Development Center,
University of Alaska, 2223 Spenard Road, Anchorage,
Alaska 99503 ($1.50; supplies are limited)

NT..... 40 p.

DE..... *Childrens Books; *Instructional Materials; *Reading
Materials; Elementary Education; *Language Instruction;
Uncommonly Taught Languages; Alaska Natives; *Eskimos;
Eskimo Aleut Languages

ID..... *Inupiat; Alaska (Buckland); Alaska (Deering)

AB..... This illustrated reader, written in Buckland and Deering
Inupiat, is intended for use at the elementary school
level. It uses a question-and-answer approach with
content relevant to daily activities in Alaskan villages.
(JB)

CP..... N

AN..... 000860

TI..... Kisum? Naliak? (Which? Whose?).

SE..... Sulhich uqayusiliksrakun (Units in Language Learning) (Series).

YR..... 77

AU..... Thomas, Evans; Sun, Susie; Boffa, J. Leslie, ill.

IN..... Alaska Univ., Anchorage. National Bilingual Materials Development Center.; Northwest Arctic School District, Alaska.

SN..... Office of Education (DHEW), Washington, D.C. (RMQ66000)

NO..... G G007605457

LG..... Inupiat

AV..... National Bilingual Materials Development Center, University of Alaska, 2223 Spenard Road, Anchorage, Alaska 99503 ($1.00; supplies are limited)

NT..... 20 p.

DE..... *Childrens Books; *Instructional Materials; *Reading Materials; Elementary Education; *Language Instruction; Uncommonly Taught Languages; Alaska Natives; *Eskimos; Eskimo Aleut Languages

ID..... *Inupiat; Alaska (Buckland); Alaska (Deering)

AB..... This illustrated reader, written in Buckland and Deering Inupiat, is intended for use at the elementary school level. It uses a question-and-answer approach with content relevant to daily activities in Alaskan villages. (JB)

CP..... N

AN..... 000861

TI..... Nunatchiagmi (Buckland).

YR..... 77

AU..... Thomas, Evans; Sun, Susie; Loon, Hanah; Boffa, J. Leslie, ill.

IN..... Alaska Univ., Anchorage. National Bilingual Materials Development Center.

SN..... Office of Education (DHEW), Washington, D.C. (RMQ66000)

NO..... G G007605457

LG..... English; Inupiat

AV..... National Bilingual Materials Development Center, University of Alaska, 2223 Spenard Road, Anchorage, Alaska 99503 ($1.50; supplies are limited)

NT..... 34 p.

DE..... *Childrens Books; *Instructional Materials; *Reading Materials; Elementary Education; *Language Instruction; Uncommonly Taught Languages; Alaska Natives; *Eskimos; Eskimo Aleut Languages; Legends; *Folk Culture; History

ID..... *Inupiat; Alaska (Buckland); Alaska (Deering)

AB..... This illustrated reader, written in Buckland and Deering Inupiat and English, is intended for use at the elementary school level. It recounts incidents relating to life in Buckland and Deering. (JB)

CP..... N

AN..... 000862

TI..... Ipnatchiami (Deering).

YR..... 77

AU..... Karmun, Mamie; Boffa, J. Leslie, ill.

IN..... Alaska Univ., Anchorage. National Bilingual Materials Development Center.

SN..... Office of Education (DHEW), Washington, D.C. (RMQ66000)

NO..... G G007605457

LG..... English; Inupiat

AV..... National Bilingual Materials Development Center, University of Alaska, 2223 Spenard Road, Anchorage, Alaska 99503 ($1.50; supplies are limited)

NT..... 32 p.

DE..... *Childrens Books; *Instructional Materials; *Reading Materials; Elementary Education; *Language Instruction; Uncommonly Taught Languages; Alaska Natives; *Eskimos; Eskimo Aleut Languages; Legends; *Folk Culture; History

ID..... *Inupiat; Alaska (Buckland) Alaska (Deering)

AB..... This illustrated reader, written in Buckland and Deering Inupiat and English, is intended for use at the elementary school level. It recounts incidents relating to life in Buckland and Deering. (JB)

CP..... N

AN..... 000863

TI..... Suna nakuagiviun? Suliqivich? (What Do You Like? What Are You Doing?).

SE..... Uqalikun ilirviksrat (Units in Language Learning) (Series).

YR..... 77

AU..... Swan, Oscar; Sun, Susie; Boffa, J. Leslie, ill.

IN..... Alaska Univ., Anchorage. National Bilingual Materials Development Center.

SN..... Office of Education (DHEW), Washington, D.C. (RMQ66000)

NO..... G G007605457

LG..... Inupiat

AV..... National Bilingual Materials Development Center, University of Alaska, 2223 Spenard Road, Anchorage, Alaska 99503 ($1.50; supplies are limited)

NT..... 42 p.

DE..... *Childrens Books; Alaska Natives; Eskimo Aleut Languages; *Eskimos; *Instructional Materials; Elementary Education; *Reading Materials; *Language Instruction; Uncommonly Taught Languages

ID..... *Inupiat; Alaska (Kivalina)

AB..... A question-and-answer format is used to teach language in this illustrated reader written in Kivalina Inupiat for the elementary grades. Content is relevant to activities in the Alaskan villages. A vocabulary list is included. (CO)

CP..... N

AN..... 000864

TI..... Suniaqpa? Suva? (What Will He Do? What Did He Do?).

SE..... Uqalikun ilirviksrat (Units in Language Learning) (Series).

YR..... 77

AU..... Swan, Oscar; Sun, Susie; Boffa, J. Leslie, ill.

IN..... Alaska Univ., Anchorage. National Bilingual Materials Development Center.

SN..... Office of Education (DHEW), Washington, D.C. (RMQ66000)

NO..... G G007605457

LG..... Inupiat

AV..... National Bilingual Materials Development Center, University of Alaska, 2223 Spenard Road, Anchorage, Alaska 99503 ($1.25; supplies are limited)

NT..... 24 p.

DE..... *Childrens Books; Alaska Natives; Eskimo Aleut Languages; *Eskimos; *Instructional Materials; Elementary Education; *Reading Materials; *Language Instruction; Uncommonly Taught Languages

ID..... *Inupiat; Alaska (Kivalina)

AB..... A question-and-answer format is used to teach language in this illustrated reader written in Kivalina Inupiat for the elementary grades. Content is relevant to activities in the Alaskan villages. A vocabulary list is included. (CO)

CP..... N

AN..... 000865

TI..... Suuva una? Sugisiñiqpiun? (What Is It? What Can You Do With It?).

SE..... Uqalikun ilirviksrat (Units in Language Learning) (Series).

YR..... 77

AU..... Swan, Oscar; Sun, Susie; Boffa, J. Leslie, ill.

IN..... Alaska Univ., Anchorage. National Bilingual Materials Development Center.

SN..... Office of Education (DHEW), Washington, D.C. (RMQ66000)

NO..... G G007605457

LG..... Inupiat

AV..... National Bilingual Materials Development Center, University of Alaska, 2223 Spenard Road, Anchorage, Alaska 99503 ($1.30; supplies are limited)

NT..... 28 p.

DE..... *Childrens Books; Alaska Natives; Eskimo Aleut Languages; *Eskimos; *Instructional Materials; *Language Instruction; Uncommonly Taught Languages; *Reading Materials; Elementary Education

ID..... Alaska (Kivalina); *Inupiat

AB..... A question-and-answer format is used to teach language in this illustrated reader written in Kivalina Inupiat for the elementary grades. Content is relevant to activities in the Alaskan villages. (CO)

CP..... N

AN..... 000866

TI..... Suvaata? Atakkii (Why? Because).

SE..... Uqalikun ilirviksrat (Units in Language Learning) (Series).

YR..... 77

AU..... Swan, Oscar; Sun, Susie; Boffa, J. Leslie, ill.

IN..... Alaska Univ., Anchorage. National Bilingual Materials
        Development Center.

SN..... Office of Education (DHEW), Washington, D.C. (RMQ66000)

NO..... G G007605457

LG..... Inupiat

AV..... National Bilingual Materials Development Center,
        University of Alaska, 2223 Spenard Road, Anchorage,
        Alaska 99503 ($1.40; supplies are limited)

NT..... 30 p.

DE..... *Childrens Books; Alaska Natives; Eskimo Aleut Languages;
        *Eskimos; *Instructional Materials; Elementary Education;
        *Reading Materials; *Language Instruction; Uncommonly
        Taught Languages

ID..... Alaska (Kivalina); *Inupiat

AB..... A question-and-answer format is used to teach language in
        this illustrated reader written in Kivalina Inupiat for
        the elementary grades. Content is relevant to activities
        in the Alaskan villages. (CO)

CP..... N

AN..... 000867

TI..... Kiña? Suliqiva? (What Are They Doing? Where Are They
        Doing It?).

SE..... Uqalikun ilirviksrat (Units in Language Learning)
        (Series).

YR..... Oct77

AU..... Swan, Oscar; Sun, Susie; Boffa, J. Leslie, ill.

IN..... Alaska Univ., Anchorage. National Bilingual Materials
        Development Center.

LG..... Inupiat

AV..... National Bilingual Materials Development Center,
        University of Alaska, 2223 Spenard Road, Anchorage,
        Alaska 99503 ($1.50; supplies are limited)

NT..... 40 p.

DE..... *Childrens Books; Alaska Natives; Eskimo Aleut Languages;
        *Eskimos; *Instructional Materials; Elementary Education;
        *Reading Materials; *Language Instruction; Uncommonly
        Taught Languages

ID..... Alaska (Kivalina); *Inupiat

AB..... A question-and-answer format is used to teach language in this illustrated reader written in Kivalina Inupiat for the elementary grades. Content is relevant to activities in the Alaskan villages. (CO)

CP..... N

AN..... 000868

TI..... Qanutun? Qavsiñik? (How Much? How Many?).

SE..... Uqalikun ilirviksrat (Units in Language Learning) (Series).

YR..... Oct77

AU..... Swan, Oscar; Sun, Susie; Boffa, J. Leslie, ill.

IN..... Alaska Univ., Anchorage. National Bilingual Materials Development Center.

LG..... Inupiat

AV..... National Bilingual Materials Development Center, University of Alaska, 2223 Spenard Road, Anchorage, Alaska 99503 ($1.50; supplies are limited)

NT..... 40 p.

DE..... *Childrens Books; Alaska Natives; Eskimo Aleut Languages; *Eskimos; *Instructional Materials; Elementary Education; *Reading Materials; *Language Instruction; Uncommonly Taught Languages

ID..... Alaska (Kivalina); *Inupiat

AB..... A question-and-answer format is used to teach language in this illustrated reader written in Kivalina Inupiat for the elementary grades. Content is relevant to activities in the Alaskan villages. (CO)

CP..... N

AN..... 000869

TI..... Kia? Nalliat? (Which? Whose?).

SE..... Uqalikun ilirviksrat (Units in Language Learning) (Series).

YR..... 77

AU..... Swan, Oscar; Sun, Susie; Boffa, J. Leslie, ill.

IN..... Alaska Univ., Anchorage. National Bilingual Materials Development Center.

SN..... Office of Education (DHEW), Washington, D.C. (RMQ66000)

NO..... G G007605457

LG..... Inupiat

AV..... National Bilingual Materials Development Center, University of Alaska, 2223 Spenard Road, Anchorage, Alaska 99503 ($1.00; supplies are limited)

NT..... 20 p.

DE..... *Childrens Books; Alaska Natives; *Eskimos; Eskimo Aleut Languages; *Instructional Materials; Elementary Education; *Reading Materials; *Language Instruction; Uncommonly Taught Languages

ID..... Alaska (Kivalina); *Inupiat

AB..... A question-and-answer format is used to teach language in this illustrated reader written in Kivalina Inupiat for the elementary grades. Content is relevant to activities in the Alaskan villages. (CO)

CP..... N

AN..... 000870

TI..... Chuna nakuagiwiun? Chulivit? (What Do You Like? What Are You Doing?).

SE..... Units in Language Learning (Series).

YR..... [77]

AU..... Komakhuk, Agnes; Boffa, J. Leslie, ill.

IN..... Alaska Univ., Anchorage. National Bilingual Materials Development Center.; Bering Strait Regional School District, Alaska.

LG..... Inupiat

AV..... National Bilingual Materials Development Center, University of Alaska, 2223 Spenard Road, Anchorage, Alaska 99503 ($1.50; supplies are limited)

NT..... 42 p.

DE..... Eskimo Aleut Languages; *Eskimos; Alaska Natives; Uncommonly Taught Languages; Elementary Education; *Reading Materials; *Instructional Materials; *Childrens Books; *Language Instruction

ID..... Alaska (White Mountain); *Inupiat

AB..... This illustrated reader in White Mountain Inupiat, like others in the same series, uses a question-and-answer approach to teach language to Alaskan children at the elementary level. Content is relevant to daily activities in Alaskan villages. A vocabulary list is included. (SH)

CP..... N

AN..... 000871

TI..... Chuliuqpa ilaa? Chuwa ilaa? (What Will He Do? What Did He Do?).

SE..... Units in Language Learning (Series).

YR..... 77

AU..... Komakhuk, Agnes; Boffa, J. Leslie, ill.

IN..... Alaska Univ., Anchorage. National Bilingual Materials Development Center.; Bering Strait Regional School District, Alaska.

SN..... Office of Education (DHEW), Washington, D.C. (RMQ66000)

NO..... G G007605457

LG..... Inupiat

AV..... National Bilingual Materials Development Center, University of Alaska, 2223 Spenard Road, Anchorage, Alaska 99503 ($1.25; supplies are limited)

NT..... 24 p.

DE..... Eskimo Aleut Languages; *Eskimos; Alaska Natives; Uncommonly Taught Languages; Elementary Education; *Reading Materials; *Instructional Materials; *Childrens Books; *Language Instruction

ID..... Alaska (White Mountain); *Inupiat

AB..... This illustrated reader in White Mountain Inupiat, like others in the same series, uses a question-and-answer approach to teach language to Alaskan children at the elementary level. Content is relevant to daily activities in Alaskan villages. A vocabulary list is included. (SH)

CP..... N

AN..... 000872

TI..... Chuuva? Chuliuqpiun? (What Is It? What Can You Do With It?).

SE..... Units in Language Learning (Series).

YR..... 77

AU..... Komakhuk, Agnes; Boffa, J. Leslie, ill.; Nassuk, Loleta, ill.

IN..... Alaska Univ., Anchorage. National Bilingual Materials Development Center.; Bering Strait Regional School District, Alaska.

SN..... Office of Education (DHEW), Washington, D.C. (RMQ66000)

NO..... G G007605457

LG..... Inupiat

AV..... National Bilingual Materials Development Center, University of Alaska, 2223 Spenard Road, Anchorage, Alaska 99503 ($1.30; supplies are limited)

NT..... 28 p.

DE..... Eskimo Aleut Languages; *Eskimos; Alaska Natives; Uncommonly Taught Languages; Elementary Education; *Reading Materials; *Instructional Materials; *Childrens Books; *Language Instruction

ID..... Alaska (White Mountain); Alaska (Council); *Inupiat

AB..... This illustrated reader in White Mountain and Council Inupiat, like others in the same series, uses a question-and-answer approach to teach language to Alaskan children at the elementary level. Content is relevant to daily activities in Alaskan villages. (SH)

CP..... N

AN..... 000873

TI..... Chuami? Qanu ataa (Why? Because).

SE..... Units in Language Learning (Series).

YR..... 77

AU..... Boffa, J. Leslie, ill.

IN..... Alaska Univ., Anchorage. National Bilingual Materials Development Center.; Bering Strait Regional School District, Alaska.

SN..... Office of Education (DHEW), Washington, D.C. (RMQ66000)

NO..... G G007605457

LG..... Inupiat

AV..... National Bilingual Materials Development Center, University of Alaska, 2223 Spenard Road, Anchorage, Alaska 99503 ($1.40; supplies are limited)

NT..... 30 p.

DE..... Eskimo Aleut Languages; *Eskimos; Alaska Natives;
Uncommonly Taught Languages; Elementary Education;
*Reading Materials; *Instructional Materials; *Childrens
Books; *Language Instruction

ID..... Alaska (White Mountain); *Inupiat

AB..... This illustrated reader in White Mountain Inupiat, like
others in the same series, uses a question-and-answer
approach to teach language to Alaskan children at the
elementary level. Content is relevant to daily
activities in Alaskan villages. (SH)

CP..... N

AN..... 000874

TI..... Kina? Chuliva? (What Are They Doing? Where Are They Doing It?).

SE..... Units in Language Learning (Series).

YR..... [77]

AU..... Komakhuk, Agnes; Boffa, J. Leslie, ill.

IN..... Alaska Univ., Anchorage. National Bilingual Materials
Development Center.; Bering Strait Regional School
District, Alaska.

LG..... Inupiat

AV..... National Bilingual Materials Development Center,
University of Alaska, 2223 Spenard Road, Anchorage,
Alaska 99503 ($1.50; supplies are limited)

NT..... 40 p.

DE..... Eskimo Aleut Languages; *Eskimos; Alaska Natives;
Uncommonly Taught Languages; Elementary Education;
*Reading Materials; *Instructional Materials; *Childrens
Books; *Language Instruction

ID..... Alaska (White Mountain); *Inupiat

AB..... This illustrated reader in White Mountain Inupiat, like
others in the same series, uses a question-and-answer
approach to teach language to Alaskan children at the
elementary level. Content is relevant to daily activities
in Alaskan villages. (SH)

CP..... N

AN..... 000875

TI..... Qanuqtun? Qapchinik? (How Much? How Many?).

SE..... Units in Language Learning (Series).

YR..... [77]

AU..... Komakhuk, Agnes; Boffa, J. Leslie, ill.

IN..... Alaska Univ., Anchorage. National Bilingual Materials Development Center.; Bering Strait Regional School District, Alaska.

LG..... Inupiat

AV..... National Bilingual Materials Development Center, University of Alaska, 2223 Spenard Road, Anchorage, Alaska 99503 ($1.50; supplies are limited)

NT..... 40 p.

DE..... Eskimo Aleut Languages; *Eskimos; *Alaska Natives; Uncommonly Taught Languages; Elementary Education; *Reading Materials; *Instructional Materials; *Childrens Books; Number Concepts; Concept Formation; *Language Instruction

ID..... Alaska (White Mountain); *Inupiat

AB..... This illustrated reader in White Mountain Inupiat, like others in the same series, uses a question-and-answer approach to teach language to Alaskan children at the elementary level. Content is relevant to daily activities in Alaskan villages. (SH)

CP..... N

AN..... 000876

TI..... Iniga (My House).

YR..... 77

AU..... Komakhuk, Agnes; Boffa, J. Leslie, ill.

IN..... Alaska Univ., Anchorage. National Bilingual Materials Development Center.; Bering Strait Regional School District, Alaska.

SN..... Office of Education (DHEW), Washington, D.C. (RMQ66000)

NO..... G G007605457

LG..... Inupiat

AV..... National Bilingual Materials Development Center, University of Alaska, 2223 Spenard Road, Anchorage, Alaska 99503 ($1.25; supplies are limited)

NT..... 25 p.

DE..... Eskimo Aleut Languages; *Eskimos; Alaska Natives; Uncommonly Taught Languages; Elementary Education; *Reading Materials; *Instructional Materials; *Childrens Books; *Language Instruction

ID..... Alaska (White Mountain); *Inupiat

AB..... An Alaskan girl shows you proudly through her house in this illustrated reader. The text is in White Mountain Inupiat and intended for use at the elementary level. (SH)

CP..... N

AN..... 000877

TI..... Chumik nailguwit? (What Can You Smell?).

YR..... 77

AU..... Pulu, Tupou L.; Pope, Mary L.; Komakhuk, Agnes; Nassuk, Loleta; Boffa, J. Leslie, ill.

IN..... Alaska Univ., Anchorage. National Bilingual Materials Development Center.; Bering Strait Regional School District, Alaska.

SN..... Office of Education (DHEW), Washington, D.C. (RMQ66000)

NO..... G G007605457

LG..... Inupiat

AV..... National Bilingual Materials Development Center, University of Alaska, 2223 Spenard Road, Anchorage, Alaska 99503 ($2.00; supplies are limited)

NT..... 48 p.

DE..... Eskimo Aleut Languages; *Eskimos; Alaska Natives; Uncommonly Taught Languages; Elementary Education; *Reading Materials; *Instructional Materials; *Childrens Books; *Language Instruction

ID..... Alaska (White Mountain); Alaska (Council)

AB..... Eight five-page sections use the same pattern to describe common scents in an Alaskan village. The illustrated reader is in White Mountain Inupiat and is intended for use at the elementary level. (SH)

CP..... N

AN..... 000878

TI..... Ilitchiliq piliksramik (Learning About Time).

YR..... Feb78

AU..... Komakhuk, Agnes; Boffa, J. Leslie, ill.

IN..... Alaska Univ., Anchorage. National Bilingual Materials Development Center.; Bering Strait Regional School District, Alaska.

LG..... Inupiat

AV..... National Bilingual Materials Development Center, University of Alaska, 2223 Spenard Road, Anchorage, Alaska 99503 ($1.00; supplies are limited)

NT..... 22 p.

DE..... Eskimo Aleut Languages; *Eskimos; Alaska Natives; Uncommonly Taught Languages; Elementary Education; *Reading Materials; *Instructional Materials; *Childrens Books; Time; *Language Instruction

ID..... Alaska (White Mountain); *Inupiat

AB..... This illustrated reader presents blocks of time, such as morning, noon, and night, and depicts activities associated with them. It is written in White Mountain Inupiat and is intended for use at the elementary level. (SH)

CP..... N

AN..... 000879

TI..... Atqit ilama (My Family).

YR..... 77

AU..... Komakhuk, Agnes; Boffa, J. Leslie, ill.

IN..... Alaska Univ., Anchorage. National Bilingual Materials Development Center.; Bering Strait Regional School District, Alaska.

SN..... Office of Education (DHEW), Washington, D.C. (RMQ66000)

NO..... G G007605457

LG..... Inupiat

AV..... National Bilingual Materials Development Center, University of Alaska, 2223 Spenard Road, Anchorage, Alaska 99503 ($1.00; supplies are limited)

NT..... 20 p.

DE..... Eskimo Aleut Languages; *Eskimos; Alaska Natives; Uncommonly Taught Languages; Elementary Education; *Reading Materials; *Instructional Materials; *Childrens Books; *Language Instruction

ID..... Alaska (White Mountain)

AB..... This illustrated reader introduces members of the immediate family in sentence form, leaving blanks for the child to fill in the names of family members. The text is in White Mountain Inupiat and is intended for use in the elementary grades. (SH)

CP..... N

AN.....	000880
TI.....	Akiligialiq (Going to the Store).
YR.....	77
AU.....	Komakhuk, Agnes; Boffa, J. Leslie, ill.
IN.....	Alaska Univ., Anchorage. National Bilingual Materials Development Center.; Bering Strait Regional School District, Alaska.
SN.....	Office of Education (DHEW), Washington, D.C. (RMQ66000)
NO.....	G G007605457
LG.....	Inupiat
AV.....	National Bilingual Materials Development Center, University of Alaska, 2223 Spenard Road, Anchorage, Alaska 99503 ($1.00; supplies are limited)
NT.....	21 p.
DE.....	Eskimo Aleut Languages; *Eskimos; Alaska Natives; Uncommonly Taught Languages; Elementary Education; *Reading Materials; *Instructional Materials; *Childrens Books; *Language Instruction
ID.....	Alaska (White Mountain); *Inupiat
AB.....	This illustrated reader relates the story of an Alaskan boy who goes to the store. The White Mountain Inupiat text is intended for use in the elementary grades. (SH)
CP.....	N

AN.....	000924
TI.....	Navajo Consonant Posters.
YR.....	Aug76
IN.....	National Dissemination and Assessment Center, Austin, Tex.; Education Service Center Region 13, Austin, Tex. (XPT82322)
SN.....	Office of Education (DHEW), Washington, D.C. (RMQ66000)
LG.....	Navajo
AV.....	National Dissemination and Assessment Center, 7703 North Lamar Boulevard, Austin, Texas 78752 ($9.00)
NT.....	28 colored posters; 13"x15"
DE.....	*Navajo; *Consonants; *Instructional Media; Visual Aids; Illustrations; *Instructional Materials; Primary Education; *Athapascan Languages; *American Indians
ID.....	*Posters; Tongue Twisters

AB..... Each of these 28 posters, intended for use at the primary
level, represents a consonant sound from the Navajo
language. A two-color illustration and tongue-twister
accentuate each consonant sound. (JB)

CP..... N

AN..... 000925

TI..... Asian American Study Prints: Teacher's Manual.

YR..... 78

AU..... Wong, Sau-Ling Cynthia, ed.

IN..... Asian American Bilingual Center, Berkeley, Calif.
(BBB15977); Visual Communications, Los Angeles, Calif.

SN..... Office of Education (DHEW), Washington, D.C. (RMQ66000)

LG..... Chinese; English

AV..... National Dissemination and Assessment Center, California
State University, 5151 State University Drive, Los
Angeles, California 90032

NT..... 125 p.
For companion study prints, see 000926.

DE..... *Asian Americans; Minority Groups; *Teaching Guides;
Curriculum Guides; Bilingual Education; Social Studies;
Self Concept; *Visual Aids; Instructional Materials;
Language Arts; *Chinese; Occupations; Cultural Awareness;
*Cultural Images; *Photographs; Minority Groups;
Kindergarten; Grade 1; Primary Education; Cultural
Education; Biographies

ID..... California (Los Angeles)

AB..... This teacher's manual provides background information,
captions, vocabulary, discussion questions, and followup
classroom activities for the 10 photo essays in the Asian
American Study Prints. The text is in Chinese and in
English, each presented in facing pages. Like the study
prints themselves, focus is on diverse occupations,
personal histories, and ethnic backgrounds of selected
Asian Americans of all ages living in the Los Angeles
area. These materials can be incorporated into social
science or language arts curriculums at the kindergarten
and first grade levels. (SH)

CP..... N

AN..... 000926

TI..... Asian American Study Prints.

YR..... [78]

IN..... Asian American Bilingual Center, Berkeley, Calif.
(BBB15977); Visual Communications, Los Angeles, Calif.

LG..... Chinese; English

AV..... National Dissemination and Assessment Center, California State University, 5151 State University Drive, Los Angeles, California 90032

NT..... 84 black-and-white photographs; 11"x14"
For companion teacher's manual, see 000925.

DE..... Kindergarten; Grade 1, Primary Education; Instructional Materials; *Visual Aids; *Asian Americans; Minority Groups; *Chinese; Social Studies; Language Arts; Bilingual Education; *Photographs; Cultural Awareness; *Cultural Images; Occupations; *Cultural Education

ID..... California (Los Angeles)

AB..... These study prints are arranged into 10 photo essays which provide a visual glimpse into the life and work of Asian Americans who reside in the Los Angeles area. Intended to reflect the diversity of peoples and communities in the United States, they represent a wide range of occupations, personal histories, ages, and ethnic backgrounds. A newspaper reporter, teacher, gardener, carpenter, doctor, artist, dancer, dentist, baker, and fireman are all shown on and off the job. Some topics covered include safety, health, communication, consumer education, food, art, community work and services, housing, career education, immigration, and the status of women. The caption for each photograph is printed on the reverse side in both Chinese and English so that the teacher can read it while showing the picture. The study prints can be used either alone or in conjunction with Chinese language arts curriculum kits at the kindergarten and first grade level. (SH)

CP..... N

Indexes

Author Index 289
Index to Languages 295
Index to Subjects 299
Index to Series Titles 309
Index to Titles 311

AUTHOR INDEX

Agard, Frederick B., 000525

Albert, Renaud S, 000181

Allen, Shauna, 000101

Almeida, Onésimo, 000119, 000120, 000121, 000122, 000123

Alvarez, Gerarda, 000019

Alvarez, Verónica, 000550

Anahonak, Carl, 000801, 000802 000803, 000804, 000805

Anahonak, Dan, 000801, 000802, 000803, 000804, 000805

Andrade, Magdalena, 000580

Astacio, Ramón, 000058

Baca, Nina 000567, 000568, 000569

Bachelier, Guy, 000067, 000068, 000069

Bachelier, Raymond, 000060 000061, 000067, 000068, 000069

Bailey, Joe, 000026

Baker, Frances S., 000110

Baker, Jean M., 000571

Begnaud, Noëmi, 000060 000061, 000062, 000063, 000064 000065, 000067, 000068, 0000069, 000180, 000182, 000183

Bergsland, Knut, comp., 000800

Besedes, Akemi, 000707

Blais, Danielle, trans., 000021, 000022

Bloomfield, Leonard, 000523

Bradley, Ruth, 000060, 000061, 000062, 000063, 000064, 000065 000067, 000068, 000069, 000180, 000182, 000183

Cadilla de Ruibal, Carmen Alicia, 000054, 000055, 000156, 000169, 000173, 000174, 000175, 000176, 000177

Calais, Gayle, 000067, 000068, 000069, 000183

Canales, Estella, 000566

Cardone, Romolo, 000687, 000688

Carmen Garcia, Maria del, ed., 000052

Casalucan, Ernest, 000710, 000711, 000712, 000713, 000714, 000715, 000716, 000717, 000718, 000719

Castañeda, Alfredo, 000646, 000647 000648, 000649, 000650, 000651, 000653

Cedillo, Gustavo F., 000532

Chabot, Grégoire, 000006

Chassé, Paul, 000181

Chatto, John, 000614

Cioffari, Vincenzo, ed., 000526

Cohen, Allen Stephen, 000052, 000053, 000109

Colón, Luisa, 000641

Cortes, Carlos E. 000652

Coussan, Odette, 000060, 000061, 000062, 000063, 000064, 000065 000067, 000068, 000069, 000180 000182

Cowan, J. Ronayne, 000529

Cox, Barbara G., 000653

Cramer, Sharon, 000119, 000120, 000121, 000122, 000123

Crespín, Emil, 000639

Curt, Carmen Judith Nine, 000563, 000564, 000669

Cushman, Dean, ed., 000026

D'Entresangle, Serge, 000183

Davis, Lorene, 000577

De la Pena, Becky, 000654

Deane, Minerva, 000660

Díaz, Luis C., ed., 000550

Dirks, Moses, 000784 000789, 000790, 000791, 000792, 000793, 000794, 000795, 000796, 000797, 000798, 000800

Dixson, Robert J., 000056

Dubé, Normand, 000034, 000658

Dugas, Donald G., 000032, 000049, 000671

Eningowuk, Johnson, 000838, 000839, 000840, 000841, 000842, 000844, 000845, 000846, 000847, 000848, 000850

Escamilla, Valentina, 000640, 000642

Factor, Susannah, trans., 000045, 000577, 000705

Fallone, Nino, 000692

Fang, Chaoying, 000527

Fanjeaux Francis, 000062, 000063, 000064, 000065, 000183

Faustino, Theodosia, 000706, 000707

Finer, Neal B., 000629, 000630

Flores Salvador, 000595, 000596, 000597, 000598, 000640, 000654, 000655

Fuller Elizabeth Valenzuela, 000059

Galindo, Angelina, 000668

García, Inés, 000566

García, María H., 000644

Garza, Beatríz de la, ed., 000566, 000657

Garza, Olivia, 000566

Geiss, Tony, 000026

Gill, Clark C., 000664

Giroux, Emile, 000035

Godoy, Viola, 000566

Golley, Nadesta, 000789, 000790, 000791, 000792, 000793, 000796

Golodoff, Dennis A., 000796

González, Josué M., 000666

Gorena, Minerva, comp., 000656

Granado, Eusebia, trans., 000027, 000028, 000481

Granger, Jean-Michel, 000060, 000061

Guardarrama, Eduardo, 000149

Hagel, Phyllis, 000184

Harjo, Edmond A., 000539

Harper, Pam, ed., 000645, 000668

Harsh, J. Richard, 000708

Haugen, Einar, ed., 000522

Hayakawa, Linda, 000569

Henio, Clyde, 000614

Herbert, Charles H., 000036, 000562

Hernández, Gloria J., ed., 000058

Herold, P. Leslie, 000646, 000647, 000648, 000649, 000650, 000651, 000653

Hockett, Charles F., 000527

Hoeflich, Carmen, ed., 000595, 000596, 000597, 000598, 000640

Holiday, Roberta, ed., 000550

Holmes, Ruth Bradley, 000486

Horne, Anne, 000665

Iribarren, Leonel O., ed., 000125, 000126

Iribarren, Norma C., 000125, 000126

Iruegas, Efraín, 000058, 000581

Jacob, Betty, 000018

John, Alfred, 000725, 000726, 000727, 000728, 000729, 000730, 000731, 000732, 000733, 000734, 000735

Johnson, Ralph, 000801, 000802, 000803, 000804, 000805

Jones, Eliza, 000152, 000720, 000721, 000722, 000723, 000724, 000756, 000757, 000758, 000759, 000760, 000761, 000762

Kari, James, 000775

Karmun, Mamie, 000862

Kingsley, Emily, 000026

Kirschbaum, Gabrielle, 000479

Komakhuk, Agnes, 000870, 000871, 000872, 000874, 000875, 000876, 000877, 000878, 000879, 000880

Korr, David, 000026

Kronby, Madeline, 000479

Kwok, Irene, 000051

Lamatino, Robyn, 000533

Laygo, Teresito M., comp., 000023, 000024

Lazos, Héctor, 000654, 000655

Leer, Jeff, 000801, 000802, 000803, 000804, 000805

Liu Sarah, 000513

López, Erleen, 000567, 000568

López, Sara, 000560, 000561

Loon, Hanah, 000861

Maldonado, Sonia, 000660

Mangino, Evangelina, 000115

Marchal, Alain, 000180, 000183

Marchal, Danièle, 000180, 000183

Markatos, John, 000057

Mata, José G., 000531

Mellenbruch, Julia K. 000664

Meneses, Fernando de, 000124, 000537

Mensoff, Olga, 000777, 000778, 000779, 000780, 000781, 000782, 000783, 000784, 000785, 000786, 000787, 000799

Milanowski, Paul, 000725, 000726, 000727, 000728, 000729, 000730, 000731, 000732, 000733, 000734, 000735

Mintz, Adin, ed., 000533

Miranda Correia, Luis de, 000108

Moonin, Arthur, 000801, 000802, 000803, 000804, 000805

Morrison, James D., 000576

Moss, Jeff, 000026

Mountain, Josephine, 000759, 000760, 000761, 000762

Nassuk, Loleta, 000828, 000829, 000830, 000831, 000832, 000833, 000834, 000835, 000837, 000877

Nevzoroff, John L., 000796

Nevzoroff, Vera S., 000796

Nichols, Lucille, 000595, 000596, 000597, 000598, 000654, 000655

Nicklas, Dale, 000018

Nouri, Fereidoun Khaje, 000528

O'Connor, Jane, ed., 000070, 000436

O'Dell, Evelyn Villa, 000550

Obolensky, Serge, 000528

Olivier, Julien, 000046, 000181

Ongtowasruk, Faye, 000850

Oozeea, Eleanor, 000807, 000808

Osborn, Faye, 000550

Otis, David L., 000036

Palandra, Maria, 000672, 000673, 000674, 000688, 000689

Panah, Kambiz Yazdan, 000528

Paukan, Andy, 000810, 000811, 000812, 000813, 000814, 000815, 000816, 000817, 000818, 000819, 000820, 000821

Peña, Becky de la, 000595, 000596, 000597, 000598, 000655

Pérez, Carlos E., ed., 000111, 000566, 000572

Pérez, Mary L., 000666

Peter, Katherine, 000573, 000736, 000737, 000738, 000739, 000740, 000741, 000742, 000743, 000744, 000745, 000746, 000747

Pétreault, Marie-Claude, 000060, 000061, 000183

Petrescu-Dimitriu, Magdalena, 000525

Petruska, Betty, 000748, 000749, 000750, 000751, 000752, 000753, 000754, 000755

Pfeiffer, Theresa, 000102

— Pipyn, Michel, 000013, 000020, 000033, 000048, 000670

Pope, Mary L., 000573, 000831, 000850, 000877

Powell, Lilia M., 000036

Price, Kathleen, 000060, 000061, 000062, 000063, 000064, 000065, 000067, 000068, 000069, 000182, 000183

Puigdollers, Carmen, ed., 000052, 000053, 000149, 000155, 000673

Pulu, Tupou L., 000831, 000850, 000877

— Quintal, Claire, 000021, 000022, 000181

Rafaelito, Johnson, 000614

Ramarui, Hermana, 000706, 000707

Ramírez, Manuel, 000646, 000647, 000648, 000649, 000650, 000651, 000653

Randall, Clint, 000103

Rechetaoch, Maech, 000707

Réndon, Clara, 000582

Rendón, René, 000578, 000579, 000581

Reno, Margarida F., 000526

Rice, Frank, 000524

Rivera, Carlos, 000641

Rivera, Lina R., 000595, 000596, 000597, 000598, 000654, 000655

Robinett, Ralph F., 000027, 000028

Rodríguez, Aurea E., ed., 000053, 000109, 000149, 000155

Rodríguez, Mary Jane, 000582

Rodríguez, Roberto, 000436, 000639

Rosenblum, Mark, 000578

Rosier, Helen Cody, 000610, 000611, 000612

Ross, Joy, 000571

Ruluke, Toyoko, 000707

Saavedra, Frances, 000569, 000570

Sáenz, Esther, 000654, 000655

Sánchez de la Vega-Lockler, Elsa, ed., 000667, 000668

Sancho, Anthony R., 000036, 000562

Santiago, Jorge, 000660

Santiago, Nick M., 000666, 000667

Santos, Richard, comp., 000684

Saslow, Joan, ed., 000693, 000694, 000696, 000697, 000699, 000700, 000702, 000703

Satre, Sharon, 000806

Satterthwait, Arnold, 000524

Schlickling, Janine, 000067, 000068, 000069

Schlickling, Jean Claude, 000182

Schmitt, Conrad J., 000693, 000694, 000695, 000696, 000697, 000698, 000699, 000700, 000701, 000702, 000703, 000704

Schuh, Russel G., 000529

Seeganna, Margaret, 000851, 000852, 000853

Serna, Leonila, 000640, 000654, 000655

Sinnok, John, 000838, 000839, 000840, 000841, 000842, 000844, 000845, 000846, 000847, 000848

Slwooko, Grace, 000809

Smith, Betty Sharp, 000486

Smith, Tana, 000036

Sones, Mary, 000580, 000582

Spencer, Betty Lou, 000018

Spiridakis, Eugenia, 000008, 000675, 000676, 000677

Stewart, Julieta, 000104

Stickman, Paulina, 000759, 000760, 000761, 000762

Stiles, Norman, 000026

Sun, Susie, 000822, 000823, 000824, 000825, 000826, 000854, 000855, 000856, 000857, 000858, 000859, 000860, 000861, 000863, 000864, 000865, 000866, 000867, 000868, 000869

Swan, Oscar, 000863, 000864, 000865, 000866, 000867, 000868, 000869

Swanson, Elvina, 000827, 000831, 000836

Thomas, Evans, 000854, 000855, 000856, 000857, 000858, 000859, 000860, 000861

Thompson, Jean, 000111

Tombari, Martin, 000115

Torres, Francisco, 000660

Tran Van Dien, 000014, 000015, 000016, 000017

Umpierre, Helga, 000436

Urzúa, Carole, 000129

Vallejo, Bernardo, 000105

Van Wagoner, Merrill Y., 000524

VanBuskirk, Sue, 000103

Villarreal, Abelardo, 000595, 000596, 000597, 000598, 000640, 000654, 000655

Vittitow, Mary Lou, 000513

Walters, Barbara, 000571

Wassillie, Albert, 000763, 000764, 000765, 000766, 000767, 000768, 000769, 000770, 000771, 000772, 000773, 000774

Weahkee, Laurie, 000066

Weahkee, Sonny, 000066

Wong, Sau-Ling Cynthia, ed., 000925

Yeats, Alid, 000567, 000568, 000569

Zayas, Madeline, 000659

INDEX TO LANGUAGES

Aleut

000777
000778
000779
000780
000781
000782
000783
000784
000785
000786
000787
000789
000790
000791
000792
000793
000794
000796
000798
000799

Aleut; English

000795
000797
000800

Arabic; English

000524

Chinese; English

000007
000051
000925
000926

Choctaw; English

000018

Creek

000705

Dena'ina Athapascan

000763
000764
000765
000766
000767
000768
000769
000770
000771
000772
000773
000774

Dena'ina Athapascan; English

000775

English; Dutch

000523

English; French

000021
000022
000479
000480

English; Gwich'in

000573

English; Hausa

000529

English; Inupiat

000861
000862

English; Mandarin

000527

English; Norwegian

000522

English; Persian

000528

English; Portuguese

000526

English; Romanian

000525

English; Seminole

000045
000539
000577

English; Spanish

000036
000057
000058
000105
000106
000112
000115
000313
000531
000532
000533
000549
000550
000551
000552
000553
000554
000555
000566
000578
000579
000580
000581

295

English; Spanish (continued)

000599
000600
000601
000621
000622
000623
000624
000625
000626
000628
000644
000657
000665
000666

English; Vietnamese

000014
000015
000017

English; Yupik

000809

French

000006
000013
000020
000032
000033
000034
000035
000046
000048
000049
000061
000062
000063
000064
000065
000067
000068
000069
000180
000181
000182
000183
000184
000185
000186
000187
000188
000189
000658
000670
000671

Greek

000008
000674
000675
000676
000677

Gwich'in

000736
000737
000738
000739
000740
000741
000742
000743
000744
000745
000747

Hualapai

000617
000618
000619
000629

Inupiat

000822
000823
000824
000825
000826
000827
000828
000829
000830
000831
000832
000833
000834
000835
000836
000837
000838
000839
000840
000841
000842
000843
000844
000845
000846
000847
000848
000850
000851
000852
000853
000854
000855
000856
000857
000858
000859
000860
000863
000864
000865
000866
000867
000868
000869
000870
000871
000872
000873
000874
000875
000876
000877
000878
000879
000880

Italian

000672
000687
000688
000689
000690
000691
000692

Koyukon Athapascan

000152
000720
000721
000722
000723
000724
000756
000757
000758
000759
000760
000761
000762

Navajo

000608
000609
000610
000611
000612
000613
000614
000615
000616
000924

Palauan

000706
000707

Portuguese

000108
000119
000120
000121
000122
000123
000124
000574
000575

Qwich'in

000746

Spanish

000019
000027
000028
000052
000054
000055
000059
000101
000102
000103
000104
000125
000126
000135
000136
000137
000138
000139
000140
000141
000142
000143
000149
000155
000156
000169
000173
000174
000175
000176
000177
000436
000481
000557
000558
000559
000565
000567
000568

000569
000570
000572
000583
000584
000585
000586
000587
000588
000589
000590
000591
000592
000593
000594
000595
000596
000597
000598
000640
000641
000642
000643
000654
000655
000659
000660
000669
000673
000678
000679
000680
000681
000682
000683
000684
000685
000686
000693
000694
000695
000696
000697
000698
000699
000700
000701
000702
000703
000704

Tagalog

000710
000711
000712
000713

000714
000715
000716
000717
000718
000719

Upper Kuskokwim
Athapascan

000748
000749
000750
000751
000752
000753
000754
000755

Upper Tanana
Athapascan

000725
000726
000727
000728
000729
000730
000731
000732
000733
000735

Vietnamese

000160

Yupik

000801
000802
000803
000804
000805
000806
000807
000808
000810
000811
000812
000813
000814
000815
000816
000817
000818
000819

INDEX TO SUBJECTS

Adolescent Literature

000023
000024

Affective Behavior

000026

Alaska Natives

000710
000711
000712
000713
000714
000715
000716
000717
000718
000719
000826

Alphabet Cards

000561

American Indian Languages

000744

American Indians

000152
000720
000721
000722
000723
000724
000725
000726
000727
000728
000729
000730
000731
000732
000734

000735
000736
000738
000739
000740
000741
000742
000743
000744
000745
000746
000747
000748
000749
000750
000751
000752
000753
000754
000755
000756
000757
000758
000759
000760
000761
000762
000763
000764
000765
000766
000767
000768
000769
000770
000771
000772
000773
000774
000775
000856

Arabic

000524

Architecture

000629
000630

Area Studies

000058

Art

000630

Asian Americans

000925

Assembly Programs

000640

Athapascan Languages

000152
000720
000721
000722
000723
000724
000725
000726
000727
000728
000729
000730
000731
000732
000733
000734
000735
000748
000749
000750
000751
000752
000753
000754
000755
000756
000757
000758
000759
000760
000761
000762

299

Athapascan Languages
(continued)

000763
000764
000765
000766
000767
000768
000769
000770
000771
000772
000773
000774
000775
000924

Autoinstructional Aids

000523
000524
000525
000527
000528
000529

Basic Reading

000561

Beginning Reading

000054

Bilingual Education

000106
000645

Bilingual Students

000479
000480

Bilingualism

000020

Career Awareness

000533

Career Opportunities

000122
000123

Careers

000122

Childrens Arts

000066

Childrens Books

000027
000028
000152
000169
000173
000174
000175
000176
000177
000481
000577
000670
000675
000676
000677
000687
000707
000710
000711
000712
000714
000715
000716
000717
000718
000719
000720
000721
000722
000723
000724
000725
000726
000727
000728
000729
000730
000731
000732
000733
000734
000735
000736
000737
000738
000739
000740
000741
000742
000743
000744
000745
000746
000747
000748
000749
000750
000751
000752
000753
000754
000755
000756

000757
000758
000759
000760
000762
000763
000764
000765
000766
000767
000768
000769
000770
000771
000772
000773
000774
000775
000781
000810
000811
000812
000813
000814
000815
000816
000817
000818
000819
000820
000821
000822
000823
000824
000825
000826
000827
000828
000829
000830
000831
000832
000833
000834
000835
000836
000837
000838
000839
000840
000841
000842
000844
000845
000846
000847
000848
000854
000855
000857
000858
000859
000860
000861
000862

Childrens Books
(continued)

000863
000864
000865
000866
000867
000868
000869

Childrens Games

000479

Childrens Literature

000052
000053
000066
000109
000110
000112
000480
000539

Children's Television

000026
000070
000436

Chinese

000007
000925

Chinese Americans

000007

Clothing

000690

Consonants

000561
000924

Conversational Language Courses

000523
000524
000525
000527
000528
000529

Course Content

000563

Course Organization

000563

Creative Activities

000070

Criterion Referenced Tests

000115

Cues

000597

Cultural Awareness

000023
000024
000119
000120
000121
000122
000123
000124
000563
000564

Cultural Background

000640

Cultural Differences

000564

Cultural Education

000021
000022
000055
000109
000124
000532
000629
000630
000640

Cultural Images

000925

Curriculum Design

000106

Curriculum Guides

000058
000060
000061
000062
000063
000064
000065

000067
000068
000069
000135
000138
000141
000531
000532
000579
000582
000654
000665

Drama

000006

Driver Education

000579

Dutch

000523

Educational Games

000479
000513

Educational Philosophy

000645

Educational Resources

000106

Educational Television

000026
000436

Elementary Education

000670

Emotional Development

000026

English (Second Language)

000056
000105
000111
000112
000533
000582

Enrichment Activities

000070
000436
000640

Eskimo Aleut Languages

000831

Eskimos

000781
000810
000811
000812
000813
000814
000815
000816
000817
000818
000819
000820
000821
000822
000823
000824
000825
000826
000827
000828
000829
000830
000831
000832
000833
000834
000835
000836
000837
000838
000839
000840
000841
000842
000844
000845
000846
000847
000848
000854
000855
000856
000857
000858
000859
000860
000861
000862
000863
000864
000865
000866
000867
000868
000869

Ethnic Groups

000109

Fantasy

000480

Filmstrips

000119
000120
000121
000122
000123

Folk Culture

000008
000023
000024
000690
000861
000862

Folklore Books

000008
000155

Foreign Students

000056

French

000006
000013
000020
000021
000022
000032
000033
000034
000035
000046
000048
000049
000060
000061
000062
000063
000064
000065
000067
000068
000069
000110
000182
000186
000187
000188
000189
000658
000670

French Photographs

000184

Games

000182

Geometric Concepts

000059

Grade 1

000069

Grammar

000035
000056
000105
000582

Greek

000008
000675
000676
000677

Group Activities

000036

Hausa

000529

Health Education

000537

History

000048

History Instruction

000021
000022

Hygiene

000654

Illustrations

000690
000691

Individual Study

000513

Instructional Materials

000006
000007

Instructional
Materials (continued)

000013
000021
000024
000027
000028
000032
000033
000035
000045
000049
000052
000053
000055
000056
000058
000070
000105
000108
000109
000110
000111
000112
000119
000120
000121
000122
000123
000125
000126
000135
000138
000141
000152
000155
000169
000173
000174
000175
000176
000177
000181
000182
000184
000185
000186
000187
000188
000189
000436
000481
000522
000523
000524
000525
000527
000528
000529
000537
000577
000579
000584
000589
000590

000591
000592
000593
000594
000613
000645
000654
000658
000659
000665
000669
000670
000675
000676
000677
000687
000688
000689
000690
000691
000707
000710
000711
000712
000714
000715
000716
000717
000718
000719
000720
000721
000722
000723
000724
000725
000726
000727
000728
000729
000730
000731
000732
000733
000734
000735
000736
000737
000738
000739
000740
000741
000742
000743
000744
000745
000746
000747
000748
000749
000750
000751
000752
000753
000754
000755

000756
000757
000758
000759
000760
000761
000762
000763
000764
000765
000766
000767
000768
000769
000770
000771
000772
000773
000774
000775
000781
000810
000811
000812
000813
000814
000815
000816
000817
000818
000819
000820
000821
000822
000823
000824
000825
000826
000827
000828
000829
000830
000831
000832
000833
000834
000835
000836
000837
000838
000839
000840
000841
000842
000844
000845
000846
000848
000854
000855
000856
000857
000858
000859
000860
000861

Instructional
Materials (continued)

000862
000863
000864
000865
000866
000867
000868
000869

Instructional Media

000924

Interviews

000046

Italian

000687
000688
000689
000690
000691
000692

Kindergarten

000062
000063
000064
000065
000106

Language Arts

000111
000112
000129
000513
000582
000597

Language Instruction

000013
000032
000033
000035
000045
000048
000105
000108
000135
000138
000140
000141
000152
000185
000186
000187
000188
000189

000522
000539
000613
000687
000688
000710
000711
000712
000713
000714
000715
000716
000717
000718
000719
000720
000721
000722
000723
000724
000725
000726
000727
000728
000729
000730
000732
000733
000734
000735
000736
000737
000738
000739
000740
000741
000742
000743
000744
000745
000746
000747
000748
000749
000750
000751
000752
000753
000754
000755
000756
000757
000758
000759
000760
000761
000762
000763
000764
000765
000766
000767
000768
000769
000770
000771

000772
000773
000774
000775
000781
000810
000811
000815
000816
000817
000818
000819
000820
000821
000822
000823
000824
000825
000826
000827
000829
000830
000831
000832
000833
000834
000835
000836
000837
000838
000839
000840
000841
000842
000844
000845
000846
000847
000848
000854
000855
000856
000857
000858
000859
000860
000861
000862
000864
000866
000867
000868
000869

Language Usage

000129

Learning Activities

000062
000063
000064
000065
000070
000129

Learning Activities
(continued)

000479
000513
000571

Learning Modules

000479

Legends

000110
000155

Lesson Plans

000036
000061
000062
000064
000065
000067
000068
000069
000111
000531
000532

Letters (Alphabet)

000054
000688

Literature

000110

Literature
Appreciation

000023
000181

Magnetic Tape
Cassettes

000480
000599

Mandarin Chinese

000527

Mathematics

000513

Mathematics Curriculum

000060
000061

Mathematics
Instruction

000060
000061

Mexicans

000629
000630

Mexican American
History

000058

Mexican Americans

000058
000531
000640

Music Activities

000182
000665

Music Education

000665

Navajo

000066
000613
000924

Nonverbal
Communication

000563
000564

Norwegian

000522

Numbers

000689

Occupations

000533

Oral History

000046

Parent Participation

000026

Pattern Drills
(Language)

000056
000125
000126
000140

Persian

000528

Photographs

000925

Physical Environment

000013

Play

000026

Poetry

000008
000034
000658

Portuguese

000108
000119
000120
000121
000122
000123
000124

Portuguese Americans

000124
000537

Preschool Education

000537
000599

Primary Education

000059

Primary Grades

000571

Pronunciation

000669

Pronunciation
Instruction

000669

Puerto Rican Culture

000055
000155
000564

Puerto Ricans

000055
000109
000564

Reading Comprehension

000125
000126

Reading Instruction

000027
000028
000045
000054
000135
000138
000140
000141
000584
000590
000591
000592
000593
000594
000613
000659
000670
000675
000676
000677
000688

Reading Materials

000006
000007
000008
000013
000020
000021
000023
000027
000028
000032
000033
000045
000048
000049
000052
000053
000054
000055
000066
000108
000109
000110
000112

000124
000140
000152
000155
000169
000173
000174
000175
000176
000177
000181
000184
000185
000186
000187
000188
000189
000481
000522
000539
000577
000584
000586
000589
000590
000591
000592
000593
000594
000613
000658
000659
000670
000675
000676
000677
000687
000707
000710
000711
000712
000714
000715
000716
000718
000719
000720
000721
000722
000723
000724
000725
000726
000727
000728
000729
000730
000731
000732
000733
000734
000735
000736
000737
000738
000739

000740
000741
000742
000743
000744
000745
000746
000747
000748
000749
000750
000751
000752
000753
000754
000755
000756
000757
000758
000759
000760
000761
000762
000763
000764
000765
000766
000767
000768
000769
000770
000771
000772
000773
000774
000775
000781
000810
000811
000812
000813
000814
000815
000816
000817
000818
000819
000820
000821
000822
000823
000824
000825
000826
000827
000828
000829
000830
000831
000832
000833
000834
000835
000836
000837
000838

Reading Materials
(continued)

000839
000840
000841
000842
000844
000845
000846
000847
000848
000854
000855
000856
000857
000858
000859
000860
000861
000862
000863
000864
000865
000866
000867
000868
000869

Reading Skills

000692

Resource Materials

000630

Romanian

000525

Sciences

000513

Second Language Learning

000020
000056
000105
000108
000522
000523
000524
000525
000527
000528
000529

Short Stories

000023
000024
000522

Singing

000182
000689

Small Group Instruction

000571

Social Development

000067
000068
000069

Social History

000531

Social Studies

000020
000110
000184
000532
000579
000629
000630

Songs

000599

Soundtracks

000480

Spanish

000027
000028
000036
000052
000054
000055
000058
000059
000125
000126
000135
000138
000140
000141
000155
000169
000173
000174
000175
000176
000177
000436
000481
000533
000537
000561

000571
000579
000582
000584
000586
000589
000590
000591
000592
000593
000594
000597
000599
000654
000659
000665
000669

Spanish Speaking

000036
000054
000126
000533

Speech Communication

000129

Speech Skills

000129

Standard Spoken Usage

000046
000523
000525
000527
000528
000529

Student Developed Materials

000066
000185
000186
000187
000188
000189

Supplementary Reading Materials

000034

Tagalog

000710
000711
000712
000713
000714
000715
000716

Tagalog
(continued)

000717
000718
000719

Teacher Education

000564
000645

Teacher Education Curriculum

000645

Teaching Guides

000022
000024
000036
000060
000061
000062
000063
000064
000065
000067
000068
000069
000111
000115
000125
000129
000135
000138
000141
000436

000537
000563
000571
000579
000582
000629
000645
000654
000665
000692
000925

Test Construction

000115

Testing

000115

Textbooks

000015
000035

Uncommonly Taught Languages

000524

Units of Study (Subject Fields)

000531

Visual Aids

000537
000597
000690
000691
000925

Vocabulary

000035

Vocabulary Development

000111
000112

Work Attitudes

000119
000120
000121

Workbooks

000119
000120
000121
000122
000123
000126
000140
000188
000189
000533

Writing Skills

000692

INDEX TO SERIES TITLES

Achixaasis (Units in Language Learning) (Series), 000789, 000790, 000791, 000792, 000793

Aguila Volante Series: Level 1, 000551

Aguila Volante Series: Level 2a, 000553

Aguila Volante Series: Level 2b, 000554

Aguila Volante Series: Level 2c, 000552

Aguila Volante Series: Level 3, 000555

Aguila Volante Series: Levels 1-3, 000550

Alutiicestun litnaurluta (Units in Language Learning) (Series), 000801

Caliarkat qaneryaramek elicalriani (Units in Language Learning) (Series), 000810, 000811, 000812, 000813, 000814, 000815, 000816

Dinaakanaaga' (Units in Language Learning) (Series), 000756, 000757, 000758, 000759, 000760

Dinaakk'a bidots'uhdil-eeghee (Units in Language Learning) (Series), 000152, 000720, 000721, 000722

Dinakinaja' ik'ats'itolnish (Units In Language Learning) (Series), 000748, 000749, 000750

Dine k'ejí naaltosoos wólta bohoaa'igii (Learning Written Navajo), 000610, 000611, 000612

Educación media básica. Primer grado (Intermediate Basic Education. First Grade), 000105

Gwich'in ginjik agwaraa'ee (Units in Language Learning) (Series), 000736, 000737, 000738, 000739, 000740, 000741, 000742

Ilisaaksrat qannuziqtuni (Units in Language Learning) (Series), 000838, 000839, 000840, 000841, 000842, 000844, 000845

Learning Achievement Packages (Series), 000057, 000058, 000578, 000579, 000580, 000581, 000582

Miami Linguistic Readers: Level 1-A (Series), 000028

Miami Linguistic Readers: Level 1-B (Series), 000481

Miami Linguistic Readers: Plateau Level 1-3 (Series), 000027

Naqenaga duch'deldih (Units in Language Learning) (Series), 000763, 000764, 000765, 000766, 000767, 000768, 000769

Naraqelleq yupigestun (Units in Language Learning) (Series), 000807

Nee'aaneegn' uudeldii (Units in Language Learning) (Series), 000725, 000726, 000727, 000728, 000729, 000730, 000731

Pag-aaral ng wika (Units in Language Learning) (Series), 000710, 000711, 000712, 000713

Programa de lectura y enseñanza del lenguaje, Unidad A (Reading and Teaching Program for Language, Unit A), 000678, 000679, 000680

Programa de lectura y enseñanza del lenguaje, Unidad B (Reading and Teaching Program for Language, Unit B), 000681, 000682, 000683

Programa de lectura y enseñanza del lenguaje, Unidad C (Reading and Teaching Program for Language, Unit C), 000684, 000685, 000686

Qué bonito es leer (How Nice It Is to Read) (Series), 000595, 000596, 000597

Qué bonito es leer II (How Nice It Is to Read II) (Series), 000135, 000136, 000137, 000138, 000139, 000140, 000141, 000142, 000143, 000557, 000558, 000559

Qué bonito es leer: Libros de lectura (How Nice It Is To Read: Readers), 000583, 000584, 000585, 000586, 000587, 000588, 000589, 000590, 000591, 000592, 000593, 000594

Sulhich uqayusiliksrakun (Units in Language Learning) (Series), 000822, 000823, 000854, 000855, 000856, 000857, 000858, 000859, 000860

Tunum achigaasingin (Units in Language Learning) (Series), 000777, 000778, 000779, 000780, 000781, 000782

Units in Language Learning (Series), 000827, 000828, 000829, 000830, 000831, 000832, 000833, 000851, 000870, 000871, 000872, 000873, 000874, 000875

Uqalikun ilirviksrat (Units in Language Learning) (Series), 000863, 000864, 000865, 000866, 000867, 000868, 000869

Villes franco-américaines de la Nouvelle-Angleterre (Franco-American cities of New England), 000020, 000184

INDEX TO TITLES

A cada paso. Lengua, lectura y cultura (At Each Step: Language, Reading and Culture). Level 1, 000693

A cada paso: Lengua, lectura y cultura (At Each Step: Language, Reading and Culture). Level 2, 000696

A cada paso: Lengua, lectura y cultura (At Each Step: Language, Reading and Culture). Level 3, 000699

A cada paso: Lengua, lectura y cultura (At Each Step: Language, Reading and Culture). Level 4, 000702

A cada paso: Lengua, lectura y cultura (At Each Step: Language, Reading and Culture). Teacher's Manual. Level 1, 000694

A cada paso: Lengua, lectura y cultura (At Each Step: Language, Reading and Culture). Teacher's Edition, Annotated. Level 2, 000697

A cada paso: Lengua, lectura y cultura (At Each Step: Language, Reading and Culture). Teacher's Edition, Annotated. Level 3, 000700

A cada paso: Lengua, lectura y cultura (At Each Step: Language, Reading and Culture). Teacher's Edition, Annotated. Level 4, 000703

A cada paso: Lengua, lectura y cultura. Cuaderno de ejercicios (At Each Step: Language, Reading and Culture. Workbook). Level 1, 000695

A cada paso: Lengua, lectura y cultura. Cuaderno de ejercicios (At Each Step: Language, Reading and Culture. Workbook). Level 2, 000698

A cada paso: Lengua, lectura y cultura. Cuaderno de ejercicios (At Each Step: Language, Reading and Culture. Workbook). Level 3, 000701

A cada paso: Lengua, lectura y cultura. Cuaderno de ejercicios (At Each Step: Language, Reading and Culture. Workbook). Level 4, 000704

A Casa do Manuel (Manuel's House), 000108

Akiligialiq (Going to the Store), 000880

Ako ay nagtatrabaho (Work in the Home), 000715

Akutanax̂ (Akutan), 000784

Alaskan Folktales (Dinjii zhuu gwandak), 000573

Alix waya? Aag̃an (Why? Because), 000779

Alqul? Mal (Why? Because), 000791

Alqus ig̃amax̂t azax̂t? Alqus maxt? (What Do You Like? What Are You Doing?), 000789

Alqus maag̃an ax̂s? Alqus manax? (What Will He Do? What Did He Do?), 000790

Alqutax̂ amaya? Alqutax̂ maasdukatxin? (What Is It? What Can You Do With It?), 000778

Alqutax̂ maduukalix inga? Alqutax̂ malix ingaya? (What Will He Do? What Did He Do?), 000777

Ang aking bahay (My House), 000714

Angalim ama amgim ilan malganas (Learning About Time), 000799

Ann ang gusto mo? Ano ang ginagawa mo? (What Do You Like? What Are You Doing?), 000710

Ano ang gagawin niya? Ano ang ginawa niya? (What Will He Do? What Did He Do?), 000711

Ano iyon? Ano ang magagawa mo diyan? (What Is It? What Can You Do With It?), 000712

Antoine ou la leçon des choses (Antoine or the Lesson of Things), 000013

Antoine ou le silence des choses (Antoine or the Silence of Things), 000048

Aprendemos con gusto. Actividades en español para niños bilingües (Let's Have Fun Learning. Activities in Spanish for Bilingual Children), 000036

Aprendemos de carreras (We Learn About Careers), 000103

Aquí se habla español (Spanish is Spoken Here), 000109

Así aprendemos: Libro I. Cuaderno de ejercicios (This Is How We Learn: Book I. Workbook), 000559

Así aprendemos: Libro I. Guía para el maestro (This Is How We Learn: Book I. Teacher's Guide), 000558

Así aprendemos: Libro I. Libro de lectura (This Is How We Learn: Book I. Reader), 000557

Asian American Study Prints, 000926

Asian American Study Prints: Teacher's Manual, 000925

Atinich ilama (My Family), 000825

Atinit ilama (My Family), 000835

Atqit ilama (My Family), 000879

Atrit ilama (My Family), 000821

Atx̂ax̂ (Atka), 000797

Au Coeur du vent (Heart of the Wind), 000658

Bai Hoc Trac Nghiem Thanh Ngu Anh Van (Tests on English Idioms), 000014

Bakit? Sapagka't (Why? Because), 000713

Beginning Cherokee, 000486

Berlin: Ville industrielle du nord (Berlin: Industrial City of the North), 000184

Beto y Tito (Beto and Tito), 000028

Bonjour papillon (Hello Butterfly), 000032

Buscando hallarás, Libro II: Cuaderno de ejercicios (Look and You Will Find, Book II: Workbook), 000137

Buscando hallarás, Libro II: Guía para el maestro (Look and You Will Find, Book II: Teacher's Guide), 000135

Buscando hallarás, Libro II: Libro de lectura (Look and You Will Find, Book II: Reader), 000136

Ca assiksiu? Calisit? (What Do You Like? What Are You Doing?), 000810

Cacaq ai? Cacamen aturnayarciu? (What Is It? What Can You Do With It?), 000801

Caciqa? Callrua? (What Will He Do? What Did He Do?), 000811

Caliaq kingunermi (Work in the Home), 000818

Cantando y aprendiendo (Singing and Learning): Primary Song Book, 000643

Caribou, mon pays blanc (Caribou, My White Country), 000020

Ch'al (Frog), 000610

Ch'ookwat zheh gwats'a' hihshyaa (Going to the Store), 000744

Ch'ukayih hits'e' (Going to the Store), 000754

Ch'utkeedn shyah ts'a' teeshyah (Going to the Store), 000734

Chaá (Beaver), 000611

Chants et danses III (Songs and Dances III), 000183

Chants et jeux K-I-II (Songs and Games K-I-II), 000182

Chasam adaan achigalix (Learning About Time), 000787

Chinese Cultural Resource Book (For Elementary Bilingual Teachers), 000051

Chiquita, 000593

Chuami? Qanu ataa (Why? Because), 000873

Chuliuqpa ilaa? Chuwa ilaa? (What Will He Do? What Did He Do?), 000871

Chumik nailguwit? (What Can You Smell?), 000877

Chuna nakuagiwiun? Chulivit? (What Do You Like? What Are You Doing?), 000870

Chuuva? Chuliuqpiun? (What Is It? What Can You Do With It?), 000872

Ciin? Tua-wa (Why? Because), 000813

Como Tú (Like You), 000588

Construindo o mundo: 5. O que e que tu vais fazer? (Building the World: 5. What Are You Going to Do?), 000123

Construindo o mundo: 1. Porquê trabalhar? (Building the World: 1. Why Work?), 000119

Construindo o mundo: 2. O Trabalho é uma forma de realizacao (Building the World: 2. Work is a Form of Realization), 000120

Construindo o mundo: 3. O Trabalho transforma o mundo (Building the World: 3. Work Transforms the World), 000121

Construindo o mundo: 4. O que há a fazer? (Building the World: 4. What is There to Do?), 000122

Coyote, the Millionaire, 000066

Crucigramas: Crossword Puzzles for Primary Grades, 000644

Cuaderno de ejercicios (Workbook), 000596

Cufe horkopv (Why the Rabbit Steals), 000577

Daily Curriculum Guide: Spanish Dame Program: Songs, 000599

Daily Curriculum Guide, The: Year I, Weeks 1-10. A Preschool Program for the Spanish-Speaking Child, 000621

Daily Curriculum Guide, The: Year I, Weeks 11-20. A Preschool Program for the Spanish-Speaking Child, 000622

Daily Curriculum Guide, The: Year I, Weeks 21-30. A Preschool Program for the Spanish-Speaking Child, 000623

Daily Curriculum Guide, The: Year II, Weeks 1-10. A Preschool Program for the Spanish-Speaking Child, 000624

Daily Curriculum Guide, The: Year II, Weeks 11-20. A Preschool Program for the Spanish-Speaking Child, 000625

Daily Curriculum Guide, The: Year II, Weeks 21-34. A Preschool Program for the Spanish-Speaking Child, 000626

Daily Curriculum Supplement: Part I, 000600

Daily Curriculum Supplement: Part II, Ditto Patterns, 000602

Daily Curriculum Supplement: Part III, Flannel Patterns, 000601

Dalla a alla z: L'alfabeto dei bambini (From A to Z: Children's Alphabet), 000688

Deeghwahtsii? Daahchy'aa? (How Much? How Many?), 000741

Deehee'yaa? Deezhik? (What Will He Do? What Did He Do?), 000737

Diagnostic Mathematics Form A, Form B, and Test Manual, 000708

Dii ch'ant'aiy? Nts'at dih'ih? (What Is It? What Can You Do With It?), 000727

Dii eh saanaih xaah iilii? Nts'at diidi'? (What Do You Like? What Are You Doing?), 000725

Dii xaah? ...eh (Why? Because), 000728

Dimaa? Dot'aanh? (What Are They Doing? Where Are They Doing It?), 000760

Diné bikéyah (Navajo Lands), 000608

Doing Things with Language: Informing, 000129

Doo ts'an ch'ant'aiy? Ndee ch'adadiinaiy? (Which? Whose?), 000731

Doo? Nts'at di'? (What Are They Doing? Where Are They Doing It?), 000729

Dotot'eek? Daaghat'eek? (What Will He Do? What Did He Do?), 000721

Dotot'eek? Daaghat'eek? (What Will He Do? What Did He Do?), 00757

Driver Education: English-Spanish, 000579

Education physique I et II (Physical Education I and II), 000180

El Camino hacia la buena salud: Cuaderno de ejercicios (The Road to Good Health: Workbook) and Posters, 000655

El Camino hacia la buena salud: Guía para el maestro (The Road to Good Health: Teacher's Guide), 000654

El Cuento de la gran piñata (The Story of the Big Piñata), 000019

El Cuento de la nota musical (The Story of the Musical Note), 000101

El Elefante y la tortuga (The Elephant and the Turtle), 000591

El Osito (The Little Bear), 000583

Elitelleq taimamek (Learning About Time), 000820

English Language Arts Units: Student's Book, 000112

English Language Arts Units: Teacher's Guide, 000111

Enka (My House), 000802

Entre dois mundos: Vida quotidiana de criancas portuguesas na America (Between Two Worlds: Daily Life of Portuguese Americans), 000124

Entre dois mundos: Vida quotidiana de criancas portuguesas na America (Between Two Worlds: Daily Life of Portuguese Americans). Teacher's Guide, 000537

Erenret casaa'it (Learning About Time), 000804

Es un fantasma? (Is It a Ghost?), 000589

Escaparate (Showcase), 000684

Escaparate: Cuaderno de trabajo (Showcase: Workbook), 000686

Escaparate: Guía para el maestro (Showcase: Teacher's Guide), 000685

Escuchando y participando aprendo (I Learn by Listening and Participating), 000598

Escucho, digo, y aprendo (I Listen, I Say, and I Learn): Spanish Reading Readiness Program for Primary Grades, 000572

Estudio cultural de Puerto Rico. A Cultural Study of Puerto Rico, 000660

Forming an Estudiantina and Symbols of Music Notation, 000665

Gabino Gatito y el siluro (Gabino Gatito and the Catfish), 000481

Games Without Losers: Learning Games and Independent Activities for Elementary Classrooms, 000513

Gennarino il pizzaiolo (Gennarino the Pizza Maker), 000687

Gin ghun? Ts'i haa-an (Why? Because), 000758

Gin gonee? Dots'il-aanee? (What Is It? What Can You Do With It?), 000152

Gin k'aa da-eent'aa? Dont'aan? (What Do You Like? What Are You Doing?), 000756

Gin kk'aa da-eent'aa? Dont'aanh? (What Do You Like? What Are You Doing?), 000720

Ginghunh ginghu? ...Ts'ahagha-ana (Why? Because), 000722

Girotondo dei numeri (Ring of Numbers), 000689

Gracejo em leitura (Fun in Reading), 000574, 000575

Graciela camina a la escuela (Graciela Walks to School), 000104

Guía para el maestro (Teacher's Guide), 000595

Guías para los carteles puertorriqueños (Guides for the Puerto Rican Posters), 000641

Gweedhaa garagwaa'ee (Learning About Time), 000746

Hááť'íísh átě? (What Is That?), 000609

Hamsi and Joker (Bright Star and Joker), 000618

Handbook on Mexico for Elementary and Secondary Teachers, 000664

Hi'il time ghots'idelt'a ts'e' (Learning About Time), 000752

Hoc Anh-Van Bang Thanh-Ngu (Learning English by Idioms), 000015

Hombres y lugares, Libro IV: Cuaderno de ejercicios (People and Places, Book IV: Workbook), 000143

Hombres y lugares, Libro IV: Guía para el maestro (People and Places, Book IV: Teacher's Guide), 000141

Hombres y lugares, Libro IV: Libro de lectura (People and Places, Book IV: Reader), 000142

How to Write Criterion-Referenced Tests for Spanish-English Bilingual Programs, 000115

Hualapai misid mispó (Learn to Read Hualapai): Book 1, 000617

Hualapai misid mispó (Learn to Read Hualapai): Book 2, 000619

Ilama atqit (My Family), 000847

Ilama atrit (My Family), 000805

Ilinniaqpaaluktuni (Learning About Time), 000826

Ilisaatuni sassaanigmik (Learning About Time), 000846

Ilitchiliq piliksramik (Learning About Time), 000878

Ilitchuksaliq piliksramik (Learning About Time), 000837

Information and Materials to Teach the Cultural Heritage of the Mexican-American Child: Grades K-9, 000656

Iniga (My House), 000876

Instructional Guide for the Home Tutor, 000627

Introduction to Choctaw, 000018

Ipnatchiami (Deering), 000862

Iyas iyasma:viyam ma:k (Eating Turkey During Thanksgiving), 000620

Jaghaii? Geh'an (Why? Because), 000739

Jidii eet'indhan? Deeni'in? (What Do You Like? What Are You Doing?), 000736

Jidii? Juu vats'an? (Which? Whose?), 000742

Jidii? Vaa deehini'yaa? (What Is It? What Can You Do With It?), 000738

Jim: L'histoire de Jim Caron jeune homme racontée par lui-même (à 101 ans) (Jim: The Story of Jim Caron the Young Man As Told by Jim Caron at 101), 000046

Juu'? Dee'in? (What Are They Doing? Where Are They Doing It?), 000740

K'qizaghetnu ht'ana (Lime Village), 000775

Kathe proi (Every Morning), 000677

Kdam ilan hunax (The Hole in the Ice), 000794

Ke medengei a omonguiu? (Do You Know What You Read?), 000707

Kia? Naliak? (Which? Whose?), 000845

Kia? Naliat? (Which? Whose?), 000816

Kia? Nalliat? (Which? Whose?), 000869

Kiapia? Naliak? (Which? Whose?), 000823

Kiapia? Nalliak? (Which? Whose?), 000833

Kiin? Alqus mal? (Which? Whose?), 000792

Kiin? Alqutax̂ malix? (What Are They doing? Where Are They Doing It?), 000781

Kiin? Qanan? (Which? Whose?), 000782

Kiko coquí 1: (Kiko the Tree Frog 1), 000173

Kiko coquí 2: Fiesta en Loiza Aldea (Kiko the Tree Frog 2: Festival in Loiza Aldea), 000174

Kiko coquí 3: En San Juan (Kiko the Tree Frog 3: In San Juan), 000175

Kiko coquí 4: Como en los cuentos (Kiko the Tree Frog 4: Like in a Story), 000176

Kiko coquí 5: El recibimiento en Nueva York (Kiko the Tree Frog 5: The Reception in New York), 000177

Kina? Calria? (What Are They Doing? Where Are They Doing It?), 000814

Kina? Chuliva? (What Are They Doing? Where Are They Doing It?), 00874

Kina? Nani? (What Are They Doing? Where Are They Doing It?), 000831

Kiña? Sugisiva? (What Are They Doing? Where Are They Doing It?), 000858

Kiña? Suliqiva? (What Are They Doing? Where Are They Doing It?), 000867

Kina? Suzruaq? (What Are They Doing? Where Are They Doing It?), 000842

Kindergarten Bilingual Resource Handbook, 000106

Kindergarten: Curriculum Guide. Kindergarten: Livre du maître, 000062

Kindergarten: Livre du maître. Avril-mai (Kindergarten: Teacher's Manual. April-May), 000064

Kindergarten: Livre du maître. Février-mars (Kindergarten: Teacher's Manual. February-March), 000065

Kindergarten: Livre du maître. Novembre-décembre-janvier (Kindergarten: Teacher's Manual. November-December-January), 000063

Kisum? Naliak? (Which? Whose?), 000860

Kiuva una? (My Family), 000853

L'Apprendimento della lettura e della scrittura (Learning Reading and Writing), 000692

L'Eau (Water), 000185

La Carrera (The Race), 000585

La Casita de Lobo (Lobo's Little House), 000586

La Choza de cotense (The Burlap Hut), 000027

La Estrella perdida (The Missing Star), 000052

La Goccolina (The Little Drop of Water), 000672

La Gotita de agua (The Little Drop of Water), 000673

La Música del sol (The Music of the Sun): Teacher's Guide, 000667

La Música del sol: Un Cuento náhuatl y una obra de teatro (The Music of the Sun: A Nahuatl Story and Play), 000666

La Rata de Rico (Rico's Mouse), 000587

La Tos de René (René's Cough), 000594

Laavkaartelleq (Going to the Store), 000819

Laavkam adan uyakux̂ (Going to the Store), 000786

Lafayette, 000189

Lahgagh ch'tuyul (Going to the Store), 000773

Laika paignidia kai tragoudia (Folk Poems and Rhymes), 000008

Language Arts: English Grammar, 000582

Language Arts: Spanish Grammar, 000580

Language Development Resources for Bilingual Bicultural Education: An Aid to Primary Teachers of Mexican American Children, 000313

Langue française: Enseignement élémentaire, 5e (French Language: Elementary Education, 5th), 000035

Las Actividades de Sesame Street (Activities of Sesame Street), 000436

Las Formas geométricas (Geometric Shapes), 000059

Las Matemáticas: Lenguaje universal. Factores y múltiplos (Mathematics: The Universal Language. Factors and Multiples), 000552

Las Matemáticas: Lenguaje universal. La Medida. (Mathematics: The Universal Language. Measurement), 000555

Las Matemáticas: Lenguaje universal. Multiplicación y división de números enteros (Mathematics: The Universal Language. Multiplication and Division of Whole Numbers), 000554

Las Matemáticas: Lenguaje universal. Números y numeración (Mathematics: The Universal Language. Numbers and Numeration), 000551

Las Matemáticas: Lenguaje universal. Suma y resta de números enteros (Mathematics: The Universal Language. Addition and Subtraction of Whole Numbers), 000553

Las Matemáticas: Lenguaje universal (Mathematics: The Universal Language). Teacher's Guide 1, 000550

Le Bois maudit (The Haunted Woods), 000670

Le Journal d'un skidoo (The Diary of a Skidoo), 000049

Le Temps: La campagne (The Weather: The Country), 000188

Le Vieil homme et l'enfant (The Old Man and the Child), 000033

Leamos sobre veinte ocupaciones! Twenty Trades to Read About, 000533

Learning English Uno: Conforme a los objetivos del programa oficial (Learning English One: Corresponding to the Objectives of the Official Program), 000105

Lenguaje. III Unidad generadora: La Convivencia. Libro del alumno (Language. Unit III: Living Together. Workbook), 000126

Lenguaje. III Unidad generadora: La Convivencia. Libro del maestro (Language. Unit III: Living Together. Teacher's Guide), 000125

Les Arts et la littérature chez les Franco-Américains de la Nouvelle-Angleterre: Module expérimental destiné aux élèves dans les écoles-secondaires américaines (Arts and Literature of the Franco-Americans of New England: Experimental Module for American Secondary School Students), 000181

Les Ressources naturelles (Natural Resources), 000186

Leyendas puertorriqueñas: Adaptaciones (Puerto Rican Legends: Adaptations), 000155

Libro de lectura: Nivel A (Reader: Level A), 000567

Libro de lectura: Nivel B (Reader: Level B), 000568

Libro de lectura: Nivel C (Reader: Level C), 000569

Libro de lectura: Suplemento (Reader: Supplement), 000570

Loca, Eco Tentokorkvtes. Terrapin Race, 000045

Los Amigos del tío Santiago (The Friends of Uncle Santiago), 000169

Los Niños (The Children), 000590

Ma'ii Wáshindoongóó deeyá (Coyote Goes to Washington), 000613

Mada heye? Hondo heye? (Which? Whose?), 000750

Mada? Dot'an? (What Are They Doing? Where Are They Doing It?), 000748

Mangteghaqa (My House), 000808

Manual de pronunciación del español para personas de habla inglesa (Spanish Pronunciation Manual for Speakers of English), 000669

Maskoke (Muskokee) onvkuce cokv enhvteceskv (Beginning Muskogee Story Book), 000705

Mathématiques I: Volume 1 (Mathematics I: Volume 1), 000060

Mathématiques I: Volume 2 (Mathematics I: Volume 2), 000061

Mexican American Studies: English-Spanish, 000058

Mexican American Studies: The Gateway and the Barrier, 000581

Mexican Experience, The: A Social Studies Approach to Art and Architecture. Resource Material, 000630

Mexican Experience, The: A Social Studies Approach to Art and Architecture. Teacher's Guide, 000629

Mga pangalan ng aking pamilya (My Family), 000717

Mi ambiente y yo (My Environment and Me): An Aural-Oral Activity Guide, 000566

Mia mikre stagona (The Little Drop of Water), 000674

Missing Star, The, 000053

Muppet Gallery, The, 000026

My New Friend, David, 000007

Náshdóí (Bobcat), 000612

Naten akitutkaa? Qafsinat? (How Much? How Many?), 000807

Navajo Consonant Posters, 000924

Nda'ihdu? Ent'i (Why? Because), 000766

Ndahqugh? Ndahdi? (How Much? How Many?), 000768

Nek'a (My House), 000817

New Approaches to Bilingual, Bicultural Education, 000645

New Approaches to Bilingual, Bicultural Education, Manual 1: A New Philosophy of Education, 000648

New Approaches to Bilingual, Bicultural Education, Manual 2: Mexican American Vaues and Culturally Democratic Educational Environments, 000647

New Approaches to Bilingual, Bicultural Education, Manual 3: Introduction to Cognitive Styles, 000646

New Approaches to Bilingual, Bicultural Education, Manual 4: Field Sensitivity and Field Independence in Children, 000649

New Approaches to Bilingual, Bicultural Education, Manual 5: Field Sensitive and Field independent Teaching Strategies, 000650

New Approaches to Bilingual, Bicultural Education, Manual 6: Developing Cognitive Flexibility, 000651

New Approaches to Bilingual, Bicultural Education, Manual 7: Concepts and Strategies for Teaching the Mexican American Experience, 000652

New Approaches to Bilingual, Bicultural Education: Self-Assessment Units, 000653

Nidaats'uh kk'a? Donaalt'aayee? (How Much? How Many?), 000759

Nidots'o hikogh? Nidots'o dinogholt'aye? (How Much? How Many?), 000749

Niigugim qalgadangis (Atkan Food), 000795

Niiĝuĝim tunugan ilakuchangis. Introduction to Atkan Grammar and Lexicon, 000800

Niivaniagvilialiq (Going to the Store), 000848

Noche del sol, Libro III: Cuaderno de ejercicios (Night of the Sun, Book III: Workbook), 000140

Noche del sol, Libro III: Guía para el maestro (Night of the Sun, Book III: Teacher's Guide), 000138

Noche del sol, Libro III: Libro de lectura (Night of the Sun, Book III: Reader), 000139

Non-verbal Communication in Puerto Rico, 000564

Nos plantations (Our Plantings), 000187

Nts'aa' eedlah? Nts'aa ihdlaan? (How Much? How Many?), 000730

Nts'at taadiil? Nts'at diidii'? (What Will He Do? What Did He Do?), 000726

Nunatchiagmi (Buckland), 000861

Oh! Canada, 000479

Oh! Canada: Piste sonore. Sound track, 000480

Olta' (School), 000615

Paca, 000584

Pag-aaral tungkol sa oras (Learning About Time), 000719

Papunta sa tindahan (Going to the Store), 000718

Phengaraki moi lampro (My Bright Moon), 000676

Pintando también se aprende: Aspectos de la cultura puertorriqueña (You Learn by Coloring, Too: Aspects of Puerto Rican Culture), 000055

Planning the Program with the Home Tutor, 000628

Poesías infantiles: Primer grado (Children's Poems: First Grade), 000565

Practice Exercises in Everyday English for Advanced Foreign Students, 000056

Presentaciones escolares: Serie de programas para conmemorar acontecimientos de valor cultural para el México Americano (School Assembly Presentations: Series of Programs to Commemorate Events of Cultural Value to the Mexican American), 000640

Pu-nvt-tv e-ten-hes-se (Animal Friends), 000539

Puedo Leer. I Can Read. Initial Reading in Spanish for Bilingual Children, 000562

Puedo Leer, Activity Supplement for: Teacher's Guide. Program for Initial Reading in Spanish for Bilingual Children, 000560

Puedo Leer, Activity Supplement for: Use of Charts Program for Initial Reading in Spanish for Bilingual Children, 000561

Puerto Rican History, Civilization, and Culture: A Mini-Documentary, 000130

Qanan sanax̂? Qanaang azax̂? (How Much? How Many?), 000793

Qanasanax̂? Qanaangasax̂? (How Much? How Many?), 000780

Qanuqtun? Qapchinik? (How Much? How Many?), 000875

Qanusiq naguaguwiun? Sulivin? (What Do You Like? What Are You doing?), 000838

Qanusit naguaguwii nigikhavgi? (What Do You Like to Eat?), 000850

Qanusiuva? Sulguwiun? (What Is It? What Can You Do With It?), 000840

Qanutun? Qapsich? (How Much? How Many?), 000859

Qanutun? Qapsinik? (How Much? How Many?), 000832, 000844

Qanutun? Qavsiñik? (How Much? How Many?), 000868

Qayutun? Qavcinek? (How Much? How Many?), 000815

Raza de tesoros (Race of Treasures), 000681

Raza de tesoros: Cuaderno de trabajo (Race of Treasures: Workbook), 000683

Raza de tesoros: Guía para el maestro (Race of Treasures: Teacher's Guide), 000682

Reading Norwegian, 000522

Resource Material for Bilingual Education, 000657

SCDC Spanish Curricula Units: Grade 1-4, 000549

Saamii (Sammy), 000798

Sam, 000803

Samayilax̂ (Sammy), 000785

Sammy, 000716, 000733, 000745, 000753, 000762, 000774

Sciences: Biology, English-Spanish, 000578

Sebechem el menguiu? Hong er a kot el skuul (Can You Read? Book for First Grade), 000706

Serie de rimas illustradas (Series of Illustrated Rhymes), 000642

Sesame Street Activities, 000070

Seven Constitutions (Anumpa vlhpisa un tuklo): Government of the Choctaw Republic, 1826-1906, 000576

Shdesnaqa izhi'a (My Family), 000771

Shizheh (My House), 000743

Shizhehk'aa eenjit ch'oozhri' (My Family), 000747

Shqenq'a (My House), 000770

Shyah (My House), 000732

Sidilnakkaa siyilniyookkaa ooza' (My Family), 000724

Sikayih (My House), 000751

Sivuqam ungipaghaatangi. St. Lawrence Island Legends, 000809

Social Living I: Curriculum Guide. Livre du maître (Teacher's Manual), 000067

Social Living I: Volume 2, 000068

Social Living: Volume 3, 000069

Social Studies, Book I: A Bilingual Multicultural Guide, English-Spanish, 000531

Social Studies, Book II: A Bilingual Multicultural Guide, English-Spanish, 000532

Social Studies: English-Spanish, 000057

Spanish as a Second Language Units, Grade 6, 000668

Spoken Arabic (Saudi), 000524

Spoken Chinese: Book One, 000527

Spoken Dutch: Basic Course, Units 1-12, 000523

Spoken Hausa, 000529

Spoken Persian, 000528

Spoken Portuguese: Basic Course, Units 1-2. A Self-Teaching Guide, 000526

Spoken Romanian: Standard Colloquial Romanian, Book One, 000525

Struggle for Independence: Mexico's Rebellion Against Spain. Social Studies. A Teacher's Guide for Grades 1-9, 000639

Strumiintas Piitram ayx̂aasii (Peter's Boat/Tools), 000796

Sua nakuagiviun? Suliqivich? (What Do You Like? What Are You Doing?), 000854

Sua nakuagiviun? Suvit? (What Do You Like? What Are You Doing?), 000827

Sua una? Sugisiniqpiun? (What Is It? What Can You Do With It?), 000829

Sua una? Sutlanayaqpiun? (What Is It? What Can You Do With It?), 000856

Suami? Qanu-ataa (Why? Because), 000841

Sugisiva? Suliqiva? (What Will He Do? What Did He Do?), 000855

Sugisiva? Suva? (What Will He Do? What Did He Do?), 000828

Suliuqpa? Suzruaq? (What Will He Do? What Did He Do?), 000839

Suluq (Sammy), 000806, 000852

Suna naguaqqhayun? Suwin? (What Do You Like? What Are You Doing?), 000851

Suna nakuagiviun? Suliqivich? (What Do You Like? What Are You Doing?), 000863

Suniaqpa? Suva? (What Will He Do? What Did He Do?), 000864

Sur les traces de l'héritage français en Nouvelle-Angleterre: Boston (In Search of the French Heritage in New England: Boston), 000021

Sur les traces de l'héritage français en Nouvelle-Angleterre: Boston. Livret du maître (In Search of the French Heritage in New England: Boston. Teacher's Guide), 000022

Sutalya na udizre ts'e' (My Family), 000755

Suuva una? Sugisiñiqpiun? (What Is It? What Can You Do With It?), 000865

Suva? Tavra (Why? Because), 000830

Suvaata? Atakkii (Why? Because), 000857, 000866

Suvaata? Takku (Why? Because), 000822

Taga the Great, 000110

Tarjetas relampago (Flashcards), 000597

Tauqsignialiq (Going to the Store), 000836

Taxidi gyro ston cosmo (Trip Around the World), 000675

Teacher Training Pack for a Course on Cultural Awareness, 000563

Tesoros de mi raza (Treasures of My Race), 000678

Tesoros de mi raza: Cuaderno de trabajo (Treasures of My Race: Workbook), 000680

Tesoros de mi raza: Guía para el maestro (Treasures of My Race: Teacher's Guide), 000679

Tets qilan (Learning About Time), 000772

Things to Do: Activities for a Bilingual Classroom, 000571

Ti-Jean et Colette (Ti-Jean and Colette), 000671

Ting ulang (My House), 000783

Tolón: El gatito glotón (Tolón: The Gluttonous Kitten), 000156

Tom k'ookkaayah nitaalyo (Going to the Store), 000761

Tsé' ádó'ii (Fly), 000616

Tsék'ina'asdzooí: Tse deiízheshígíí baa hane' (Inscription Rock: Eroding of a Rock Formation), 000614

Tuaqsigñiaqtilialiq (Going to the Store), 000824

Tupiga (My House), 000834

Un Jacques Cartier errant: Pièce en un acte (An Errant Jacques Cartier: One-Act Play), 000006

Un Libro de pinturas de la revolución de México (A Picture Book of the Mexican Revolution), 000102

Un Mot de chez-nous (A Word from Our Home), 000034

Un Niño llamado Manuel: Lectura en español, educación primaria (A Boy Named Manuel: Reading in Spanish, Primary Education), 000659

Un po' d'Italia (A Bit of Italy), 000691

Un Sueño musical (A Musical Dream), 000149

Una cauga? Caksuumasiu? (What Is It? What Can You Do With It?), 000812

Vada idi? Ndan'i? (Which? Whose?), 000769

Vada? Yada tul'il? (What Are They Doing? Where Are They Doing It?), 000767

Vamos a jugar con letras (Let's Play with Letters), 000054

Van Pham Anh Ngu Thuc Hanh: Bai Hoc (Practical English Grammar), 000016

Van Pham Anh Ngu Thuc Hanh: Bai Tap (English Grammar Exercises), 000017

Vestiti femminili di un tempo (Traditional Women's Costumes), 000690

Vina, la víbora (Vina, the Viper), 000592

Well of Time, The: Eighteen Short Stories from Philippine Contemporary Literature, 000023

Well of Time, The: Teacher's Handbook, 000024

Xa' dakthan iin huu'oosi' (My Family), 000735

Yada di? Nda'ich' q'u vel tghit'il? (What Is It? What Can You Do With It?), 000765

Yada q'u nel yagheli? Yada q'u t'enl'an? (What Do You Like? What Are You Doing?), 000763

Yada q'u tul'il? Yada q'u tghil'an? (What Will He Do? What Did He Do?), 000764

Yah hukk'o-eeneeya' (Work in the Home), 000723